Creating Conversos

CREATING CONVERSOS

The Carvajal–Santa María Family
in Early Modern Spain

ROGER LOUIS MARTÍNEZ-DÁVILA

UNIVERSITY OF NOTRE DAME PRESS
NOTRE DAME, INDIANA

University of Notre Dame Press
Notre Dame, Indiana 46556
www.undpress.nd.edu

Library of Congress Cataloging-in-Publication Data
Names: Martínez-Dávila, Roger L., author.
Title: Creating conversos : the Carvajal/Santa Maria family in early modern Spain /
Roger Louis Martínez-Dávila.
Description: Notre Dame, Indiana : University of Notre Dame Press, [2018] |
Includes bibliographical references and index.
Identifiers: LCCN 2017056500 (print) | LCCN 2017055957 (ebook) |
ISBN 9780268103217 (hardcover : alk. paper) | ISBN 0268103216 (hardcover :
alk. paper) | ISBN 9780268103231 (pdf) | ISBN 9780268103248 (epub)
Subjects: LCSH: Carvajal family. | Crypto-Jews—Spain—Castile—History. |
Jews—Spain—Castile—History. | Castile (Spain)—History. | Spain—History.
Classification: LCC CS959 . C32 2018 (ebook) | LCC CS959 (print) |
DDC 929.20946—dc23
LC record available at https://lccn.loc.gov/2017056500

∞ *This paper meets the requirements of ANSI/NISO Z39.48-1992*
(Permanence of Paper).

CONTENTS

ABBREVIATIONS OF ARCHIVES AND LIBRARIES

ABAMT	Archivo-Biblioteca Arquidiocesanos Monseñor Taborga (Bolivia)
ABNB	Archivo y Biblioteca Nacionales de Bolivia
ACP	Archivo de la Catedral de Plasencia (Spain)
ACV	Archivo de la Catedral de Valladolid (Spain)
AGI	Archivo General de Indias (Spain)
AGN	Archivo General de la Nación (Mexico)
AGS	Archivo General de Simancas (Spain)
AHCB	Archivo Histórico de la Catedral de Burgos (Spain)
AHMB	Archivo Histórico Municipal de Burgos (Spain)
AHPC	Archivo Histórico Provincial de Cáceres (Spain)
AHN	Archivo Histórico Nacional (Spain)
AHNSN	Archivo Histórico Nacional, Sección Nobleza (Spain)
AMP	Archivo Municipal de Plasencia (Spain)
ARCV	Archivo de la Real Chancillería de Valladolid (Spain)
ASAV	Archivum Secretum Apostolicum Vaticanum (Vatican City)

AUS	Archivo de la Universidad de Salamanca (Spain)
BNE	Biblioteca Nacional de España (Spain)
BUS	Biblioteca de la Universidad de Salamanca (Spain)
HL	Huntington Library (U. S. A.)
RAH	Biblioteca de la Real Academia de la Historia (Spain)

ILLUSTRATIONS AND TABLES

FIGURES

CHARTS

TABLES

ACKNOWLEDGMENTS

During the innumerable research trips I undertook during the preparation of this book—over forty archives in Spain, Latin America, and the United States—there is one that will remain the most intellectually and personally meaningful to me. It was March 2009, and I had traveled from my new academic home, Saint Joseph's University in Philadelphia, to the Archivo Histórico Nacional in Madrid to continue my research on converso families. There, as so many scholars of Spain do when they visit the Sala de Investigadores, I encountered a dear friend. On that occasion it was Sabine MacCormack, whom I had the pleasure of meeting several years before at the University of Texas at Austin when I was a doctoral candidate. Although I was just commencing my dissertation research at the time, she immediately granted me, like so many other grateful students, her undivided attention. Having lived a previous professional life in the Texas legislature and the Democratic political consulting world, I had encountered every type of person—genuine, devious, sincere, calculating, and ideological, just to name a few. What struck me immediately about Sabine, both in my first and all later encounters, was her willingness to listen intently, advise thoughtfully, and, most important, offer encouragement. Now that I have the time to reflect, some four years since her death in 2012, I remain grateful for her stewardship of this manuscript at the University of Notre Dame Press. Hoping to preserve her memory and her exceptional role in the development of many scholars, I am pleased to acknowledge her and to share her good counsel: "Don't be discouraged." When I believed this text would never find its place, Sabine made it a reality.

This book is a search for my extended family's historical identity. My Carvajal family settled in San Antonio de Bejar, Texas, in 1703. Although our oral family history imparted that we were related to Luis de Carvajal "the Younger," who was executed by the Holy Office of the Inquisition in Mexico City in 1596 for Judaizing, we had no tangible historical record to connect us to this Sephardic Jewish lineage. Furthermore, as intensely devoted Roman Catholics with a carefully documented genealogy leading back to Mateo de Carvajal from Santiago de la Monclova, Mexico, in the late 1600s, we did not know how to reconcile our disparate Christian and Jewish histories. For his passion to understand who we were, where we came from, and what we had become, I acknowledge my father, Eugene Albert Martínez-Carvajal, and offer this book as an answer to his questions.

As an American of Mexican ancestry, there is no more meaningful community to thank than my maternal and paternal extended families: the Dávila, González, Martínez, Carvajal, Mora, and Burnsides. In particular, I am grateful to my loving mother, Mary Louise Dávila; my brother and sister-in-law, Mark Eugene Martínez and Patti Maldonado; and my nephews, Mark Andrés and Ian Alexander. No uncle was ever more devoted to my upbringing than Alfonso Dávila; I am pleased that I can now return his attentiveness to my cousins, Sonia Villarreal and Román Gracia. My other aunts and uncles always showed me great affection, including Rudolfo Dávila II, Dorothy Dávila, Frank Dávila, and Kathy Dávila, as did my cousins, Rudolfo Dávila III and Rosette Dávila. Similarly, I recognize the contentious but important Martínez-Carvajal arm of my family, especially my grandmother, Josephine Carvajal, and great-aunts, Esther Carvajal and Janie Carvajal. All were impressive matriarchs. Among those sharing this path of family discovery are my paternal uncles, Hector Martínez and Arthur Martínez, as well as my paternal cousins, Greg Martínez, Pamela Martínez, Ryan Martínez, Matthew Martínez, and Jeff Martínez.

Now married for over twenty years, I am thankful to be a part of my spouse's family. For her dear friendship and always welcoming home in Santa Fe, New Mexico, I recognize my mother-in-law, Pat Mora, as well as my fathers-in-law, William Burnside and Vern Scarborough. For their generosity of spirit and good family company, I acknowledge Terry Henry, Stella Mora Henry, and their son, Christopher. To the sister I never had, Cecilia Burnside, and her husband, Brad Cason, and their daughter, Bonny Lilac, and my brother-in-law, Bill Burnside, I express my thanks for sharing many holidays together and challenging days as well. I also thank those friends who I consider my family, especially James Aldrete, Elma Cantú, Susan Hays, Joseph Sawin, James Ray, Rene Lara, Jerry and Kristin Haddican, Catarino Felan, Mike Trimble, John Warren, Travis James, David Seidman, Celeste Giuliano, Robert Mittman, Frances Levine, Josef Díaz, and Sonya Loya.

For encouraging me to search for Spain's concealed Jewish past, as well as my own, I thank Denise A. Spellberg, my undergraduate adviser and first dissertation adviser at the University of Texas at Austin. I gratefully acknowledge Ann Twinam for stewarding my doctoral dissertation to completion and Cory Reed for his unflinching loyalty on my dissertation committee. I thank L. J. Andrew Villalón, Julie Hardwick, and Neil Kamil for ensuring this book manuscript was superior to the dissertation. For their past and continuing roles in my development as a historian at the University of Texas, I thank Janet Meisel, Geraldine Heng, Caroline Castiglione, Madeline Sutherland-Meier, Michael Harney, and Alison Frazier. For their camaraderie and counsel as fellow doctoral students, I am grateful to Carla Roland, Mónica Vallin, Lisa Lacy, Saad Abi-Hamad, Hanan Hammad, Kristi Barnwell, Christine Baker, Lauren Aptner Bairnsfather, Frances Ramos, Amber Abbas, Michael Bednar, Paul Conrad, Andrew Paxman, Anna Taylor, Christopher Albi, Roy Doron, Ken Ward, José Barragán, Matt Heaton, Meredith Glueck, Michael Anderson, and Rais Rahman.

For welcoming me as their inaugural David H. Burton Postdoctoral Fellow at Saint Joseph's University (2008–10) and supporting my book research, I fondly remember and thank my cherished colleagues in the Department of History—in particular, Alison Williams Lewin, Richard A. Warren, Jeffrey Hyson, James Carter, Randall M. Miller, Katherine A. S. Sibley, Phil Smith, Thomas M. Keefe, Susan McFadden, Paul Patterson, Joseph F. Chorpenning, and David H. Burton.

In addition, I wish to acknowledge the guidance of my colleagues in many other disciplines. I especially thank Stanley M. Hordes, who served as a wonderful mentor in life and scholarship. Similarly, this book could not have found its voice without the intellectual and collegial camaraderie of Carla Rahn Phillips, William D. Phillips Jr., Jane Gerber, Ron Duncan Hart, Francisco García Serrano Nebras, Sean Perrone, Victor R. Schinazi, Gretchen Starr-LeBeau, Michael Ryan, Paddington Hodza, Seth Kunin, Seth Ward, Alicia Gojman, David Alonso García, Jodi Campbell, Elizabeth Lehfeldt, Jessica Fowler, Luis X. Morera, Daniel Wasserman, Alison Parks Weber, Anthony Puglisi, Anne Marie Wolf, Katie Harris, Jorge Cañizares-Esguerra, David Coleman, Liam Brockey, Elizabeth Bishop, Fernando Feliu-Moggi, and Ofer Ben-Amots.

To my colleagues and friends at the University of Colorado at Colorado Springs (UCCS), I cannot begin to express the extent of my gratitude. I thank my dear friends Paul Harvey, Christina M. Jiménez, and Robert Sackett, who read and offered constructive suggestions on the many revisions of this manuscript. I also wish to acknowledge the genuine support of my colleagues in the Department of History, including Christopher Hill, Bernice E. Forrest, Brian Duvick, Yang Wei, G. Carole Woodall, Judith Price, Janet Myers, Roy Joy Sartin, Leah Davis-Witherow, Barbara Headle, Christopher Bairn, Nicole Emmons, Michaela Steen, and Peter R. Brumlik. For his incomparable counsel, I acknowledge Raphael Sassower. And I am grateful to many other colleagues at UCCS who generously offered their good wishes, including Jane Rigler, Glen Whitehead, Colin McAllister, Kimbra Smith, Zak Mesyan, Kee Warner, Ian Smith, Rebecca Laroche, Thomas Napierkowski, Fernando Feliu-Moggi, Peg Bacon, Mary Cousson-Read, Rex Welshon, Perrin Cunningham, and Michael Calvisi. For assisting with my research and listening endlessly to discussions about the conversos and Spain, I want to thank my students Joseph Sandoval, Kim Sweetwood, Kyle Clark, Jennifer Broderick, Max Pelz, Tawnie Mizer, and Andrew Roome.

At the Universidad de Carlos III de Madrid, where I am presently a CONEX–Marie Curie Fellow (2015–18), I thank my adviser, Jaime Alvar Ezquerra, and my colleagues María Jesús Fuente Pérez and Antón Alvar Nuño.

For their friendship and assistance in discovering the lives of the Carvajal–Santa María family confederation, I thank the Placentinos Esther Sánchez Calle and her husband, Francisco; Isidro Felipe Iñigo; Don Fernando Pizarro García-Polo; Cristina Sánchez Hernández; Ángel Custodio Sánchez Blázquez; Don Francisco Rico Bayo; Don Juan Manuel Ramos Berrocoso; Don Francisco González Cuesta; Alfonso Párraga; Marciano de Hervas; María del Carmen Fuentes Nogales; and José Luis García Araujo and his wife, Puerto. In Burgos, I thank Don Matías Vicario Santa María, archivist at the Cathedral of Burgos, for his kindness and deep knowledge of the cathedral's manuscript collection.

For their editorial counsel, I recognize Stephen Wrinn, Eli Bortz, Stephen Little, and Harv Humphrey at the University of Notre Dame Press. Similarly, for their editorial, production, design, and marketing efforts at the press, I thank Rebecca DeBoer, Matthew Dowd, Maria Herrera, Wendy McMillen, Kathryn Pitts, and Elizabeth Sain. Most important, I commend and thank Kathy Kaiser and Sheila Berg for their exceptional copyediting.

For their generous financial support of my research, I would like to acknowledge the University of Texas at Austin, the University of Colorado at Colorado Springs, the University of Colorado System, the Council for European Studies at Columbia University, the Andrew W. Mellon Foundation, the Program for Cultural Cooperation (Gobierno de España, Ministerio de Educación, Cultura y Deportes), the International Institute for Jewish Genealogy and the Paul Jacobi Center Research Grant at the National Library of Israel, and the Maurice Amado Program in Sephardic Studies and Center for Jewish Studies at the University of California, Los Angeles. My final revisions of the manuscript, completed in Madrid, were funded by the Universidad Carlos III de Madrid, the European Union's Seventh Framework Programme for research, technological development, and demonstration under Grant No. 600371, Ministerio de Economía y Competitividad (COFUND2013-51509), and Banco Santander.

Most significantly, I acknowledge and thank Libby Martínez, my wife, for sharing this journey with me.

NOTE TO THE READER

The Castilian Spanish spellings of persons, places, and things, as well as grammatical forms, used in this book are taken from original fourteenth- through eighteenth-century manuscripts. As a historian, as opposed to a linguistic specialist who studies the nuances of language, accurately communicating the essential content of the documents was my primary concern. To this end, I have preserved the archaic Spanish forms for surnames like Estúñiga (or Zúñiga) and words like chantre (or cantor).

Antonio de Nebrija's *Gramática de la lengua castellana*, the first effort to standardize the use of a European vernacular language, did not appear until 1492. Before this date, and in almost all of the manuscripts I have evaluated, spellings varied, terminology was interchangeable, and grammar was quite flexible. Manuscripts generally followed local and regional preferences. In addition, diacritical marks rarely appear on the page. For the benefit of the reader, I have selected the most common spellings and, where appropriate, introduced diacritical marks in accordance with contemporary Spanish standards.

English translations are my own and closely follow the original Spanish sources.

This work is not free of language errors, however, and I encourage other scholars to improve on my efforts.

INTRODUCTION

A GRASP FOR THE PAPACY

This is the history of familial aspirations that fell short. This family's ultimate goal was to secure the praiseworthy status of elite Spanish Christians, religious and governmental leaders who would serve Queen Isabel and King Ferdinand. Theirs was an outrageous wager. In an age of increasing hostility to and discrimination against Jews and conversos, they explicitly agreed to craft a new identity, a new way of life and self-perception, by blending their Jewish and Christian lineages. The fundamental impediment they encountered was the pernicious fifteenth-century belief that ancestry and blood lineage, not professed beliefs, defined one's identity. Jewishness could not be erased—even after sincere conversion or generations of Christian belief. The culmination of their explicit efforts took form in their progeny, the Spanish cardinal Bernardino López de Carvajal, who sought the highest achievements on his and their behalf at the opening of the sixteenth century.

Only a few weeks before a damp October evening in 1511, the Florentine Machiavelli labored to persuade Bernardino López de Carvajal to delay his actions at the schismatic Roman Catholic Council of Pisa. The question remained unanswered: could Carvajal capture the papacy for himself and thus thrust this son of a blended Jewish-Catholic lineage into the center of European affairs? The excommunicated French king Louis XII, the Florentines, and a scattering of cardinals promised to support Carvajal's initiative. A native of the Spanish western frontier town of Plasencia and a descendant of the intermarriage of Old Christian knights and conversos, or New Christians, Carvajal would not deny himself what he had failed to seize only eight years earlier. Fatefully, he ascended the papal throne at the schismatic Council of Pisa and there sat in opposition to Pope Julius II. An initiative, begun in the late fourteenth century by his ancestor, Solomon ha-Levi, a rabbi who became Pablo de Santa María and bishop of Burgos, Spain, had come to fruition. Through collective dedication and concerted action, the converso Carvajal–Santa María family reached for the highest office in Christendom (figs. 0.1, 0.2). Together, these two families mingled blood and faith and adapted to a new way of life—a middle path that required compromises of their Jewish and Catholic origins. This new way of life publicly proclaimed Catholicism, shifted attention away from a hidden Jewish past, and radically transformed the families' professions and religious practices in order to advance the clan in a rapidly changing world.

Bernardino López de Carvajal and his family's thirst for the grandest Christian pedigree was extraordinary but not nearly as noteworthy as their Jewish blood. Castilian Old Christians considered the mere existence of a single drop of Jewish blood anathema and incompatible with the Spanish Christian faith. In effect, early sixteenth-century Castilians viewed New Christians as fundamentally defective because of the principle of *limpieza de sangre* (blood purity), which held all persons of Jewish and Muslim descent spiritually flawed. Ever since the 1450s, when blood purity statutes began to be implemented in Spanish church, royal, and municipal institutions, Spanish Christians had come to equate religious identity with genealogy. Even converts who were the most faithful servants of the Roman Catholic Church and Queen Isabel and King Ferdinand were banned from holding ecclesiastical or governmental offices. Bernardino López de Carvajal became Pope Bernardino in 1511 because the Carvajal–Santa María family had effectively concealed all evidence of his Jewish ancestry while masterfully promoting their Christian identity through dedication to church and crown.

But this triumph was short-lived. Due to unforeseeable circumstances, including the rapid recovery of Julius II from a near-fatal illness and King Ferdinand's withdrawal of support for Bernardino, the co-conspirators at the Council of Pisa failed to force Pope Julius out of office.[1] Further, although Maximilian I had initially supported Bernardino's grasp for the papacy, he too renounced the actors in the council.[2] Unable to hold a viable coalition together, the French and Cardinal Carvajal's co-conspirators concluded the council without success. To penalize the five schismatic cardinals for their actions, Pope Julius II excommunicated them at the Fifth Lateran Council of 1512.[3] Although the pope deprived Bernardino of his ecclesiastical titles and his income from the Diocese of Sigüenza for a short period, in 1513 Bernardino and his associates rehabilitated themselves when Julius II died and Pope Leo X assumed the mantle of the papacy. Pope Leo X reconciled Bernardino and the four other men to the church and restored them to their status as cardinals.[4]

Bernardino López de Carvajal's failure to capture the papacy is not only telling of the political intrigue of the early 1600s; it is a revealing history of the formation of

FIGURE 0.1. Portrait of Cardinal Bernardino López de Carvajal. Source: Biblioteca Nacional de España. Used with permission.

FIGURE 0.2. Portrait of Bishop Pablo de Santa María. Source: Biblioteca Nacional de España. Used with permission.

early modern identities. He was an exemplar of a maligned but highly influential religious minority: the conversos of Spain. His blood and faith combined to create a multifaceted identity, one that found its origins in the mid-fourteenth-century Spanish Kingdom of Castile and León.

CREATING IDENTITIES: FROM MEDIEVAL SPAIN TO THE EARLY MODERN IBERIAN WORLD

From mid-fourteenth-century Iberia to mid-seventeenth-century Mexico and Bolivia, blood, faith, and family persisted in shaping the identities of the descendants of Old Christians and Sephardic Jews. Navigating from the medieval world to the nebulous early modern one of conversos is not a linear task. Rather, it is characterized by a descent into cultural and religious disorder, on which early modern people desperately attempted to impose order. When the new social and religious structure did not correspond to the realities of genealogy and faith in early modern Spain, the agents of this new world revisited their own pasts and remodeled them to fit the constraints of the sixteenth century. Put simply, conversos such as the Carvajal–Santa María family were aggressive concealers of their Jewish ancestries and bloodlines and skillful promoters of their Christian credentials.

I argue that through the successful intermarriage and integration of the Jewish ha-Levi (converso Santa María) lineage of Burgos with the Old Christian Carvajal line of the knights of Plasencia, a new identity—a hallmark of the early modern age—took root as early as the late 1300s. Their decisions, perspectives, relationships, and actions constitute what I refer to as "identity." Further, because the Carvajal–Santa María family derived this identity from two distinct origins—Jewish and Christian—their collective approach was one that was hybridized. It was dominantly Christian, but remnants of Jewish ways of life persisted. This active process of self-selecting the religious and cultural characteristics they wished to promote, as well as those they attempted to conceal, is a harbinger of early modern identity. Why? The medieval age did not encourage and support the ability to choose a unique family or personal pathway: the son of a tailor would be a tailor, for example.

Uncovering their identity is a frustrating task because what we might wish to locate in the historical record of the fourteenth through early sixteenth centuries, definitive information on personal and family identities, rarely exists. No family diaries, recanting of sins or exposing of hearts, remain for these women and men of the late medieval period. Wills follow formulaic patterns of distributing wealth to children and clan, dictating burial instructions and memorial services, and settling the affairs of the deceased. However, louder than words, the Carvajal–Santa María family's deliberate actions—marriage patterns, residential arrangements, professional associations, financial affairs, and religious practices—speak forcefully of life choices that shaped who they were and what they were to become. There is truth in the Spanish *dicho*, or saying, "Dime con quién andas y te diré quién eres," "Tell me who you walk with and I will tell you who you are." Together, the Carvajal–Santa María family members walked a new path and created a new identity that paid respect to Judaism but adapted to a Christian way of life.

The story of the Carvajal–Santa María family is of crucial historiographical interest because it turns back the scholarly clock on the origins of early modern identities. Before Jacob Burckhardt's Italian Renaissance identities or Stephen Greenblatt's English self-fashioning occurred, Spanish conversos engendered the complicated and fractured identities that defined early modern Europe. Iberian Jews and Christians, especially those with the greatest incentives to take risks and experiment with new cultural forms, created converso identities that harnessed Jewish and Christian ways of life and expertise to outcompete, socially and politically, both Old and New Christians. Their cultural ingenuity and craftsmanship was born out of crisis, opportunity, innovation, turmoil, memory, and loyalty. Some scholars might argue that the converso Carvajal–Santa María were nothing more than self-interested opportunists of the early modern era, and perhaps they were, but I leave that judgment to the reader.

To uncover how conversos actively molded their identities from the mid-1300s through the mid-1600s, I first explore the creation of medieval multireligious Iberia. Chapter 1 evaluates the transformation of Jews, Catholics, and conversos in the Spanish Extremaduran city of Plasencia and the broader Spanish Castilian world by contextualizing the roots of the Spanish Middle Ages. These origins are tied to the complex history of the Iberian Peninsula—a dynamic Jewish, Christian, and Muslim environment. In many respects, distinct religious norms, not ethnic and genealogical pedigree, dictated pre-fourteenth-century religious identities.

In chapter 2 I discuss how the old order of narrowly defined religious identities and stable social stations were radically altered by the appearance of new types of Spanish Christians. The willing conversion of a few elite Jewish clans, the uneven disintegration of communal relations during the anti-Jewish pogroms of the 1390s, and the Castilian king Enrique II's creation of the "New Nobility" (a different generation of social and political elites crafted from lesser families) all added to this period of crisis. The unsettled environment also initiated a brutal contest for political power among Castile's New Noble houses who were ascending as they garnered wealth through newly bestowed royal privileges. In the midst of this turmoil, a new type of Christian was created by blending formerly Jewish families (like the ha-Levi) with existing Christian clans (such as the Carvajal). This phenomenon was a precursor to accepted scholarly perspectives of individualized and fragmented identities championed by great theorists such as Jacob Burckhardt, Stephen Greenblatt, and Guido Ruggiero, among others. Emerging at this time was the Carvajal–Santa María family confederation, which was a harbinger of early modern European identities.

Chapter 3 delves into the aftermath of the destructive anti-Jewish riots of the 1390s and the changing religious and social character of Castile's elite. The residents of Plasencia, the focal point of this text, must have believed they were an isolated vessel sailing through troubled waters. Castile's principal cities were distant, whether it was Burgos, the royal administrative city, or the expanding commercial center of Sevilla to the south. Transformative opportunity, namely, the successful intermixing of Jewish and Christian elites, was on full display as the Castilian Trastámaran dynasty's New Noble and converso clans, especially the Álvarez de Toledo (*señores de Oropesa*), and the Estúñiga (*condes de Béjar*), asserted their political and economic clout across Castile and even in smaller cities such as Plasencia. In this critical chapter, I evaluate the dynamic processes and the unexpected opportunities that opened a clear path of metamorphosis for the intermarried Carvajal and Santa María (ha-Levi) clans. From two they would become one—a formidable confederation of converso families intent on securing a prosperous future built on Christian and Jewish ancestries and practices.

In chapter 4, the Carvajal–Santa María confederation's dominance in Plasencia is documented and evaluated. In practice, the formerly Old Christian Carvajals began to imitate and learn the basics of bureaucratic operations from the formerly Jewish ha-Levi, who had been royal treasurers and rabbis in Castile during the fourteenth century and now brought those skills and expertise to the Cathedral of Plasencia. The family confederation's endeavors also reflected a new converso mind-set—*mentalité*—that advanced family power but also communicated intense respect for Jewish-Christian relations and institutionalization of new ways of governing the broader community. This chapter investigates the fundamentally different cultural designs the family confederation planned for Plasencia's Jews, Christians, and Muslims. The family largely rejected previous local church leaders' exclusion of Jews and Muslims from certain economic activities (e.g., lucrative leases on vineyards and productive lands) that were reserved for Christians. The confederation's ideology of coexistence and hybridized Jewish-Christian practice brought about an entirely novel identity that had not existed previously in Castile, much less in most of Western Europe. This self-conscious converso identity was definitively Christian in belief, but their familial approach always drew Jews close to them and sought to shield them from predatory conversos, like the New Noble Estúñiga.

Chapter 5 charts kingdomwide political violence that was reflected in a regional conflict between the residents of Plasencia and neighboring seigniorial lords. In effect, elites returned to their normative competition with each other, except now many of the elites leading Castile were New Nobles and therefore an entirely new entity, composed partly of conversos. Although all conversos were of mixed religious pedigree, there were significant variances in how they conceptualized their identities. Some, like the Carvajal and the Santa María, seemed committed to defending mixed bloodlines in Castilian society, whereas others, like the Estúñiga, became predators on Spanish Jewry.

As the disorders of the late 1430s through 1460s were unfolding, the converso ascendency in Castile abruptly collapsed. In the aftermath of anticonverso riots in Toledo in 1449, new limpieza de sangre ordinances were promulgated across the kingdom to exclude conversos from lucrative church and government offices.[5] Contextualizing these events is a complicated task, but the Sephardic historian Jane Gerber expertly explains that fifteenth-century conversos lived in a perpetual state of cultural marginality. Gerber's position is critical because she accurately describes how Castilians viewed conversos:

> By the middle of the fifteenth century, there simply was no easy answer to the question of who was a Jew or a Christian. But for most of the population, the conviction began to spread that Jewish ancestry or "race," not professed religious belief, defined who was a Jew. . . . The *conversos* were now isolated as a new class, neither Jewish nor Christian, that was inassimilable and could not be redeemed.[6]

Gerber's position, one that I subscribe to, exposes the troubled identities of conversos. Conversos, and for that matter *moriscos* (Muslim converts to Christianity), could only be described as hybrid identities that drew from a mixture of religious, lineage, and biological identifiers. For the Carvajal–Santa María family confederation, the Álvarez de Toledo, and even the Estúñiga, identity was no longer something that could be easily delineated or categorized because of the Jewish question. As a result, increasingly these conversos forcefully demonstrated their Christian identities through their overt actions and hidden activities.

Thus, in chapter 6, I demonstrate how conversos like the Carvajal–Santa María sought to prove their Christian and noble worthiness to the public. By means of intensive religious programs and family devotions, they created a distinctive Christian memory to proclaim their identity. Their motivation for doing so was closely tied to a swelling Castilian interest in weighing Christians' virtue based on their blood cleanliness—namely, whether or not they were contaminated by Jewish or Muslim ancestries. Over time, Old Christians saw conversos as insincere converts to Christianity. They also believed that these New Christians had amassed too much influence in royal affairs and over the Trastámaran dynasty.

In response to this dangerous cultural landscape, the Carvajal name began to assume more authority in the Carvajal–Santa María confederation. This was necessary because the Santa María lineage was a genealogical dead end; the New Christian Santa Marías were simply too well known as a formerly Jewish family. In the personage of Cardinal Juan de Carvajal, as well as numerous religious endowments championed by clansmen and clanswomen alike, the family confederation began a methodical initiative to shelter itself and seal others' perception of it as Old Christian. Curiously, the previously Jewish Santa María lineage initially developed these public demonstrations of Christian piety, which the Carvajal simultaneously emulated, perfected, and perpetuated. In many respects, it was among the most ingenious constructions of family heritage and identity because it overtly declared Old Christian piety and roots while privately communicating a hybridized Jewish-Christian heritage within the family confederation.

Chapter 7 examines the momentous affairs of early modern Spain, Europe, and the Americas. This contentious period was punctuated with religion, politics, and encounters with new and old peoples. Spanish imperial successes were reflected in the achievements of the Carvajal–Santa María family confederation, which by the late fifteenth century had effectively laundered its Jewish ancestry and transformed itself into a prominent Old Christian identity.

Among their numerous efforts to solidify a culturally homogeneous Spain, Isabel and Ferdinand sought to imprint a strict Christian identity on all of their subjects— Christians, Jews, and Muslims. In 1478, by means of a papal bull, the Catholic monarchs secured the establishment of the Holy Office of the Inquisition, and just two years later, in 1480, the Holy Office began its efforts to seek out suspected heretics, especially Judaizers within the Christian ranks. Caught in this cleansing apparatus were conversos of all lineages—Jewish commoners and merchants turned Christians, lower nobles and clerical leaders like the Carvajal and Santa María, and even elites like the New Nobles, the Estúñiga and Álvarez de Toledo families.

By 1492, the march of history claimed its Christian victories as well as historic Muslim, Jewish, and Native American losses. After a ten-year war to reclaim Islamic Nasrid Granada and Isabel and Ferdinand took up residence in the ornate Alhambra palace (January 1), the remaining Jews would be exiled from Spain (July 31) and Cristóbal Colón and his crew would land on Hispanola in the Americas (December 25).[7] As witness and participant in this history, the Carvajal–Santa María family must have understood their unique and privileged position in the making of the early modern period. As cardinals, bureaucrats, and knights, family members participated in almost every monumental affair in Spanish history from the 1480s to the 1530s.

It is within this remarkable historical setting that the Carvajal–Santa María family entered the terminal stage of its perfection of a fragmented early modern identity. Since the end of the 1300s, their conversion exuded a progressive sense of change and hope. The Jewish ha-Levi rabbinic family had become the converso Santa María clan of churchmen, and the Old Christian knightly Carvajal family had transformed into a converso ecclesiastical and royal bureaucratic one. Through their intermarriage, the families seemed to believe they could create and mold their future from the bits of bewildering times. With the arrival of the sixteenth century, the Carvajal–Santa María confederation pushed forward as Spaniards and Christians. They labored to forget their

Jewish past and, in doing so, assisted the Spanish monarchy and nobility in disavowing the family's hybrid religious pedigree so that there would be "one, eternal Spain."[8]

In chapter 8 I briefly follow the long-term outcomes for the Carvajal–Santa María family in Spain and the Americas. Because of the inflexible environment of the limpieza de sangre statutes and in the aftermath of the formal expulsion of all Jews from Spain and Portugal, contrasting outcomes materialized for those who remained in Spain and others who migrated to Spanish America. Universally, the confederation's response in Plasencia and in colonial Mexico and Bolivia focused on public denials of their Jewish ancestry and any connection to Jewish religious practices. While the Spanish and Bolivian families largely blocked investigations into their limpieza de sangre and questions pertaining to the sincerity of their Christian practices, the story of those in Mexico is entirely different. There the identities of the family confederation were on full trial. New archival research I present here suggests that the staunchest of the Christian family confederation members in Mexico actively participated in the quieting and ultimate execution of Judaizing arms of their own extended clan; the family killed its own members in order to save itself from further official investigations and other inquisitorial penalties. Thus, by no means was the Carvajal–Santa María family confederation's identity a monochromatic or uniform one. Rather, the longue durée of their familial history suggests that while some elements of the clan were definitively Christian, others either maintained or adopted Judaism as late as the seventeenth century. In this respect, the permutations of their mixed ancestry and faith revealed an early modern world.

1

ORIGINS

Fourteenth-century Plasencia bore the cultural weight of Jewish, Christian, and Muslim influences. Fairly well-developed although not entirely rigid religious norms shaped the pre-fifteenth-century identities of Placentinos, residents of Plasencia. In essence, Jews were Jews, Christians were Christians, and Muslims were Muslims. Religious mixing certainly occurred, but it was normative for each group to view other religious groups as different from themselves. Families descended from long-standing noble lineages enjoyed more prominence than did common ones. The blood lineage preoccupations of the fifteenth century—a world obsessed with distinctions between Old Christians, or those who claimed ancient Christian roots, and New Christians, or those who were recent converts to Christianity—had yet to form.

Iberia's medieval cultural conditions molded how Castilians and Placentinos perceived their world and their identities. Their perspectives establish why Placentinos, both Old Christians like the Carvajal clan and Jewish families such as the de Loya and ha-Levi, would be shaken to their spiritual cores by a late fourteenth-century transition to more fragmented familial and cultural identities. This transformation resulted in contests for control of Iberia's Christian future with the creation of new clans such as the converso Estúñiga, Santa María, and Álvarez de Toledo as well as the rapid ascent of minor Old Christian houses, such as the Carvajal, a family who hybridized its identity as it integrated converso lineages into its own.

RELIGIOUS IDENTITIES

During the Middle Ages, Spanish Christians and their European contemporaries conceived of themselves in relation to other groups that they persecuted.[1] David Nirenberg brought contemporary scholars' attention to this observation in *Communities of Violence*, which discusses the Christian Kingdom of Aragón's relationship to subjugated Jewish and Muslims in the twelfth through fifteenth centuries. The crown recognized and tolerated Jews as a religious minority group because they served "as abject witnesses to the truth and triumph of Christianity."[2] Jews were a social tool used by Christians to define themselves. Analogously, Christians set themselves apart from Muslims by imposing burdensome taxes, prohibitions on clothing, and restrictions on social interactions with Christians.[3] Furthermore, because of interreligious competition for political authority and economic resources, in addition to "collective anxieties" about the polluting effects of sexual encounters between groups, Christians utilized violence against Muslims and Jews to enforce social boundaries.[4] Thus, late medieval Iberia maintained strict boundaries that reinforced distinct religious identities.

Another important work that captures the nature of medieval Christian perspectives of Jews is R. I. Moore's *The Formation of a Persecuting Society.* In particular, the Catholic Church and political elites wrought a permanent change in the social fabric of the eleventh and twelfth centuries by sanctioning and directing "habitual" violence against other religious groups.[5] Persecution was driven by the "zeal" of the ruling elite.[6] Further, the change in the medieval mind-set advanced by the "new, literate, clerical element" was instrumental in building new governmental institutions that focused on social control, especially "suppressing resistance to authority and legitimating that same authority."[7] This discriminatory view was advantageous to the clerical elites as they positioned themselves to outmaneuver Jews in court life. In this medieval world, Christian states and the Catholic Church created the administrative processes to identify, separate, and punish "groups of people deemed to be foreign and in some ways harmful to *societas Christiana.*"[8]

Within Christian Iberia, thirteenth-century legal codes such as the Siete Partidas are a consequential example of persecution as institutionalized in Castile. These laws were also likely to provide comfort to those occupying the lowest social and political rungs of Christian society—commoners and laborers—who could claim that their Christian identity at minimum placed them above the "debased" Jewish and Muslim communities. These fundamental elements of the belief systems of Spanish Christian societies demonstrate that religious identities were by and large fixed and stable prior to the fourteenth century.

Scholars of Sephardic Jewry and conversos articulate corollary arguments about religious differences. Yitzhak Baer's *A History of the Jews in Christian Spain* describes Castile at the end of the thirteenth century as a place where Jews were well integrated in the Castilian royal court, overseeing much of its administration, but their prominence instigated religious competition with the nobility and the church.[9] From the fifteenth century on, a change occurred in Spanish society that was a result of growing anti-Semitism, Baer argues.[10] For example, during the 1300s, Gonzalo Martinez, a master of the military Order of Alcantara, planned to "annihilate" Castile's courtly Jews.[11] An outcome of this change in Christian attitudes toward Jews was a steep rise in conversions. If nothing else is certain in Christian Spain prior the 1400s, religious identity and institutionalized negative perspectives of Jews and Muslims were pervasive realities of life.

FAMILY, KINSHIP, AND CLAN IDENTITIES

A fundamental component of identity within medieval Europe and Spain were notions of family, kin, and clan identities. Group perceptions based on "blood relationships" emerged in medieval Europe from a variety of diverse cultural origins.[12] In *Feudal Society*, Marc Bloch observed the complexity of these origins and the terminology of family:

> In the whole of feudal Europe . . . there existed groups founded on blood-relationship. The terms which served to describe them were rather indefinite—in France, most commonly, *parenté* or *lignage*. Yet, the ties thus created were regarded as extremely strong. . . . A legal document of the eleventh century originating from the Ile de France enumerates them thus: "His friends, that is to say his mother, his brothers, his sisters and his other relatives by blood or by marriage." . . . The general assumption seems to have been that there was no real friendship save between persons united by blood.[13]

Friendship through blood also reinforced personal oaths and loyalty within a family. Bloch highlights one Castilian example in which "four kinsmen, who at Usagre in Castile, were required to swear with a woman who declared she had been the victim of rape."[14] Kinship, therefore, intricately connected families in visible public, official settings and delineated those persons as collective units. Georges Duby argued similarly that aristocratic culture, and later "common culture," by the tenth century was organized along "the basis of lineage, or as a 'house', with genealogy based on strict agnatic rules of filiation, strictly patrilineal."[15] From this origin, families progressively developed extended customs relating to "matrimonial customs, primogeniture, patronymic surnames, and heraldic signs."[16] By the fourteenth century, the family structure was deeply engrained in Europe.

In the medieval Spanish context, as Michael Harney advances in *Kinship and Marriage in Medieval Hispanic Chivalric Romance*, many authors communicated notions of family in well-known chivalric romances such as *El Libro del caballero Zifar* (ca. 1300),

Curial e Güelfa (written between 1435 and 1462), *Tirant lo Blanc* (1490), and *Amadis de Gaula* (1490s).[17] In these works, a strong sense of group lineage orientation is present. Family awareness and solidarity were often expressed through terms such as *maison* (house) and *lignage* (lineage), as well as *cohermano* (cobrother) and *deudo* (relative by blood).[18] Thomas Bisson reports that in twelfth-century Catalonia, "everywhere people lived the experience of family. . . . [T]hey spoke for and about kinsfolk male and female: about wives, husbands, daughters, sons[,] . . . infants[,] . . . uncles and aunts."[19] Every imaginable category of family relationship was an important organizing aspect of group identity because it offered human "trust and support" as a "remedy of impotent life."[20]

As might be expected, scholars identify ancestry as a vital tool in the structure of group identities in Castile and the Extremadura region.[21] Marie-Claude Gerbet's *La noblesse dans royaume de Castille* states that the Siete Partidas made Castilians keenly aware of lineage.[22] Further, house and bloodlines (*sang*) communicated vital information about the nobility and social status of a family unit.[23]

Helen Nader's foundational work, *The Mendoza Family in the Spanish Renaissance 1350–1550*, stands out because it explores contemporary views of family identities and discusses an elite clan connected to the Plasencia Carvajal family. For example, Fernán Pérez de Guzmán, the prominent royal historian and author *of Generaciones y semblanzas*, stated that the Castilians' noble character of "loyalty" and "action" was firmly seated in the social structure of family.[24] In the case of the Mendoza clan, men such as Pedro González de Mendoza, cardinal of Santa Croce, perpetuated a "family tradition" of leadership in the intellectual, social, and political realms.[25] The Mendoza family were counterparts and patrons of the lesser-known Carvajal clan. Bernardino López de Carvajal would become cardinal of Santa Croce at the end of the fifteenth century. In such ways family identities channeled the activities of the group and extended into broader collective family networks.

Jewish and Muslim communities had an equal or even heightened attention to family identity within Christian domains. José Amador de los Ríos, in his fundamental study of Jewish life, *Historia social, política y religiosa de los judíos de España y Portugal*, maintained that Spanish Jews always placed "the father," and thus the family, at the center of group life.[26] Therefore, a paternally led family characterized the most immediate Jewish identity, which then was subsumed within the collective Jewish perception. Similarly, through the lens of women's lives, María Jesús Fuente argues, in "Christian, Muslim and Jewish Women," that Jewish culture utilized the domestic space of the home to bind the immediate family together. Jewish rituals relating to cooking and bread making, cleanliness, marriage and child rearing, and prayer all contributed to "safeguarding the cultural identity of community."[27]

Although outside the purview of this chapter, it should be noted that family identities remained pervasive well after the Spanish Middles Ages. The final chapter of this book, which addresses Spanish conversos' departure to the Americas, shows that family remained a powerful integrator of groups in Europe and the Americas during the sixteenth century.[28] Stephen Greenblatt determined that family could serve as an intermediary that linked the "individual experience and the alien . . . public world."[29] This was the case for comparable communities such as those in early sixteenth-century England; some Protestant families in Oxford, for example, held "intense familial emotion toward one another" as they endured in a Catholic community.[30] Even as new forms of religious self-perception were taking holding in Reformation Europe, family remained a bulwark against change. Likewise, in Italy, the social glue of the clan remained especially resilient among the aristocracy. Neapolitan nobles like the Caracciolo di Bienza "strove to ensure the continuation of the family name" and the maintenance of hereditary lands (entails) in Italy, as well as France and England.[31] Family-centered identities were a continental phenomenon that never lost relevance in early modern Europe.

FOUNDATION OF THE CHRISTIAN CITY AND THE DIOCESE OF PLASENCIA

With this medieval history in place, we can understand better multicultural Plasencia — its foundation, geography, and people — and the way in which Castilians adapted to the societal changes that transpired after the fourteenth century.

Plasencia is located in the rocky and oak-covered Spanish province of Extremadura, a territory formerly known as the Roman and Visigothic region of Lusitania. It was a hub of social and commercial life in the northern portion of the province. To the north was the university city of Salamanca, to the east was Toledo on the Tajo River, to the south was the ancient Roman city of Mérida, and to the west lay Portugal (fig. 1.1).

Placentinos conceived of themselves as inheritors of the Roman-Visigothic tradition, although Muslims dominated the area from 713 to 1189.[32] Muslim supremacy over the region began when the Visigoths, and their commercial capital of Mérida, capitulated to the Muslim governor Musa ibn Nusayr in a pitched battle.[33] At this time, Plasencia was not a major settlement, and, as the Islamic rulers learned, most of Extremadura was sparsely populated, with scattered minor fortifications and castles.[34] The province remained relatively uncontested up until the end of the twelfth century, when the Castilian king Alfonso VIII (r. 1158–1214) challenged the Almohad caliph Abu Yusuf Ya'qub al-Mansjur (r. 1184–99) for frontier territories separating the Kingdom of Castile and León from al-Andalus.[35]

Not until the sixteenth century do Christian sources speak about the city in any detail; the annals describe events that occurred at the end of the twelfth century (1189–96). Castilians think of this era as one marked by the triumphant capture and renaming of the city. For the Islamic Almohads, it was a short-term loss. The earliest

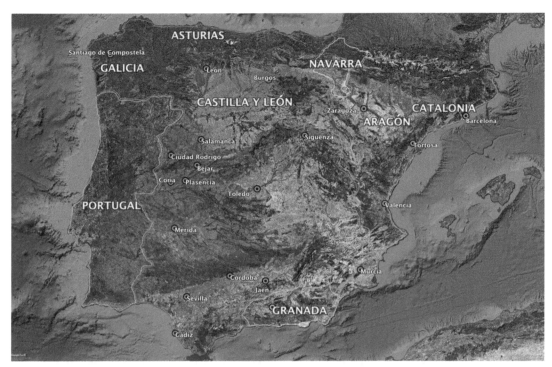

FIGURE 1.1. Late medieval Iberia. Author-created map. Google Maps Pro.
Used with permission.

historical source from Plasencia that speaks to this twelfth-century event is the 1579 manuscript titled "Anales de la Santa Iglesia Catedral de Plasencia desde su fundación," by Dr. Juan Correas Roldán, the church headmaster. The unpublished "Anales" is a critical original source for all later historians regarding the history of Plasencia. It records the capture and conversion of Plasencia from an Islamic-ruled city to one governed by Christians. An important component of the event was the rechristening of the city and the regeneration of the local church leadership. Correas Roldán declares in his "Anales," "In 1189, the thirty first year of [King Alfonso VIII's] reign . . . and in the Province Lusitania, which the Ancients called Vetonia and we now call the Extremadura, you [King Alfonso VIII] won from the Moors . . . the ancient city called Ambroz. There, you established the city of Plasencia by your royal privilege."[36]

In 1627, approximately fifty years after the appearance of Correas Roldán's history of Plasencia, Friar Alonso Fernández enlarged that account by drawing on an older and critical Castilian chronicle dedicated to the aggrandizement of King Alfonso VIII. Friar Alonso cites don Rodrigo Jiménez de Rada, archbishop of Toledo and an instrumental chronicler during Alfonso VIII's lifetime. Fernández quotes the archbishop's description of the city: "[King Alfonso VIII] directed his efforts to building a new and divine city . . . and he called her Plasencia. He converted those persons living in her villages [to the Christian faith] and exalted the Pontifical Tiara."[37]

However, on further examination, it appears that King Alfonso VIII was not simply transforming the thriving Islamic city of Ambroz into Plasencia but establishing a strategic Christian hamlet as a bulwark against the Islamic south. An 1188 royal donation of property from the king to Pedro Tajabor, archpriest of Ávila and archdeacon of Plasencia, just one year before its reconstitution, reveals the limited resources of the city. As Tajabor described it, "I encountered a dam in Plasencia, on the Jerete River,[38] situated close to the city's gate of Santa María. The city's dam was intact in its totality and it had a watermill and aqueducts constructed there. . . . [Y]ou, [King Alfonso VIII], also made a donation of an ancient church in the city. . . . We found the undisturbed church where the ancient city was first established."[39]

Tajabor was able to convert Plasencia's modest amenities (a dammed river, a watermill, some cultivable lands, and a church that was "still undestroyed") into a consolidated resource. At its best, Plasencia presented settlers with the opportunity to improve their economic circumstances by receiving land and property donations.

With the refoundation of the Christian city in the twelfth century, a castle was erected, as well as multiple city gates and walls, with as many as sixty-eight towers (referred to as "cubos").[40] The partially walled community, which appears to have been smaller than its late fourteenth-century footprint, could accommodate up to one thousand persons "at times of war."[41]

Unfortunately, no contemporaneous source from the period or any of the earliest Christian chroniclers of Plasencia indicate the religious makeup or population size of the city. The remarkably silent record recounts nothing about the Jewish population, and the only reference to Muslims is one that victoriously recalls "the expulsion of the Moors."[42] However, other sources disclose that as late as 1400 Plasencia remained primarily a Jewish and Muslim-populated city with a minority Christian population. According to archival tax records from the Diocese of Plasencia, in 1400 there were only 119 adult men and their families—40 Christians (34 percent), 50 Jews (42 percent), and 29 Muslims (24 percent)—who resided there.[43] Historians speculate the total population of the city was roughly 800 to 1,000 souls by 1400, although Luis de Toro reports that the city's population did not reach "almost 1,000 persons" until the 1570s.[44] Thus Jews and Muslims were a key component of the population base throughout the local economy. The Christians of Plasencia, on the other hand, are remembered in modest details. The Christian knights (of the Order of Alcantara), churchmen, and families who settled in Plasencia "came from the mountains of Burgos," the political-religious capital of the Kingdom of Castile and León.[45]

What most local chroniclers of Plasencia exclude from their ecclesiastical histories is a particularly significant moment in its formation: the recapture of the city by Caliph Abu Yusuf in 1195–96.[46] Not only was the Castilians' triumphant establishment of

Christian Plasencia derailed for as many as twenty-six years (through 1221), but even the details of its destruction and the fate of the clergy were either not clearly understood or misrepresented by Christian historians.

Refounding of Plasencia

Although the Christians advanced against the Spanish Muslims in a critical victory at the Battle of Las Navas de Tolosa in 1212, it was an additional nine years before royal and papal authority was restored to Plasencia. On November 10, 1221, a new Castilian king, Fernando III (r. 1217–52), "conceded and confirmed" the royal privilege that King Alfonso VIII had previously granted to the city of Plasencia in the form of a royal city charter, or *fuero*.[47] The comprehensive legal document governed all aspects of life, including local public offices, clerical roles, criminal acts, civil disputes, trade, festivals, and public spaces, to name a few.

While the Fuero de Plasencia was very important to the community because it established the rights and privileges of the king and the city and its inhabitants, it also informed the separation enforced between Christians, Muslims, and Jews. Over thirty of its individual laws and decrees pertained to the distinctive Jewish and Muslims communities, thus reinforcing the well-established norm of separate religious identities in medieval Iberia.[48] Among the more prominent religious issues in the Fuero was religious conversion. It welcomed and encouraged Muslim families to convert to Christianity and enjoy the privileges of a Christian identity. Specifically, the king instructed, "I mandate that all of those men that are Muslims and become Christians . . . that as their lord, I will receive and think well of them."[49] In the Plasencia context, this was the first indication that religious identity could change, and the Fuero served as an origin point for the creation of the fifteenth century's demarcations of "Old" versus "New" Christians.

However, conversion was not necessary to participate in civic life, as the king dictated that Christians as well as Jews and Muslims could serve as royally appointed city councilmen (*corredores*) and retain the privilege of bearing weapons and arms in the city.[50] Therefore, Plasencia's Fuero created a representative role for religious minorities in Castilian affairs. Last, the king required disputes that involved persons of different faiths to be settled in a specific manner at a church located in the Jewish quarter of the city. Law VII stated, "In all disputes involving Jews and Christians, they will be heard at the Church of St. Nicholas and no other place. The cases will be heard at the hour of the regular mass of the church. And when these cases are considered closed, then their settlement cannot be vacated."[51]

This aspect of the Fuero, and others, showed that Christian society viewed each religious community (Jews, Christians, and Muslims) separately but nonetheless a part of the city. In the same year that King Fernando III issued his renewal of Plasencia's Fuero, official papal recognition came with a bull confirming the creation of the Diocese of Plasencia.[52] In 1221, Pope Honorius III acknowledged the king's efforts by declaring:

In Rome, we praise your royal effort to expand the Christian religion. And with the apostolic authority that is invested in the Holy See . . . we recognize . . . the valor of your strong arm against the Muslims. We now establish this cathedral of Plasencia with its own diocese, and all rights and privileges. . . . and it shall include the Villages of Trujillo, Medellín, Montfrague, and Santa Cruz. . . . We, therefore, confirm upon you, our beloved son in Christ, Fernándo III, King of Castile, your request for a bull that places you under our protection.[53]

Physical and Cultural Geography of the City

The physical boundaries of the city became more evident after 1221, when Plasencia would remain indefinitely in Christian hands. The Jerete River enclosed the city's southern flank from the west to the east. Along the banks of the river, in the city and north to the village of Béjar, were sizable agricultural plots. The sixteenth-century observer Luis de Toro, a physician and student at the University of Salamanca, described the city in great detail and prepared the first stereographic etching of it (fig. 1.2). His ebullient language characterized the richness of the city, the region, and its primary river, the Jerete: "It supports innumerable farming plots, vineyards, olive groves, and chestnut trees, but principally, there are apple groves. . . . They have the apples of the sweetest taste and size. . . . There are also every variety of lemon trees . . . and all types of cherry, pear, and peach trees."[54]

The eventually fortified, walled city relied on five gates both to facilitate the flow of people and goods and to deny access to enemies. Four of the city's gates (*puertas*), the Puerta de Talavera, Puerta de Trujillo, Puerta de Coria, and Puerta de Berrozana, led to nearby villages and territories. The fifth, the Puerta del Sol, was oriented to the sunrise. Flowing inward from these exterior points, like spokes on a wheel, were several major streets that led to the Plaza Mayor. Figure 1.3 shows the late medieval city of Plasencia with its city gates, castle, and respective religious quarters.[55]

Although the city had a Jewish quarter (*judería*) and a Muslim quarter (*morería*), Muslims and Jews also lived in other parts of Plasencia. Many religious minorities chose to live in these loosely defined zones. The city was an open community where Jews, Christians, and Muslims resided alongside one another. The large judería dominated the western portion of the city and could be entered via the Puerta de Coria or the Puerta de Trujillo. Under Christian rule, the Muslim population contracted and found itself settled in the eastern part of the city, between the Puerta de Talavera and the Puerta del Sol.

The Plaza Mayor was both the center of civic life and the location of surrounding residences for Jews, Christians, and Muslims. In the ideal Spanish Christian world, this should have been an exclusively Christian zone. When the city council (*consejo*) announced critical decisions, like that affecting the local taxation of wine, the city crier (*pregonero*) made these pronouncements in the Plaza Mayor.[56]

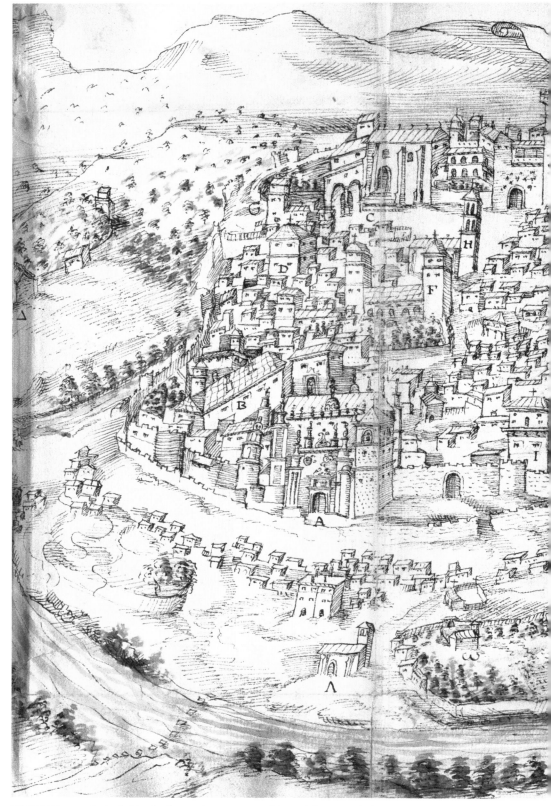

FIGURE 1.2. Luis de Toro's sixteenth-century etching of the city of Plasencia. Source: Biblioteca de la Universidad de Salamanca (BUS), MS 2.650. Descripción de la Ciudad y Obispado de Plasencia por Luis de Toro, fols. 25–26. Used with permission.

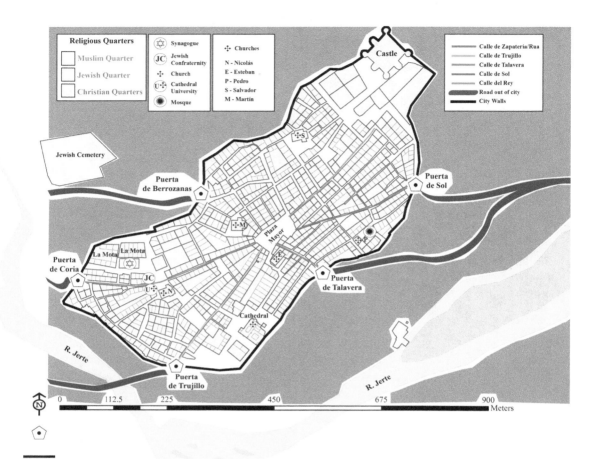

FIGURE 1.3. Map of the city of Plasencia. Source: Revealing Cooperation and Conflict Project. Used with permission.

Entering the city from the east would take one through the Puerta de Sol and west-ward along Calle de Sol to the central plaza. The eastern section of the city was desig-nated the Muslim quarter (*aljama*). Yet this was not a religiously one-dimensional space. On this primary thoroughfare, the cathedral owned numerous houses, many of which were close to the Plaza Mayor.[57] In the vicinity of these homes and close to the Puerta de Sol was the Islamic mosque, which during the late fifteenth or early sixteenth century was converted to the Church of Saint Peter (Iglesia de San Pedro).[58] According to one of the principal historians of the city, D. Jose Benavides Checa, the first reference to Chris-tian artwork and a chapel in the former mosque was not recorded until 1562. Thus it ap-pears the mosque remained a Muslim house of worship at least into the late 1400s.

From the southeast, one entered through the Puerta de Talavera and passed along Calle de Talavera to the center of the city. On this lane was one of the oldest parishes, the Church of Saint Steven (Iglesia de San Esteban), which the clergy had reportedly founded as early as 1254.[59]

Between the southeastern Puerta de Talavera and the southern Puerta de Trujillo, was the cathedral of Plasencia, which was stylistically Romanesque.[60] Peppering the streets and alleys adjacent to the cathedral were more church-owned houses as well as stables (*establos*).[61] Church canons and prebendaries resided in most of these homes and leased them for as little as five *maravedís* (silver coins) a year during the 1410s.[62] This was a relatively modest sum when contrasted to the taxes (*portazgo*) assessed on goods transported into and through the city of Plasencia. For example, a trader passing through the city's gates would pay two maravedís to the city council to bring high-quality honey into the city for sale.[63] This southeastern section of the city was one of the few zones populated exclusively by Christians.

Entering the city from the south, one traveled through the Puerta de Trujillo and on to Calle de Trujillo. Along this road, which led directly to the Plaza Mayor, were houses with corrals and stables. The church also owned many of these, often leasing them to church officials and local residents.[64] The street also served as a boundary between the Jewish quarter to the north and the Christian sector closest to the cathedral.[65]

North of the Calle de Trujillo was the Puerta de Coria, which led to the Jewish quarter filled with Christian nobles. The two roads connecting this western gate to the Plaza Mayor, Calle de Coria and Calle de la Rua/Zapatería, ran through the center of the Jewish quarter. In actuality, by the 1300s this section of the town was not exclusively Jewish. Both Jews and Christians lived and owned property here. The Church of Saint Nicholas (Iglesia de San Nicolás) and the Jewish synagogue were also located on this road. Established in 1326, the church was built on the foundation of an old Roman temple.[66]

As previously noted, the Church of Saint Nicholas was an important venue because interfaith disputes were resolved at its front doors (fig. 1.4).[67] In "extraordinary circumstances," a Jewish judge and a Christian judge heard and adjudicated cases on the church's steps that involved conflicts between individuals of these different faiths.[68] The synagogue of Plasencia, the Jewish confraternity (*cofradía de los judíos*), and a large block of enclosed Jewish residences (Apartamiento de La Mota) sat across from the church. Although this was a predominantly Jewish section of Plasencia, Christian clans such as the Carvajal and the Estúñiga had constructed homes there by the 1400s.[69] In 1493, this section of town lost its center of Jewish life when the Catholic monarchs forced the Jewish community to "hand over the keys of the synagogue" to local Christian leaders.[70] (Figs. 1.4–1.6.)

The Christian sector of the city was accessed via the northwestern gate (Puerta de Berrozana), which provided a circuitous route to the Plaza Mayor and reached the city's castle. Within this part of the city stood two churches: the Church of Saint Martin (Iglesia de San Martín), founded before 1273 as the community's second parish, and the Church of the Savior (Iglesia del Salvador). Several noble Christian families resided here, such as the Martínez and the Trejo, who also favored these churches for

FIGURE 1.4. Digital painting of the Church of Saint Nicholas. Source: Revealing Cooperation and Conflict Project. Painting by David Seidman.

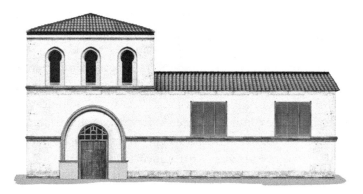

FIGURE 1.5. Digital painting of the synagogue of Plasencia. The synagogue is no longer in existence. This visualization uses the original footprint of the synagogue and incorporates architectural elements from other fifteenth-century synagogues that remain intact in Ávila, Córdoba, and Toledo. Source: Revealing Cooperation and Conflict Project. Painting by David Seidman.

FIGURE 1.6. Digital painting of the plaza of Saint Nicholas. Church of Saint Nicholas (left), synagogue of Plasencia (center), and Palace of Mirabel (right). Source: Revealing Cooperation and Conflict Project. Painting by David Seidman.

their entombments and the saying of memorial masses for their families.[71] Like most of the city's other neighborhoods, this one claimed a mixed Muslim-Christian pedigree. Although Spain's Islamic and Christian roots dictated strict delineations of the three religious communities and their identities, within the city of Plasencia different peoples lived alongside one another.

Christian Families in Plasencia before 1400

Like the physical boundaries of the city, during the remainder of the thirteenth century, the social fabric of Plasencia changed little. Increasingly, however, two principal classes of men and their families began to dominate its historical trajectory: knights and members of the cathedral chapter, hereafter referred to as churchmen. Still silent, the archival record yields no information about the foundational Muslim and Jewish families of the thirteenth and fourteenth centuries.

During this period, King Fernando III continuously dispatched Plasencia knights to the south, where they participated in the reconquest of the Muslim cities of Jaén (1246), Baeza (1247), and Sevilla (1248).[72] Almost four decades later, in the service of King Sancho IV, knights from Plasencia besieged Jérez de la Frontera for six months.[73] Among the leading Plasencia families participating in the siege were the Carvajal, the Monroy, and the Almaraz.[74]

From the mid-thirteenth century into the early fourteenth century, the region witnessed the rise of several Christian families from the lesser aristocracy, as well as other more established families who began to form their own seigniorial lands (*señorios*) with the approval of the monarchy. This "old" aristocratic class would soon be eclipsed, when the Castilian monarchy in the late 1300s unleashed a grand social-religious experiment that entailed the creation of a new aristocracy composed of New Christian families. (See ch. 2.) Most of these Old Christian families were heavily intermarried, as social status reinforced a desire by elite clans to maintain exclusivity.

In 1252, the Old Christian Carvajal clan first appears in the local historical record when the knight Diego Gonzalez de Carvajal founded the Monasterio de San Marcos.[75] Local chronicles note that Diego and his father resided in Plasencia and were in the service of King Fernando III. The two men participated in the king's military campaigns against the Iberian Muslims and reportedly attended to the king's mother, doña Berenguela, as her stewards (*mayordomos*).[76] After the reconquest of Sevilla (1248), Diego retired to Plasencia; the family continued to reside there as a minor noble clan of modest means up through the fourteenth century.[77] Spanish nobility genealogies maintain that the Carvajal family of Plasencia was descended from the line of King Bermudo II of León (r. 982–99) and through these noble origins entered knightly service.[78]

Although the Carvajal house was the fountainhead of many intermarried noble clans, what was special about it was its prized Old Christian status and ability to incorporate New Christians clans. In essence, as Castilian society increasingly viewed new converts to Christianity with suspicion, the Carvajal family would use its ancient Christian surname to hide less desirable New Christian ones. These included, during the fourteenth through fifteenth centuries, the González, Trejo, Quiros, Sotomayor, Villalva, Bermudez, Chavez, Garcia, Bejarano, Tamayo, Ulloa, Espadero, Yanguas, Galindez, Girón, Loaysa, Almaraz, Álvarez de Toledo, Fernández, Cabreros, Gutiérrez, and, most important, Santa María families.[79] The origins of the distinct Santa María family, who converted from Judaism to Christianity during the fourteenth century, is discussed in depth in chapter 2.

By the beginning of the 1300s, the region began to generate its own elite Old Christian aristocracy. For example, in 1262, the king named the Old Christian Pedro Sánchez the first señor de Grimaldo.[80] Twenty years later his señorio passed to the Bermudez and Trejo houses.[81] The señores de Grimaldo integrated with the Bermudez, Trejo, Gutiérrez, López, Carvajal, Sande, Paniagua, Villalobos, Toro, Barca, and Gasca clans.[82] In 1295, the king named don Nuño Pérez de Monroy señor of Valverde.[83]

The first decade of the 1300s would see additional local knights converted into lords by the king. First was Fernán Pérez de Bote, who formed the señorio de Belvis.[84] Juan Alonso de Almaraz followed him as the señor de Almaraz. The house of Almaraz would grow to include the Bote, Fernández, Monroy, Pérez, Godinez, Rodríguez, and Garcia families.[85] In 1309, King Fernando IV granted Fernán Pérez de Monroy, a knight, the privilege to establish seigniorial lands near a farmhouse in Monroy.[86]

Notably absent from this accounting of noble houses in the vicinity of Plasencia were the New Noble families that the Castilian monarchy created at the tail end of the fourteenth century. Although the new nobility was not exclusively New Christian, several families were indeed intermarried with Jews or had Jewish origins. Among these clans were the Álvarez de Toledo, who became the señores de Oropesa; the Estúñiga, who became the condes de Béjar y Plasencia; and the Santa María, a noble family of elite church leaders and royal administrators. Each of them would achieve meteoric ascendance during the 1400s in spite of their Jewish ancestries.

The ecclesiastical counterpart of nobles and knights in pre-fifteenth-century Plasencia was a reliable collection of church leaders, of which little is known. The first bishop of Plasencia, who led the city through the period of Christian and Muslim reconquests of the region (1189–1212), is only known as "Don Bricio."[87] He initiated the construction of the first cathedral in the city (now known as the Old Cathedral), but other than this detail, there is no record of his family or his church deacons and other officials. Following his administration, the first named cathedral clan was that of Bishop "Don Domingo" (r. 1212–33), a member of the house of Jimenez.[88]

Shortly after Bishop Domingo's term, the cathedral's churchmen began to solidify the organization and administration of the diocese. The church finally received its Foundational Statute (Estatuto Fundamental) in 1254, establishing its structure and operations.[89] In a papal bull, Pope Innocent IV authorized ten canon positions for the

FIGURE 1.7. Facade of the Old Cathedral of Plasencia. Photo by author.

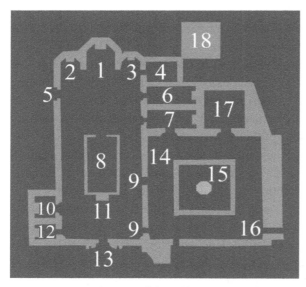

KEY POINTS OF INTEREST
1. Main altar
2. Altar of the Crucifixion
3. Altar of Our Lady of Mercy
4. Sacristy
5. Door of Mercy
6. Chapel of Saint Vincent
7. Chapel of Holy Mary "The Fair"
8. Choir
9. Doors to the Cloister
10. Chapel of Saint Catherine
11. Altar of the Choir
12. Chapel of the Doctors
13. Main door
14. Cloister
15. Plaza of the Oranges and Fountain of Juan de Carvajal
16. Altar of Our Lady of the Cloister
17. Chapel of Saint Paul and the Cathedral Chapter Hall
18. Bell Tower

FIGURE 1.8. Diagram of the Old Cathedral of Plasencia. Prepared by author.

cathedral. The document also created five dignitary offices (*dignidades*). The dignitaries included the dean, the archdeacon of Plasencia, the archdeacon of Trujillo, the cantor, and a treasurer. In addition, the statute created eight prebendary (*racionero*) positions and detailed the separate responsibilities of priests.

The church's locus of authority was the cathedral, and its governing chapter routinely convened in the Chapel of Saint Paul to conduct church business (figs. 1.7, 1.8). These meetings involved, among other tasks, the leasing of church properties, the management of tax collections, the distribution of church revenues to its membership, and the preparation of new statutes to govern its internal affairs.[90]

While the physical and organizational structure of the cathedral is well documented, there is almost no information about the men who inhabited it. No family surnames survive in the historical chronicles or in archival manuscripts from the mid-1200s through the close of the 1300s. Not until the start of the late 1390s did the cathedral's notaries consistently report on the clan affairs of the most powerful Plasencia church family—the Fernández. In its brief appearance over the course of two decades, 1390 to 1410, the Fernández clan would find its rule over the cathedral contested by the Carvajal and Santa María families (see ch. 3).

But before the local ecclesiastical authority in this northern reach of the Extremadura would be challenged, all Castilians would have to endure the fourteenth century's trials of plague, climate change, and civil war. The historian Teofilo F. Ruiz calls this period the beginning of "Spain's centuries of crisis" during which "dramatic and cataclysmic events" led ultimately to brutal conflicts "about power, and strife over who would, in the end, wield authority."[91] The issue of Castilian secular and ecclesiastical leadership was decisively shaped by a new king, Enrique II of Trastámara, and new families that sparked the creation of a novel and fragmented Spanish identity— a converso identity.

2

CRISIS AND IMPETUS

This investigation of Castilian crises and the impetus for cultural change commences with an exploration of late fourteenth-century affairs—plague, civil war, and anti-Jewish riots. From their ruinous outcomes, the local Placentino families, both Jewish and Old Christian houses of lesser knights, experienced significant religious and economic pain that may have served as the decisive impetus for radical experimentation by Old Christians and conversos to form new networks and alliances to compete for political and economic success. These events establish the cultural baseline against which new identities can be understood. Converso and New Noble families stood in stark contrast to past delineations of Jews and Christians. As this book's narrative unfolds, especially in the following chapter, the details reveal how many of Spain's noteworthy families came not only from Old Christian backgrounds but from Jewish and Muslim ones as well. The untold history of the Carvajal, the Santa María, and the Estúñiga illuminates the trajectories of such families.

As the fourteenth century drew to a close, the old order of tightly defined religious groups and stable social stations was radically altered. The willing conversion of a few elite families from Judaism to Christianity, the uneven disintegration of Jewish and Christian communal relations, and Castile's King Enrique II's testamentary actions creating a class of New Noble families all contributed to a crisis of old religious identities and the impetus to create new hybridized Jewish-Christian ones. The unexpected outcome of this political and social experiment was the generation of a new identity, a new way of self- and group perception, that blended Christian norms with selected Jewish customs. In effect, this was a transition from traditional, recognizable medieval religious identities, Jewish versus Christian, to ones that would become officially sanctioned as based on ethnic, racial, and blood lineage characteristics. Spanish Christians would come to view religion not as a matter of conscience but as explicitly tied to genealogy. Because the crucial and all-encompassing issue of blood lineage is so formative for the fifteenth century, it cannot be presented neatly in one chapter. Rather, it must be discussed chronologically and as the phenomenon of blood purity unfolded, which was especially momentous during the 1450s and the implementation of government-enforced blood purity statutes. But before Spanish Christians would turn to blood ancestry to define and categorize peoples, it first would pass through many difficult days.

THE TROUBLED FOURTEENTH CENTURY

The seeds of change began with the sudden and unexpected death of King Alfonso XI in 1350 from the Black Plague.[1] Between 1347 and 1350, the plague claimed the lives of approximately 25 million in Europe, or 25 percent of the population.[2] In fact, the pandemic returned two more times in Castile, in 1374 and 1384. Over the course of the fourteenth century, the Iberian population withered from an estimated 5.5 million to 4.5 million.[3] Across Europe, Jewish communities were implicated as the cause of the illness. Samuel M. Cohn Jr. writes that "Jews were accused of poisoning food, wells and streams, tortured into confessions, rounded up in city squares or their synagogues, and exterminated en masse."[4] In Germany, southern France, and Spain, in particular, the "burning of Jews" was carried out.[5]

The *Crónica de los reyes de Castilla* did not implicate the Jewish community in the death of Alfonso XI, however. Instead it relates that the monarch was one of the many victims of the plague: "[While laying siege to Gibraltar and] after the battles and conquests by the noble prince Lord King Alfonso of Castile and León . . . it was at the village and the noble, notable, very strong castle of Gibraltar, the plague entered among the Muslims and Christians. . . . By the will of God this pestilence of the greatest mortality returned and fell upon our most noble Lord King Alfonso."[6]

On Alfonso's death civil war broke out, with the king's legitimate son Pedro I "the Cruel" battling his half brother Prince Enrique II of Trastámara for the kingdom and crown.[7] Neither of the competing claimants could secure the kingdom. Pedro I was only fifteen years old, and many leaders considered him too young to rule, whereas his older half brother was the son of the deceased king's mistress, Leonor de Guzmán.[8]

In 1350, as Pedro I attempted to consolidate his rule, a member of the Jewish ha-Levi family served as his chief treasurer.[9] Among Samuel Levi's efforts on behalf of Castilian Jewish communities was the founding of El Tránsito Synagogue in Toledo in 1357, which was commemorated with a stucco plaque bearing the royal Castilian coat of arms (center shield with lions and castles), as well as the genealogical-heraldic device adopted by the ha-Levi–Santa María clan, the *flores de lilio* (fig. 2.1; left side,

FIGURE 2.1. Stucco plaque commemorating the founding of El Tránsito Synagogue (Toledo, Spain). Source: David Bláquez. Used with permission.

above castle).[10] By 1360, however, Pedro had Samuel executed on the rack; this may have had a bearing on the ha-Levis' abandonment of Pedro and subsequent support of Enrique II.[11]

Hostilities between the half brothers commenced as early as 1353, when Enrique fielded 600 knights and 1,500 Asturian men-at-arms in the village of Cigales to meet Pedro I's military companies coming from the nearby city of Valladolid.[12] Joining Enrique II's endeavor to unseat Pedro I were many noble families, including that of Count Juan Alfonso de Alburquerque.[13] The count's allegiance to Enrique II reflected the challenges and choices that the Old Nobility faced during the civil war. Who should they support—the legitimate heir to the throne, Pedro I, or the illegitimate Enrique II? Also complicating the political environment and battlefield was Pedro I's war with Pere III, king of Aragon, who had his own design for control of the Iberian Peninsula.[14]

The civil war that Pedro I waged was, according to Villalón, a "bloody Iberian episode"; "the monarch employed terror as a major military strategy, an external terror directed against the enemy and an internal one aimed at inspiring his own followers to greater efforts."[15] Royal directives ordered Castilians loyal to Pedro I "to wage the cruelest war you can."[16] Supporting his efforts were Old Noble families like the Fernández de Henestrosa, Suárez de Figueroa, Fernández de Toledo, and Benavides.[17]

By 1360, after he had three of his half brothers executed and signed a peace accord with the Kingdom of Aragon, Pedro I seemed to be in a strong position to gain the upper hand.[18] The remaining impediment to his consolidation of control of Castile was his brother, Enrique II. Among the many complaints raised by Enrique II was that his half brother was far too sympathetic to religious minorities and was overly dependent on Jewish advisers and Muslim men-at-arms.[19] On several occasions during the civil war, Enrique II besieged Jewish communities in Toledo and Burgos.[20] It was ironic that in his eventual victory over Pedro I, Enrique II would turn to Jewish converts to Christianity as he rebuilt his devastated prize, the Kingdom of Castile and León.

The royal contest was also an international conflict as several Spanish Christian kingdoms, England, and France politically and militarily wrestled with each other on the continent during the opening of the Hundred Years' War.[21] England and France both courted Castile as a strategic ally in their continental war, which in 1362 pulled Pedro I into an alliance with King Edward III's England and in 1363 prompted France to recognize Enrique II as the legitimate heir to the crown of Castile.[22]

Not until 1369 was the conflict for the crown resolved, when Enrique II and Pedro I fought the fateful Battle of Montiel.[23] Supporting Enrique II were Toledo archbishop Gómez Manrique, Pedro González de Mendoza, Ferrand Pérez de Ayala, Diego García de Toledo, Diego Gómez de Toledo, Juan Alfonso de Guzmán, Alfonso Fernández de Montemayor, Gonzalo Fernández de Córdoba, Mosén Beltrán de Calquín, and Gonzalo Mejía, among others.[24] At Montiel, Pedro I was defeated and took refuge in his castle.[25] When Enrique II sent his emissary, Mosén Beltrán, to his half brother to negotiate, Pedro sought Beltrán's assistance to betray Enrique II, making him a generous offer. As the chronicler Pedro López de Ayala reported, "Pedro . . . said if he [Mosén] will liberate him from here, safely and securely . . . he would give to him, and those who succeeded him, the villages of Soria, Almazán, Atienza, Montagudo, Deza, and Serón . . . as well as two hundred thousand Castilian *doblas*."[26]

Beltrán agreed to the treachery but informed Enrique II of the plan and led him to Pedro's refuge. There the two met face-to-face. According to Pedro López, the bitter war had inflicted damage on both men's memory, and Enrique II did not recognize his half brother. In the presence of Pedro I, one of Beltrán's knights said to Enrique II, "This man is your enemy," and to this statement Pedro I replied, "I am. I am."[27] With a dagger, Enrique II struck his half sibling in the face; "the two fell to the ground . . . and there died King Pedro on the twenty-third day of March of the said year."[28] With Pedro's death in 1369, Enrique II became the fountainhead of the Trastámaran dynasty, culminating in the unification of Spain under Isabel of Castile and Ferdinand of Aragón in 1469.[29]

With the death of Pedro I, the Navarrese, Portuguese, and Catalonian-Aragonese quashed the Castilians' desires for total Iberian control. On the continent, the English stood as a hostile power just to the north as they ruled much of France from Bordeaux.[30] Likewise, in the 1370s, Fernando of Portugal challenged Enrique II's claims for the Castilian crown, as did John, duke of Lancaster, who was married to Pedro I's eldest living daughter, Doña Constanza.[31] Only after Castile's successful invasion of Portugal and support of French efforts to retake La Rochelle, Normandy, and Brittany in 1372 and 1373 did Enrique II ensure his rule and the succession of his progeny.[32]

The twin stresses of political disintegration and disease facilitated a unique political and cultural change in Castilian cultural history. The Castilian nobility were exhausted by almost two decades of civil war.

CREATIVE ACTION: NEW FAMILIES AT THE OPENING OF THE FIFTEENTH CENTURY

Under the typical constraints of most medieval European monarchs who had the power to grant titles but lacked financial resources, Enrique II and his three heirs devised an ingenious method to regenerate the noble class. Their approach and calculation were simple: in return for political loyalty and financial assistance, Enrique promoted lower-class noble Christian families and elite Jewish and New Christian clans to become his new nobility. The social experiment was wildly successful, even if it came at the expense of the traditional old nobility and ran counter to anti-Jewish polemics during the civil war and thus angered Christian commoners. At the heart of rebuilding the nobility was the rapid integration of elite conversos into royal and church institutions. Henceforth, conversos would rapidly secure new opportunities, and Jews who maintained their religion would face an uncertain future.

The explosive 1390s, characterized as one of the most prominent times in the de-cline of Spanish Jewry, and the first two decades of the 1400s present a perplexing his-tory that defies artful explanations. On the one hand, Jewish converts to Catholicism, especially those who had successfully intermarried and collaborated with the Chris-tian elite, experienced an unprecedented social and political ascendency; on the other, Sephardim experienced intense communal pressure and uneven outcomes across the Iberian Peninsula. Many Jewish communities were annihilated. Others weathered a storm of Christian persecution. And yet some, like those in Plasencia, managed to sur-vive due to economic need and cultural respect for *convivencia* (coexistence) on the part of Old Christians and conversos.

While the Sephardim suffered, their former coreligionists found new opportuni-ties as a result of the political disintegration of the old nobility during the late four-teenth century. There was significant transformation of the nobility during this era as the crown bankrupted and disempowered the older feudal nobility and replaced them with new elite families such as the Estúñiga, Mendoza, and Álvarez de Toledo. While the new elite, who were quite powerful themselves, could spar with the crown for au-thority and resources, lesser families like the Carvajal and Santa María remained the creatures of the king.[33]

Prior to the rule of Pedro I, the older Christian nobles of Castile prospered through control of family feudal lands, which were not indissoluble *mayorazgos* (en-tailed lands). These territories, given to feudal families by the crown, generated rents and natural resources and created the conditions for them to prosper financially. These families included the Aguilar, Álvarez de Asturias, Arana, Aza, Camero, Cas-tañeda, Castro, Cerda, Cisneros, Enríquez, Girón, Guevara, Guzmán, Haro, Hinojosa, Lara, Manrique, Manuel, Manzanedo, Marañón, Mendoza, Meneses, Osorio, Ponce de León, Rojas, Saldaña, Traba, Valencia, Vega, Villalobos, and Villamayor.[34]

The older noble families were responsible for contributing men, resources, and taxes to the Castilian crown. Pedro I's reign disenfranchised these families by relying on local municipal administrations instead of his nobles, preventing the Cortes (par-liament) from meeting, actively controlling the military orders, and relying on foreign Genoese administrators and Castilian Jewish advisers.[35] These restrictions on the Old Noble families, in addition to the Castilian civil war between Pedro I and Enrique II and the war with Aragón, left Castile in a vulnerable position.

Bartolomé Clavero's seminal text, *Mayorazgo: Propiedad feudal en Castilla 1369–1836*, provides an expansive discussion of this heir- and wealth-protection sys-tem.[36] Clavero argues that the Castilian development of the mayorazgo was built on the preexisting concept of *concesión feudal* (feudal concession).[37] Under this system, the king granted vassals conditional dominion over their individual patrimonial vil-lages and lands and, more critically, the right to benefit (materially and financially) from control of these territories.[38] The first feudal concessions in Castile, prior to 1374, were known as *mercedes enriqueñas*, later enhanced to their mayorazgo form by

Enrique II.[39] On March 23, 1374, the king specified in the twenty-third clause of his testament that his royal *donaciones* and *mercedes* (donations and gifts) to his noblemen were to pass to their firstborn sons; should one of his noblemen die without an heir, the rights to the lands would revert to the crown.[40]

Salvador de Moxó argues that a key feature of the mercedes enriqueñas was a transition from the norms of the thirteenth and early fourteenth centuries. In the past, "the nobilities' principal font of wealth and patrimonial status was built on their territorial dominions," which were accumulated during the Christian expansion during the Reconquista.[41] However, this fundamentally changed in the late fourteenth century as the king resorted to another source of wealth creation, the granting of economic privileges to New Nobles, such as *portazgo* (city gate tax) and *cabeza de pecho* (poll tax on Muslims and Jews).[42] Based on Enrique II's testament, from 1380 to 1488 eight New Noble families individually collected and combined their royal rights, donations, and gifts and formed familial mayorazgos (table 2.1).

The fifteenth century saw the new nobility having an unprecedented oligopoly on political and economic power. The converso upper class was by no means alone, as other great noble houses benefited from the Trastámaran dynasty's concessions, such as the Enríquez, Jajardo, Guzmán, Manrique, Medinacelli, Quiñones, Velasco, and Villena clans.[43] This disturbance in the old order "led to waves of violence and instability" as the crown was consistently tested by its noble houses and as the latter challenged one another.[44] Therefore, it is at this historical moment that Spanish Christian elites and commoners began to see themselves in a new light. Elite clans became a dynamic mix of Old and New Christians and and Old and New Nobles—all of which used every political and cultural tool at their disposal to outcompete one another.

PLASENCIA'S FUTURE: OLD CHRISTIAN, CONVERSO, AND NEW NOBLE FAMILIES

Plasencia could not escape the transformations that transpired in the Castilian world during the late 1300s. Among the newly arriving families in the city were the converso Santa Marías of Burgos. Other important clans included the converso and New Noble Estúñigas, condes de Béjar y Plasencia. The wealthy and militarily powerful Estúñigas began as Carvajal collaborators during the 1410s. However, after disputes over the condes' treatment of local nobles during the early fifteenth century, the two became bitter enemies. To a lesser extent, other converso and New Noble families such as the Álvarez de Toledo (señores de Oropesa) coexisted with the Carvajal and Santa María—sometimes at odds and sometimes building new collaborative networks. On the whole, each of these Castilian houses represented different family pathways that were molded by Christian and Jewish histories.

Table 2.1. New Elite Family Mayorazgos in Castile, Fourteenth to Fifteenth Centuries (converso families denoted with an asterisk*)

Founder	Year of Foundation	Title	Notes
Pedro Fernández de Velasco	1380	Conde de Haro	Formation of the mayorazgo was started in 1371 but not completed until 1458.
Pedro González de Mendoza*	1380	Duque de Infantado	
Rodrigo Ponce de León*	1392	Duque de Arcos	By 1469 the Ponce de León and Estúñiga families intermarried. The grandson of Rodrigo Ponce de León, also known as Rodrigo, married Teresa de Estúñiga, a member of the Conde de Béjar family.[a]
Diego Lopez de Estúñiga*	1397	Conde-Duque de Béjar	
Rodrigo Alfonso de Pimentel*	1440	Conde-Duque de Benavente	
Fernán Ruiz de Alarcón	1451	Señorío de Valverde	The basis for a mayorazgo was tied to the family patriarch, Fernán Ruiz de Alarcón.
Pedro Girón	1466	Duque de Osuna	
Casa de Borja	1488	Duque de Gandía	

Source: Clavero, *Mayorazgo*, 37–44.
[a]See AHNSN, Osuna, Caja124, doc. 2 (a, b, c, d) for details of the high-level intermarriage of the Estúñiga (Zúñiga) and Ponce de León clans. As the Estúñiga family is clearly converso, this marriage "corrupts" the main lineage of the Duques of Arcos in 1469.

The Old Christian Carvajal

The Old Christian Carvajal, unlike the elite New Noble families or the converso Santa María, were still a minor noble family that persisted as knights with limited resources. The Carvajal are clearly identifiable as originating from the Extremaduran towns of Plasencia, Trujillo, and Cáceres during the thirteenth century, although near the fifteenth century they expanded into Talavera de la Reina and eventually Sevilla.

However, there are indications that the Carvajal family may have included a Jewish lineage that was located in the same place as where the Santa María originated—

the city of Burgos. The Carvajal clan may have been early Jewish converts to Catholicism (prior to the 1200s), and some branches of the family (those in Plasencia) were indeed New Christians. In 1429, Yucef Carvajal, a member of the Jewish community in Burgos, was recorded as a community leader when he and fellow Jews confirmed the payment of religious poll taxes to Bishop Alonso de Cartagena, the son of Pablo de Santa María.[45] There is no additional information about the Jewish Carvajal of Burgos, but it raises interesting questions about the ancestral origins of the family and their earlier connections to the Jewish ha-Levi–Santa María.

Spanish genealogies report that the Carvajal family of Plasencia is descended from the line of King Bermudo II of León (982–99) and entered knightly service on the basis of this noble origin.[46] The earliest tangible evidence connecting the Carvajal family to Plasencia is a mixture of narrative and physical evidence. According to Friar Alonso Fernández, a sixteenth-century local historian of Plasencia, Diego González de Carvajal and his father resided in Plasencia and were in the service of Ferdinand III (1217–52). The two men participated in the king's military campaigns against the Iberian Muslims and reportedly attended the king's mother, Doña Berenguela, as her stewards (*mayordomos*).[47] Further, after the reconquest of Sevilla (1248), Diego González and his father retired to Plasencia.[48] Friar Alonso bolsters his claim that the Carvajal family resided in Plasencia by noting that Diego González gave a donation to the nuns of the Monastery of Saint Mark (Monasterio de San Marcos), which allowed the nuns to establish their order in Plasencia in the 1230s.[49] In the monastery's church and at its main altar, Friar Alonso reported, an inscription on a sepulcher read, "Diego Gónzalez de Carvajal, family founder."[50] He cites this as tangible evidence of the early connection of the Carvajal family to this region: "From these words recorded on the epitaph, we know that Diego González de Carvajal was the progenitor and propagator of the Carvajal family in Plasencia."[51] Unfortunately, the nuns abandoned the monastery in the mid-fourteenth century, and there is no longer any way to verify Friar Alonso's account. Nonetheless, the friar's history of Plasencia provides tantalizing evidence of the origins of the Plasencia line of Carvajal knights.

Roughly one hundred years after the death of Diego González, the Carvajal family name appears frequently in the personal testaments, royal documents, and church accountings in the Archivo de la Catedral de Plasencia. The progenitors of the Plasencia lineage investigated in this book are the noble Diego González de Carvajal y Vargas and his spouse, Sevilla López de Villalobos, both of whom died before 1400. Only one significant detail is known about these two individuals: Sevilla López chose to be interred in the Church of Saint Nicholas, which is in the heart of the Jewish quarter.[52] After her death, the Carvajal family continued to patronize the church, and well into the sixteenth century many descendants selected the Church of Saint Nicholas as their final resting place.

Although the couple were nobles, they were not extremely wealthy, nor did they hold the title of lord of any city, village, or land. Unlike the Estúñiga and Álvarez de

Toledo clans, the Carvajal family lacked commanding incomes and extensive property bases. While it is difficult to determine Diego González de Carvajal y Vargas's personal wealth, the property of his eldest son, Diego, is quantifiable, suggesting that the Carvajal family's holdings were quite modest in comparison to those of the Estúñiga and the Álvarez de Toledo. For example, in his will of 1455, Diego González de Carvajal documented that he possessed 62,000 maravedís, owned an extensive housing complex in the city of Plasencia, and held a varied portfolio of properties in the region, including several vineyards, a grain mill, twenty-three *caballerías* (lands given to him by the king), and over two dozen other houses and various lands.[53] This was substantial wealth in comparison to commoners but little in relation to the Estúñiga or Álvarez de Toledo clans. As previously mentioned, in roughly the same year, the count of Béjar and Plasencia (Pedro de Estúñiga) earned 3.6 million maravedís from his property holdings, and Pedro Suárez de Toledo earned an annual royal salary of 80,000 maravedís.

Nevertheless, Diego and his wife, Sevilla, were successful in producing a distinguished family lineage with significant mobility into royal and especially ecclesiastical offices (fig. 2.2). Their son Diego served on the king's city council in Plasencia and produced multiple heirs from three separate marriages.

Diego's first marriage, to Juana García de Ulloa, a New Christian, assisted in the integration of the Ulloa and Carvajal clans, in addition to introducing the merchant Espadero family into the Carvajal extended family.[54] Juana García de Ulloa was a member of the Espadero clan, which was likely also a recent New Christian family.[55] In addition, through this marriage the Carvajal family shared a distant family connection to the converso Santa María family of Plasencia. Juana García's first cousin, María Gómez de Almaraz, was married to Juan González de Santa María.[56] More important, Diego González de Carvajal's second marriage, to Catalina González, produced children that would further enhance the family's fusion with other knightly clans, such as the Camargo and the Trejo (fig. 2.3).[57]

The Santa María, Rodríguez de Maluenda, and Gutiérrez de la Calleja

The converso Santa María were a well-known, potent political and ecclesiastical family at the opening of the fifteenth century. They are the focus of a contested historical debate: were they model converts to Christianity or traitors to Judaism? Their history in Extremadura, which is neither well documented nor well understood, is a central focus of this book. They were distinct from all other notable families in Plasencia, who, while elite, were not among the new nobility with ostentatious wealth. The family does not appear in Plasencia's archival documents before 1406.

The chain of events that brought the Santa María clan from its ancestral lands in Burgos to Plasencia commenced as early as 1390, the year Rabbi Solomon ha-Levi converted to Catholicism and took the name Pablo de Santa María.[58] Pablo was a de-

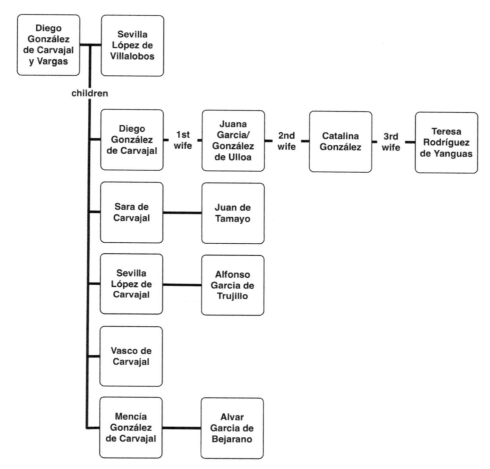

FIGURE 2.2. Genealogy of Diego González de Carvajal y Vargas and Sevilla López de Villalobos (early fifteenth century).

scendant of Samuel ha-Levi, the executed treasurer of Pedro I. Throughout the first three decades of the fifteenth century, Pablo was an ever-present force in the court of Juan II and was presumably related to the king.[59] He began as the young king's tutor and subsequently became his senior chancellor. The king also named him bishop of Cartagena (1403–15) and bishop of Burgos (1415–35). Pablo de Santa María's converso siblings, children, and relatives assumed various Castilian surnames, including Santa María, de Burgos, de García, de Cartagena, Rodríguez de Maluenda, and Gutiérrez de la Calleja (fig. 2.4).

Scholars in various disciplines have shaped Pablo de Santa María, the historical person, into several archetypal figures ranging from vicious persecutor of Jews to successful convert to Christianity. My position lies somewhere in between and is tied directly to the

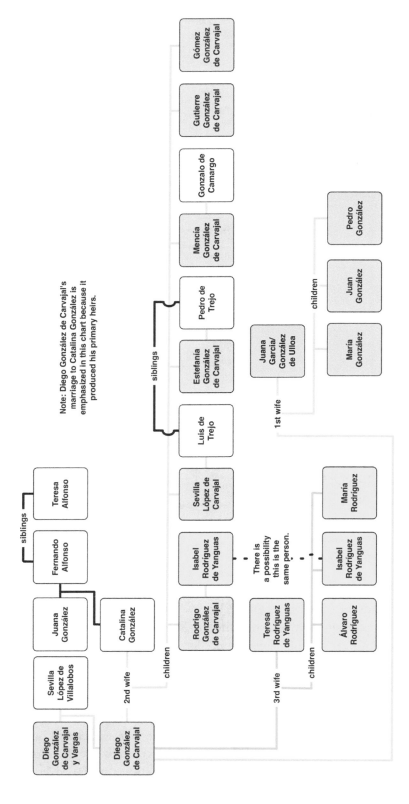

Note: Diego González de Carvajal's marriage to Catalina González is emphasized in this chart because it produced his primary heirs.

FIGURE 2.3. Genealogy of Diego González de Carvajal, his three wives, and his children.

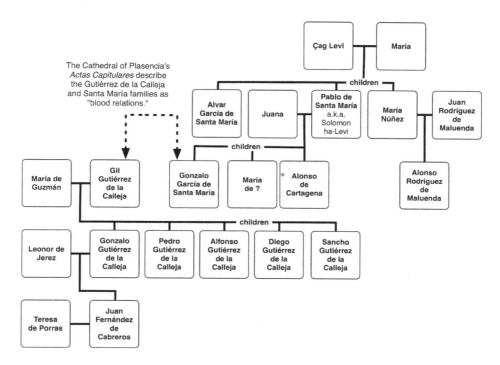

FIGURE 2.4. Genealogy of the Santa María family in Plasencia (fourteenth and fifteenth centuries).

archival record of royal and church administrative actions taken by him and his kin. Archival manuscripts from Burgos and Plasencia present a convincing account of a converso family intent on more than surviving after the degeneration of Jews' status in Christian Spain during the 1390s. Their activities in Extremadura demonstrate a single-minded focus on political ascent through carefully crafted family alliances, administrative achievements and collection of economic benefits from their church positions, and a tempered and relatively tolerant position vis-à-vis their former Jewish neighbors and family.

Perhaps one of the most carefully gauged evaluations of the font of the converso Santa María family is that of Henry Charles Lea:

> The most prominent among the new Conversos was Selemoh Ha-Levi, a rabbi who had been the most intrepid defender of the faith and rights of his race. On the eve of the massacres, which perhaps he foresaw, and influenced by an opportune vision of the Virgin, in 1390, he professed conversion, taking the name of Pablo de Santa Maria, and was followed by his two brothers and five sons, founding a family of commanding influence. . . . He wrote his *Scrutinium*

Scripturarum against his former coreligionists. . . . It is more moderate than is
customary in these controversial writings [of the period] and seems to have
been composed rather as a justification of his own course.[60]

Lea's assessment is a helpful one because it is not tainted with the scholarly hostility
seen in other works like those by José Amador de los Ríos and Yitzhak Baer (see below).
Lea states the historical details of the clan's conversion and contextualizes them in the
anti-Jewish violence of the era.

R. P. Luciano Serrano's *Los conversos D. Pablo de Santa María y D. Alfonso de Cartagena* and Francisco Cantera Burgos's *Alvar García de Santa María y su familia de conversos* also addressed the role of this most prominent converso family. These groundbreaking texts opened the door to a more open-minded perspective on the converso
experience, namely, that some conversos were actively managing their futures while
acknowledging their Jewish pasts. In doing so, the Santa María and other distinguished
New Christian families redefined what it meant to be Christians of Jewish ancestry. The
mere act of stepping outside the prescribed traditional religious boundaries, and doing
so as a Jewish leader, signaled a conspicuous break within the Jewish community.

Serrano argues that the Jewish community and peninsular rabbis received the
news of Pablo de Santa María's baptism on July 21, 1390, with "amazement" and as an
indication of a Christian apostolic plan in motion.[61] If the ha-Levi clan would convert,
who else would follow voluntarily? More significantly, would willing Jewish conversion to Christianity allow for a subset of the Jewish people to not only survive but also
thrive? With "sincerity, loyalty, and founded exclusively in doctrinal motives," Pablo
found Christianity, Serrano argued, and began a spiritual transformation that included a dreamlike vision of the Virgin Mary and a physical journey to the University
of Paris, where he earned his doctorate in theology.[62]

Without explicitly stating it, Serrano advanced the position that Pablo de Santa
María, and by extension other conversos, acted with individual agency and actively
formed new identities. The bishop's family, which included his sons, Bishop Alonso
de Cartagena and Bishop Gonzalo García de Santa María of Plasencia, subsequently
contributed to this identity remolding process as they demonstrated to Castile how
faithful converts could nobly serve the crown and the Roman Catholic Church. Cantera Burgos's text on Alvar García de Santa María largely communicated the same
themes of conversos framing their own futures.

But as can be expected from the controversial nature of this topic, these fundamental texts have not been received with universal endorsements. Norman Roth, an
important scholar of conversos, argues that Serrano's book is "full of misinformation
and romantic fantasy. . . . [T]he claim that as Solomon ha-Levy, rabbi of Burgos, Pablo
had established a huge 'school of Hebrew studies' which attracted students from all
Spain is sheer imagination for which there is not the slightest evidence."[63] Roth's fasci-

nating approach to critiquing this colleague demonstrates how each and every work that explores the lives of the Santa María family receives especially critical evaluation. Roth does seem to endorse Cantera Burgos's book, describing it as "the only balanced and factual treatment of this important converso family."[64]

Roth's own perspective on the ha-Levi/Santa María is an intriguing one that carefully dissects the genealogical and documentary confusion surrounding this family, which is often connected to the Benveniste, the Cavallería, and the Alazar,[65] specifically, whether we can precisely identify Pablo, and his activities, during his previous Jewish identity as Solomon ha-Levi.[66] One of the most interesting arguments that Roth offers about Pablo relates to his life as a Christian but before he became a leader in that faith. The author insinuates that Pablo was paid for his conversion to Christianity: "What has not been hitherto noticed is that among those listed as receiving payments from [Pope] Benedict XIII in March of 1396 was Pablo de Santa María."[67]

Ultimately, Roth seems to find that Pablo was a committed and loyal servant to Enrique III and Juan II and an aggressive defender ("fanatic zealot") of the Christian faith in his writings and his actions.[68]

Other historians have charged Pablo de Santa María and his lineage as treacherous defectors. Amador de los Ríos castigates Pablo by connecting him to Vicente Ferrer, the intense proselytizer of Jewish communities. Amador de los Ríos argues that Ferrer's mission to convert Jews closely corresponded with Castile's implementation of the anti-Jewish Ordinances of Valladolid, which Queen Mother Catalina and Prince Fernando de Antequera proposed in 1412 to regulate Jews.[69] Amador de los Ríos argues that Pablo de Santa María developed these policies as a means to attack his former coreligionists; the ordinances focused primarily on limiting Jews' social and economic interaction with Christians and conversos, as well as moving Jews to separate neighborhoods.[70] He proposes that both Pablo and his son, the Placentino bishop Gonzalo García de Santa María, were intent on "squeezing and reducing to sterility" the Jewish community throughout Castile.[71]

However, the historical record in fifteenth-century Castile demonstrates that these assessments do not neatly align with the facts on the ground. Yitzhak Baer states that Castilians implemented just two of the laws' comprehensive provisions, "namely, the removal of Jews to separate quarters, and their exclusion from tax farming and from the service of the State and the court."[72] Though draconian, at minimum, these provisions do not seem to have been uniformly enforced.

Within Castile, the Santa María clan appears far less ruthless than Amador de los Ríos argues. Rather, the Santa María were also authors of new protections for Jewish communities. The majority of the violence against Jews concluded at the end of the fourteenth century after Enrique III of Castile repeatedly demanded that his subjects cease their harassment of both Jews and new converts to Christianity.[73] In a July 30, 1392, royal decree sent from the city of Segovia, the king mandated the following to all persons living in the kingdom: "No person shall obligate Jews to become Christians by force, nor make them listen to a sermon against their will, nor mistreat them, because it is counter to Christian charity."[74]

As the king was still three years from the age of majority, his royal advisers and tutors likely had a profound impact on the decision to call an end to the violence.[75] Among those advisers were the converso Estúñiga and Santa María. In other specific cases, Enrique sent communiqués that enhanced these basic religious protections. Not only would the youthful king refuse to tolerate the forced conversions, but he directed Alvar García de Santa María (the historian-bureaucrat) to enforce his decision to allow forced converts to return to Judaism. On this issue, the king's pronouncement stated, "Many [Jews] had converted and now wanted to return [to their faith]. . . . Not one person should harass them, and if some amount of them were to return [to Judaism], no one should seize them."[76]

Although the monarch was concerned about the safety of the Jewish community, the call to protect Jews also explicitly acknowledged their vital role in the economy. For instance, the crown used a religious poll tax levied on Jews to pay for its wars against Islamic Granada, as well as to fund other royal initiatives.[77] In this way, the juderías in each community contributed to the royal coffers. For example, in the early 1400s, the Jewish community of Plasencia paid the king 10,250 maravedís annually in cabeza de pecho.[78] Jewish subjects were valuable assets that necessitated royal protection on economic grounds.

As I demonstrate throughout this book, the Santa María family did not uniformly persecute their former Jewish brethren and were not necessarily accomplices to Ferrer's hateful preaching but actively protected them in certain instances. Likewise, Baer's certainty that the implementation of the Ordinances of Valladolid segregated Jews into separate quarters appears to be inaccurate. This was particularly the case in Plasencia.

While many Santa María family members elected to stay in Burgos, others routinely traveled to Plasencia, with some settling there permanently. The most prominent of the Santa María clan in Plasencia and Extremadura were Pablo de Santa María's son, Gonzalo García, and his brother, Alvar García.[79] From the 1420s through the 1440s, Gonzalo García de Santa María served as Plasencia's bishop. Alvar García de Santa María traveled to Extremadura in the 1430s on court affairs. However, neither of these men was the first Santa María family member to travel to or settle in Plasencia. A church prebendary, Gil Gutiérrez de la Calleja, married to María de Guzmán, is the first documented Santa María to come to Plasencia, establishing his family just prior to 1406.[80] Church records verify the relationship of the Gutiérrez de Calleja to the Santa María clan: church notaries refer to Gil Gutiérrez and his sons (Alfonso, Diego, Pedro, and Sancho) as the "family" of Gonzalo García de Santa María.[81]

Gil Gutiérrez was also the first Santa María family member to find a position in the cathedral's leadership chapter. In 1407, he appeared to be a well-established and respected member of the church hierarchy. The chapter acknowledged his continued services as one of its prebendaries and, more important, reelected him to a new term as dean.[82] However, Gil Gutiérrez was not the only Santa María in the city at this time. Juan González de Santa María was married to María Gómez de Almaraz, the daughter of the knightly family of Diego Gómez de Almaraz.[83] Gil Gutiérrez, Juan González, and María Gómez were close family members. In one case, Gil Gutiérrez and Juan González defended María's interests in an ongoing property conflict (1406–21) with her aunt, Leonor Sánchez.[84] As discussed in the next chapter, the first extended family relations that would connect the converso Santa María to the Old Christian Carvajal clan would appear via this internal family conflict.

The Maluenda family, also present in Plasencia, was related to the Santa María via the marriage of Pablo's sister, María Núñez, to Juan Rodríguez de Maluenda. In the 1420s, María and Juan's son, Alonso Rodríguez de Maluenda, occupied the archdeaconship of Coria, a city in the Diocese of Plasencia. He later served simultaneously as the vicar general for Bishop Santa María and the abbot of Castro at the Cathedral of Burgos.[85] The affinities of the Carvajal, Santa María, and Maluenda are demonstrated by the fact that between 1425 and 1427, Gonzalo Rodríguez de Maluenda of the Cathedral of Burgos named extended family members from Plasencia to oversee affairs in Burgos. Specifically, Gonzalo tapped Gonzalo García de Carvajal, archdeacon in Plasencia, and Gonzalo Gutiérrez de la Calleja, shield bearer for the bishop of Plasencia, to serve as church procurers.[86]

The Estúñiga, Future Condes de Béjar y Plasencia

The Estúñiga (or Zúñiga), a New Noble and converso family, appear in Plasencia at the end of the fourteenth century.[87] Originally from the Kingdom of Aragón, the family later enjoyed success as royal bureaucrats in the Kingdoms of Navarra and Castile.[88] In the late fourteenth century, the clan found solid footing in Castile when Diego López de Estúñiga, founder of the condes de Béjar, became part of a new generation of powerful elites that surrounded King Enrique III (r. 1390–1406). At that time, the key men advising the adolescent king were Diego López, *justicia mayor* (chief justice); Juan Hurtado de Mendoza, mayordomo of the royal house; and Ruy López Davalos, constable of the army.[89] Enrique III facilitated the entry of the Estúñiga family into the Diocese of Plasencia when he granted Diego López permission to establish a family mayorazgo in the village of Béjar in 1397.[90] The Estúñiga clan utilized its already accumulated wealth to move its family holdings from Burgos to the region that included Béjar and Plasencia.

At the time Diego López established his mayorazgo in Béjar, the family owned extensive properties across Castile. The primary beneficiary of these lands was his eldest son, Pedro, who received the seigniorial territories in the village of Béjar, as well as others in Burgos, Valladolid, Burguillos, Algaba, Urbel, and other cities.[91] The wealth of the Estúñiga was unsurpassed in Castile, except for the house of Haros. For example, by the mid-fifteenth century, in a single year Count Pedro de Estúñiga collected 3.6 million maravedís in rents and taxes alone from his seigniorial lands.[92] King Juan II appointed Diego López de Estúñiga's other son, Gonzalo de Estúñiga, bishop of Plasencia in 1414.[93] (See fig. 2.5.) In 1441, King Juan II granted Pedro de Estúñiga the title conde de Plasencia, as well as regional authority over Plasencia in exchange for the village of Trujillo.[94] Over the course of the fifteenth century, the Estúñigas would prove to be aggressive competitors for control of the Cathedral of Plasencia and for dominance over other nobles in the region, as well as economic predators on the surviving Jewish communities.

Tantalizing indications of the Estúñiga's Jewish lineage are revealed in both the original fourteenth-century testaments and copies, as well as Cardinal Francisco Mendoza y Bobadilla's sensational text, *El tizón de la nobleza: O maculas y sambenitos de sus linajes* (The Stain of the Spanish Nobility; Or the Blemishes and Disgraces of Its Lineages), a memorial published in 1560 that was a form of converso fratricide. The strongest evidence is found in Diego's testament of 1397, which names his wife as Juana Garcia de Leyva, a member of the Jewish Leyva family of Burgos.[95] There are also indications that Diego inherited several houses from Don Yucef, a Jewish nobleman in Sevilla.[96] Other extended family relations indicate a broad connection to the converso world, such as the intermarriage of the Ponce de León, a New Noble and converso house, with the Estúñiga family during the first half of the fifteenth century.[97]

Another provocative element of the Estúñiga Jewish heritage is disclosed in sixteenth-century writings of other elite conversos and in official histories. During the sixteenth century, these families used limpieza de sangre laws forbidding Jewish and Muslim converts to Christianity from holding public and church offices to limit their competitors' aspirations. Put simply, though all conversos and moriscos had impure blood, they used this fact against one another. This was a contest to determine which families could most effectively use blood lineage information against each other in the public realm. From these interfamilial conflicts, evidence emerges that a large number of New Noble families were of converso origins. This was especially evident in the case of *El tizón de la nobleza*. After learning that his nephew would be denied the honor of entry into any of the three leading Christian military orders because of his Jewish ancestry, the cardinal penned *El tizón* as an indictment of the hypocrisy of the nobility.[98] In the opening of his memorial, directed to King Philip II, the cardinal claimed, "The knights, dukes, counts and marquises of the republic, those that illuminate the republic and who are the petals of the rose that all can see[,] . . . in these noble hearts there is infamy and backbiting and scandal that separates them from the people."[99]

Francisco Mendoza claimed that "ignobility" separated the noble houses from the commoners. For sixteenth-century Spaniards, this was the worst category of cultural

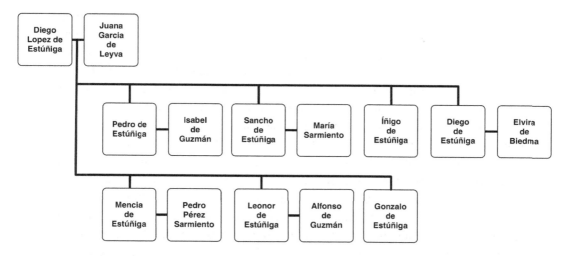

FIGURE 2.5. Genealogy of the Estúñiga and the Leyva Families (early fifteenth century).

pollution because it was the result of the Catholic nobility's intermarriage with Muslim and Jewish families. In his text, the cardinal named the countless lineages that descended from Jews and Muslims.[100] His language aggressively sought to expose the humble and religious origins of everyone in his path.

In *El tizón*, Cardinal Mendoza noted that his information from Canon Diego de Guzmán indicated that "the sons of Lord Pedro de Zúñiga" were descended from Jews, as were later descendants, such as Alvaro de Estúñiga (a church prior), who came from families with *sambenitos*, the penitential garb worn by conversos convicted of practicing Judaism.[101] To add insult to injury, when referring to some of the lowly beginnings of these families, the cardinal also reported that another relative, Teresa de Zúñiga, had married Francisco Sotomayor, conde de Benalcázar, who was related to a "Portugese shoemaker."[102]

The Álvarez de Toledo, Señores de Oropesa

The Álvarez de Toledo family, both New Noble and converso, was yet another important Plasencia clan that upset the settled state of religious and political affairs. They descended from García Álvarez de Toledo, master of the Christian military Order of Calatrava.[103] In 1366, Prince Enrique II (the future king) conceded the villages of Oropesa and Valdecorneja to García Álvarez and named him a señor. In the 1390s, while not as prosperous or influential as his brother, Fernán Álvarez de Toledo (founder of the House of Alba), García Álvarez left his family the señorío de Oropesa, which generated significant rents and income.[104]

In 1398, the señor de Oropesa collected about 26,000 maravedís in annual rents and taxes from his seigniorial lands near Talavera.[105] In addition, his property holdings included houses, lands, mills, and vineyards in Oropesa, Jarandilla de la Vera, Tornavacas, and Torralba.[106] Likewise, García Álvarez earned revenues from his livestock: 1,600 sheep, 288 cattle, 140 swine, 88 goats, 21 oxen, and 126 beehives.[107] By the 1450s, the señor de Oropesa also collected a healthy salary from the king. For example, in 1452, Señor Pedro Suárez de Toledo earned an annual salary of 81,200 maravedís as the chief collector (*recaudador mayor*) of royal taxes in the Archdiocese of Talavera.[108]

The Jewish ancestry of the Álvarez de Toledo was well known within noble circles, as at least two family members were investigated by the Holy Office of the Inquisition during the sixteenth century.[109] Similarly, *El tizón* named the señores de Oropesa as related to the House of Portocarrero, which was descended from a Jewish convert to Christianity, Ruy Capón.[110] Thus, like the Estúñiga and Santa María clans, the Álvarez de Toledo were another important converso family in the Plasencia region during the late 1300s.

ANTI-JEWISH POGROMS OF THE 1390s AND THE DISPUTATION OF TORTOSA (1413–1414)

Since the publication of the influential works of Amador de los Ríos, Lea, and Baer, the history of Jewish and Christian relations in Spain during the late fourteenth and early fifteenth centuries has remained a stable picture of increasing Christian hostility to Jews.[111] There is little doubt this is an accurate assessment of the period. These fathers of Sephardic historiography critically evaluated the devastation inflicted on juderías during the notorious anti-Jewish riots of the 1390s, which began in Sevilla and swept across Spain over the course of several years. These historians contributed in immeasurable ways to our understanding of how Jews were systematically targeted for persecution and murder and their juderías for eventual dismantling during the fifteenth century. Amador de los Ríos argued, "The horrid butchering that occurred in the Spanish *juderías* during the year 1391 was a vast conspiracy that had as its objective their total annihilation; however it was a conspiracy made in the light of day and proposed with vehement desire."[112] Other scholars have echoed this haunting assessment. Lea has pointed out that "in the paralysis of public authority . . . one city after another followed the example; the *Juderías* were sacked, the Jews that would not submit to baptism were slain and fanaticism and cupidity held their orgies unchecked."[113]

It is estimated that as many as 100,000 Jews were killed, 100,000 converted to Christianity, and another 100,000 fled to Muslim territories or went into hiding.[114] Perhaps because of the incontrovertible historical evidence of the horrors exacted on Jews such as those who resided in the cities of Sevilla, Córdoba, and Valencia, as well as its distastefulness, this difficult era in Spanish history continues to be treated as a settled debate that does not need to be examined further.[115] For example, Benzion Netanyahu summarizes the era as follows: "The losses of Spain's Jews in 1391 far surpassed those the Jews had borne elsewhere [in Europe]. . . . Within two or three years from 1391, Spain's Jewish community, the largest in the world, was reduced by nearly one-third— in both geographic and numerical terms, the greatest catastrophe that had hitherto befallen European Jewry."[116] Unfortunately, such definitive statements have all too often reduced the granularity, richness, and complexity of interreligious relations in the first half of the fifteenth century to these universalistic assumptions in Sephardic historiography. More important, they deny us a fuller understanding of what occurred and create opportunities for some to deny the Christian violence against the Sephardim.

We would be remiss if we did not consider the period immediately after the 1390s, during which physical violence was replaced with spiritual violence. Vicente Ferrer's intense efforts to convert Jews across Aragon and Castile led to the disappearance of juderías in Salamanca, Valencia, for example, as well as the cruelty of the Disputation of Tortosa.[117] The impact of the Disputation of Tortosa cannot be underestimated in terms of the chilling effect it had on European Jews. Although previous efforts, like one in Paris (1240) and another in Barcelona (1263), had established a precedent for forcing Jewish religious leaders to debate the validity of their religion, the coerced debate in the Aragonese city of Tortosa was exceptionally effective.[118] On the heels of Vicente Ferrer's efforts to refute Judaism and convert Jews to Christianity, Cardinal Pedro de Luna (or Antipope Benedict XIII) called for this new debate in 1413 to undermine Talmudic teachings.[119] Over the course of sixty-nine sessions, Vicente Ferrer, Jerónimo de Santa Fe, and other Dominican friars battled Jewish scholars like Rabbi Ferrer, Salomón Ishaq, Rabbi Astruch ha-Levi, and Profiat Duran, attacking the living embodiment of Judaism, the Talmud.[120]

Jerónimo de Santa Fe, who was previously known as the learned Jewish scholar Joshua al-Lorqi, was among the principal leaders of the "anti-Jewish polemics" of the era and likely had been convinced to convert by Pablo de Santa María,[121] who also participated in the public spectacle. On the Christian side of the dispute, he engaged in arguments relating to original sin, the eternal nature of God, and whether or not it was proper for one to investigate the basis of one's religious beliefs.[122] The effectiveness of this campaign was tangible: over the course of the year and a half sessions, many elite Jewish leaders and thinkers converted to Christianity, including the poet Solomon de Peira, Vidal Joseph (of the Benveniste and Cavallería families), and Fernando de la Cavallería.[123]

Plasencia's Jewish Community

Violence and collaboration, conflict and tolerance were all present during this historical period. Plasencia was no different, and peaceful coexistence of different religious

groups no longer obtained. With serious disruptions to the traditional residential intermixing of Jewish and Christian families, Plasencia was not free of anti-Jewish sentiment. Beginning in the 1390s with the anti-Jewish riots, Jews in Plasencia resided in a
religiously charged environment that placed their communities in economic, religious, and physical jeopardy. Sometime before 1416 (the exact date of construction is
unknown), several Jewish families found it necessary to live in a fortified and gated
collection of homes known as the Apartamiento de La Mota (fig. 2.6).[124] This enclosed
section of homes was located across from the Church of Saint Nicholas. Contemporaneous militant Christian evangelization of Jewish communities in the region during
the early fifteenth century may have been the impetus for the creation of La Mota. In
1411, Vicente Ferrer preached in the cities of Zamora and Salamanca, which are located north of Plasencia.[125] He even preached his message of conversion in these communities' synagogues.[126]

In response to these Christian initiatives, Plasencia's Jewish community built La
Mota, which was secured with stone walls surrounding its homes and synagogue.[127]
The large wooden doors of La Mota were likely festooned with bronze or steel hard-
ware, and at night they could be closed and locked from within by a heavy metal bar
(aldaba).[128] In 1416, there were two zones within the apartamiento: one area contained the synagogue and a number of Jewish homes, and the other area included the
dwellings of Tel Díaz de Vega, a Christian city councilman.

Why Tel Díaz was the sole Christian property owner inside La Mota is not clear,
but it suggests that he may have been a recent Jewish convert to Christianity. When the
city council forced Tel Díaz to forfeit his properties inside La Mota to Álvaro de Sande,
due to unpaid debts, many details about the apartamiento and its inhabitants
emerged.[129] An accounting of properties conducted by Mayor Juan Sánchez and the
scribe Fernando Rodríguez revealed that Tel Díaz owned approximately five homes in
the walled community.[130] Jewish families occupied all of Tel Díaz's properties; those
families included Rabbi Abraham Deloya, Yucef Castaño, Symuel Abenabibe, Yuce
Abencur, Cag Pardo, and Hayn and Symuel Daza.[131]

In April 1416, the city council supervised the initial liquidation of Tel Díaz's holdings in order to settle Álvaro de Sande's petition. Fernando de la Mota purchased all of
these homes but allowed the families to continue to reside in them. In an interesting
display of the process involved in taking possession of a house, the scribe recorded:

> Fernando entered into the houses lived in by Yucef Castaño [and other Jewish
> residents]. These houses, the best of all of them, had been owned by Tel Díaz.
> [Fernando] took possession of the homes by physically walking into them . . .
> and then he closed all of its doors. He then opened the doors and shook the
> hands of Ledicia and her husband, Symuel Abenabibe, and all of the other Jews
> living in these homes.[132]

FIGURE 2.6. Three-dimensional visualization of Apartamiento de La Mota (fourteenth century). Source: Revealing Cooperation and Conflict Project, Virtual Plasencia, v1.6.

Unfortunately for these families, less than eight months later the properties were sold again, purchased for 100,000 maravedís by Iñigo de Camudio, shield bearer of Alonso de Sande.[133] By 1426, less than a decade later, the new owner forced all of the Jews out.[134]

The dismantling of La Mota was not necessarily part of a Christian plan to prevent Jewish families from isolating themselves from the rest of the city's population. Rather, it appears to be the product of brewing competition among the region's local knights, the Cathedral of Plasencia, and the Estúñiga family. Specifically, Iñigo de Camudio's purchase of these homes in La Mota appears to have been part of a secret arrangement for the Estúñiga family to acquire property in Plasencia. Iñigo had served a critical role, some might say a deceptive one, when he executed the purchase of this section of La Mota not for himself or his lord, Alonso de Sande, but for Alonso's superior—Pedro de Estúñiga, count of Béjar, who was positioning himself to extend his political influence in the region.[135] After the mid-1420s, the Estúñiga clan would quickly consolidate its landholdings in this section of the Jewish quarter, which would in turn lead to conflict with the Carvajal–Santa María confederation. The Estúñiga clan's effort to secure properties in La Mota was only the beginning of more convoluted times for Plasencia's Jews, Old Christians, and conversos.

At the Mercy of the Older Order in Plasencia

Trouble visited the lower aristocracy of Old Christian houses of knights in Plasencia as well; in their case, however, the immediate problem was the local cathedral and the pervasive strength of the Old Christian Fernández family that ruled it. In the battle for economic wealth may lie the crucial moment when the Old Christian Carvajal clan recalculated their future and formation into a converso family. The house of Carvajal learned that while knights might have political and military power, they were no match for the church. To succeed in the future, and take advantage of the changing social and cultural dynamics in Castile, the family would need to shapeshift and adopt new ways of making their livelihood.

In the late fourteenth century, the Carvajal learned that the Cathedral of Plasencia was a potent entity with judicial powers that could humble even elite Castilian seigniorial lords. In 1396, the cathedral's churchmen successfully appealed to Enrique III for help enforcing the church's right to collect a *diezmos* (tax) from the region's New Noble families, such as the señores de Oropesa, as well as lower noble Old Christian families such as the Carvajal. After the receipt of this royal decree, the knights complied, but in 1403 the tax affair repeated itself, with dire consequences for the Carvajal clan. In Christian kingdoms local lords and bishops had battled over diezmos since the thirteenth century.[136] Cathedrals and churchmen highly prized the right to collect diezmos because they were entitled to keep excess tax revenues that were not paid to the Castilian crown and the Roman Curia.[137]

This ecclesiastical-secular conflict highlights the nature of late fourteenth-century economic competition between Castile's knightly families and church clans, both of which pursued wealth generation but using fundamentally different approaches. Petty nobles, like the Carvajal family, generated a sizable portion of their incomes from agricultural and pastoral activities as well as property leases. In this respect, the Carvajal were very much lower-level old nobility who were tied to territorial lands. Seigniorial lords, or those high noble families with titles and secular jurisdiction over the local communities in which they resided, also collected income through secular taxes, such as the portazgo. These economic benefits were especially on display after the mercedes enriqueñas (royal favors bestowed by King Enrique II) empowered the new nobility to gather these types of taxes. On the other hand, families that depended on the church for their livelihood, such as the Old Christian Fernández clan, relied on church tax collections and the leasing of church assets to fund their cathedral salaries. It was within this late fourteenth-century social and economic competitive framework that the Carvajal family aspired to increase their stature in the Kingdom of Castile and León.

WEALTH AND INCOME IN PLASENCIA:
CHURCHMEN VERSUS KNIGHTS AND MERCHANTS

At the beginning of the fifteenth century, the petty nobles in the Diocese of Plasencia were the Camargo, Carvajal, Monroy, Orellana, Ovando, and Trejo.[138] As minor members of the Castilian aristocracy, these houses relied exclusively on agricultural and pastoral production and property leasing to generate their livelihoods and accumulate wealth. Specifically, 90 percent of their revenues were derived from vineyards, agricultural production, and herding, whereas 10 percent was accumulated from housing and land leases.[139]

Also in the region were two converso houses that were among the Castilian high nobility—the Estúñiga, condes de Béjar, and the Álvarez de Toledo, señores de Oropesa. These New Noble clans derived their titles and generous economic privileges, such as the right to tax their individual patrimonial villages and lands, by virtue of royal privilege and feudal concession.[140] Unlike their petty knight counterparts, these families derived the majority of their income from seigniorial taxes and duties:[141] 57 percent from trade tariffs (portazgo, alcabala, *montazgo, tercias*) and only 43 percent from rents and cultivation of their lands.[142] Thus, the señores' and condes' decision to comply with Enrique III's 1396 royal order to pay diezmos to the cathedral was likely in order to guard against losing their more important source of revenue— seigniorial taxes. On the other hand, lower noble clans did not benefit from these same royal taxation privileges and as a result were disproportionately affected by and vulnerable to the financial pressures imposed on them by church diezmos.

The independent Christian kingdoms likely derived this church taxation system, which began in the twelfth century, from the secular, seigniorial tax structure used by the Visigoths.[143] At the Council of Peñafiel, held in 1302, the Spanish church specified that a 10 percent tax would be assessed on goods produced in the countryside, such as grain, wine, fruit, livestock, and milled products. These revenues provided a considerable sum for the cathedral's operations. A decade after the Council of Peñafiel, the Cathedral of Plasencia held its own constitutional synod. There, Bishop Domingo and the cathedral chapter's officials agreed to distribute two-thirds of these annual tax revenues to themselves and reserve the remaining one-third for the "works of the church."[144] Thus, families employed by the church, for example, the Fernández, depended on these revenues to fund both their salaries and the patronage opportunities they showered on their relatives and associates. When tax collections did not meet expectations, they had a direct impact on the financial well-being of the cathedral's churchmen.

An investigation of the earliest church financial records of the Cathedral of Plasencia, dating to the 1390s, also reveals that minor knights, as well as local merchants, bore the brunt of church taxation, while local churchmen were largely unaffected. While many knights, such as Diego González de Carvajal, earned salaries as regidores in their local communities of as much as 1,000 maravedís a year, their greatest source of income came from their lands.[145] In contrast, Plasencia's clerics and canons derived their compensation from a mix of diezmos revenues, the leasing of church lands, and the production of goods from church lands.

A review of the *Actas capitulares* (books recording day-to-day diocesan church and business affairs), which commence in the 1390s, reveals that diezmos had a disproportionately negative effect on knights and merchant families, as compared to clergymen's

Table 2.2. Cathedral of Plasencia's 1390s Accounting of Church Properties (named landowners with property adjacent to church properties)

Primary Landowners (occupation)	Properties Owned
María Pérez, wife of Martín Domínguez (merchant)	10
Sons of Diego Pérez de Granada (knights)	8
Gonzalo García de Carvajal (knight's son)	7
Gómez Fernández of Abala (clergy)	6
Mateo Sánchez, royal servant (knight)[a]	6
Diego Martínez, of Calle de Trujillo	5
Juan Pérez de Buenaventura	3
María Martín (merchant)	3
Gracia (wife of García González de Plasencia)	3
Miguel Sánchez of Aceituna, of Calle de Coria (knight)	3
Diego Muñoz, of Calle de Trujillo	3
Fernán Pérez de Monroy (knight)[b]	3
Ximena (spouse of Duran González)	3

[a] Don Mateo also donated three properties to the Cathedral of Plasencia. See ACP, *Actas capitulares*, tomo 1, fols. 1–1v.

[b] Given the time period in which the *Actas* property records were generated, around the 1390s, this Fernán Pérez de Monroy is very likely the knight who served under Kings Alfonso XI and Pedro I during the mid- to late 1300s. Friar Alonso Fernández notes that Fernán Pérez was a well-known knight in the Diocese of Plasencia during this period. In 1369, Fernán Pérez, who was loyal to Pedro I during the Castilian civil war, attacked and killed Blasco Gómez de Almaraz, who is listed in the *Actas* as the property owner of a house in the Pueblo de Albala. See ACP, *Actas capitulares*, tomo 1, fol. 6v; Fernández, *Historia y anales*, 121–23; González Cuesta, *Obispos de Plasencia*, 77.

houses, because knights and merchants tended to own more land than churchmen.[146] In addition to recording ecclesiastical properties, the *Actas capitulares* list local property owners. Interestingly, the cathedral's accounting does not provide a complete picture of the region, as it does not give information about the seigniorial lands of the Estúñiga and the Álvarez de Toledo. This might suggest, as highlighted in Bishop Pedro de Fernández de Soria's 1396 tax complaint against regional lords, that the cathedral had difficulty documenting their property ownership.

However, the accounting records reveal that the Carvajal family relied heavily on agricultural lands and vineyards to generate their wealth and therefore were subject to diezmos tariffs. Of the thirteen wealthiest individuals in Plasencia, five were from knightly families, two were from merchant families, and only one was from a churchman's family (table 2.2).[147] The five remaining families in the accounting, whose occupations cannot be determined, were not members of the church leadership.[148]

As the king typically compensated knightly clans with land for their military service, it is not surprising that the Carvajal, Pérez de Granada, Pérez de Monroy, and

Sánchez owned the majority of income-producing properties in the diocese. Among the merchants, who also claimed noble titles, only one extended family—the Martín and Pérez-Domínguez—is recorded. The only clerical family with any recorded amount of land wealth was the well-established Fernández.

Unlike cathedral officials and their families, Plasencia's merchant clans relied on a broad mix of real estate holdings to provide for themselves. In the *Actas capitulares*, the landholdings of María Pérez, a noble lady and merchant, are especially noteworthy.[149] She, not her husband, Martín Domínguez, owned ten properties consisting of "arable plots, lands," and vineyards. All of the goods produced from her lands—wine, vegetables, wheat, and the like—were subject to the diezmos. María Pérez's extended family owned fourteen additional parcels, the most of any local family. Her extended merchant clan also incorporated the Pérez-Domínguez and Yáñez lineages. However, Plasencia's merchants did not bear the brunt of the church tariffs as they only accounted for two of the thirteen wealthiest families in the diocese.

On the other hand, as lower noble houses of mounted warriors accounted for five of Plasencia's thirteen most affluent families, as a group they were the primary target of ecclesiastical taxation. For instance, second in wealth to María Pérez were the sons of the city councilman and knight Diego Pérez de Granada, who jointly owned eight properties.[150] Diego Pérez's sons held a significant and diverse mix of real estate that included houses, arable plots, vineyards, and irrigated plains. The eight properties were located in the cities and villages of Plasencia, Coria, Galisteo, and Puerto de Castaño. Together, the extended Pérez de Granada clan held twelve properties. The Carvajal were also among the wealthier low noble clans in Plasencia. Gonzalo García de Carvajal's extended family, which included the Orellana, Espadero, and Ulloa lineages, was the third wealthiest group of landowners in the diocese (table 2.3).[151] In total, Gonzalo García de Carvajal owned seven distinct properties, and his extended family owned ten parcels.[152]

The Carvajal and their extended relations concentrated their financial efforts in the profitable but taxable enterprises of agricultural and livestock production. In the village of Trujillo, adjacent to the vineyards of Albaladejo owned by the priests, the brothers Diego García de Béjarano and Gonzalo García de Carvajal possessed one parcel with vineyards.[153] Gonzalo García also owned agriculturally productive lands in Torrejón adjacent to the Jerete River and the cathedral's smaller plots and four sizable plots in the Valle de Milaña and El Pico, both near the village of Coria, that were adjacent to church farmlands. These larger parcels likely would have been utilized for livestock grazing. Therefore, most of the lands owned by Gonzalo García and the extended Carvajal family were subject to church diezmos.

The Carvajal knights supplemented their income from agricultural activities through their intermarriage with merchant families. For example, Gonzalo García was married to the daughter of Rui Pérez, a local merchant and shopkeeper. The record tells little about Rui Pérez's livelihood, although he owned two pieces of land, one in

Table 2.3. Three Key Landowners Named in the Cathedral of Plasencia's 1390s Accounting of Church Properties

Landowners	María Pérez	Sons of Diego Pérez de Granada	Gonzalo García de Carvajal
Social status and occupation	Noble merchant	Noble knight	Noble knight
Total properties owned by the individual	10	8	7
Location of properties			
Plasencia, Riobermejo, Aldeanueva	4 parcels of land (tierras) 1 arable plot (aza)	1 house (casa) 1 parcel of land 1 arable plot	none
Coria, Galisteo, Puerto de Castano	3 parcels of land	1 irrigated parcel of land with gardens (huerta) 1 parcel of land 1 arable plot (aza)	4 lands
Torrejón, La Penuela	1 parcel of land 1 vineyard (vinas)	1 parcel of land	2 parcels of land
Trujillo	none	none	1 vineyard
Albala	none	1 vineyard	none
Total properties owned by extended family	14	12	10

the Pueblo de San Esteban and another in the Campo de Calamoco.[154] A ravine on his land in the Pueblo de San Esteban reportedly contained a valuable natural resource—quartz rock laden with silver and gold deposits. However, the Carvajal were primarily dependent on their farming and herding lands for income. It is no wonder, then, in the calamities of the late 1390s and the general disorder that surrounded the Kingdom of Castile and León, that New Noble lords and lower noble knights chose to fight the Cathedral of Plasencia's taxation efforts.

The First Diezmos Rebellion, 1396

Plasencia's New Nobles and knights engaged the Cathedral of Plasencia's churchmen by refusing to pay church taxes. When Bishop Pedro Fernández de Soria, patriarch of the Fernández family, pleaded in 1396 with Enrique III to intervene in the church's diezmos conflict with local knights, his petition represented much more than an issue of jurisdiction and taxing authority. His complaint straddled a fault line separating Plasencia's houses. On one side were elements of the nobility and armed knights.[155] Among these individuals were Gastón de Béarn y de la Cerda (conde de Medinaceli), Gonzalo González de Herrera, Fernán Álvarez de Toledo (señor de Oropesa), Diego Gómez de Almaraz, Fernándo Rodríguez de Monroy, and Gutierre González de Trejo.[156] Of these men, Gastón de Béarn and Fernán Álvarez were members of the aristocracy, as they held both titles and seigniorial lands.[157] Noticeably absent from the list were the Carvajal clan, which included Diego González de Carvajal of Plasencia and Alvar García de Bejarano of Trujillo.[158] Perhaps the bishop did not name these men in his appeal to the Castilian monarch because they chose to pay their diezmos or because they lacked sufficient wealth to be of importance to the Cathedral of Plasencia.

Opposing this group of high and low nobles was a determined group of church families whose salaries were dependent on the successful collection of church tariffs and rents. The key families in the cathedral chapter at this time included the Blásquez, Domínguez, Fernández, García, González, Martínez, and Sánchez. More than their compatriots, the Fernández family enjoyed a long-established presence in the local church; as early as 1338 Sancho Fernández held the office of prebendary.[159] Not only did Pedro Fernández de Soria serve as bishop of Plasencia, but his nephew, Martín Fernández de Soria, held the influential archdeaconship of Plasencia and Béjar.[160] In general, the knights and church families did not share immediate family relations, nor did they overlap professionally. Thus the two groups had decidedly different perspectives on the payment of taxes.

At the heart of this church-secular tax conflict were the deceptive practices employed by the nobles to obscure the accounting of income generated from their taxable lands and territories. In his appeal to Enrique III, the bishop stated that the noblemen were "interfering" with the collection of diezmos by transporting bread, wine, and other goods to be stored in locations outside of the diocese.[161] The transfer of goods meant that the cathedral could not accurately account for these items and therefore could not tax them. To remedy this situation, the king ordered his knights "to no longer lease or rent houses or storehouses or storage casks in places other than your lands."[162] The monarch insisted further, "Just like other landholders and residents in other places . . . you must pay diezmos for bread and wine and other things."[163] According to the bishop, another tactic utilized by the knights to deny the cathedral its fair revenues was their recording of agricultural products and livestock "at half of their actual value" or simply their refusal "to pay the appropriate amounts."[164] As a result of these perceived infringements on the church's tax collection rights, the bishop argued that "much of the diezmos collections for these seigniorial lands had been lost and were progressively dropping each year."[165]

The king's order on February 11, 1396, further stipulated:

Bishop Pedro Fernández de Soria wrote to me and informed me that some of
you, my vassals and señores[,] . . . will not consent to the collection and leasing
of church taxes in your seigniorial lands [and] . . . that you do not wish to pay
even half of their valued amount. . . . From this point forward, none of you will
cause interference, act with impunity, or hold back any of these church taxes. If
you fail to comply with my orders, you will suffer the loss of my grace and a
penalty of 10,000 maravedís.[166]

With the jurisdictional authority of the church bolstered by Enrique III, the
churchmen would ultimately prevail on the taxation issue. Although the multiple
overlapping jurisdictions—royal, church, municipal, and local seigniorial—complicated the issue of levies, the king forced a resolution between his nobles and the
churchmen. With this order, the Carvajal, a long-standing noble family that had failed
to rise to the upper aristocracy in spite of its two centuries of military service, appeared to learn a valuable lesson: ecclesiastical power had certain advantages and created opportunities. Perhaps they surmised that in this newly evolving Castilian world
perhaps they, like elite Jewish families, could enter the class of New Nobles.

The Second Diezmos Revolt, 1403–1410

In 1403, led by Diego García de Bejarano (a Carvajal clansman), a different group of
knights resumed the diezmos dispute after a newly installed bishop, Vicente Arias de
Balboa, took the helm of the diocese. Although the diezmos disagreement of 1396 had
ended relatively quickly with the pronouncements of Enrique III, this new conflict
spanned seven years.

The quarrel was so bitter that Bishop Vicente temporarily excommunicated Diego
García de Béjarano as punishment for leading the tax revolt.[167] Diego García was the
son of the *caballero* (knight) Alvar García de Bejarano and Mencía González de Carvajal, daughter of the caballero Diego González de Carvajal y Vargas.[168] For seven years,
Bishop Vicente was unable to compel Diego García and his compatriots to pay their
diezmos.

Only when the bishop threatened them with permanent excommunication did
the stalemate conclude through a legal settlement. On May 15, 1410, Bishop Vicente,
Diego García, and several other important men from the region appeared in front of
Alfonso López, a member of King Juan II's royal court, and Fernando, bishop of Córdoba.[169] Diego García conceded that he had "obfuscated the truth, retained, and did
not want to pay in any manner the diezmos[,] . . . nor had he informed the church for
what amount he had sold the products from the meadows, mountain, and pastures of

his inherited properties."[170] Bishop Vicente added that the knight's actions were part of a "conspiracy" and that Diego García "had participated in a depraved crime against the bishop, the dean and the cathedral chapter, and its clergy . . . and his actions were a violation of the church's privileges." The notary recorded that Diego García was humbled by the judicial ordeal: "[Diego] appeared to be contrite in his conscience and displayed great humility. He was now a faithful son of the holy mother church and a faithful Christian of the religion . . . and he swore not to rebel against this judgment or fail to pay the taxes."[171]

In the final act of that day, Alfonso López of the royal court approved the settlement, which granted the knight spiritual absolution in exchange for full payment of seven years of unpaid diezmos. Also present at the hearing was Diego García's uncle, Diego González de Carvajal, who served as a witness to the terms of the settlement. While Alfonso López did not record Diego García de Bejarano's financial penalty, he did note that his co-conspirators were also in arrears on their taxes. On June 10, 1410, four of these men also "confessed" their crimes and agreed to pay the diezmos owed to the cathedral (Francisco Gil, 1,285 maravedís; Juan Sánchez, 730 maravedís; Gil García, 1,507 maravedís; and Gil Blásquez, 63 maravedís).[172] Presumably, Diego García had owed a significantly larger amount, given that he was Bishop Vicente's primary target. Just as in the tax dispute of 1396, Diego García's conflict with the church was a symptom of a broader social competition for wealth and status. Both groups, nobles and churchmen, were steadfast in their desire to build and protect family wealth.

An unusual outcome of the tax revolt is that it appears to have initiated the Carvajal family's entry into the ecclesiastical and royal administrative world. Unlike other Placentino clans, the Carvajal recognized that if they could secure leadership positions in the Cathedral of Plasencia they could enhance their family's authority, stature, and economic position in the region. In fact, in a transformative sequence of events, Diego García's brother, Gonzalo García de Carvajal, would become the cathedral's archdeacon of Plasencia and Béjar in the 1420s. This was the first step in the family's exploration of an identity not tied to their service as knights; it was a break with this family's specific medieval tradition.

Facilitating the Carvajal family's entrance into the cathedral were internal divisions and fissures in the cathedral's leadership chapter. During this era, the converso Santa María clan, newcomers to Plasencia, gained initial access to the cathedral chapter. However, the Fernández family of churchmen, the strongest clan in the chapter, largely excluded the Santa María from the church's lucrative patronage and wealth-building opportunities. This environment created an opening for the Carvajal clan to form an alliance with the Santa María family to garner access to, and ultimately control, the Cathedral of Plasencia. By acquiring mastery of the chapter, the Carvajal and Santa María families could harness the church's impressive ecclesiastical authority for familial gain, as well as benefit from new patronage and financial enhancement opportunities. More important, as the Carvajal and Santa María integrated their extended houses through intermarriage, they began an experimental process of creating a new, hybridized converso identity, one that required the Carvajal to incorporate new administrative traditions and religious practices used by the Santa María pulled the Santa María into armed confrontations as means to resolve conflicts and further intermarriage with Old Christians.

3

OPPORTUNITY

In the aftermath of the anti-Jewish riots of the 1390s and the changing religious and social character of Castile's elite, Placentinos must have believed their city was an isolated
vessel sailing through troubled waters. Castile's principal cities were distant, whether
Burgos, the royal administrative city, or, to the south, the burgeoning commercial center of Sevilla. Perhaps the waves of change might just wash past them; after all, in 1400
the city remained as it had for nearly two centuries. It was a stable collection of Christian families of knights and churchmen (accounting for approximately 34 percent of
the population) who governed a larger religious minority (42 percent Jewish and 24 percent Muslim).[1] In many respects, the configuration of the three religious groups had remained constant since the Christian reconquest of the city in the late twelfth century.
However, the Castilian political and cultural revolution submerged the old social and
religious order while revitalizing some positive forms of religious coexistence. Transformative opportunity, namely, the successful intermixing of Jewish and Christian elites,
was on full display as the Trastámaran dynasty's New Noble and converso clans asserted
their political and economic clout across Castile and even in smaller hamlets such as
Plasencia.

In this chapter, I evaluate the dynamic processes and the unexpected opportunities that opened a clear path for the Carvajal–Santa María family confederation to secure a prosperous future for their collective interests in the Cathedral of Plasencia. In
many respects, their efforts signaled that an identity shift was afoot for these two families. Stepping into the mind-set of Castilians at the beginning of the 1400s is a challenging task for historians because we are not diviners of hearts but only interpreters

of records. First, I consider the historiographical impact of the work of Jacob Burck-hardt, Stephen Greenblatt, John Jeffries Martin, and Guido Ruggiero on nascent frag-mentary identities in early modern Europe. Subsequently, an expeditious review of European and Sephardic historiography contextualizes these broader findings and helps us understand the peculiarities of Castile's Jewish and Christian identities. After this brief discussion of relevant historiography and converso motivations for seeking new opportunities, I document the intermarriage of the extended Carvajal and Santa María lineages, a previously unknown familial partnership that would come to shape the royal and ecclesiastical policies of Queen Isabel and King Ferdinand's Catholic Spain. The evidence for this partnership, which draws from more than two centuries of documents (testaments, dowry letters, chapel foundations, and property records), unravels the clans' highly effective fifteenth- and sixteenth-century efforts to hide Jew-ish lineages within Old Christian ones.

From this foundational documentation of the genealogical integration of the two families (and several others), I explore the doors of opportunity that opened in early fifteenth-century Plasencia. Principally, this was due to the failure of the Old Christian Fernández family to consolidate control over the Cathedral of Plasencia and the shrewd ability of the Carvajal–Santa María family confederation to step into the leadership void to its full advantage. Although capturing the Cathedral of Plasencia required a short-lived collaboration with the New Noble house of Estúñiga, the political risks ap-peared to be well worth it to this confederation.

HISTORIOGRAPHY: BETWEEN EUROPEAN
AND SEPHARDIC WORLDS

Old Christians, New Christians, Jews, New Nobles, and Old Nobles—all had much to lose as the 1300s came to a close. No person or community was spared the unpredictable political and cultural turbulence created in the wake of anti-Jewish violence, the earlier civil war, or the plague. This dynamic environment spawned the conditions for what Eu-ropean historians envisioned as the opening for new identities—fragmented and self-fashioned—that would take root much later, during the late fifteenth and early sixteenth century. What is so unusual about the Castilian experience of identity is that it disrupted and upset traditional religious and cultural norms much sooner, perhaps as early as the late 1300s. What made this possible were the unique conditions generated by the Trastá-maran dynasty's actions pertaining to conversos and Jews and the Old Christians' violent reaction against them.

Equally intriguing are the developments captured by historians of the Sephardim, who characterize the late 1300s–early 1400s as a pivotal period in the future of Spanish Jews and their descendants. In essence, Jews were just as suspicious of New Christians as were Old Christians. Forced into a liminal state, where religious boundaries became more fluid, converso houses would begin a period of cultural experimentation with their identities. There is a growing consensus among historians that social and personal identities profoundly shifted during the fifteenth and sixteenth centuries. In short, these social transformations were revolutionary because they shattered medieval religious identities—Jewish versus Christian—and replaced them with the multilayered and overlapping category "converso." During this era, group identity constructions fractured into individualized identities.

Jacob Burckhardt, the nineteenth-century historian who authored the influential text *The Civilization of the Renaissance in Italy,* initiated historians' discussion of the issue of identity. He contended that early modern people, unlike their medieval counterparts, perceived themselves as "spiritual individuals" distinctly separate from social groups. One of his most pointed observations on the matter is as follows:

> In the Middle Ages both sides of human consciousness—that which was turned within as that which was turned without—lay dreaming or half awake beneath a common veil. The veil was woven of faith, illusion and childish prepossessions, through which the world and history were seen clad in strange hues. Man was only conscious of himself as a member of a race, people, party, family, or corporation—only through some general category. In Italy this veil first melted into air; an objective treatment and consideration of the state and of all the things of this world became possible. The subjective side at the same time asserted itself with corresponding emphasis; man became a spiritual individual, and recognized himself as such.[2]

Burckhardt's observation sheds light on how conversos, those of mixed Jewish and Catholic lineages and beliefs, might create new forms of individual perceptions. Stephen Greenblatt, author of *Renaissance Self-Fashioning: From More to Shakespeare,* extends this argument, postulating that "there were selves and they could be fashioned."[3] He presents a compelling case that clarifies how the monotony of medieval group identities, such as Christian or Jewish ones, could give birth to new, individual identities. Put simply, individuality created opportunities for great variability in identity. Nonetheless, it would be inaccurate to suggest that any member of a Castilian converso family was by any means an "individual," as this is understood in the twenty-first century. Rather, the idea of individuality was far more nuanced. As Greenblatt writes, these were not "expressive individuals" but rather "cultural artifacts" who were molded by social institutions. In the case of the Castilian conversos, they were artifacts generated by unique historical circumstances, Christian violence against Jews, and laws, such as the Ordinances of Valladolid. Conversos, some of whom practiced a mix of Jewish and Christian beliefs, were a direct by-product of these convoluted events.

John Jeffries Martin's *Myths of Renaissance Individualism* enhances our understanding of the multimodal nature of early modern identities, arguing that the Renaissance "self" was not a "thing" but a collection of relations between the internal and external experiences of the individual.[4] Early modern men and women viewed their identities as an array of "possible permutations": in essence, the self served as a flexible intermediary between an individual's interior and the social networks surrounding him.[5] Martin's neatly delineated model proposes that Renaissance men and women understood the self as existing in five forms: socially conforming, prudential, performative, possessed, and sincere. He asserts that some of these identities offered people "at least an illusion of control" over the self, whereas other identities either diluted the self into an unwilling host, as in the case of the demonically possessed, or brought forth a precursor of modernity.[6] Through the lens of the late sixteenth-century thinker Montaigne, Martin locates the generation of the sincere self in the Renaissance reconciliation of the twelfth-century notion of the concordia of God and humanity, the Reformation's concern with sincerity but preoccupation with human sinfulness, and the new sense that men and women as "agents" were responsible for their actions and assertions. With respect to conversos, there is good evidence to support the position that they had many paths to choose from; for example, the converso Estúñiga tended toward repression of Jews, whereas the converso Carvajal–Santa María family confederation leaned toward accommodation. These different approaches of conversos to how they would treat Jewish communities indicate distinct variations in their identities.

Finally, Guido Ruggiero's *Machiavelli in Love* explores early modern sexual identities in the context of broader social groups. For example, he notes that a woman might hold more than one identity—that of a prostitute as well as that of an honorable lady, for example. In one context, a married woman of modest means who turned to prostitution for financial sustenance was a whore, and in another, she was viewed as a good and honorable neighbor.[7] Ruggiero writes, "The relativity of such socially shared 'consensus identities' explain much about the apparently fluid nature of Renaissance identity and what has been labeled Renaissance self-fashioning. In the end, . . . there was perhaps less of the latter and more identity negotiation by individuals in dialogue with the various social groups with which they lived, played, and worked."[8]

This variability in identity seems highly applicable to the New Christian identities that formed in Spain. Depending on the context, conversos could be *buen cristianos* (good Christians) or *judaizantes* (Judaizers). Conversos held multiple identities that they themselves shaped and that were also shaped by others. For example, the Carvajal would come to be viewed simultaneously as exemplary knights and as crafty imitators of the Santa María churchmen.

New Fragmented Identities Constructed around Religious Differences

The conventional wisdom on medieval European religious historiography is well articulated in Herbert Grundmann's *Religious Movements in the Middle Ages*. It explores the Roman Catholic Church's organization, its lay and cleric leaders, key religious movements, and piety during the twelfth and thirteenth centuries.[9] At the heart of the text is an exploration of popular religious movements and their lasting impact on the formation of a distinct Christian and common culture.[10]

Embedded in Grundmann's approach to the Middle Ages is what John Van Engen characterizes as "the common presupposition that medieval culture was essentially 'Christian' or 'Catholic,'" a position that he, along with scholars such as Carlo Ginzburg, contests on the basis of the prevalence of Indo-European folklore.[11] Regardless of the outcome of the continuing debate on the matter, there is little space to counter the opinion that there was an ecclesiastical elite and that many laypersons constructed their identities based on a Catholic, religious worldview. The previously discussed texts, R. I. Moore's *The Formation of a Persecuting Society* and Marc Bloch's *Feudal Society*, both contribute to and bolster the position that European society deeply valued Christian group identification. In Spain, Christian identity was even more pronounced. Spain was simultaneously Christian and "other," but religious purity was a difficult social practice to guard over the course of eight hundred years of Jewish, Catholic, and Muslim interaction, especially for converted Jews at the end of the fourteenth century.

Spanish Jews and Conversos

The intellectual counterweight to the Christian perspective is an intriguing Sephardic historiography that has shifted from polemical to more nuanced evaluations. The history of Sephardic and converso identity is controversial because of the persistence of the debate about the "one, eternal Spain": is Spain an outcome of many cultures and faiths, or is it pure, Catholic, and Castilian? Likewise, for the Jewish community, what was to be made of the conversos? Were they fully Christianized, or did they retain their Jewish identity? One of the prominent outcomes of this debate is the disjointed, problematic, and polemical tone as scholarship evolved from the 1800s to the 2000s. It is as if fifteenth- and sixteenth-century souls inhabit and possess modern scholarship and remain unwilling to concede or acknowledge the complexity of history.

As discussed in chapter 2, Amador de los Ríos (1876) and Baer (1961) appear to subscribe to a black-and-white view of Sephardic Jews and conversos: they were either defenders or betrayers of Judaism. Lea (1907) complicated this view by arguing that conversos' self-perceptions and religious identities were tied the historical circumstances of this era of anti-Semitism. Like Lea's earlier work, Serrano's *Los conversos* (1942) and Cantera Burgos's *Alvar García de Santa María y su familia de conversos* (1952) focused the academic debate on conversos' specific activities, as opposed to offering fictional strawmen to knock down. Serrano's and Cantera Burgos's conversos are active agents of their futures, albeit heavily constrained by the fifteenth-century fixation on limpieza de sangre.

Twentieth-century Sephardic and converso histories also have an intense and combative tone that closely corresponds to the critique of the Nazi regime's systematic extermination of Jews and post–World War II anti-Semitism. Of these, the most important contributions to the evaluation of Spanish Jewish identities are those of Baer, Julio Caro Baroja, Netanyahu, and Roth. The more recent scholarship of George Mariscal, David Nirenberg, Ann Laura Stoler, Norman Roth, and María Elena Martínez, which focuses on identities tied to blood and race, is presented in chapter 6. These scholars' findings on identity are very interesting in the context of how conversos' shaped and managed their public personae in life and death through religious memorials and foundations.

Juan Ignacio Pulido Serrano, in his review of the life and work of Caro Baroja, captured the sense and spirit of those authors who perceived more pervasive historical connections: "The allusions of Julio Caro Baroja to the Nazi Holocaust are present in his works pertaining to Jews, many times implicitly, and at other occasions explicitly. . . . Caro Baroja exposed the great similarity between what occurred in Spain during the fifteenth through seventeenth centuries and what, after a great deal of time later, took place in Germany. . . . [T]he impact of the Holocaust caused these intellectuals to reflect on the reasons for this tragedy and the history of victimization."[12] Perhaps it is because of this attention to oppression and survival that an interest in crypto-Judaism, or the distinct converso identity that publicly practiced Christianity while retaining Jewish faith and practice in private, developed within scholarship.

Briefly, it should noted that Caro Baroja's *Los judíos en la España moderna y contemporanea* points out that conversos occupied high offices and status in fifteenth-century Spain but also suffered abuse that was "not less violent" than that visited on Jewish communities.[13] Cornered, and considered "a separate class . . . or nation," he writes, the conversos' identity would be shaped by "a united campaign of demagoguery . . . by discontented nobles and clergy."[14]

In the nineteenth century, the study of Spanish Jewry and conversos began with full force, intent on distinguishing itself as a vital field in Jewish and European history.[15] This first took form in the study of the Holy Office of the Inquisition in Spain, commonly referred to as the Spanish Inquisition. In his pivotal work, *Historia crítica de la Inquisición en España*, first published in French in 1817–18 and then in Spanish in 1822, Juan Antonio Llorente presented the first comprehensive investigation of the formation of the church institutions dedicated to identifying and castigating heretics in Spain. The exhaustive four-volume study traces inquisitorial activities from the fourth century through its terminal point in the early nineteenth century, which was during Llorente's lifetime. Although Llorente discusses events in other European countries, his focus is on the minutiae of the Spanish Inquisition, tracing its establishment, its methods and operations, and its outcomes across Spain. His work provides some of the first statistics on the impact of the Spanish Inquisition on conversos tried for heresy.

Although Llorente does not explicitly discuss identity, he explains that Old Christians were highly suspicious of Jewish converts to Catholicism. He argues that in the early fifteenth century "more than 200,000 families, or more than a million persons of the 'Law of Moses' [Judaism], were baptized" as Christians. Thus it was believed "that the vast majority of the New Christians had not converted because of an interior belief, but only for the reason that they feared death."[16] Further, Castilians believed that conversos continued to practice Judaism in secret. At this historical moment—the first decades of the 1400s—Old Christians imposed a new group identity on a vast swath of the Spanish population because they believed conversos were not sincere Christians.

It was in this cultural environment that a new converso identity began to take form because of social transitions within the Sephardic community. Jane S. Gerber's *The Jews of Spain*, a sweeping and artful history of the Sephardic people from their pre-Roman inception through the twentieth century, argues that the fifteenth century was a crucial period for Spanish Jewry. At the outset she states, "The experience of the Sephardim raises the issue of acculturation and assimilation like no other community."[17] She argues that the high degree of Jewish acculturation and assimilation under the Muslims and Christians, the "breakdown of communal discipline," and the "cynicism of Spain's assimilated Jewish courtier class" must have had an impact on Jews' mass conversion to Christianity.[18]

David Graizbord notes that conversions in the period from 1391 to 1492 were due in part to a "crisis of leadership throughout Castilian and Aragonese *kehillot* [local Jewish community leadership]."[19] Elite, educated Jews had in fact become separated from the "affective piety of the Sephardic masses."[20] Elite Jews, he writes, were "'ripe' for defection to the Christian enemy" because of their sense of distinctiveness from the masses and their "intellectual and moral degeneration in the form of rationalism" or "spiritually deracinated Averroism."[21] Thus, it appears that conversos, especially Jewish elites like the ha-Levi/Santa María clan, had splintered off as a new community and identity that was distinguishable from Sephardic Jews.

These first-generation conversos represented a novel community that would come to be defined as they integrated with and mixed with Old Christian families such as the Carvajal. What is exceptional here is that this was not a one-way relationship that entailed former Jews sacrificing who they were and replacing it with a Christian identity. Rather, Old Christian families who intermarried and collaborated with the recent converts experienced their own form of identity transformation as they adopted new ways of worshipping and living. Religious and cultural purity was simply not a realistic option for new Christian-Jewish clans such as the emergent Carvajal–Santa María family confederation in Plasencia.

AT THE FRONTIER OF A NEW FAMILY: THE ORIGINS OF THE CARVAJAL–SANTA MARÍA CONFEDERATION

It was roughly in the year 1400 that the Carvajal ceased to be an exclusively Old Christian knightly family by marrying into the converso Santa María clan. But this was just the beginning of their shifting identities of both families as they began to support each other's claims in disputes, select elements of each other's practices and beliefs, and continue the practice of intermarriage over subsequent generations.

During the late fifteenth and sixteenth centuries the label "New Christian" could destroy a clan's social, religious, political, and economic future, as evidenced by the period's limpieza de sangre statutes prohibiting conversos from holding public and church offices as well as the Holy Office's skepticism about their true conversion.

The Carvajal–Santa María family confederation was established precisely when the Trastámaran dynasty was creating its New Nobility and large numbers of elite Jews were converting to Christianity. Quite shockingly, large numbers of the nobility and their families were of mixed religious heritage, and this truth remains obscured due to the successful whitewashing efforts of early fifteenth-century historians like Lorenzo Galíndez de Carvajal. Key members of this amalgam of church leaders, royal administrators, and knights were the Almaraz, Álvarez, Bejarano, Burgos, Cabrera(o)s, Camargo, Cartagena, Carvajal, Cervantes, Fernández, Galíndez, Gutiérrez, Maluenda, Sandi, Santa María, Trejo, Ulloa, Vargas, Villalva, and Villalobos clans.

At the core of this book is the previously unearthed evidence that demonstrates the Carvajal and Santa María family confederation was a robust converso network that would come to dominate Plasencia, and broader Spanish affairs, in the early fifteenth century. More important, this was the inception of a collective Christian-Jewish identity that borrowed from both religious and cultural traditions. Unfortunately, after the mid-fifteenth century families were required to hide their Jewish ancestry. Families who bore the name Santa María, however, were well known and could not hide without the aid of families like the Carvajal. In fact, it was not until the early seventeenth century that the descendants of the Santa María received a special dispensation from Pope Clement VIII (r. 1592–1605) declaring them of Old Christian lineage.[22]

Creating an intricate family partnership as early as 1406, the Carvajal and Santa María clans shared family relations through the intermarriage of the houses of Santa María, García de Ulloa, González de Espadero, Sánchez, and González de Carvajal. There is also suggestive evidence that the extended clan, visible in the 1395 testamentary actions of Gonzalo Lorenzo de Espadero, may have been affluent Jewish merchants who had converted to Christianity.[23] Espadero was one of the primary genealogical trunks that integrated undocumented Jewish relations into the Carvajal's family tree.

Reinforcing the connectedness of the Carvajal–Santa María confederation was its sixteenth-century propensity to pursue endogamous marriages for several generations, which was a well-known Jewish practice. Collectively, the families operated as one, defending each other's economic interests, residing together, transferring property to and from each other, and holding ecclesiastical posts in the Cathedral of Plasencia over generations.

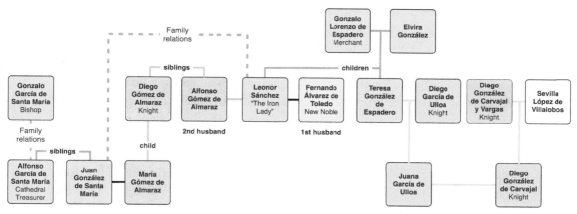

FIGURE 3.1. Carvajal, Santa María, and Sánchez family relations.

Exposing a Family Rift and Genealogical Connections

The Carvajal–Santa María relationship first came into public view in 1421, when the Carvajal clan intervened in a property dispute in Plasencia.[24] A collision of family interests pitted Leonor Sánchez, also known as "the Iron Lady," against her niece, María Gómez de Almaraz, who was the spouse of Juan González de Santa María.[25] Interestingly, Leonor also claimed to be a blood relative of Juan González, indicating that the Almaraz, Espadero, Gómez, González, and Sánchez families all had a blood relationship with the Santa María family (see fig. 3.1). At issue in this conflict was the property known as the Corral del Medio that Leonor Sánchez had donated to the Cathedral of Plasencia. In return for this customary land donation, the cathedral assured her that ten masses a year would be said in her memory.[26] Given that most properties donated to the cathedral typically produced only one mass a year for the benefactor, this was likely a substantial property that included highly specialized structures and lands meant for the housing and care of horses.[27] Unfortunately, according to María Gómez, the property was not Leonor's to give; María claimed that her father, Diego Gómez de Almaraz, had left it to her.[28] To determine the ownership of the property, the ecclesiastical judge Pedro González summoned the parties to the cathedral and required that all in attendance "defend and abide by his decision or face the penalty of excommunication."[29]

Leonor Sánchez argued that her late husband, Alfonso Gómez de Almaraz, had granted her the property. To this claim, María Gómez responded, "I do not agree this is the truth and it is my understanding that many witnesses that live in the vicinity of el Corral del Medio will confirm that my father gave this land to me more than twenty years ago."[30] In a defining moment in the resolution of the dispute, the knight Diego

González de Carvajal, along with María Gómez's spouse, Juan González de Santa María, testified that, in fact, "more or less thirty years ago," Maria's father had bequeathed the land to his daughter.[31] At this juncture, it is clear that the Carvajal and Santa María family interests were comingled and that perhaps the clans had had extended relations with one another for several decades. By supporting María's position, Diego González took a deliberate step toward creating the family confederation's identity. Although it might be argued that he was only speaking the truth on the matter, he was doing much more: he was choosing to "walk with" the Santa María at the cost of more closely related extended family members. This is the essence of identity: making conscious decisions that not only affect one's own life, but the lives of one's immediate and extended family. From this point forward, the Plasencia Carvajal began to display growing faithfulness to the Santa María house that typically only existed between two closely related families.

After weighing the differing accounts presented by both parties, the judge ruled, "That with the recording of this judgment, I offer remediation to María Gómez. That in defense of her rights the church chapter will pay her 100 gold *reales* for her lands."[32] On that day, standing alongside the victorious María Gómez and her husband were her relatives Prebendary Gil Gutiérrez de la Calleja and Diego González and his nephew, Diego García de Bejarano. While Gil Gutiérrez elected not to testify in the case, probably to avoid the appearance of inappropriate church pressure on the ecclesiastical judge, the Carvajal chose to support the Santa María–Almaraz over the Sánchez-Almaraz clan's claim.

The Villalva Connection: Mid- to Late Fifteenth-Century Family Relations

By 1450, it appears that the Plasencia Carvajal also shared another collection of extended family relations with the Santa María clan through the Villalva family.[33] Through these connections, prior clan relationships were reinforced (fig. 3.2). Specifically, in 1438, the Cathedral of Plasencia's notary recorded that church official Juan de Villalva was a "family" member of Bishop Gonzalo García de Santa María. Juan was a progenitor of the Plasencia Villalva family, which intermarried with the Carvajal clan.[34] Several noteworthy family leaders included the cathedral cantor, Christóval de Villalva, Juan de Villalva, and Juan's son, Coronel Christóval de Villalva (ca. 1450–1520).

These family connections came into view once again during the 1480s and 1490s, when Estefanía de Trejo Carvajal was reportedly married to Christóval de Villalva, an important personage in the military Order of Santiago.[35] Francisco de Carvajal, señor de Torrejón, was Christóval's second cousin. Through the marriage of Estefanía and Christóval, the prior Espadero-Sánchez-Almaraz relationships linking the Santa María and Carvajal clans were also reinforced.

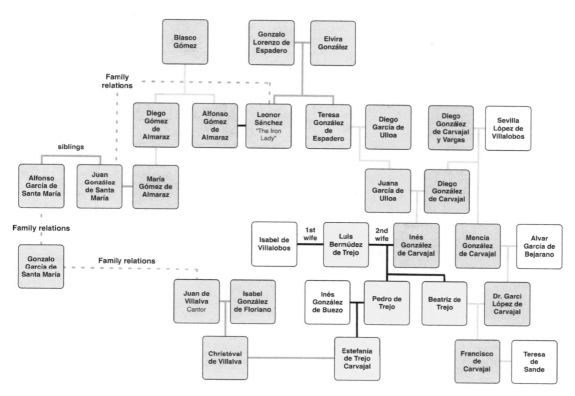

FIGURE 3.2. Villalva, Almaraz, Trejo, Carvajal, and Santa María family relations.

The Gutiérrez Connection: Intermarriage, Mid-Fifteenth through Early Sixteenth Centuries

The Carvajal family also sought integration with the Santa María lineage via its previously undocumented Gutiérrez de la Calleja (Maluenda) line that resided in Plasencia. For example, in 1470, in the Carvajal stronghold of the village of Cáceres, Juan de Carvajal "the Elder" is named the spouse of Mariana Gutiérrez de Álvarez, who was a significant beneficiary of a family estate.[36] A thorough review of the archival records of the Cathedral of Plasencia indicates that no other clan, Old or New Christian, utilized the Gutiérrez surnames in this region of Extremadura except for this converso one (fig. 3.3).

Church records verify the relationship of the house of Gutiérrez de Calleja to the family of Santa María. Specifically, the church notary Gil Gutiérrez and his sons (Alfonso, Diego, Pedro, and Sancho) were recorded in the Cathedral of Plasencia's day-to-day business records, the *Actas capitulares*, as the "family" of Gonzalo García de Santa María.[37]

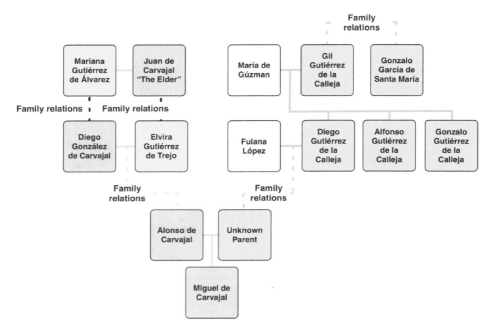

FIGURE 3.3. Gutiérrez, Carvajal, and Santa María family relations.

The Jewish and converso practice of endogamy is also revealed in the Carvajal-Gutiérrez lineage. Several manuscripts document two Carvajal-Gutiérrez marriages during the fifteenth century. This finding is unusual because the Cathedral of Plasencia's archives seem to have been purged of almost all Gutiérrez and Santa María testaments, dowry letters, and other family documents. In contrast, there is a large collection of personal legal documents for most of the noble families of Plasencia. In an accounting of property holdings in 1497, another Diego González de Carvajal was named one of the patrons of the memorial chapel for his relative, Juan de Carvajal "the Elder," and Mariana de Gutiérrez de Álvarez.[38] Mariana's relative, Elvira Gutiérrez de Trejo of Plasencia, was married to this Diego González de Carvajal of Plasencia.[39]

Another revealing marriage that ties the Carvajal line to this formerly Jewish ancestry is that of Miguel de Carvajal, the Spanish Golden Age playwright from Plasencia. The story of Miguel is intertwined with his controversial play, *Tragedia Josefina* (The Josefina Tragedy), which he brought to the stage in Plasencia on Corpus Christi Day in the 1530s.[40] His work was controversial because he allegorized the biblical story of Joseph being sold into bondage by his brothers in order to speak of the plight of conversos.[41] (Miguel's *Tragedia Josefina* and his relationship to his contemporary family members are discussed further in chapter 8.)

Miguel was descended on his father's side from Diego González de Carvajal and on his mother's side from Fulana López and Diego Gutiérrez de la Calleja, described as "noteworthy New Christians."[42] Thus it appears that Miguel's paternal and maternal roots can be traced back to the Carvajal–Santa María family confederation.

KNIGHTS' AND CONVERSOS' CONTROL OF THE CATHEDRAL OF PLASENCIA

The catalyst for the Carvajal–Santa María religious and familial experiment was not a grand literary work, great social unrest, or even deadly illness. It was the miscalculations of an Old Christian clan that had overstepped its bounds in the Cathedral of Plasencia and the readiness of the family confederation to exploit an institutional window of opportunity.

Affairs of the church had been outside the realm of the house of Carvajal's experiences and way of life. Family members were knights and petty noblemen who held modest territories and accumulated wealth via agricultural and animal production from their lands. Before the 1410s, it appears that the Carvajal clan had neither the inclination nor the ability to gain access to the Cathedral of Plasencia's chapter of canons and prebendaries. There is no mention in the Carvajal recorded history before this date of a family member branching out from traditional military service into church service.[43] It was not until after the tax revolts of 1396 and 1403–10, and most likely due in part to limited opportunities for social and economic advancement, that the Carvajal family began to appreciate the political and economic possibilities that could be garnered as a member of the Cathedral of Plasencia's leadership chapter. If the clan could find a path into the cathedral's leadership ranks, it could benefit financially from the church's patronage opportunities, resources, and taxation authority. Blocking its access was the Fernández family of churchmen, as well as bishops sympathetic to the Fernández clan.

Leadership and Management of the Cathedral of Plasencia

Fundamental to the ecclesiastical strength and autonomy of Catholic dioceses in the Kingdom of Castile and León during the late fourteenth and early fifteenth centuries were the significant local powers that the Catholic Church bestowed on them. In each of Spain's regional ecclesiastical benefices, including the Diocese of Plasencia, a bishop and cathedral chapter (*cabildo de la catedral*) had jurisdiction. Although the bishop was the titular leader of the diocese, the cathedral chapter often played a role in the appointment of the bishop, and the chapter could significantly circumscribe the bishop's authority in local matters.

From 1375 to 1422, there was considerable tension and turbulence within the administration of the Plasencia diocese. In at least three cases, Plasencia's bishops found themselves in conflict with the cathedral chapter and the local community. For instance, between 1375 and 1401, Bishop Pedro Fernández de Soria attempted to gain control of the membership of the local church council to benefit his own family, but the chapter successfully rebuffed his efforts until his death. Likewise, Bishop Vicente Arias de Balboa (r. 1401–14) battled local noble families and knights repeatedly over church taxes. Finally, and to the detriment of the diocese, Bishop Gonzalo de Estúñiga (r. 1415–22) sold large tracts of church lands in the village of Béjar to his powerful brother, Pedro de Estúñiga, conde de Béjar and justicia mayor of King Juan II.[44] Across Castile the relations between bishops and cathedral chapters were problematic at best.[45] Not until the leadership of Bishop Gonzalo García de Santa María (r. 1423–46), and the harmonious bishop-chapter relations under his administration, did stability return to the administration of the Diocese of Plasencia. Critical to creating the conditions necessary for a smoothly operating cathedral was the bishop's tacit acceptance of the chapter's authority over the diocese.

Local cathedral chapters and bishops derived their specific authority to govern their dioceses from the pope.[46] In theory, bishops held absolute ecclesiastical and sacramental authority within their respective geographic jurisdictions, and only the pope could remove them from office.[47] However, by the thirteenth century, cathedral chapters retained their own competing authority over their dioceses.[48]

Castilian kings found themselves equally constrained by the local authority of churchmen. Since King Alfonso X's creation of the Siete Partidas in the thirteenth century, monarchs obligated themselves not only to protect and guard but also not to interfere with church property and goods.[49] This policy of secular noninterference was first brought to a head in the late eleventh through early twelfth centuries during the investiture controversy, when the Holy Roman Emperor finally succumbed to the power of the Roman Catholic papacy to name diocesan bishops. Thus, an intricate web of relationships bound the king, pope, bishop, and cathedral chapter. Although royal and papal authority were supreme in their own rights, those powers weakened and local power grew with each step away from the royal and church centers in Burgos and Rome. In this manner, the Cathedral of Plasencia had much in common with other late thirteenth-century Castilian "frontier" ecclesiastical centers, such as the Cathedral of Segovia, where "ecclesiastics [were] liberated by distance and environment and from the constraints of authority."[50]

The cathedral chapter governed every aspect of the Diocese of Plasencia's ecclesiastical activities, including regular masses but also payment of church officers, management of church properties, and collection of church rents and taxes. While the bishop was the local "lord" of the church, the chapter had considerable control over the administration of the diocese. Often Placentino bishops hailed from other cities in

Spain and were physically absent from Plasencia while attending to affairs in the king's royal court (*real audiencia*).[51] In fact, for more than thirty years (from the 1390s to 1423) not a single sitting bishop of Plasencia appeared to be physically present at any of the recorded meetings of the cathedral chapter.[52] Pedro Fernández, Vicente Arias, and Gonzalo de Estúñiga were mostly absentee bishops who left the cathedral chapter to attend to its affairs.[53] The first bishop to appear in the cathedral chapter's meeting records was the interim bishop, Friar Don Diego Fernán Sánchez de Seradilla, who occupied the chair for only part of 1424.[54] This routine absence of bishops from the Diocese of Plasencia generally promoted a strong self-identity and reliance on self-governance in its cathedral chapter.

In the Castilian western frontier of Extremadura, far from Burgos and Rome, the Diocese of Plasencia perceived itself as a self-administering local institution. When the dean and church officers met to discuss administrative matters, in most cases in the Chapel of Saint Paul (Capilla de San Pablo), they did so by invoking their own authority, in the name of "the Dean and the Cathedral Chapter," not in the name of the king, the pope, or even the bishop.[55] They acted under their own authority for they, not the bishop, "owned" the church's property, "leased" it to other parties, "gave" and "exchanged" it for other lands, and "obligated" themselves to the terms of their negotiated contracts.[56] Further, the Cathedral of Plasencia's Estatuto Fundamental of 1254 dictated that the cathedral chapter controlled the naming of local church officials, such as canons.[57]

Typically, in the Kingdom of Castile and León, a cathedral chapter's membership was composed of a dean, who served as its presiding officer; archpriests (*arciprestes*), who oversaw the clergy and religious services; archdeacons (*arcedianos*), who administered all church business affairs and participated in religious services; a cantor (*chantre*), whose role included overseeing and leading the choir but also other unspecified duties; a church treasurer (*tesorero*); and a headmaster of the church school (*maestrescuela*).[58] Cathedral records often refer to this group as the diocese's ecclesiastical dignitaries (*dignidades eclesiásticas*). Bishops were highly dependent on the chapter, primarily composed of prominent families from the local community, for advice on the particulars of governing their territories.

Since the late fourteenth century, the Diocese of Plasencia's church organization mimicked this standard form, except that Plasencia's cathedral chapter operated in a highly decentralized manner. Further, its archdeacons, canons, and prebendaries had considerable independent decision-making authority. The *Actas capitulares* reveal that the most important members of the Plasencia cathedral chapter were its dean, archdeacons, cantor, treasurer, canons (*canónigos*), prebendaries (*prebendados*), notaries (*notarios*), attorney (*abogado*), and vicar general (*vicario general*). The archpriests were not active members of the decision-making chapter, and the diocese had no school headmaster. The Cathedral of Plasencia's archdeacon of Plasencia and Béjar and archdeacon of Trujillo and Medellín oversaw their respective regions with the assistance of their hand-selected canons and prebendaries. The archdeaconship of Coria also appeared to be part of the diocese during this period.[59]

The *Actas capitulares* indicate that the church's canons and prebendaries managed most of the routine administrative affairs relating to church property, taxes, and salaries. From its cadre of canons, the chapter selected its archdeacons, who had the authority to hire their own prebendaries, often family members or close associates. In all business transactions, one of several church notaries recorded the critical elements and terms of transactions and documented the church officials who presided over these events and other attending parties and witnesses.

Within the Diocese of Plasencia, the ill-defined role of cantor was nonetheless a key chapter post. According to the *Diccionario de historia eclesiástica de España*, although the cantor was the leader of the choir, his responsibilities could extend beyond this role.[60] In Plasencia, the cantor appeared to have broader administrative duties as he dispensed two canon positions to family and associates. In addition, the cantor worked with other chapter members to develop church statutes and served as a high-level witness when the cathedral leased substantial properties.[61] On occasion, the Cathedral of Plasencia appointed an attorney to handle legal issues surrounding church jurisdiction and tax collection.[62]

Given that the cathedral chapter appointed its own members and was not obligated to accept the bishop's input on the naming of canons and prebendaries, the only post over which the bishop had total control was that of vicar general. The vicar general represented the bishop's interest in local issues, especially as they related to managing the clergy and enforcing church statutes.[63] Often, the bishop selected senior and well-respected family members and friends to serve as his vicar. When a bishop died in office, his vicar general would serve in his position until the appointment of a new bishop.

The lack of centralized control within the Cathedral of Plasencia meant that no one party—the bishop, the vicar general, or the chapter dean—exercised control of the diocese. It also spoke to the communal—some might say, conciliar—approach to decision making. Throughout the late fourteenth to mid-fifteenth century, Plasencia's church leaders seemed to distrust the idea of vesting too much authority in one position. Unlike cathedral chapters in other dioceses, such as Ávila and Valencia, Plasencia's dean was not the most powerful member on the council or the most likely to negotiate agreements and resolve problems for the church.[64] When the chapter confronted difficult decisions or complicated financial transactions, more often than not Plasencia's two main archdeacons and not the dean were the senior officials who oversaw these matters.[65] The limitations placed on Plasencia's dean are evident in the cathedral chapter's decision never to grant the deanship to any man for life, therefore preventing him from exerting the full force of his office over other members. Rather, senior members of the council rotated through the dean's post, often while they held other permanent church positions.[66]

At times, the chapter left the deanship vacant, presumably because this post was not necessary to manage the day-to-day operations of the diocese. For instance, on October 6, 1403, Pedro Fernández, archdeacon of Trujillo and Medellín, leased several church houses on Calle de Zapatería in Plasencia for 150 maravedís to Fernán Álvarez de Toledo, señor de Oropesa, "on behalf" of the Plasencia dean and chapter.[67] Theoretically, the dean or the archdeacon of Plasencia and Béjar should have overseen this transaction for Plasencia properties. Because the cathedral chapter relied on a decentralized approach to manage the church's affairs, it also opened new pathways for local families with administrative backgrounds, such as the Santa María, to gain access to the chapter. However, in most cases, it required family or patronage connections to obtain a position in the Cathedral of Plasencia.

Access and Patronage

Between the late 1300s and the 1420s, the Plasencia cathedral chapter membership underwent considerable change as a result of the rise and decline of several family networks within the city. With these radical shifts in family fortunes, the cathedral's authority and patronage opportunities passed out of the hands of the Old Christian Fernández family of churchmen and into those of the converso Carvajal–Santa María family confederation. Prior to this change, the ecclesiastical patronage network in Plasencia had revolved around four key families—the Fernández, Estúñiga, Santa María, and Carvajal. Since the 1370s, the Fernández family had attempted to control the cathedral through its participation in the chapter and had seen one of its clansmen named bishop. The New Noble Estúñiga, which was forming a base of power and property in the village of Béjar in the late fourteenth century, entered the ecclesiastical fray in the 1410s and had its greatest influence on the church under Bishop Gonzalo de Estúñiga. During the first decade of the 1400s, the Santa María family joined the local church hierarchy but did not achieve prominence until the naming of Bishop Gonzalo de Santa María in the 1420s. Similarly, the Carvajal family's entry into the church patronage structure was late and not evident until the early 1420s.

From 1391 to 1424, before the arrival of converso Bishop García de Santa María in Plasencia, local church leaders effectively locked both the Carvajal and Santa María families out of most cathedral leadership positions and patronage opportunities. Similar to the governing chapter of the Cathedral of Valencia, Plasencia's churchmen aggressively competed for the "lucrative and honorific" posts of archdeacon, sacristan, and cantor.[68] Exclusion from these roles denied families access to superior salaries and the privilege of controlling church decision making relating to church assets, such as the leasing of houses, vineyards, agriculturally productive lands, and other real estate. Ultimately, though, neither the established Fernández family of Plasencia nor the prominent and powerful newcomers to Extremadura, the Estúñiga clan, was able to exclude the emergent family confederation. The converso Santa María clan had ecclesiastical credentials linked to its noteworthy family head, Pablo de Santa María, bishop of Burgos and member of the king's royal council. Furthermore, the Carvajal family used its high regional stature, earned through their services as knights, to gain control of the Cathedral of Plasencia. Through shrewd local politicking and patience, the family confederation weathered this transitional period and then placed their family members and friends in the cathedral chapter. Although each of these four families made every effort to mold the Cathedral of Plasencia to their personal needs, the Santa María and Carvajal clans proved the most effective at directing the institution for their enrichment and advancement.

Patronage was among the defining characteristics of the cathedral's operations. This socioeconomic system, which allowed ambitious men ("clients") to advance in return for "reliable and useful service" to their patrons, was shaped by family networks.[69] Patrons and clients formed associations through their extended families, as well as with their close associates. Individuals looked to their clan relations—uncles, cousins, and distant relatives—to access the wider realm of occupational opportunities.[70]

If familial relationships proved fruitful, men could also turn to the families of their allies. Within these networks, clients sought better professional positions, advancement, and access to new social and financial resources from the patrons they served.[71] In the late fourteenth and early fifteenth centuries, the Santa María and Carvajal families' social and economic worlds overlapped significantly, especially in the area of patron-client relations in the Cathedral of Plasencia. Specifically, the lords of the local church—the bishop and the cathedral chapter—utilized their positions to bestow the most coveted church roles on each other's immediate family members.

The Fernández Family

Prior to the establishment of the Carvajal–Santa María family confederation, the Fernández were the most powerful family in the cathedral chapter (1380s–1410s). The Fernández family's best chance at leading the church was under the guidance of their family elder, Pedro Fernández de Soria, who became bishop of Plasencia in 1375.[72] The first indication of the family's attempt to build a loyal membership in the cathedral chapter was the appointment of one of the bishop's nephews, also named Pedro Fernández, as a prebendary in 1380.[73] Given that the archdeacons selected their own prebendaries, this appointment is a good indication that the bishop had allies in the governing chapter. Over the next four years, the canons Juan Fernández and Toribio Fernández concurrently served with Pedro Fernández in the cathedral.[74]

Yet, in spite of the Fernández clan's success in securing these appointments, the family did not have full control of the leadership council. During the 1380s and 1390s, the membership of the cathedral chapter remained highly diversified and included the Martínez, Blásquez, González, García, Sánchez, Domínguez, and Gutiérrez de la Calleja clans.[75] Among these, only the Gutiérrez de la Calleja were conversos. The Fernández family persisted, and their efforts gained some ground between 1396 and 1401, when Martín Fernández de Soria, the nephew of the bishop, assumed the archdeaconship of Plasencia and Béjar. [76] With this position, Martín Fernández could name men of his choosing to other salaried offices under his jurisdiction. For example, Martín Fernández employed Alfonso Fernández, his nephew, as his personal page.[77]

Just as the family's control of the diocese appeared to come to fruition, it effectively collapsed. Although Pedro Fernández became archdeacon of Trujillo and Medellín in 1401, he would die on October 18 of that year.[78] If the family had captured all three positions—bishop of Plasencia, archdeacon of Plasencia and Béjar, and archdeacon of Trujillo and Medellín—it could have utilized these posts to consolidate its family power over the cathedral.

With the Fernández family unable to fully dominate of the Cathedral of Plasencia at the end of the fourteenth century, Plasencia's ecclesiastical leadership began to fragment as new families began to secure roles in the administration of the cathedral. Beginning with Bishop Arias de Balboa's term and continuing through the end of Bishop Gonzalo de Estúñiga's stewardship, a consequential shift in family power occurred in Plasencia. This transitional environment was crucial to the entrance of the Carvajal and the Santa María families into the cathedral chapter. Little is known about Bishop Arias de Balboa and his tenure, but what is evident is that he inherited a diocese in difficulty. This climate impeded the monopolization of church positions by any one family. Instead, the cathedral chapter defaulted to an uneasy sharing of posts.

Immediately on arriving in Plasencia in 1404, Bishop Arias de Balboa faced several governing challenges that required the acquiescence of the cathedral chapter. The key families in the chapter at this time were the Blásquez, Fernández, González, Gutiérrez de la Calleja, Martínez, Pérez de Alfaros, and Sánchez.[79] In April 1410, when the bishop personally proposed local church statutes to address problems with "slanderous" talk in Plasencia, as well as rules relating to the collection of diezmos, he did so with "the consensus of the cathedral chapter."[80] The bishop and the chapter most likely deemed both statutes necessary, given the continuous history of conflict between the cathedral and local knights.[81] The cathedral chapter promulgated these statutes soon after Diego García de Bejarano, a member of the house of Carvajal, conceded his position in the diezmos tax rebellion of 1403–10.[82] Even though the bishop was able to convince the chapter to enact these new church laws, the local churchmen were displeased with the way in which they were applied. The late sixteenth-century Placentino cleric and historian Friar Alonso Fernández stated, "Although [he] . . . was very learned, he was unfair in their application and used these anti-slander statutes on all occasions and without reservation."[83]

In order to impose his will on the Cathedral of Plasencia, the bishop required the assistance of the chapter's strongest family faction, the Old Christian Fernández. The

Fernández clan's local ecclesiastical power resided in their control of the archdeacon-ships of Plasencia and Béjar and of Trujillo and Medellín.

The Fernández family's motivation for supporting the bishop's initiatives, especially those intended to constrain knightly families like the Carvajal who resisted paying diezmos, was primarily an issue of church authority and finances. To enjoy the fruits of its archdeaconships, and the posts below those positions, the Fernández clan's livelihood depended on a financially stable diocese. The two Fernández archdeacons likely earned individual annual salaries comparable to the dean's, 800 maravedís.[84] However, the salary was just one of the benefits of these positions. As most of the cathedral's employment opportunities fell under the Fernández family's authority, they also stood to suffer the most from reduced tax collections. For instance, in 1405, Archdeacon Pedro Fernández collected 3,224 maravedís in taxes and other earnings from his parish churches Santa María de Trujillo and San Martín de Trujillo.[85] In return for providing these monies to the cathedral chapter, its membership rewarded him with six canonships to grant to church members. Each of the archdeacon's hand-selected canons earned an annual salary of 230 maravedís.

When an archdeacon successfully performed his administrative duties, such as gathering critical church rents and taxes, the entire cathedral chapter benefited. With the funds collected by the archdeacon of Trujillo and Medellín in 1405, the cathedral chapter generated fourteen new canon positions for its other members. The archdeacon of Plasencia and Béjar received two new canons; the dean, two canons; the cantor, two canons; and five lesser chapter officials shared funding for eight canons. Through this distribution, the Fernández clan secured nine new dedicated jobs for its family and friends. These offices were in addition to the two archdeaconships and the two preexisting church canonships awarded to Gil Fernández and Alfonso Fernández. Thus the Fernández house continuously utilized its position in the cathedral chapter to create additional opportunities for its family members.

Other families benefited from the church collections but not as generously. Canons Juan Sánchez and Christobal Sánchez shared one and a half canonships. Fernán Martínez garnered one canon position. The Fernández clan awarded the remaining half-time canonships to lesser men such as Andrés Domínguez, Juan Gutierre, and Pedro González. Noticeably missing from the cathedral's distribution of new patronage opportunities to current members of the chapter was Prebendary Gil Gutiérrez of the Santa María clan. Perhaps because of his exclusion from these benefits, the Santa María were not enthusiastic supporters of the dominant Fernández.

Converso Alliances: The Santa María

New alliances revealed themselves in the first and second decades of the 1400s as multiple converso families acted collectively against Old Christian leaders. This was among the first indications that conversos, on occasion, would find unity so that they could displace Old Christian families from their customary posts in the church. The Santa María family, which included the Gutiérrez de la Calleja, Fernández de Cabreros, and Salamanca, led the charge. Finding a post in the cathedral chapter was a challenge, but the first family member to do so was Gil Gutiérrez. On December 24, 1406, the chapter acknowledged his continued services as a prebendary but, more important, in 1407 reelected him as its dean, or mayordomo.[86] On his reelection, he took an oath "to serve as is the custom, faithfully and justly," and in return his colleagues provided him with a rich annual salary of 800 maravedís,[87] three times a canon's income of 230 maravedís a year.[88] Further, its purchasing power is evident considering that the average annual lease for a centrally located house in the city of Plasencia was 104 maravedís and a pair of chickens. For at least a decade, Gil Gutiérrez was the lone member of the Santa María family to penetrate the close-knit leadership chapter of the cathedral.[89] However, in 1414, when Bishop Arias de Balboa left his post in the diocese and Gonzalo de Estúñiga became the new bishop of Plasencia, the fortunes of the Santa María family began to improve substantially. An uneasy alliance of New Nobles, conversos, and knights began to unfold.

The first important shift in the cathedral chapter's membership occurred when the converso and New Noble bishop Gonzalo de Estúñiga initiated a series of actions to transition the leadership of the cathedral chapter away from the Old Christian Fernández family. Although he had no direct authority to make those changes, other families had an interest in displacing the Fernández family. One step in carrying out his plan was to appoint Gil Martínez de Soria as his vicar general and personal representative in the chapter.[90] Gil Martínez was an educated doctor of the law and a seasoned canon from the Church of Calahorra. On June 19, 1417, he demonstrated his ability to influence the members of the cathedral chapter when he proposed and led the implementation of new church statutes.[91]

It was an unusually well-attended meeting that drew the interests of twelve men to the cathedral's Chapel of Saint Paul. The Fernández family appeared with their two archdeacons and two canons, and the rest in attendance were a mix of the other representative families, including Gil Gutiérrez. The men gathered to address what appeared to be a recurring problem—the embezzlement of church assets and income. Vicar General Gil Martínez de Soria explained:

> Some of the favored individuals of this church have interfered and taken the fruits and monies and other things that belong to the church for themselves . . . and without the approval nor the command of the Dean and the Chapter. We do not know the allocations or the amounts of these things or to whom they were due or given to. [In the future] no individuals who serve this church will have or borrow or take that which is rightly deserved by the church without the approval of the Dean and the Chapter. We will pay everyone what they deserve because in the end we are all one.[92]

The enactment of the statutes indicates that the cathedral's leadership conceptualized itself as communal entity that treated its members fairly. As a whole, they believed corrupt practices needed to end immediately.

Although the chapter did not name the guilty parties, it was an inescapable truth that, since 1401, the Old Christians Martín and Pedro Fernández had held the church's two primary archdeaconships. It is likely that the Fernández family was the guilty party. Although cathedral families routinely utilized church assets for their own benefit, such as when they personally rented church properties at reduced rates and subsequently leased them to other individuals at higher rates, theft was an entirely different matter.

The conversos subsequently acted to solidify their position in the cathedral chapter. The unrecorded events that led to the enactment of the embezzlement statutes promoted a desire for change in the governing chapter, which created another opening for the Santa María family, which was facilitated by Bishop Estúñiga. One way the bishop and the chapter implemented this organizational shift, without overtly confronting the Fernández clan, was by expanding the cathedral's leadership positions. In a move that gave equal status to the other two archdeaconships, the bishop and the church council named Alonso Rodríguez de Maluenda to the newly created position of archdeacon of Coria. A converso, Alonso Rodríguez was a relative of the local Santa María clan and the prominent Pablo de Santa María of Burgos. He was a well-respected church leader who later served simultaneously as the vicar general for Bishop Santa María and the abbot of Castro at the Cathedral of Burgos.[93] With Alonso Rodríguez taking the archdeacon's post, the Santa María family gained another vote on the cathedral chapter, which allowed them access to new financial resources and patronage opportunities.

Seismic cultural and familial shifts were in play as conversos began to position themselves to outmaneuver Old Christians. The ascent of the Santa María from Burgos, alongside the New Nobles, meant that the Old Christian Fernández clan could be pushed out of its own cathedral. In this specific instance, we can see how the conversos' improved political status in Castilian society was a direct threat to Old Christians.

What was unusual about the next steps the conversos took in the Cathedral of Plasencia was that they did not choose to empower another converso clan to confront the Fernández churchmen. Instead, in a break in their unity, and perhaps to appease some of the Old Christians who remained in the cathedral chapter, the conversos turned to the Old Christian Carvajal family of knights some of whom had just begun to marry into converso families. The importance of this decision—to empower the Carvajal—demonstrated that the conversos perceived these Old Christians as good partners, partners who were unafraid of confrontation and willing to adjust their identities to match those of conversos like the Santa María.

By 1421, the cathedral's membership was in full transition. The church's leaders forced Martín Fernández out of his position as archdeacon of Plasencia and Béjar and replaced him with Gonzalo García de Carvajal.[94] This occurred more than three years before the elder Fernández had even planned his retirement from the cathedral.

As most archdeacons held their positions for life, Gonzalo García's appointment in-dicated that the Fernández clan's power had substantially weakened in the cathedral chapter.[95]

Nonetheless, before the reforming Bishop Estúñiga left office, he too abused his office and initiated a seventy-year conflict that pitted his family against most of Plasen-cia's other clans. This demonstrated that the converso alliance within the cathedral was fragile. Ultimately, the Estúñiga clan became the enemies of the Carvajal–Santa María family confederation. In 1417, Bishop Estúñiga assisted his family with its consolida-tion of property in the village of Béjar when he sold the bishop's housing complex to his brother, Pedro de Estúñiga, King Juan II's justicia mayor.[96] The sum his brother paid was sizable (2,350 Aragonese gold florins), but it was not likely that the amount offset the symbolic loss of these important homes or the physical displacement of church leaders from this area of the diocese. According to the local Placentino historian Domingo Sánchez Loro, this event marked the beginning of the Estúñiga clan's nega-tive impact on Extremadura.[97] Friar Alonso de Fernández also stated that this highly controversial property sale angered Placentinos because it provided the Estúñigas with even more power in the diocese.[98]

During the 1410s and 1420s, there was an unstated quid pro quo among the Es-túñiga, Santa María, Carvajal, and Martínez. While the Estúñiga acquired an impor-tant church housing complex in the village of Béjar, the Santa María increased its stature in the cathedral chapter through Gil Gutiérrez's and Archdeacon Alonso Ro-dríguez's roles in the church. At the same time, the Martínez and Carvajal families found their first church patronage opportunities with the naming of Gil Martínez de Soria as vicar general and Gonzalo García de Carvajal as archdeacon. Together, these parties effectively displaced the Fernández family's twenty-year attempt to dominate the cathedral chapter and created the political environment necessary for the forma-tion of a new robust alliance of families, the Carvajal–Santa María family confedera-tion, which would take control of the cathedral in the mid-1420s.

Not until after his death, still two decades away in the 1420s, would it be apparent that the house of Carvajal had made momentous decisions about their future along-side their Santa María partners. With his appointment as archdeacon, Gonzalo García de Carvajal initiated the Carvajal family's first significant identity transition. Genera-tions of Carvajal men had served as knights in the king's armies, although none had ever pursued a churchman's livelihood.[99] For several hundred years, the Carvajal clan had labored, like the Mendoza family, as "military entrepreneurs."[100] However, only those soldiers with personal wealth, proven military talent, and the desire for financial and social advancement could readily enter the upper echelon of Castile's nobility.[101] Unfortunately, the Carvajal lacked significant wealth and could boast of only modest successes on the battlefield, in contrast to others like the Estúñiga who owned great armies.[102] Further, like all noble families, its social and economic status was always in jeopardy. A noble clan could rapidly decline in status if the family's size exceeded the economic capacity of its resources or if it failed to generate sufficient male heirs to perpetuate the clan's lineage.[103]

Sometime after the Plasencia knights' tax revolts of 1396 and 1403–10, the Carvajal family guided Gonzalo García de Carvajal toward ecclesiastical service. This decision forever redirected the trajectory of the Carvajal of Plasencia and began the family's religious, social, and economic metamorphosis as it adapted to their relationship with the Santa María ecclesiastics. With these early initiatives in place by the first decade of the 1400s, the Carvajal clan was at the forefront of identity change among Castile's knight clans; other noble families such as the Mendoza delayed their entry into the ecclesiastical world for another fifty years.[104]

What remains frustrating is our limited knowledge about the family's and Gonzalo García de Carvajal's decision to enter ecclesiastical service, as no other Old Christian Carvajal, or extended family member, had served the church. His father, Alvar García de Bejarano, was a knight, and his brother, Diego García de Bejarano, had been excommunicated for his role in a recent tax revolt. His mother, Mencía González de Carvajal, was the daughter of a knight.

The one clue that may point to why Gonzalo García de Carvajal was guided toward the church was that his father was more than a knight; his full name and titles were Alvar García de Bejarano "el Rico" and Señor de Orellana de la Sierra.[105] In fact, in appears that Gonzalo García de Carvajal's father was a minor and previously undocumented member of the new nobility. There is virtually nothing known about his origins, but the nickname "the Rich" and his ownership of seigniorial lands signals that he was likely among the generation of New Noble houses created by the mercedes enriqueñas, and possibly a first-generation converso. Further investigation reveals that this single family within the extended Old Christian house of Carvajal was the first to become religious leaders. As I explore in subsequent chapters, Gonzalo García de Carvajal had other siblings that departed from the long-standing knightly profession of the extended family. This included Dr. Garci López de Carvajal, who would become a royal bureaucrat, and Sancho de Carvajal, future archdeacon of Plasencia.[106] As a group, these siblings were initially an anomaly, but soon they would be joined by their maternal first cousins.

The family decisions that led these men to join the church evade us, but what is clear is that the clan had prioritized this immediate family unit as responsible for developing highly educated leaders, men who could bridge the relationships between Old Christian knights and the converso Santa María churchmen who were their extended relatives. This was a shift in religious and professional identities to a new path working alongside first-generation conversos and trading swords for wax seals.

Asserting Control in the Cathedral of Plasencia

Exploring the Carvajal–Santa María entry into the leadership of the Cathedral of Plasencia reveals how this converso confederation gained access to church positions and their attendant rewards. The addition of Archdeacon Alonso Rodríguez to the cathedral chapter introduced a rising Santa María leader to Plasencia's community. Alonso Rodríguez's converso pedigree was impeccable from the Santa María's perspective, as his mother, María Núñez, was the sister of Bishop Pablo de Santa María, the influential senior chancellor of King Juan II.[107] Like the Santa María, the knightly Carvajal clan gained new prominence in the chapter. The cathedral chapter appointed Gonzalo García de Carvajal archdeacon of Plasencia and Béjar sometime before 1422.

Swift changes in the diocese's leadership shifted power in favor of the two families, and their fortunes improved after the departure of Bishop Estúñiga in 1422 and the short tenure of Bishop Friar Diego de Badán.[108] Between 1424 and 1425, the membership of the cathedral chapter changed and the king named Gonzalo García de Santa María bishop of Plasencia.[109]

To hold cathedral power, the family confederation needed to decrease the power of its Old Christian rivals and place even more of its members in key positions. When the chapter selected Gil Martínez as the new archdeacon of Trujillo and Medellín,[110] this change in leadership effectively marked the end of the Fernández family's influence on the chapter. It was the opening that the Carvajal and Santa María had patiently awaited. With Gil Martínez's cooperation, the new makeup of the chapter fell decidedly into the arms of the family partners. The Santa María, Carvajal, and Martínez families equally shared the council's three commanding archdeacon titles. In the early 1420s, of the fourteen identified members of the cathedral's governing chapter, four were Santa María (Gil Gutiérrez and Alonso Rodríguez), one was a Carvajal, one was an Almaraz (married into the Santa María), and two were Martínez clansmen.[111] At this moment the united families, who had participated in the 1421 intrafamilial property dispute between Leonor Sánchez and María Gómez de Almaraz, acted together.

Only one Old Christian Fernández remained in the chapter, severely diluting the clan's influence. Thus, the cathedral chapter's power was not simply autonomous and institutionally separate from its membership but a reflection of local clans' ability to impose their authority over the local church and the community.[112] Put simply, a family's canonships equaled power (table 3.1).

With a dominant position in the cathedral chapter, the family confederation now shared a common interest in creating a working majority that would ensure the successful nomination of its candidate for bishop. The Santa María wished to enhance their growing prominence in the chapter. Like their counterparts, the Carvajal and Almaraz families desired new patronage opportunities for their immediate clansmembers but also hoped to shield their houses from further church tax investigations. The Martínez and Estúñiga clans also shared this interest of continued participation in church benefits. The Estúñiga family, while increasingly estranged from the Plasencia churchmen, was indebted to those who now ruled the chapter.[113]

The naming of Bishop Santa María, as well his first actions, suggest that the bishop's interests were aligned with those of the cathedral chapter. In 1425, just after

Table 3.1. Cathedral Chapter Membership, 1424–1425

Members	Position(s)
Gonzalo García de Carvajal	-Archdeacon of Plasencia and Béjar -Dean (part of 1424)
Gil Martínez de Soria	-Archdeacon of Trujillo and Medellín -Vicar General
Alonso Rodríguez de Maluenda	Archdeacon of Coria
Gonzalo Gutiérrez de la Calleja	Treasurer
Sancho Ortiz de Estúñiga	-Canon -Dean (part of 1424)
Diego Blásquez	-Canon -Dean (part of 1425)
Andrés Pérez	-Canon -Dean (part of 1425)
Gil Gutiérrez de la Calleja	Prebendary
Alfonso Gutiérrez de la Calleja	Prebendary
Diego Martínez de Soria	Prebendary
Blasco Gómez de Almaraz	Prebendary
Pedro González	-Prebendary -Notary
Juan Sánchez	Sacristan
Gómez Fernández	Canon

the chapter named Gil Martínez as archdeacon, the bishop rewarded him with the vicar general's seat.[114] While the vicar general was a member of the cathedral chapter, he was the bishop's only personally appointed local authority.[115]

Likewise, the Castilian bishop appointment process positioned the Santa María–Carvajal-dominated cathedral for an exponential growth in power and unity. Although the king was not required to consider a cathedral chapter's input, customarily he would take into account its recommendation for bishop.[116] Although no records detailing the politics surrounding Bishop García de Santa María's appointment are preserved, it is likely that the family confederation recommended him as its candidate for bishop to the king. Subsequently, the pope confirmed the king's choice.

Unlike the three bishops appointed prior to his term, Bishop Santa María's placement was indicative of the development of a new alliance of families in the Cathedral of Plasencia.[117] His selection as bishop was also ideal from the perspective of those who had King Juan II's ear in Burgos, including the new bishop's father, Pablo de Santa María. The coalescence of royal and local agreement on one candidate virtually assured that the Cathedral of Plasencia and its dominant families would rule the bishopric with little external or internal interference.

If the Castilian king did take into account the Plasencia chapter's recommendation for bishop, then Bishop Santa María's engagement with the cathedral is significant because it attests to his family's distinct role in shaping the Extremaduran church. Gonzalo García de Santa María's selection as bishop of Plasencia is not only further evidence of the rapid expansion of the converso Santa María family inside the royal administrative and ecclesiastical center in Burgos, but it also indicates that its leadership reached into the Castilian periphery of Extremadura. Perhaps the Placentino leaders' decision to recommend him to be their bishop also reveals that these men recognized the value of favoring this administratively and royally connected family. The rewards were not insubstantial; by accepting the position of bishop, Gonzalo García de Santa María was entitled to one-third of Plasencia's collection of diezmos.[118]

Once the family confederation controlled the bishop's position and the majority of positions in the cathedral chapter, in 1425 it began rewarding the chapter membership. Crucial among such benefits was the authority to lease its tax collection authority to extended family members. Customarily, the chapter might elect to use this financial tool so that the church could both guarantee itself a precise income and expedite the collection of that income. Specifically, the churchmen leased to Juan Ruiz de Camargo the cathedral's collection of the annual church tax assessed on locally produced goods such as wine, wheat, cattle, and hogs.[119] This lease was a valuable opportunity granted to the Carvajal clan's extended family, the Camargo.[120] From these tax proceeds, the Cathedral of Plasencia distributed one-third directly to the chapter, paid one-third to the bishop, and reinvested the last third in "the works of the church."[121] Thus the church received an "advance" on future tax levies.

Individuals like Juan Ruiz chose to rent these tax collection powers with the expectation that they could realize a profit by collecting more tax revenues than the purchase price of their lease. In the four-year agreement with Ruiz, the Cathedral of Plasencia leased the right to collect and keep one-eighth of the annual church taxes for a portion of the diocese.[122] On December 26, 1425, the chapter gathered to disburse the proceeds from this contract.[123] Juan Ruiz paid the dean and cathedral chapter 18,000 maravedís, which the Carvajal–Santa María confederation promptly divided among the thirteen church canonships. After four years of proven loyalty and with the benefits of their partnership in the Cathedral of Plasencia now beginning to pay tangible dividends, the family confederation extended its efforts onto the stage of papal and royal affairs.

From Knights to Tax Collectors

In the 1420s, as its converso alliance unfolded and the confederation prospered, the Santa María rewarded their Carvajal kinsmen with the honor of collecting papal monies to present to the king. What was so unusual about this moment is that it brought different experiences to each side of the family confederation. The Carvajal adapted to becoming bureaucrats like the Santa María, who had been Jewish tax collectors and treasurers. The Santa Maria, members of a subjugated Jewish leadership class, were now Christian vassals much like the Carvajal knights. The Santa María–Carvajal had a new identity, one in which they could claim Christian noble origins and valuable administrative expertise.

New financial arrangements also reveal how complex patronage chains linked families, the crown, and the papacy. In 1425, rather than personally delivering taxes to the king or appointing an immediate family member to do so, Bishop Gonzalo García de Santa María elected Archdeacon Gonzalo García de Carvajal to deliver a cathedral payment of 45 gold Aragonese florins to King Juan II.[124] Pope Martín V (r. 1417–31) offered these monies to reaffirm the church-royal relationship and to bestow patronage on the king. The florins were much more than a simple payment to the king; they were a formal papal expression of approval and appreciation. As such, Bishop Santa María could not entrust this offering to a minor local church leader. Thus the bishop's tapping of Archdeacon Carvajal to perform this task was an explicit act of personal faith and family unity. What is extraordinary about this minor episode in the history of the Catholic Church and the Kingdom of Castile and León is that it signaled to the king, the New Nobles of Castile, and other elite conversos that the Santa María and Carvajal families were steadfastly bonded to one another.

Bishop Santa María's actions also placed the Carvajal in the enviable position of serving as intermediaries between the papacy and the crown. The bishop's promotion of the Carvajal family was also a selfish act on behalf of his kinsman, as it likely enhanced the relationship between royal adviser Dr. Garci López de Carvajal and the Santa María family members serving in the Castilian court. Certainly, the bishop could have chosen a man with more prestigious and noble credentials, such as the Placentino canon, Sancho Ortiz de Estúñiga, whose family he knew well. That he did not reveals the tightly constructed relationship of the Carvajal and Santa María houses.

By selecting the Carvajal for the honor of serving the king, Bishop Santa María communicated a powerful symbolic message to Burgos and Rome: the Carvajal–Santa María confederation was now an important link in the patronage chain binding the papacy to the Castilian crown. Not only did the two families focus their attention on these kingdom-level patronage initiatives, but they also directed their mutual efforts at leveraging their local authority in the Cathedral of Plasencia. Thus by 1425 the Carvajal–Santa María family confederation was poised to actualize their new vision of identity—one built on Christian and Jewish precedent—and to safeguard interreligious coexistence within the political and cultural constraints of this era of rapid change.

4

INNOVATION

With the Carvajal–Santa María dominance in full force as of 1425 in the Cathedral of Plasencia—Bishop Gonzalo García de Santa María guiding the institution, four Santa María family members occupying key roles in the cathedral chapter, and Gonzalo García de Carvajal serving as archdeacon of Plasencia and Béjar—new practices of converso ideology and identity were actualized. Over the course of the next twenty years, unprecedented change percolated through the Placentino cathedral, the city, and the region. The family confederation's endeavors reflected a new converso mentalité that advanced family power but also communicated intense respect for Jewish-Christian relations and institutionalized new ways of governing the broader community. This chapter investigates these changes and the fundamentally new cultural designs the family confederation had in mind for Plasencia's Jews, Christians, and Muslims. I am not arguing that the family confederation brought about perfect interreligious relations; rather I am suggesting that the Carvajal–Santa María seemed to approach interfaith relations with pragmatism and open-mindedness. Promoting the demographic and economic health of local Jewish and Muslim families was good for Plasencia and thus good for the family confederation.

Ideologically, the family confederation promoted cooperative governance of civic and church institutions while preserving the benefits of patronage and personal wealth creation for its extended family members. The families were neither saints nor opportunists; they were self-interested but appeared to avoid the worst corruption that had driven the Fernández from power in the cathedral. With improvements in governance, the Placentino Carvajal and Santa María clans advanced religious tolerance and opportunities for Jewish and Muslim community members via housing and commercial opportunities. Likewise, they used their local authority to integrate conversos into the Jewish quarter of Plasencia, as well as to promote mixed residence of Jews, Christians, and Muslims in private and church-owned housing in the prominent public square. This mentalité can only be understood as a cultural repudiation of the anti-Jewish Ordinances of Valladolid of 1412.[1] The ordinances focused primarily on limiting Jews' social and economic interaction with Christians and conversos, as well as on moving Jews to separate neighborhoods.[2] This point—the confederation's actions focused on interreligious residential zones—cannot be underestimated in light of the vitriolic language of the era that was driving a wedge between conversos and Jews.

As discussed previously, the historian Amador de los Ríos blamed the development of these anti-Jewish policies on the Santa María family and suggested it promulgated them as a means to attack its former Jewish coreligionists. Yet the historical facts belie this supposition. The Carvajal–Santa María confederation in Plasencia was intent on preserving a balanced, interfaith approach in this age of increasing intolerance of Jews, Muslims, and recent converts to Christianity (both conversos and moriscos). There was a good economic reason for this tolerance too: Jews and Muslims could pay more for residential and agricultural leases than could Christians.

In practice, the formerly Old Christian Carvajal family began to imitate and learn the finer details of bureaucratic operations from the formerly Jewish ha-Levi (Santa María) clan members, who had been Jewish royal treasurers and rabbis in Castile during the fourteenth century and now brought that expertise to the Cathedral of Plasencia. Before their association with the Santa María, the Carvajal had no prior secular or religious administrative experience; they were knights skilled with swords, not seals. This occupational shift of the Carvajal appears to be one of the hallmarks of families pursuing social and political mobility in Castile. What is quite unusual here is that it was a formerly Old Christian family imitating and mimicking the traditional roles of courtly Jews.

Conscientious about protecting its growing local religious and political authority, the Carvajal–Santa María confederation began to adopt unusual practices within the cathedral. It is what we might call a converso identity and way of life because it was a blending of Christian and Jewish practices. With deliberate official acts, family members imposed cathedral statutes that ensured secrecy among select converso members of the cathedral chapter and began a practice of conducting chapter gatherings on Friday, the eve of the Jewish Sabbath. Although their Friday activities are intriguing, the scant historical record leaves the interpretation of their meaning and purpose incomplete. This change would culminate in a modified "Christian" practice with special masses said in honor of the Virgin Mary on Saturdays, thereby focusing the family's religious activities on Fridays and Saturdays, as opposed to the Christian focus on Sunday (see ch. 6).

Cumulatively, this ideology of coexistence and intermingled Jewish-Christian practice brought about a created identity that had not existed previously in Castile, much less in most of Western Europe. This self-conscious converso identity was definitively Christian in belief, as the family confederation would promote Marianism (veneration of the Virgin Mary) in its future church policies and family devotions, but its familial approach always drew Jews close and sought to shield them from predatory conversos, such as the New Noble Estúñiga clan. In essence, it appears that the family confederation was intent on creating a converso identity that could honor both faiths and families but with an overt Christian veneer.

This experimentation with a blended Jewish-Christian identity would not last. It entered a fifty-year decline starting as early as the 1440s and 1450s as Old Christian religious intolerance increased toward both conversos and Jews. In addition, there was no universal approach to converso identity as different clans pursued different plans, as in the case of the New Noble Estúñiga family, who became bitter enemies of the Carvajal–Santa María family confederation. In particular, as is explored in chapter 5, the family confederation suffered a debilitating and strategic political loss in 1441 when the Castilian king named Pedro de Estúñiga count of Plasencia; this former New Noble ally would become the bane of the family confederation's existence until the 1490s. With the entry of the new count into Plasencia, the confederated family would witness the dilution of its political and economic domination of the local city council. Utilizing the authority they had amassed in the Cathedral of Plasencia, the Carvajal–Santa María would have to position themselves as the weaker counterbalance to the Estúñiga family's surging political power in the region.

IMPROVING CIVIC AND RELIGIOUS GOVERNANCE

Benefits of Identity Hybridization

One of the first indications that Plasencia was culturally and politically evolving under the leadership of the Carvajal–Santa María family confederation was the advancement of collective community action. The family confederation did not confine its initiatives to the church alone but also promoted new collaborations between the knight-dominated city council and the cathedral chapter. Over the course of two days in 1428, the Carvajal and Santa María clans and their extended family overcame previous impediments to cooperation by promoting a communal identity and righteousness. Together, they steered the city council and the cathedral through a revenue-collaboration arrangement and through a potentially explosive dispute over wine and taxes. Their success in leading these specific Plasencia city-church negotiations is noteworthy because in other Castilian communities, such as Ávila and Ciudad Real, similar community issues often turned into tense jurisdictional battles.[3]

The first of these initiatives involved the Cathedral of Plasencia's lease of its portion of the portazgo, or royal taxes assessed on goods passing through the city's gates and its periphery, to the city council.[4] In Plasencia, as in other cities in the kingdom, residents were subject to several forms of annual taxation. The most important of these were church taxes on goods and livestock (diezmos), royal sales taxes (alcalaba), and city gate taxes (portazgo).[5] In Plasencia, the portazgo was assessed on a wide assortment of items. Among the named items subject to the toll tax were livestock, honey, olive oil, vinegar, herbs, chestnuts and other nuts, fruit, cheese, butchered meats, bacon, salted fish, linen, wool, cloth, iron and iron objects, timber, and glazed tile.[6]

The mayor and the bishop did not necessarily lead the sensitive business lease negotiations between the city council and the cathedral; instead men from the community's new leading families often conducted these affairs. Acting on behalf of the city council, Dr. Garci López de Carvajal negotiated and finalized the city's lease of one-third of the church's portazgo collections for 1,600 maravedís with his family member and counterpart, Gonzalo Gutiérrez de la Calleja, treasurer of the Cathedral of Plasencia. As a de facto member of the cathedral who had directly benefited from Bishop Santa María's favor and patronage, Garci López had an affinity for the Cathedral of Plasencia.

Adding his voice to the acceptance of this agreement was the elder knight and councilman, Gutierre González de Trejo, who was related to both the Santa María and Carvajal families. His presence and his expressed approval of the city-church partnership was evidence of an astonishing transformation of knight-churchmen relations. Less than thirty years earlier, Bishop Pedro Fernández de Soria had personally written to King Enrique II to complain about Gutierre González's recalcitrance and failure to pay diezmos.[7]

The Carvajal family proved that the knights and the cathedral could coexist and thrive together, as the clan's own members had set aside their past conflicts with the church and now secured canonships and other cathedral benefits. Because several local families participated in both the city council and the cathedral chapter, the portazgo contract was more than an institutional agreement; it was also an interfamilial accord. To some extent, the medieval Old Christian identities, "those who pray" and "those who fight," began to fuse into a more complex existence as churchmen and knights worked toward a new collective good for the city, which was dependent on the converso families' integration.

The many family members surrounding Gutierre González likely helped spur and gain his acquiescence to the agreement. After all, the Carvajal family hailed from similar knightly stock but now had integrated with converso churchmen. Garci López's father, grandfather, and brother, Diego García de Bejarano, were knights. These men, especially Diego García, who had his own brush with excommunication by Bishop Arias de Balboa, remembered and understood the Plasencia knights' troubled past with the church. From the perspective of Gutierre González, the new leadership of the Cathedral of Plasencia, led by his extended relations, must have appeared less threatening and potentially long-term partners.

Personal family relationships also likely influenced Gutierre González because two of his sons married daughters of Diego González de Carvajal (fig. 4.1). Luis de Trejo

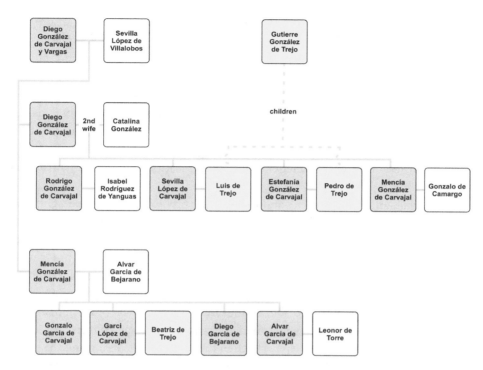

FIGURE 4.1. Carvajal and Trejo family relations.

married Sevilla López de Carvajal, and Pedro de Trejo married Estefanía González de Carvajal.[8] The proximity of these relations could only have helped convince Gutierre González that the portazgo lease was favorable for all parties to the agreement.

The final member of the city council's leaders negotiating the arrangement with the church was Alfonso Fernández de Logroño. Like the Carvajal clan, his family had a close association with the church. Pedro Fernández de Logroño, who was related to Fernández de Logroño, served as a prebendary in the cathedral chapter.[9] Thus the relationship between the three city councilmen and treasurer Gonzalo Gutiérrez de la Calleja likely helped them advance the portazgo agreement. These families, especially the family confederation, were part of a restoration of church and city relations that had not existed since 1385, the last year the two parties had consented to a similar portazgo contract.[10]

Shedding light on this city-church collaboration was a simultaneously negotiated agreement regarding churchmen's illicit transport of wine into the city.[11] Unlike the portazgo arrangement, the wine issue was a simmering and festering conflict. Tensions rose when the city council suspected that unnamed churchmen were abusing their church privileges. These liberties allowed the cathedral's men to bring wine into the city free of locally imposed tariffs, provided the wine was for church or personal use.[12] However, the city's representatives believed that churchmen were transporting wine under the guise of church or personal use but then selling it below the cost of taxed wines. Not only were wine merchants affected by this alleged covert activity, but, more important from the perspective of the city council, the city was cheated out of these revenues. The city's public notary reported the following: "The lords of the cathedral are allowing the transportation of wine by its clergy into the city. This occurs in opposition to our ordinances, as the city council has not consented to this. Further, when wine tax collectors confront the clergy carrying the wine in, the clergy threatens to present them with a letter of excommunication. Now, we remain at this impasse."[13]

Rather than attack the church's abuse of its wine privileges, Garci López, Gutierre González, and Alfonso Fernández emphasized the importance of protecting the rights of the church and promoting harmony in the community. They stated that "the council will always protect the church's right to bring wine into the city," but that it has "always been understood that this privilege must be secured with a written order of a councilman."[14] The matter was discussed on January 2, 1428. The next day the city councilmen came to a decision on how best to address the circumstances. Each of them made the sign of the cross and placed their hands on their hearts. They explained their decision as follows: "Because God came to help us, both in this world of the living and the other world of the spirit, it is our duty to do what God demands. We are charged with the responsibility of doing what is right. So, we order that from this time forward that for those churchmen that have permission to bring wine into the city, they will only pass through the Gate of Talavera" (see fig. 4.2).[15]

For all parties, it was a fair and face-saving measure that promoted community consensus and harmony. It ensured that the city would still collect its wine taxes and that the movement of wine into the city could be easily monitored at one city gate, the Gate of Talavera. For the churchmen, it required no admission of illegal dealings. Lending credence to the belief that the agreement was acceptable to both parties was the presence of two church officials at the reading of the official order. Later that day, in the city's Plaza Mayor, Juan Cadino, the city crier, announced the city council's new rules on wine transportation to and from the city. Noted among the prominent witnesses at the reading of the agreement were cathedral prebendary Martín Fernández de Logroño, a relative of city councilman Alfonso Fernández, and members of the Santa María clan. The Santa María family members present included Canon Juan Fernández de Cabreros and his young son, also named Juan, who was being raised and trained to be a future member of the cathedral chapter. The appearance of Canon Juan Fernández, the son of the cathedral treasurer, Gonzalo Gutiérrez, was an explicit acceptance by Bishop García de Santa María and the family confederation of the terms of the new city council's orders.

Near the end of the day, a second and private component of the city-church negotiations concluded. Retreating to the quiet of the Chapel of Saint Paul in the cathedral,

KEY │ A │ Cathedral of Plasencia   │ Z │ Puerta de Talavera   │ O │ Plaza Mayor

FIGURE 4.2. Map detail from Luis de Toro's sixteenth-century etching of Plasencia (fig. 1.2). Source: Biblioteca de la Universidad de Salamanca (BUS), MS 2.650. Descripción de la Ciudad y Obispado de Plasencia por Luis de Toro, fols. 25–26. Used with permission.

Bishop Santa María convened the church chapter. Gathered were his extended family members—Treasurer Gonzalo Gutiérrez, Canon Juan Fernández, Archdeacon Rodríguez de Maluenda, Archdeacon Gonzalo García, and Garci López. Mayor Alonso Arias attended the meeting and confirmed the city council's commitment to protect the church's wine privileges. Bishop Santa María invoked his authority as well as asserted the chapter's authority, which was required for the resolution of the matter, and ordered the implementation of new church statutes governing churchmen and their wine. The bishop explained:

> All churchmen can freely bring wine into the city. Even taking one or two measures of wine [*azumbres*] to any person that you wish is acceptable. However, if you are to bring more than this amount, you are not to sell it to anyone for any price, whether that is in the public square or on the street corner. Further, I order my Provisor and Vicar General to check routinely with the wine tax collectors to see if any churchman is transporting hidden wine along with livestock, whether that is in the city or at its periphery. If any churchman violates this order or the city ordinance, we will present them with a letter of excommunication.[16]

The church notary recorded no discussion of the matter. Likewise, the cathedral chapter and its nominal leaders, Archdeacon Gonzalo García, Archdeacon Martínez de Soria, and Archdeacon Rodríguez de Maluenda, voiced no dissent to the proposal. Rather, "all of them [in attendance] judged the statute to be right."[17]

With one voice, the family confederation advanced a harmonious and judicious practice of better governance for Plasencia's future. These two events—the city's leasing of the church's portazgo and the collaborative orders to prevent clerical abuses of church privileges—indicated that the Santa María–Carvajal family confederation greatly influenced church and city council affairs in Plasencia and the surrounding region. In the coming years, these houses would confront more aggressive challenges, including cathedral reforms and the consequences of growing anti-Jewish sentiments in the city. However, these changes had limits. The family confederation never allowed reforms to impede its initiatives to expand opportunities for patronage and wealth.

The Dual Benefits of Professionalizing Memorialization of the Deceased

By the 1430s, the family confederation readily understood that a well-managed and professionalized cathedral not only enhanced the church's mission, a further indication of their Christian identity, but also had corollary benefits for its relations. Through the implementation of multiple church reforms and initiatives—affecting staffing, masses, accounting practices, loans, and chapter meetings—the family renovated the Cathedral of Plasencia to create a better balance between the spiritual and economic needs of the church and those of their immediate family members. Here we can see that these conversos were committed to a public Christian life that distanced themselves further from Judaism. In essence, they consistently and methodically evangelized the Christian message of forgiveness and redemption through Christ.

One of their earliest initiatives relying on this dual-benefit approach addressed the need for a dedicated clergy to officiate at funerals as well as daily masses. In this way, the conversos showed a preference for promoting Christian ritual in the public arena. In 1433, Bishop Santa María established six religious benefices for new clergy with revenues earmarked from specific church property leases.[18] These monies funded six new priests and six altar boys who were responsible for celebrating regular masses and anniversary masses for the deceased.[19] This was a resourceful initiative: it not only funded new church positions, but communicated an enticing message to prospective church donors. That is, if an individual bequeathed properties or funds to the church so that memorial masses could be said for his soul, the donor knew that priests and altar boys would be there to perform the services. As a result, donations and endowments readily flowed into the church's coffers.

Memorial masses served as a robust conduit for encouraging parishioners to bequeath property and other financial gifts to the church in their last testaments. Typically, a wealthy knight or his spouse would will between 200 and 300 maravedís to the cathedral for a one-time funeral mass, the equivalent of the annual salary of a cathedral canon.[20] On the other hand, a family could arrange a more elaborate annual memorial service, which might include a procession and masses said at different liturgical hours, by donating real estate or annual payments.[21] For example, in August 1430, Teresa López donated her estate of Cuadrilleros to the church so that priests would sing six masses each year for the soul of her husband, Lope Ortiz de Montoya.[22] In 1459, the Fernández-González clan chose only to obligate themselves to pay 200 maravedís a year for memorial masses for their deceased family members, Alfonso Fernández and Teresa González.[23] In return for these annual payments, the church would celebrate two masses each year for their relatives. Thus personal property donations, as opposed to one-time or annual payments, yielded substantially more care for one's soul. Just as church statutes created a dedicated staff to sing memorial masses for the deceased, the cathedral chapter implemented initiatives to improve day-to-day management of the cathedral.

During the 1430s, the Cathedral of Plasencia also committed itself to performing memorial services for deceased canons, prebendaries, and other local church officials.[24] The names and memories of departed family members would continue to be sung in perpetuity—an overt reminder of their idealized Christian identity.

Other innovative procedures introduced by the Carvajal and Santa María placed a high priority on the professionalization of the cathedral's operations. This facilitated further transformation of the knightly Carvajal clan as it followed the lead of the house of Santa María. For instance, before the family confederation assumed the management of the cathedral in 1424, the governing chapter did not require its clerical administrators to be physically present in the diocese. In 1438, the cathedral chapter promulgated its first mandatory residency requirements (six of every twelve months) for church canons and prebendaries.[25] This reform was particularly timely as absenteeism was a common problem in most church dioceses across Europe.[26] It also was an indication that the Cathedral of Plasencia was beginning to establish stricter requirements and encourage ecclesiastics to perform their required responsibilities. Both were necessary for the cathedral to maximize its sacred as well as economic effectiveness.

Reining in Church Corruption

The family confederation also pursued reforms intended to prevent or resolve financial irregularities and increase churchmen's compensation and benefits. For example, a 1440 statute required the cathedral's canons, prebendaries, chaplains, and other church officials to turn over to the church their rent collections in a timely manner—specifically, no more than eight days after the funds were received.[27] In this manner, the chapter could reduce both the temptation and the likelihood that church officials would improperly use church monies or keep any portion of the proceeds.

Perhaps it was past experience that convinced the Carvajal–Santa María confederation that it was necessary to implement these financial practices. After all, it was because of financial irregularities in the church during the 1410s that the Fernández family fell into disfavor in the cathedral chapter.[28] Their abuse of their cathedral positions prevented them from successfully rehabilitating either their name or their previous influence in the chapter.

The strict payment policy came with an important benefit, as another church rule authorized the cathedral to make interest-free personal loans to the dean, archdeacons, cantor, treasurer, canons, and prebendaries.[29] Specifically, the cathedral could lend these individuals monies for the term of one year and eight days at no cost. However, if the individual failed to pay back the loan on time, he was subject to unspecified fines. Again, the thrust of these two church statutes—the timely payment of collected rents and access to interest-free loans—highlights the chapter's fundamental belief that if churchmen performed their duties with honesty, then all could enjoy the church's resources; church assets and funds were not the personal property of the chapter members. Further, chapter members could not easily embezzle or indefinitely retain the church's assets for personal use. Fundamentally, the family confederation was a reforming entity, even if it did so to enhance its own converso family lineage.

During the mid-1440s, the chapter enacted additional statutes to improve compensation for its members, doubling some churchmen's salaries and creating new high-paying appointments for others. The key beneficiaries of these changes were the canons. This was the first major improvement in their salaries since 1407, when their pay rate was set at 230 maravedís a year.[30] In 1442, the chapter increased a canon's annual compensation to 500 maravedís.[31] In addition, during the 1440s, the salaries of cathedral notaries rose to 300 maravedís per year.[32] The institution, in effect, rallied to secure the material prosperity of these converso clans.

Among the new church positions, which both extended the administrative capabilities of the chapter and offered new opportunities for family members and associates, was that of church attorney, assumed first by Canon Ruy García de Salamanca, a Santa María family member.[33] In his first year of service, because of financial shortfalls in cathedral income, Ruy García received a partial salary of 1,000 maravedís; thereafter, he earned 1,200 maravedís a year. At the same time, the dean and chapter crafted new posts to professionalize the collection of rents from church properties in Plasencia, Trujillo, Béjar, and Medellín.[34] This task, previously overseen by canons and prebendaries, now passed to the church's accountants. For local properties in the city of Plasencia, the church hired two accountants at 200 maravedís each per year. However, to administer the collection of rents in the diocese's other regions, much larger salaries were set aside. Trujillo's and Medellín's individual accountants earned an annual salary of 800 maravedís, whereas Béjar's accountant collected an annual salary of 1,500 maravedís. In this manner, the savvy tax collection and accounting tradition of the Santa María clan was fully harnessed and shared with its extended relatives, the Carvajal family, which had known only the art of war.

The cathedral may have established these new accounting roles in response to a church financial scandal that occurred in 1444. These financial irregularities appear directly related to the confederated family's strict adherence to a family patronage system. Because the Carvajal and the Santa María valued loyalty over competence, they had appointed a number of canons to posts they could not effectively perform. On this matter, the chapter's notary recorded:

> In just one year there has been much dissension and discord and scandal relating to the offices held by some members. . . . It has caused great concern among us. Some persons are not apt to hold these offices responsible for collecting rents for the chapter. Because we wish to avoid these difficulties and scandals in the future, and as we wish to live in peace and harmony as brothers, we now agree and order the accountants to be responsible [for collecting these rents]. . . . We do this to eliminate derision and to conserve our good brotherhood.[35]

Although the family confederation had avoided the graft and corruption issues that plagued the cathedral in the 1410s, it had not fully appreciated the limitations of its closed patronage system. Rather than require Archdeacon Rodrigo de Carvajal and Archdeacon Alfonso García de Santa María to remove their hand-selected canons and thus disrupt the families' patronage network, the chapter elected to fund three new positions to solve the rent-collection problem. As for the canons who had created this problem, the archdeacons neither fired them nor imposed any punitive reduction of their salaries. Instead, they and the rest of the chapter rewarded themselves financially for making these necessary changes. In the same agreement approving the new accountants and their salaries, the churchmen arranged to distribute 2,200 maravedís a year among its membership. From that point forward, this money, which was derived from annual rent collections, would be shared among men with at least three years of official membership in the church council. It appears the chapter attempted to placate everyone with these changes. The ineffective canons kept their titles, the archdeacons received five new positions, and the senior members of the chapter shared in the collection of rental incomes. Clearly, even with some governance problems, the family confederation had mastered the cathedral enterprise since earnings continued to grow.

Rewards of Chapter Membership

The families of the cathedral chapter enjoyed exclusive privileges in the management of the diocese's diverse property, which they could utilize for the direct advancement of the church's mission or for the financial sustenance of administrators. During

Chart 4.1. Comparative Average Lease Rates for Church Officials and Community Members, 1399–1453

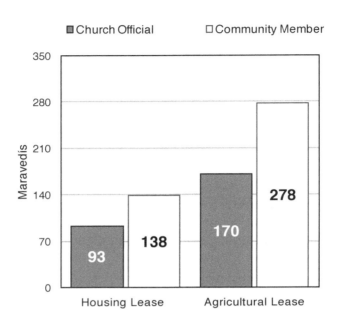

the 1420s and 1430s, the Carvajal and Santa María began an extensive program of utilizing the cathedral's assets for family enrichment. The church's property holdings comprised houses, land formerly granted by the king to knights, arable plots, irrigated land and gardens, pastures, vineyards, water- and land-based mills, and fishing weirs.

Industrious church officials could profit from these property assets by leasing them from the cathedral, often at below fair market value, and then subletting them to other parties at higher rates. This practice was similar to tax farming, except in this arrangement the Cathedral of Plasencia granted church officials license to "property farm" for lower fees but required those officials to assume personal financial risks. For example, although cathedral chapter families could lease a house from the church for an average rate of 93 maravedís a year, a local community member with no ties to the cathedral chapter paid, on average, 138 maravedís, or 45 percent more, for the same lease (chart 4.1).[36]

A more pronounced difference in leases is evident for agriculturally productive lands such as vineyards. While church members rented these properties to their relatives for 170 maravedís a year, community members paid 278 maravedís for their leases (a 64 percent difference).[37] It is evident that the churchmen who negotiated fixed, lifelong rates from the cathedral planned to use these commercial properties as personal investments.

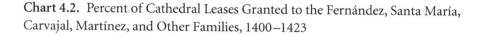

Chart 4.2. Percent of Cathedral Leases Granted to the Fernández, Santa María, Carvajal, Martínez, and Other Families, 1400–1423

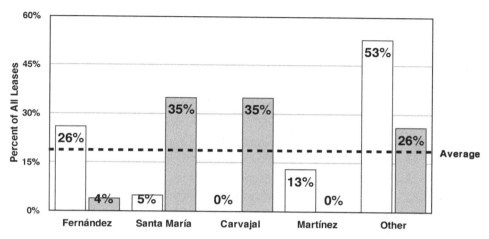

☐ **1400–1423 (Corresponding to the terms of Bishop Arias de Balboa and Bishop Estúñiga)**
☐ **1424–1431 (Corresponding to the term of Bishop Santa María and before reforms)**

The cathedral was concerned about steady income streams and preventing its members from overexposing themselves to cash flow risks. For example, many church contracts specified that the churchman renting the real estate "could benefit from its fruits year in and out" but did so "at their own risk, at whatever danger, and in all cases of fortune were obligated to pay the cathedral chapter the agreed to maravedís."[38] In the case of houses leased by churchmen, some church contracts named the initial lessee, as well as the ultimate tenant of the house (the sublessee).[39] To help offset any uncertainty, the churchmen crafted agreements that delayed their payments to the church for as long as a year or separated them into two installments.[40]

Initially, the Santa María and Carvajal clans found it difficult to take advantage of these leases because the previously dominant family in the chapter, the Fernández, limited most churchmen's access to them. Before the installation of Bishop Gonzalo de Santa María, from 1400 through 1423, the Santa María family was able to rent only 5 percent of all church properties. During the same period, the Carvajal clan was unable to lease a single piece of church property (chart 4.2).

Bishop Vicente Arias de Balboa (r. 1401–14) and his supporters, the Fernández family, never granted the Santa María and Carvajal clans meaningful access to these properties. However, from 1400 to 1423, the Fernández family secured 26 percent of all leased church properties and the Martínez clan about 13 percent. At that time, the cathedral chapter's practice of renting the majority of church properties (55 percent) to ordinary community members suggests that the church greatly limited churchmen's access to discounted property contracts. It is remarkable that although the Santa María clan was a member of the cathedral chapter during this period, the chapter almost totally excluded its members from these lucrative property transactions.

Under Bishop Estúñiga (r. 1414–22), the Santa María family fared slightly better. In 1416, prebendary Gil Gutiérrez de la Calleja (a member of the Santa María family) rented his first houses on Calle de Talavera from the church for 5 maravedís a year, well below the average lease rate of 138 maravedís a year.[41] As the record indicates, Gil Gutiérrez did not live in these houses but sublet them to prebendary Fernán Sánchez.

It was not until the cathedral came under the authority of Bishop Santa María that the Carvajal and Santa María families' fortunes substantially improved. During the first seven years of the bishop's term, 1424 to 1431, the period before the cathedral's local church reform efforts, the two families rapidly gathered church leases.[42] They secured 70 percent of all church property leases for their personal and economic use. Instead of the meager 5 percent of church contracts they held from 1400 to 1423, the Santa María clan now collected 35 percent of property agreements with the chapter. The Carvajal family, which had never secured a church property before this period, also acquired 35 percent of all church leases.

In contrast to the significant gains made by the Carvajal and Santa María houses, the loss of seats by other families on the chapter resulted in a subsequent exclusion from church lease opportunities. The displaced Fernández family lost almost all access to these transactions, dropping from 26 to 5 percent of all property contracts. Because the family had failed to retain its two archdeaconships under the new administration of Bishop Santa María, the chapter effectively denied it the ability to compete for church leases. Unexpectedly, the Martínez family also did not fare well under the new bishop, despite the fact that Dr. Gil Martínez de Soria was the archdeacon of Trujillo and Medellín.

In addition to the losses experienced by the Fernández and Martínez families, local community members with no relatives in the cathedral chapter lost a significant share of church leases. Under Bishop Arias de Balboa and Bishop Estúñiga, these "outsiders" rented 55 percent of all cathedral properties. Under Bishop Santa María, their share dropped to 25 percent. The Santa María and Carvajal intercepted these profits as they pursued an aggressive policy of acquiring church property leases.

From the perspective of the converso family confederation's identity, what is remarkable is the extent to which the Carvajal and Santa María adapted to the economic opportunities available to them. In just seven short years, the family confederation found that its mastery of the Cathedral of Plasencia demanded familial and economic innovation and flexibility. Family members became highly effective converso property farmers, gaining their wealth through complex legal and financial arrangements, as opposed to earning their livings as Jewish tax collectors and knights securing winnings in battle. During the remainder of Bishop Santa María's term, which ended in 1446, the family confederation continued to leverage substantial financial and patronage opportunities from the Cathedral of Plasencia. It devised increasingly creative ways of leasing church properties for personal gain by using atypical partnerships, transferring contracts to their descendants, and exchanging personal assets for church assets. Diversification of economic specialties was a characteristic of this converso confederation. These actions also appear to confirm what blood relations and marriage arrangements had already demonstrated: the Santa María and Carvajal were becoming one house but with subspecialties. While the Santa María side of the clan focused on diversified leasing strategies, the Carvajal family relied on agricultural and pastoral leases. Another intermarried converso family, the Camargo, became tax farmers. For example, in 1426, their relative, Juan Ruiz de Camargo, signed a limited, four-year lease for 18,000 maravedís for a portion of church tax collections; his annual payment was only 4,500 maravedís a year.[43]

Prior to its involvement in the Cathedral of Plasencia, the converso Santa María family was neither a significant landowner nor did it rent and manage sizable agricultural or animal-herding lands in the region. In this manner, its members were similar to other local Jewish individuals who owned only a few commercial properties such as vineyards.[44] In Plasencia, Jewish families typically made their livelihoods in the trades (blacksmiths, shoemakers, military arms makers), as well as through leasing royal tax collections.[45] However, the Santa María made a considerable break from the traditional economic activities of Plasencia's Jews by engaging in personal property management efforts to generate wealth. From 1424 to 1431, the Santa María family secured a diverse collection of eight church leases, including two houses, two vineyards, and four leases for lands of various sizes.[46] Seven of these newly acquired properties were income generators.

For example, Gonzalo Gutiérrez, a Santa María family member, rented a church-owned house with a subterranean storehouse or wine cellar on Calle de Santa María.[47] Since the home was strategically located two blocks south of the Plaza Mayor and two blocks north of the cathedral, finding a sublessee for the property was not difficult. In fact, the house was a favorite residence of church officials. Gonzalo Gutiérrez leased the property from the cathedral for 10 maravedís a year, well below the average amount charged to church officials (about 93 maravedís) and significantly below the average amount charged to local community members (about 138 maravedís) (see chart 4.1). As he acquired the lease near the end of the year, the cathedral only required him to pay half of the agreed on amount, 5 maravedís, by Christmas and the remainder by the Feast of San Juan in June 1426.

The Santa María family diversified its wealth-generating activities into the countryside. It began to participate in the land-management activities customarily engaged in by property-rich Old Christian knights and New Nobles. For example, it secured other income-producing church properties that included three small vineyards and other types of real estate. Before the arrival of the planting season, in January and February 1425, Gil Gutiérrez rented three smaller vineyards (*parrales*) situated among larger vineyards (*vinas*) in the region surrounding Plasencia.[48] Interestingly, Gil Gutiérrez named his son, Alfonso, as his cosigner for one of the transactions. By making him a party to the real estate agreement, Gutiérrez began the process of introducing his son to the business dealings of the cathedral. By paying only 40 maravedís a year for one small vineyard with an arroyo and 50 maravedís a year for two small vineyards, Gil Gutiérrez realized an 80 percent discount on the typical community contractual rate for similar properties. In addition to reduced rent on the vineyards, Gil Gutiérrez reaped profits from the production of grapes and wine.

The benefits of the larger pieces of real estate rented by the Santa María clan are more difficult to ascertain. Because these agreements specified that the lands were subject to diezmos and alcabalas, it is certain that all of them were used for agricultural production, grazing purposes, or other taxable economic activities.[49] Put simply, they were income-producing lands. Most likely, the Santa María family pursued these transactions knowing that cattle, sheep, and pigs already grazed on these pastures and lands—a typical use for large parcels in the vicinity.[50] The largest of these tracts was the Heredad de Fresnodoso, which Juan Rodríguez de Sevilla, the controller for Bishop Santa María, leased for 1,000 maravedís in 1431.[51] More than thirty years earlier, Bishop Arias de Balboa had donated the immense parcel, with its collection of houses, to the church for his memorial masses.[52]

Although Juan Rodríguez, a close Santa María associate, paid a significant sum for this heredad, the Santa María clan secured three other properties (yugadas or caballerías) at reduced rates.[53] For comparison, consider that the cathedral leased two yugadas in the Heredad de San Pedro to Diego de Solís, a man with no connections to the church leadership chapter, for 400 maravedís a year.[54] Therefore, the average rate charged to the community for one yugada or a caballeria, was approximately 200 maravedís a year.

This comparative rate suggests that the Santa María family secured its remaining leases at below fair-market rates. For instance, Juan Fernández de Cabreros (a Santa María family member) leased four yugadas for only 200 maravedís a year. Furthermore, Gil Gutiérrez acquired four caballerias for 280 maravedís a year, and the previously mentioned Juan Rodríguez rented an entire *heredad* (homestead) with houses for 150 maravedís a year.[55] In each of these property transactions, the Santa María family paid considerably less for its leases than Diego de Solís, a man who lacked family connections on the cathedral chapter.

The other component of the family confederation, the Carvajal, drew on their traditional knightly expertise of managing and collecting rents from their feudally obtained agricultural and herding lands. With access to prime real estate, the cathedral clan now vigorously sought church contracts for large parcels of land.[56] In total, from

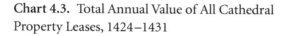

Chart 4.3. Total Annual Value of All Cathedral
Property Leases, 1424–1431

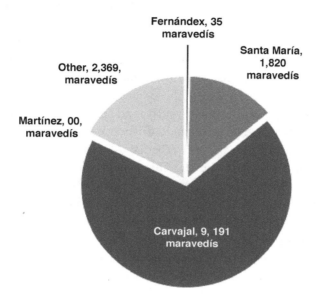

1424 to 1431, the Carvajal clan signed eight property agreements with the church (representing 35 percent of all church leases). The family dedicated most of its attention to the cathedral's large properties, such as pastures, meadows, irrigated lands, gardens, and some vineyards, becoming the Cathedral of Plasencia's largest and most valuable client as well as administrator of church-owned properties. Between 1424 and 1431, the annual value of the Carvajal family's cathedral lease agreements was 9,191 maravedís (chart 4.3).

A significant difference between the confederated families was the liquid wealth each was willing to invest in church transactions. From 1424 to 1431, the Santa María family signed eight leases valued at 1,820 maravedís a year. On the other hand, the Carvajal clan negotiated eight contracts for 9,191 maravedís a year. While both branches the confederation shared equally in the number of church rental agreements they acquired, the Carvajal invested about five times more of their wealth in these efforts than the Santa María. Further, it can be argued that the Carvajal had a higher tolerance for risk than did the Santa María, perhaps because, having been knights, they were more accustomed to facing great perils in return for financial rewards. Besides, the Carvajal had more personal wealth to risk

In addition to pursuing higher financial risks, the Carvajal family sought church property contracts that leveraged its existing expertise in overseeing vineyards like those they owned in the village of Trujillo.[57] For example, in 1424, Archdeacon Gonzalo

García de Carvajal signed the clan's first lease with the chapter for the vineyards of Los Barriales in Plasencia for the amount of 350 maravedís annually.[58] With the vineyard, Gonzalo García began to cultivate a new income source, even though the rent was above the average rate for a vineyard, 278 maravedís a year.

Curiously, even though Gonzalo García held the high-status post of archdeacon, the cathedral chapter took the unusual step of requiring him to secure a cosigner for the vineyard of Los Barriales. Before the 1430s, the church tended to require cosigners for some but not all contracts. Most of those agreements pertained to property trans-actions conducted by first-time renters, such as archpriest Pedro Fernández de Soria, who was the nephew of Prebendary Juan Rodríguez de Fuenteveros, and for individu-als who lived outside of Plasencia, such as Fernán Álvarez de Montealbán (aka Fernán Álvarez de Toledo).[59] Perhaps the church required Gonzalo García to provide a cosigner because he was a relatively new member of the chapter and had limited expe-rience in property farming or because his brother had led the knights' church tax re-bellion of 1403–10. To comply with this requirement, Gonzalo García, indicating the tightly knit nature of the family confederation, relied on Archdeacon Alonso Rodrí-guez de Maluenda, a Santa María family member, to serve as his cosigner. This action was just one of many that would emerge as the confederated family integrated their personal fortunes and business practices.

After this first business arrangement, the Carvajal clan acted aggressively to extend its financial tentacles into the church. Just three years after Bishop Santa María took the reins of the Diocese of Plasencia, Archdeacon Gonzalo García and his brother, Gómez González de Carvajal (a knight), rented eight separate properties in the village of Tru-jillo and its periphery.[60] This single transaction included the church's longest-held pas-tures in Trujillo, known simply as the "pastures and land that is called the church's," the Heredad de Valnegro, the Heredad de Pizarral, the pasture of Toribio Gil, and a pasture and a house and part of a vineyard on the outskirts of Trujillo. For 8,500 maravedís a year, plus the diezmos and alcabala, the brothers acquired the church's most significant holdings in Trujillo. As expected, the favorable terms negotiated by the Carvajal clan and facilitated by the Carvajal–Santa María who controlled the cathedral chapter en-sured that the contract was not payable until one year after its signing. Thereafter, the conditions became even more desirable: the annual payment dropped by 500 mara-vedís. This moment was significant for the extended family and the Cathedral of Pla-sencia because the contract was the largest annual lifelong property agreement recorded in the sixty years detailed in the *Actas capitulares*, tomo 1 (1390–1453). In revolution-ary fashion, the Carvajal–Santa María family confederation shifted its occupational outlook to a future as church leaders and bureaucratic administrators.

These generous church contracts only hinted at what lay below the surface of the family collaborations occurring in the Cathedral of Plasencia. Through successive and increasingly complex property and payment arrangements, Bishop Santa María cemented the families' partnership. This alliance would extend well into the sixteenth century when the Santa María clan's ancestry and blood lineage would be carefully obscured with surnames and, more important, this Jewish ancestry would be laundered into the Old Christian name, Carvajal.

Many of the hopes of the converso family confederation were pinned on a rising leader who demonstrated that the Carvajal clan could properly transition from knightly service and adapt to royal administrative service. Bishop Santa María singled out and promoted Garci López de Carvajal, the brother of Archdeacon Gonzalo García, for this opportunity. The doctor, son of a moderately powerful house in the region, was a fixture in local affairs in Plasencia as well as in the Castilian royal court. King Juan II appointed Garci López one of the twelve regidores of the city council of Plasencia. As it had done for his brother the archdeacon, the family confederation had directed him into a learned career. His family provided him with the opportunity to obtain the most prestigious university credential one could earn in the early fifteenth century—a doctorate, most likely in canon law, which required at minimum seven to eight years of education.[61] Garci López ushered in an entirely new administrative class of Carvajal who would successfully serve in Queen Isabel and King Ferdinand's administration at the end of the fifteenth century. Like his brother Gonzalo García, who was the first ecclesiastical leader in the family, Garci López was the first of many family members to become royal bureaucrats and to follow in the footsteps of their Santa María clansmen.

The doctor was also the precursor of the rise of Castile's professional (*letrado*) class, which did not begin until the reign of Isabel and Ferdinand.[62] The letrados posed a threat to the traditional position of high noble families in the royal administration. During the fourteenth and early fifteenth centuries, powerful New Nobles, some of whom were conversos, and knightly families like the Mendoza populated most of the monarchs' administrative posts, such as admirals of fleets, military governors (*adelantados*), chief notaries (*notarios mayores*), municipal councilmen (*corregidores*), and military governors (*alcaides*).[63] However, as the letrado class developed during the late fifteenth and early sixteenth centuries, the monarchs minimized the bureaucratic participation of high noble families.[64] Thus the Carvajal clan's early fifteenth-century engagement in the royal bureaucracy was an exceptional event, not only because the family used education to outcompete higher-status nobles, but also because the family's administrative initiative represented a precursor of the development of the letrado class.

Although Garci López was well educated, he was an untitled noble and relatively powerless in Castilian affairs. Thus he, like the Santa María clan that had converted from the politically weak position of Spanish Jewry, was of unique utility to the Castilian king. Lacking the political, economic, and war-making power of high noble families like the Mendoza and Estúñiga, the doctor's immediate family was of little consequence and thus would not pose a threat to the king. Like the administratively successful Santa María family, which was beholden to the king for its positions, the Carvajal clan was an ideal familial extension for the king to recruit for administrative posts. It is not surprising, then, that Juan II made Garci López a judge in his royal court around 1423–24,[65] a seat not typically awarded to lower-ranking noble families.[66]

As a close personal associate of Bishop Santa María, Garci López enjoyed a unique connection to the Cathedral of Plasencia. Although not a sitting church administrator, like his brother Archdeacon Gonzalo García, he was a continuous presence in the cathedral. At times he served as a character witness for church property transactions and at times as a party to delicate business negotiations between the city council and cathedral.[67]

The relationship between Garci López and Bishop Santa María is important to our understanding of the converso Carvajal–Santa María family confederation because it is one of the few historical moments when we can see how closely the families were integrated. Bishop Santa María's comments in March 1427 bring life to what is not apparent in the countless but sterile property transactions recorded in the Cathedral of Plasencia. In an act of ecclesiastical homage that celebrated the ties of the family confederation, Bishop Santa María called the chapter together in the cathedral's Chapel of Saint Paul to honor and compensate Garci López for his efforts on behalf of the cathedral.[68] In all of the recorded meetings of the cathedral chapter, this was only the second time the bishop was physically present.[69] In most cases, he conducted business or communicated with the chapter through correspondence.[70] His participation and direction of the event was unusual and significant; the public message was inescapable: the Santa María family was proud and appreciative of its union with the Carvajal clan. Together, they were demonstrating, in a world of exceptional social and cultural change dictated by Jewish-Christian tensions and animosities, that a new, hybridized converso identity could thrive in Castile.

Although the cathedral chapter usually met for the purposes of conducting business affairs, this particular event took on the formal qualities of a religious ceremony. Pedro González, the notary, reported, "The Lord Bishop calls us together, the Lords of the cathedral chapter, with the tolling of the bells and by the verger and the symbols of his office." Alongside the bishop and Garci López were the archdeacons, prebendaries, treasurer, notary, and other officials. With all gathered, Bishop Santa María pronounced, "The chapter and I are indebted to you, Dr. Garci, especially for all of your assistance and counsel on specific affairs at the royal court. As from this point forward we will be in need of your advice on future affairs and the chapter will pay you 300 maravedís every year."[71]

By acknowledging his personal debt to the doctor and granting him this financial benefice, Bishop Santa María invoked feudal-like bonds that tied two men together. However, unlike a traditional act of homage in which one man was beholden to the other, neither the bishop nor Garci López was subordinated. This was a ceremonial act that signaled gratitude. Although not an official functionary of the cathedral,

Garci López thereupon became a de facto member of the cathedral leadership and a respected dignitary and advocate. No other person in the cathedral enjoyed these privileges.

Unlike any other previous church act, the bishop and the cathedral chapter also compensated Garci López with church lands, an indication of how the confederated family would initiate a process of privatizing church resources for its personal use.[72] His property compensation took the form of a convoluted land exchange (*cambio*) pertaining to the Heredad de El Berrocal. Earlier in his life, Garci López had traded two-fifths of his ownership of the heredad to the cathedral for some ancestral homes (*casas solares*) behind his own homes on Calle de Trujillo. Since that trade, the church had reportedly earned a meager 15 maravedís annually from these lands—a disappointing rate of return given that houses in Plasencia on average fetched a minimum of 138 maravedís annually. Ancestral houses, the prestigious historic homes previously owned by noble families, garnered as much as 400 maravedís a year.[73]

Unwilling to part with the ancestral homes he now owned but wanting to reconstitute the entire heredad, Garci López agreed to lease back from the chapter his two-fifths of El Berrocal. For this lease, the doctor would pay 600 maravedís a year—an indication that perhaps the land generated much more income than the 15 maravedís the church claimed. It would be highly unusual for Garci López to lease the property for such a substantial sum when it only supposedly generated a minimal amount in annual rents. After all, the Carvajal family had demonstrated impressive business acumen throughout this period and expertly maneuvered the church to act in their favor. This payment was unique because the cathedral rarely sold lands, as evidenced by the Santa María clan's loss of Corral del Medio in 1421.[74]

All questions about the rationale for the exchange evaporated when the notary recorded the bishop's final orders on the transaction. Under the terms of the final agreement, the doctor would receive his annual salary of 300 maravedís, keep the ancestral houses, and assume a lifelong lease of the church's two-fifths portion of El Berrocal for a single payment of 315 maravedís. These financial rewards to Garci López de Carvajal are further evidence of the unprecedented familial partnership between the Carvajal and Santa María families.

Now stewarding the Cathedral of Plasencia as a family monopoly, between 1433 and 1434, its treasurer, Gonzalo Gutiérrez de la Calleja, implemented an unusual financing mechanism to lease two large parcels from the church.[75] In 1433, when the Heredad de Visñuela and the Heredad de Malpartida became available for lease, he jumped at the opportunity because of their desirable "pastures and river access."[76] The properties likely generated lucrative profits from animal grazing because Gonzalo Gutiérrez took the unprecedented step of entering into a limited two-year partnership with an outsider to acquire them. On June 6, 1433, he and Diego Sánchez de Riotortillo, a knight, leased the heredades for 600 maravedís annually.

In fact, this partnership is the only one of its kind for either a Carvajal or a Santa María family member recorded in the *Actas capitulares* for the years 1390 to 1454. Because the first payment for the two properties was due on the Feast of San Miguel in September 1433—just three months after the contract was signed—which amounted to 600 maravedís, approximately what Gonzalo Gutiérrez earned annually as treasurer, the churchman probably required an outside partner to secure the property in the short term.

Apparently, Gonzalo did not intend to keep his partner for the long term. In November 1434, a full seven months before the expiration of the partnership's lease, he returned to the cathedral chapter and renewed the contract as the sole renter. Further, the dean and his church associates converted the property agreement into a lifelong one, reduced the rate by 17 percent (100 maravedís), and delayed Gonzalo's payment for ten months. His successful conversion of the property agreement demonstrated that cathedral membership had its privileges for its dominant converso family confederation.

Securing church contracts for oneself was not the only goal of these churchmen. At other times, the chapter members devised mechanisms to convert their existing nontransferable cathedral contracts into new lease agreements for their relatives and each other. In 1433, for example, Gonzalo Gutiérrez transferred his 60-maravedís annual lease of houses and a corral on "the street they call the ugly one," which was next to the Church of the Savior (Iglesia de San Salvador), to his son, Canon Juan Fernández de Cabreros.[77] It appears that with this lease transfer, this arm of the Santa María family would settle into this section of Plasencia for the long term as it later chose to endow a family chapel in the adjacent church.[78] After Gonzalo Gutiérrez's death, in 1448, the cathedral chapter transferred his property contracts for several houses with orchards, cultivation tools, and storage vessels to his relative, cantor Ruy García de Salamanca.[79] The cantor was allowed to continue paying the rate Gonzalo Gutiérrez had previously negotiated, which was 350 maravedís and two pairs of chickens. Likewise, Carvajal family members also shared and transferred some of their leases to the younger members of the Santa María clan. In November 1434, the cathedral chapter transferred Archdeacon Gonzalo García de Carvajal's annual lease for irrigated land (*huerta*) with olive trees to Canon Alfonso García de Santa María.[80]

Another innovative tool the families employed for personal gain were property exchanges in which they traded less valuable personal lands for more beneficial church real estate. For instance, with only confederation members in the room, on April 26, 1438, Gonzalo Gutiérrez de la Calleja convened the church council to implement the bishop's instructions to transfer the entire Heredad de los Carrascales in exchange for one yugada of land in Garci López de Carvajal's portion of the Heredad de Rio Bermejo in Plasencia.[81] López not only kept most of his property, but he also obtained another good-sized property.[82] As if the agreement needed sweetening, the vicar general also added the lease of several additional houses on Calle de Trujillo for 15 maravedís a year. Approving and witnessing the transaction were Gonzalo Gutiérrez de la Calleja, Archdeacon Alfonso García de Santa María, and Ruy García de Salamanca. Moreover, and as in all cases, Garci López brought his servants (*criados*) and family members, Miguel de Trujillo and Juan de Carvajal, to witness and learn how the cathedral operated.[83] This moment provided Juan de Carvajal, who had recently become a canon in the Cathedral of Zamora, a valuable introduction to the bishopric that he would later inherit. In 1446, the king and pope would name him bishop of Plasencia.[84]

Three years after this property transaction, the same men and the recently appointed Archdeacon Rodrigo de Carvajal (brother of Juan) returned to the Chapel of Saint Paul to provide the doctor with another special opportunity. On January 2, 1441, again acting on the guidance of the bishop, the cathedral exchanged "some of its houses on the street that runs from the cathedral to Calle de Trujillo, with its corrals, and the statue in the street," for one of Garci López's yugadas in the Heredad de Rio Bermejo.[85] To guarantee that there was no confusion regarding this contract and the previous transaction, the notary reported that "this [property] is separate from the other yugada that Dr. Garci López had given to the cathedral chapter in exchange for the Heredad de los Carrascales."[86] Subsequently, Garci López effectively disposed of his less valuable peripheral lands and created an interlocking collection of homes close to the cathedral. In these incremental ways, the Santa María and Carvajal families consistently channeled the cathedral's assets into their own coffers.

After capturing the Cathedral of Plasencia's leadership chapter in the 1420s, the family confederation aggressively sought church positions for its families and associates (table 4.1). This indicates that the confederation intended to place its collective, multi-generational identity within the framework of the Roman Catholic Church. During the 1430s and 1440s, it accelerated this practice by monopolizing almost all of the cathedral positions. What emerged from its collective efforts was a specific patronage-sharing arrangement. While the Santa María family took the majority of the chapter roles for themselves (cantor, prebendary, provisor and vicar general, and treasurer), the Carvajal clan occupied the archdeaconship of Plasencia and Béjar and controlled the positions (accountants, canons, and prebendaries) assigned to it.[87]

This indicates that the Carvajal had now fully adopted the Santa María clan's administrative training and livelihood. In a strange twist of fate, Old Christians began emulating former Jews. As the Santa María and Carvajal families ascended the patronage ladder, the cathedral awarded increasingly central roles to them at the expense of others. Upon the death of the respected Gil Martínez de Soria, archdeacon of Trujillo and Medellín, the church council decided not to give his title to another Martínez but instead bestowed it on Alfonso García de Santa María.[88] Gil Martínez had guided the council through an extraordinary embezzlement controversy in the 1410s and had served as Bishop Santa María's personal representative in the chapter, but this service was not sufficient reason to make his ecclesiastical position into a hereditary one for his

Table 4.1. The Carvajal–Santa María Family in the Cathedral of Plasencia, 1420s–1440s (All color-coded cells are confederation members.)

Decade	Bishop	Archdeacon of Plasencia and Béjar	Archdeacon of Trujillo and Medellín	Archdeacon of Coria	Cantor	Treasurer	Vicar General (appointed by bishop)
1420s	Gonzalo García de Santa María	Gonzalo García de Carvajal	Other Family	Alonso Rodríguez de Maluenda	Other Family	Gonzalo Gutiérrez de la Calleja	Other Family
1430s	Gonzalo García de Santa María	Gonzalo García de Carvajal	Alfonso García de Santa María	Alonso Rodríguez de Maluenda	Gonzalo Gutiérrez de la Calleja	Gonzalo Gutiérrez de la Calleja	Juan Fernández de Cabreros
						Gonzalo García de Carvajal	Gonzalo Gutiérrez de la Calleja
							Alonso Rodríguez de Maluenda
1440s	Gonzalo García de Santa María	Gonzalo García de Carvajal	Alfonso García de Santa María	Alonso Rodríguez de Maluenda	Gonzalo Gutiérrez de la Calleja	Gonzalo Gutiérrez de la Calleja	Juan Fernández de Cabreros
	Juan de Carvajal	Rodrigo de Carvajal			Ruy García de Salamanca	Juan Fernández de Cabreros	
						Alfonso García de Santa María	

family. By February 1436, the Martínez family did gain a new canonship, although it was lesser compensation, for the deceased archdeacon's relative, Juan Martínez.[89] Fourteen months later, Archdeacon Alfonso García entrusted him with the collection of rents and diezmos for Trujillo and Medellín.[90] In the future, the Martínez family would marry into the Carvajal and Santa María clans, thus expanding the converso family confederation.

As stated previously, another church role monopolized by the family confederation was that of vicar general, the bishop's official representative in the diocese during his frequent absences. After 1436, this position became a critical stepping stone for training younger members of the Santa María family. For example, immediately after the death of Gil Martínez, the bishop appointed his relative, Canon Juan Fernández de Cabreros, as his vicar general. Juan Fernández was the teenage son of the churchman Gonzalo Gutiérrez de la Calleja, and the grandson of the churchman Gil Gutiérrez de la Calleja. The teenager held the position for only a portion of 1436 as it appears he spent the next several years earning his doctorate in canon law. In his place, his father served as vicar general from the end of 1436 to 1445.[91] In 1444, after earning his degree, Juan Fernández returned to Plasencia, and, by 1446, reassumed the title of vicar general at the end of Bishop Santa María's term.[92]

Because the Santa María family occupied many of the senior posts in the cathedral of Plasencia, the younger Carvajal men relied on their relatives' willingness to extend patronage opportunities to them. This seems further evidence that the two houses had integrated their families in almost every way. Most important, this extended to training each other's adolescents. For instance, in 1437, Bishop Santa María created a new deputy vicar's position for the up-and-coming bachiller Alfonso de Carvajal.[93] When Archdeacon Alonso Rodríguez de Maluenda needed to fill a canonship in the village of Coria, he selected a younger Carvajal clansman, Juan Ruiz de Camargo, for the post.[94]

This family partnership did not end in 1446, the year Gonzalo García de Santa María left his position in Plasencia and was named bishop of Sigüenza. Rather, when Juan de Carvajal was appointed as Gonzalo García's successor in Plasencia, the family confederation continued on this path of integrated action and sponsorship. As one generation of Santa María and Carvajal family members aged and retired, their sons, nephews, and cousins dutifully replaced them.

REFLECTIONS OF IDENTITY:
SECRECY, HYBRIDITY, AND TOLERANCE

With its consolidated control over the Cathedral of Plasencia, remarkable changes began to transpire that reflected the deliberate self-consciousness of the family confederation. Essentially, this new converso identity began to blend Christian and Jewish traditions while maintaining the traditional importance and centrality of family. Their actions ranged from subtle to overt, and they constituted elements of what it meant to worship and live as conversos in the mid-fifteenth century.

From early 1431 to 1446, the two families thoroughly transformed the cathedral into a bulwark to protect their family as well as church interests. Further, they propagated a converso ideology that insisted on secrecy, hybridity, and tolerance toward Jews. Unlike their predecessors, these conversos were intent on institutionalizing new ways of governing. Likewise, they continued to conduct the cathedral's operations as a family business, being certain to grant themselves personally beneficial arrangements while also advancing their next generation of leaders inside the cathedral.

Already, across the kingdom mistrust of conversos was growing. Most notably, Castile's ruling elite and Old Christian families were suspicious of powerful conversos such as Constable Álvaro de Luna, who during the 1430s and 1440s was the favorite of King Juan II.[95] By 1432, de Luna had already successfully isolated competing power centers like Aragonese families who were part of the Trastámaran dynasty. This ensured that Castilians would control their future. It was accomplished by rewarding converso New Nobles like the Estúñiga and the Ponce de León with titles and political and economic privileges.[96] This general suspicion of conversos permeated Plasencia as well.

By the 1430s in Plasencia, it is true that the Carvajal–Santa María confederation was publicly operating as the dominant family in the cathedral and the municipal council. But what was not known to the vast majority of the community of Christians, Jews, and Muslims was the extent to which the confederated family began to operate in secrecy and institute new religious and administrative practices that harkened back to Jewish ways of living and worshipping. Was this a new converso religion? Yes, but the evidence of their practices is fragmentary, and we can only interpret, at the macrolevel, their intention to preserve and integrate Jewish customs into Christian practice. The Carvajal–Santa María confederation had something to hide: the creation of a new identity that borrowed traditions from Judaism.

Jewish Memory and Action: Friday Gatherings and the Saturday Sabbath

Under the direction of the key leadership of the cathedral chapter—namely, Archdeacons Gonzalo García de Carvajal, Alfonso García de Santa María, and Alonso Rodríguez de Maluenda—the family confederation initiated a new institutionalized practice that required its churchmen to meet at the cathedral every Friday to conduct church business, celebrate Mass, and be together as a group.[97] The cathedral statute, which presently only exists as a transcribed document and therefore may be incomplete, follows.

Statute relating to Friday celebrations of the cathedral chapter, recorded Friday, 12 of October of 1431 [Julian calendar]

The cathedral chapter and titular leaders of the Church of Plasencia are gathered together in the Chapel of Saint Paul . . . and they are ordered that from this time forward on all Fridays that all of the titular leaders who are in the city are required to come to the cathedral chapter. Without excuse, and only in the case of necessity and because they cannot come of their own free volition, they will come to the cathedral chapter and there will be a penalty if they do not come regardless of the excuse.

With this selection of Friday as the appointed time to meet and with strict penalties for nonattendance, the converso family confederation unveiled its unusual acceptance of a communally important day for Judaism. Friday gatherings were not a prior practice of the cathedral's leadership; this was an innovation. Thus the collective converso Carvajal and Santa María clans met in preparation for the coming Saturday, just as their Jewish ancestors had done. By celebrating a mass at the gathering, these conversos used Christian cleansing rituals (washing of hands) and fresh vestments that would have been necessary to receive Christian communion and were compatible with prior Jewish practices,[98] for they were used by Iberian Jews during the fifteenth century, as well as by the Judaizing conversos in Ciudad Real and Lisbon who were investigated by the Inquisition in the sixteenth century.[99] By celebrating on Friday, the converso churchmen also overlaid the Jewish religious practice of Friday afternoon prayers.[100] This was the nature of converso religious hybridity: familiar Jewish customs and practices that dovetailed into Christian ones. There is corollary evidence to suggest their selection of Fridays was not accidental or lacking in religious purpose.

What is quite interesting about the Friday statute is how it interrelates to other Carvajal–Santa María family confederation efforts that centered the collective family's spiritual attention on Saturdays, the Jewish Sabbath. First, consider that this statute was not included in the Cathedral of Plasencia's official *Actas capitulares* but as loose folios inserted in the separately bound Calendar or Book of Anniversary Masses for the Holy Church of Plasencia.[101] Therefore, the Friday practices were intentionally and physically connected to Saturday-based memorial masses in the Book.

The Book of Masses, a fifteenth-century leather-bound vellum text that was considered lost until the mid-2000s, is a record of all the memorial masses that were sung in the name of deceased churchmen and parishioners. The Book of Masses was created in 1433 in response to Bishop Santa María's and the cathedral chapter's new policy that memorial masses were to take place on Saturdays. This enabled the conversos to limit their participation in work and concentrate their day's activities on worship, which is another element of Jewish custom.[102]

Assembling this evidence together, we can appreciate that during 1430s the family confederation initiated a converso approach to worship in the Cathedral of Plasencia. It ordered all of its family churchmen to meet for Friday evening services and then called on all community members to celebrate mass on Saturday to remember their ancestors. Like a hand in a glove, Jewish Friday preparations and Saturday Sabbath worship fit into new Christian practices.

Through the Book of Masses, as well as other records left behind by the Placentino churchmen, we also learn that, like the recently deceased family patriarch, Pablo de Santa María (aka Solomon ha-Levi), had done, the Placentino clan had instituted Saturday as their day of worship devoted to the Virgin Mary.[103] In fact, in 1435, Pablo's sons, Bishops Garcia de Santa María and Alonso de Cartagena, established a religious endowment at the Cathedral of Burgos on behalf of their father and in the name of the Virgin Mary.[104] As conversos, theirs was a devotion to Mary and not Christ. As conversos, they were modeling a middle way of worship and life—recentering their spiritual existence from the traditional Christian Sunday to Friday and Saturday.

A second consideration pertaining to the October 12, 1431, statute is the special religious significance of this specific Friday, which occurred on Heshvan 13, 5198, of the Jewish calendar, and its connection to Jewish hopes for a Messiah. This day was approximately two weeks after the celebration of Sukkot (the Feast of Booths), which emphasizes the repentance of sins, the last day of spiritual judgment (Hoshana Rabbah), and prayers for the arrival of the Messiah.[105] As late as the twelfth century in Spain, the Jewish poet Zerahya wrote in his *Seder ha-Ma'or* on the practice and expectations of religious holidays like Sukkot with verse that "ends with the hope that the Messiah will appear soon."[106] Therefore, this well-known rabbinic family, the ha-Levi or Santa María, was bridging the divide from Judaism to Christianity through the conduit of the Christian Messiah.

For the Carvajal clan, who had become conversos through their intermarriage with the Santa María, Sukkot served as a corollary path to experience Judaism as demonstrated in the Gospel of John, chapter 7, about when Christ taught in the Temple of Jerusalem and proclaimed himself the Messiah. These passages read:

> Feast of Booths. 1. After this, Jesus moved about within Galilee. He had decided not to travel in Judea because some of the Jews were looking for a chance to kill him. 2. However as the Jewish feast of the Booths drew near, 3. his brother had this to say: "You ought to leave here and go to Judea so that your disciples there may see the works you are performing. . . ." First Episode. 14. The feast was half over by the time Jesus went into the temple area and began to teach. 15. The Jews were filled with amazement and said, "How did this man get this education when he had no teacher?" 16. This was Jesus' answer: "My doctrine is not my own; it comes from him who sent me."[107]

Therefore, that Friday, October 12, 1431, was an important creative moment for the converso family confederation, which committed itself to perpetual Friday services.

These conversos shared a hope for redemption based on two religious rationales—one Jewish and one Christian—that transformed Fridays and Saturdays into hybridized days of family significance.

Secrecy in the Cathedral

Just a few short years later, the Placentino conversos enacted a second cathedral statute that hinted at their desire to insulate themselves from outsiders and turn the institution into a protective cocoon. On Monday, August 12, 1437, the cathedral chapter promulgated its first rule of secrecy; prior to this date, the cathedral chapter had never instituted a rule that limited access to information. Only a select group of churchmen gathered for a private meeting in the smaller Chapel of Santa Catalina, as opposed to the traditional convening location, the Chapel of Saint Paul.

Those in the room collectively agreed that "not all of the chapter needed to be included in all matters."[108] With the exception of the sacristan, Sancho Ortiz de Estúñiga, the only canons or prebendaries present at the meeting were Santa María and Carvajal family members. These two families' converso clans deliberately excluded any of the remaining Old Christian churchmen. As Sancho Ortiz had been a canon in the cathedral chapter since 1420 and had participated in the transition of the cathedral's leadership to the family confederation, he presumably remained a trusted confidant.[109] Sancho was also a converso. In addition, he appeared to possess limited resources and thus posed little threat to the cathedral's leadership. Unlike his affluent distant relatives, the future New Noble counts of Plasencia and Béjar, Sancho had the financial means to lease only one home from the church.[110]

Gathered together, the Carvajal and Santa María clans and Sancho Ortiz pledged their commitment to the secrecy agreement by "raising their right hands" and then making the sign of the cross, indicating their Christian fealty and commitment to Catholicism. In this sense, we understand that these conversos had left the practice of Judaism and were not crypto-Jews but true believers in the Christian message. They swore "never to reveal their secret discussions to any person . . . and to take these things from this world to their deaths and with their souls."[111] Further, violation of this statute would result in "penalties imposed by the chapter that could not be reduced."[112] Among the penalties was a two-month period of shunning during which no one would receive or speak with the churchman. Therefore, the secrecy statute seems to have been enacted to protect and shield the family confederation's activities—economic, political, and, possibly, cultural—from other members of the Cathedral of Plasencia.

One unresolved question is why the secrecy statute was recorded in a well-known official record of the cathedral, the *Actas capitulares?* By 1437, the family confederation was in full control of the cathedral leadership and likely acted with impunity. The statute was recorded in book 2 of the *Actas*, covering the 1430s and 1440s, which was

protected by one of the attending churchmen and disappeared from the archival collection. The account of the secrecy agreement is known only through an innocuously
titled document, "1445. Statutes relating to the naming of tax and rent collection com-
missioners."[113] With book 2 missing, one wonders what the secrecy statute intended to
hide besides financial and political decisions.

With closer command over the proceedings of the governing chapter of the cathedral, the united clan also moved to limit the participation of other families in critical
leadership roles. From 1436 to 1442, Archdeacon Gonzalo García de Carvajal, Canon
Gonzalo Gutiérrez de la Calleja, and Archdeacon Alfonso García de Santa María passed
the treasurer's job back and forth while holding their other official roles.[114] Likewise,
Bishop Santa María rotated the vicar general's title between his immediate blood relations, Canon Gonzalo Gutiérrez, Archdeacon Alfonso García, and Juan Fernández de
Cabreros.

More important for the Carvajal clan, the cathedral chapter took the unprecedented step of converting the archdeaconship of Plasencia and Béjar into an unofficial
hereditary office. This action seemed to counter some of the reform-minded aspects
of the cathedral's agents, but it also appeared to be a long-term strategy and investment in the publicly promoted Old Christian lineage of the Carvajal. This action
would prove vital to the family confederation as societal antagonisms targeted conversos for exclusion from church roles after the propagation of Castilian blood purity
statutes during the 1450s.

As Gonzalo García de Carvajal advanced in age, he elected to step down as archdeacon, and in the winter of 1440 his younger cousin, Rodrigo de Carvajal, assumed his
title and jurisdiction.[115] For the next seven generations, the family held the archdeaconship.[116] Thus the allied families so heavily weighted the cathedral chapter in their
favor that from the 1430s on the chapter's goals closely mirrored their goals. In essence,
the clans and the local church were one and the same as they shaped the institution in
their hybridized converso image. Their identity reflected a focus on protecting Jewish
and Christian ideas, beliefs, and communities. This position was on full display when
the family confederation remade Plasencia, especially its Jewish quarter, the ecclesiastical section near the cathedral, and the Plaza Mayor into multireligious residential zones.

Indications of Jewish Sympathies: A Revival of Convivencia

How the Carvajal–Santa María family confederation utilized their tight bonds clearly
exposes their converso values, beliefs, and sympathies for the Jewish people. Unlike the
New Noble Estúñiga family, which would march aggressively into Plasencia during the
1440s and assert its secular authority, this blended clan valued their Jewish neighbors
economically, politically, and culturally. The residential patterns they promoted in
Plasencia indicate that these conversos had a preference for religious diversity and, it
would appear, the neighborly company of Jews and Muslims.

Throughout the early and mid-1400s, the collective family demonstrated an uncommon respect and appreciation for positive forms of convivencia—the cooperative and competitive tension bred by the commingling of Jewish, Muslim, and Christian peoples on the Iberian Peninsula. According to the historian Thomas Glick, "*Convivencia* . . . carries connotations of mutual interpenetration and creative influence, even as it also embraces the phenomena of mutual friction, rivalry, and suspicion."[117]

As we remember, Jewish-Christian convivencia began to unravel in the Kingdom of Castile and León during the 1390s when Christians unleashed devastating violence upon Jewish communities and forced large numbers of religious minorities to convert to Christianity. After the attacks on Jewish communities across Christian Spain, it is estimated that 100,000 Jews were killed, 100,000 Jews converted to Christianity (by force and choice), and another 100,000 fled to Islamic lands.[118] The scale of Christians' violence against Jews—murder, intimidation, and expulsion—cannot be underestimated because they speak to the intense hatred of Jews during the fourteenth and fifteenth centuries. Although these events cast a dark shadow on the acceptance of Jewish communities in Christian Spain, they created an opening for some elite Jews in Castile, such as the ha-Levi/Santa María, who converted to Christianity to access new identities. Further, the Carvajal–Santa María family confederation's rejection of the prevailing anti-Jewish mentality indicated they intended to reinstate better relations with religious minorities.

The majority of the violence against Jews concluded at the end of the fourteenth century after Enrique III (r. 1390–1406) repeatedly demanded that his subjects cease their harassment of both Jews and new converts to Christianity.[119] In a July 30, 1392, royal cédula sent from the city of Segovia, he mandated, "No person shall obligate Jews to become Christians by force, nor make listen to a sermon against their will, nor mistreat them, because is counter to Christian charity."[120]

The Castilian monarchy's concern for Jewish communities harkened back to the traditional political and social norm of convivencia; the call to protect Jews was also an acknowledgment that Jews were a vital component of the economy. At the kingdom level, the crown relied on Jewish communities to pay a religious poll tax to finance royal activities.[121] In this way, each local Jewish community contributed to the royal coffers. For example, in the early 1400s, the Jewish aljama of Plasencia paid the king 10,250 maravedís annually in poll taxes.[122] Thus the Placentino Jewish community was a valuable asset that necessitated royal protection on economic grounds.

Plasencia's sizeable Jewish community was critical also to the city's economic vitality. Although an exact population census for the city and Diocese of Plasencia is not available for the period between the 1420s and 1440s, tax records from the year 1400 indicate only 119 persons—40 Christians, 50 Jews, and 29 Muslims—resided in the city.[123] Thus, within the city's walls, Jews were a fundamental component of the population base. However, the diocese's outlying villages and countryside had a population of 881, dwarfing the city's population by a factor of 1 to 8. By the end of the fifteenth century, the city's population grew almost ninefold to approximately 1,000 persons, while the diocese's countryside population increased fivefold to 4,890 persons.[124] Unfortunately, no estimates of the total number of Jewish residents in Plasencia or the surrounding area are available for the late fifteenth century.

In total, these statistics suggest that the city's population from the 1420s to 1440s might have numbered roughly 300 to 500 persons, assuming a linear population growth rate. While the Jewish community probably did not grow as fast as the Christian community due to the harsh realities of anti-Jewish sentiment in the kingdom, Jews remained a substantial part of the total population of the city, as evidenced by property ownership and leasing records.

From the 1420s through the 1440s, the city's Jewish residents became a strategic economic and cultural asset promoted by the Carvajal–Santa María family confederation—one that the Cathedral of Plasencia and noble landowning families relied on as a steady source of income and political fealty. While the Castilian king and seigniorial lords enjoyed the unique financial rewards of a religious poll tax imposed on Jewish (and Muslim) subjects, local communities benefited from the leasing of homes and property to Jewish families. Even though Plasencia's Muslim population was much smaller than the Jewish community, Muslim residents also rented homes from the cathedral and local Christian families. While some Jewish and Muslim families, such as the Cohens and Serranos, owned homes and property in Plasencia, many others leased their residences from the cathedral and noblemen.[125] Although there are no records that reveal why Jews and Muslims chose to rent properties from the church and nobility, it seems likely that both religious groups did so to reduce the likelihood of becoming targets of Christian harassment and violence. Because Jewish families of substantial economic means owned property in Plasencia, as did Muslims, we can appreciate that Jews and Muslims exercised some degree of choice in their living arrangements.

During Bishop Santa María's term (1424–46), a period when the Carvajal–Santa María confederation dominated the cathedral chapter, the church departed from prior local church policies by increasing access to housing leases for Jewish and Muslim families. This not only exposes the converso family's tolerance for religious minorities but good economic thinking. In a sense, elite and well-off Jewish clans not only gentrified Plasencia but also financed the expansion of the Cathedral of Plasencia's patronage and employment opportunities for the family confederation. It was a hand-in-glove relationship, although arguably it is hard to determine whose was the hand directing the glove.

While the prior cathedral leadership only leased 4 percent of church houses to religious minorities, the Carvajal–Santa María family confederation actively directed 22 percent of all leases to Jews and Muslims.[126] This amounted to an almost sixfold increase in access for Jewish and Muslim tenants (table 4.2). Thus this converso family confederation displayed a growing preference of providing housing leases to Jews and

Table 4.2. Cathedral Housing Leases, 1401–1446

Years	Cathedral Leadership	House Leases to Christians		House Leases to Jews/Muslims	
		Number and Percent of Total	*Average Lease Rate*	*Number and Percent of Total*	*Average Lease Rate*
1401–1423	Bishop Arias de Balboa, Bishop Estúñiga, and the Fernández family	27 houses (96%)	55 maravedís	1 house (4%)	150 maravedís
1424–1446	Carvajal–Santa María family confederation	25 houses (78%)	109 maravedís	7 houses (22%)	191 maravedís
Percent Change 1401–1423 vs. 1424–1446	7% decrease in Christian leases	98% increase in Christian leases	600% increase in minority leases	27% increase in minority leases	7% decrease in Christian leases

Muslims as compared to their church predecessors, Old Christian bishop Arias de Balboa and converso bishop Gonzalo de Estúñiga.

Perhaps, the Carvajal–Santa María openness to renting properties to religious minorities was related to their own unique relationship. That is, in spite of the intense societal and religious animosity directed at conversos and Jews after the 1390s, the Carvajal family of Old Christian pedigree readily collaborated with and married into the Santa María clan of New Christians. In the deeply contradictory Castilian mindset, conversos could simultaneously be noble and elite (like the New Nobles) and considered "less" Christian; hence the designation, New Christian.

The Carvajal family did not appear to espouse or subscribe to Castilians' negative perceptions of Jews and conversos; after all, they had become conversos by mixing their bloodline with the Santa María. In sum, the Carvajal–Santa María confederation's decision to lease property to Jews and Muslims in Plasencia at a greater rate than their contemporaries indicates an inclination to support peaceful coexistence of the three faiths and to accept an uncertain cultural and political future for themselves— one financed and facilitated, as will be seen, by Jewish friendships and partnerships.

The decision to increase Jewish and Muslim tenancy appears to have been a strategic one. When the Santa María and Carvajal families gained control of the cathedral chapter in the mid-1420s, they inherited a collection of housing lease agreements with Christian, Jewish, and Muslim families. In the period before the family confederation's administration, from 1401 to 1423, Christian tenants on average paid 55 maravedís each year for a cathedral-owned home, whereas Jewish and Muslim tenants paid on average 150 maravedís per year. Thus, during this era, religious minorities paid almost three times more than Christians did for housing agreements. Put succinctly, it was more profitable for Christian landlords to lease to Jews and Muslims.

Under the families' management of the chapter, all new rental agreements increased in price. However, Christians experienced a 98 percent increase, while Jewish and Muslim residents experienced only a 27 percent increase. The latter lower increase was offset by the fact that from 1424 to 1446 Jewish and Muslim tenants on average paid 191 maravedís for a housing contract, whereas Christians paid 109 maravedís. This demonstrates that the family confederation was not uncomfortable certain discriminatory practices. There were limits to coexistence, especially if the rental market could be segmented for greater profit for the cathedral.

Typically, the cathedral's Jewish and Muslim tenants were tradesmen, as opposed to religious leaders like Plasencia's rabbis, who tended to live in Jewish-owned homes.[127] The cathedral's clients included a Muslim family of tailors and merchants (the Chicala), as well as Jewish shoemakers (the Aruso), clothing shearers (the Caces/González), blacksmiths (the Arrañon), and military arms makers (the Escapa). These trades—especially arms making—were critical to bolstering the military power of the evolving Carvajal family of knights and churchmen (table 4.3; figs. 4.3a–d).

The cathedral signed seven church leases with Jews and Muslims during the 1430s. Church administrators were also surprisingly open-minded about leasing houses to families of mixed faiths—those with Jewish and converso members. For instance, the Caces and González family were a mixed religious household in which Pedro González, a converso, lived with his son, Yuda Caçes, who had retained his Jewish faith, in a house on the very public Plaza Mayor.[128]

In effect, the converso-led Cathedral of Plasencia fully sanctioned blended Jewish-Christian lives in the most prominent public space—the city's main square. As all actions of the cathedral were undertaken with the full authority of the Roman Catholic Church, the cathedral's willingness to facilitate the Jewish-converso Caces-González residence was tantamount to an official blessing for religious blending.

In 1442, another particularly interesting residential lease was the one granted to Çag Escapa, which showed economic, social, and interfaith interconnections.[129] Çag Escapa, a Jew, was most likely a recent arrival to the city because the Cathedral of Plasencia's chapter required him to present a cosigner for his housing lease.[130] By the 1430s, the practice of requiring a cosigner was limited to cases involving new members of the local community or younger men procuring their first church lease.[131] In this 1442 agreement, Çag Escapa produced Rabbi Abraham de Loya of Plasencia, a well-known member of the community, as his cosigner. This contract also demonstrates that the cathedral did not require Jewish or Muslim parties to present Christian cosigners but viewed well-known members of other religious communities as trustworthy and legally recognized. Equally fascinating is Çag's trade—that of an arms maker—which meant that he provided weaponry to the region's large collection of knights, such as

Table 4.3. Cathedral Housing Leases to Jews and Muslims, 1430s–1440s

Year	Lessee	Religion	Annual Lease	Location (See figs. 4.3a–4.3d.)
1434	Abraen Chicala and Amat ("the tailor" and "the merchant")	Muslim	320 maravedís and 2 pairs of chickens	Plaza Mayor/White box with green border labeled "M." Adjacent to red "DGC" box.
1436	Yusefe Champus Arrañon; his son, Abraham Arrañon ("the blacksmith"); and Yefada Daza	Jewish	110 maravedís and 2 pairs of chickens	Calle de Zapatería/Red boxes labeled "J." Adjacent to red "DGC" box.
1438	Simuel Aruso and Abraham ("the shoemakers")	Jewish	400 maravedís and 3 pairs of chickens	Plaza Mayor/White box with blue border labeled "J" and adjacent to white box with purple border labeled "C."
1441	Abraham Arrañon ("the blacksmith")	Jewish	110 maravedís and 2 pairs of chickens	Calle de Zapatería/White box with blue border labeled "J" and directly across from red boxes labeled "J."
1441	Yusefe Champus Arrañon (lease transfer from his brother, Abraham)	Jewish	110 maravedís and 2 pairs of chickens	Calle de Zapatería/White box with blue border labeled "J" and closest to brown box labeled "Alamaraz."
1442	Çag Escapa ("the chainmail maker")	Jewish	120 maravedís and 2 pair of chickens	Calle de Zapatería/White box with blue border labeled "J" and closest to Cathedral University.
1444	Yuda Caçes, son of Pedro González ("the clothing shearer")	Jewish/ converso	170 maravedís and 2 pairs of chickens	Plaza Mayor/White box with blue border labeled "J" and directly across from red "DGC" box.

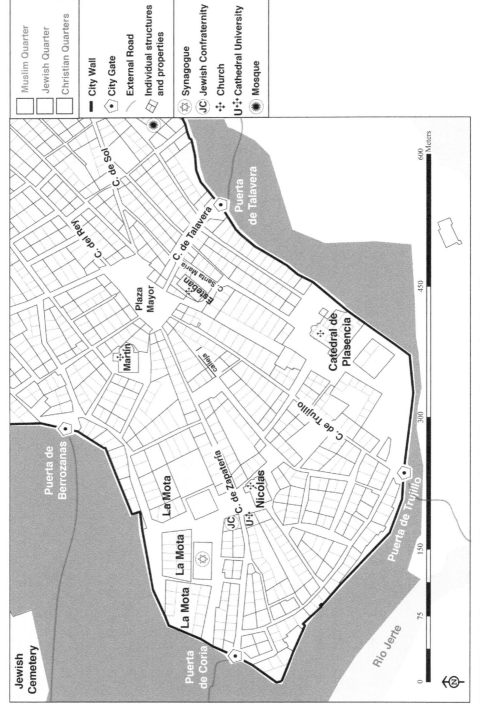

FIGURE 4.3A. Overview map (from fig. 1.3) of Jewish, Muslim, and Christian residence and interaction patterns in Plasencia, 1420s–1440s.

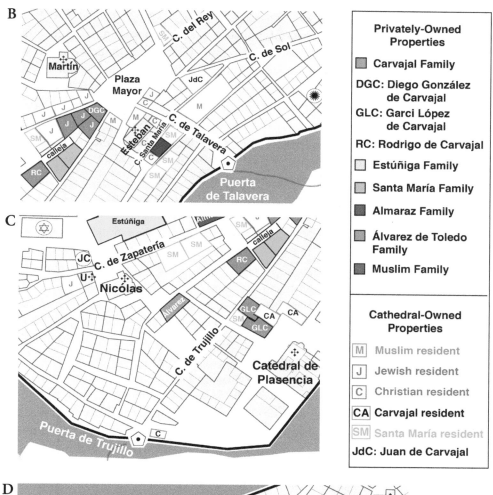

FIGURE 4.3B. Plaza Mayor and Muslim quarter; 4.3C. Cathedral area and Calle de Trujillo; 4.3D. La Mota and Calle de Zapatería.

the Carvajal, Álvarez de Toledo, Almaraz, Camargo, and Monroy. This indicates that Jewish residents provided both financial contributions to the community, in the form of rents, and tools of war used by Castilians still pursuing the reconquest against Islamic Granada. More important, this transaction showed that the church, and its patron families, perceived the Escapa family as a key link in efforts to defend their local interests when the Carvajal knights would find themselves engaged in conflict with the Estúñiga clan.

Church homes leased to the Jewish Escapa and other religious minorities also reveal the significant residential intermixing of the three faiths in Plasencia (see fig. 4.3). Although the Escapa family's homes were located on Calle de Rua/Zapatería in the Jewish quarter, they were also adjacent to venues that were important to the Carvajal, Santa María, and Estúñiga clans. The Church of Saint Nicholas was of tremendous importance for the Carvajal because it held the remains of the family's progenitors and is where subsequent generations interred their family members.[132] This church, located in the Jewish quarter, was also especially vital to Plasencia's resolution of interfaith disputes.[133] Specifically, according to the Fuero de Plasencia (city charter), in "extraordinary circumstances," during this era a Jewish judge and a Christian judge stood on the church's steps and adjudicated cases that involved conflicts between individuals of different faiths.[134] In this respect, even though this was the core of the Jewish quarter, it was a prominent interfaith venue for both personal and communal reasons.

At this location was the heart of the Jewish community, the synagogue, as well as the houses of the Jewish confraternity (cofradía de los judíos) and the remaining portion of La Mota neighborhood.[135] For the Carvajal–Santa María family confederation, this city quarter was equally critical as it housed the leadership chapter for the cathedral's University of Plasencia (Universidad de Plasencia).[136] This location of the cathedral university within 50 meters of the Synagogue of Plasencia is intriguing as it seems that this center of Christian learning would have been located at the distant cathedral structure. It implies notions of shared, perhaps collective, Jewish-Christian intellectual space. The historically and spatially accurate digital reproduction of the Plaza de San Nicolás, prepared by the Revealing Cooperation and Conflict Project (RCCP), displays the intimacy of this Jewish-Christian environment (fig. 4.4).[137]

More noteworthy is that this confined area in the Jewish quarter was populated by King Enrique II's late fourteenth-century innovation—the New Noble class, including the Carvajal, Almaraz, Álvarez de Toledo, and Estúñiga. The intensity of their daily interactions and shared life should not be underrated, especially along major thoroughfares like Calle de Zapatería. During the late 1420s, the Estúñiga family, the future counts of Béjar and Plasencia, positioned their first homes and palace (Palace of Mirabel) in La Mota.[138] Similarly, the Álvarez de Toledo family, señores de Oropesa, and the Almaraz clan owned homes in this area.[139] The Álvarez de Toledos' housing complex, an elaborate structure with a "tower," was either purchased by or transferred to the Carvajal family by

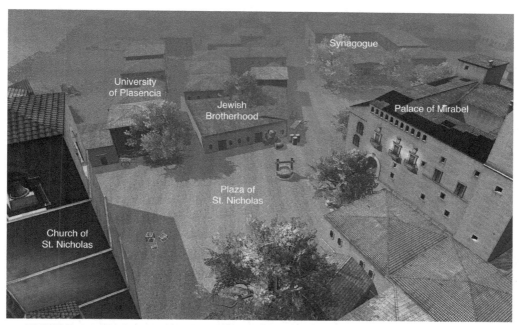

FIGURE 4.4. Digital reproduction of the plaza of Saint Nicholas, mid-fifteenth century. Source: Revealing Cooperation and Conflict Project, Virtual Plasencia, v1.6.

the middle of the fifteenth century.[140] The 1469 marriage of Councilman Diego de Carvajal to Elvira de Toledo likely facilitated this property transfer.[141] Thus, from the 1420s through the 1440s in this portion of the Jewish quarter, a mixture of Old Christians, conversos, and Jews worshipped, labored, and resided together.[142]

Most of the homes owned and leased by the cathedral were located in the Jewish quarter, adjacent to homes owned and occupied by the Carvajal and Santa María. This suggests that no rigid social norms enforced the physical separation of Jews and Christians in Plasencia. The Carvajal, Santa María, and Jewish families all lived in a collection of closely clustered homes near the Plaza Mayor, between Calle de Zapatería and Calle de Trujillo. Members of the extended Carvajal–Santa María family confederation residing in these homes included Diego González de Carvajal (a knight), cathedral treasurer Gutiérrez de la Calleja and his sons (a Santa María family), and Archdeacon Rodrigo de Carvajal.[143] A Muslim family—the Barro—lived in the immediate vicinity.[144] (See fig. 4.3 for locations of these homes.)

In addition to the residential relationship promoted by the Carvajal–Santa María-dominated cathedral, the Carvajal family leased its own private property holdings to religious minorities. Like his first cousins in the cathedral chapter, Diego González earned valuable income from Jewish families that rented houses from him.[145] Just behind his personal residence on the Plaza Mayor, he leased three collections of homes to the Jewish individuals Yaco Zafia, Eza Harruso, and Yuce Pando (see fig. 4.3, "J"). For Jewish residents, a likely benefit of leasing homes from the cathedral or a Christian landlord was protection from harassment by Christians. Thus, a lease contract purchased more than shelter; it also shielded Jewish residents from Christian violence. For example, with Jewish families living in Christian-owned dwellings, they were less susceptible to the type of mob violence that characterized the 1390s. The leases also indicate that Diego González made deliberate decisions to lease homes, with which he shared a common wall, to Jewish residents. Not only had the Carvajal embraced the Santa María as family, but they also seemed to prefer the immediate and personal companionship of Jewish individuals like Yaco, Eza, and Yuce. In this period of religious and ethnic discrimination, González's decision to rent homes to Jewish residents was akin to religious residential desegregation during the Spanish Middle Ages.

Deeper in the Jewish quarter along Calle de Zapatería but not more than a two-minute walk from the prior collection of homes, several Santa María clansmen resided in another three homes. This residential zone included a large housing complex rented by Diego Jiménez de Burgos, nephew of Bishop Santa María, as well as the homes of Ruy García de Salamanca, another Santa María relative.[146]

The bonds of family confederation were so intimate that at times Santa María and Carvajal families lived together in collective clan houses and family compound-like structures. The remaining family resided along Calle de Trujillo and close to the cathedral, which was at the periphery of the Jewish quarter. Included in this area were homes owned by Garci López and other houses leased by Archdeacon Alfonso García de Santa María, all of which were across the street from the cathedral and on Calle de Iglesia.[147] The bonds between the Carvajal and Santa María families were so secure that, during the 1430s, the elderly archdeacon Gonzalo García de Carvajal resided in a home with his family member, Alfonso García de Santa María, and Alfonso's wife and children.[148]

In the Christian quarters, Amat Moro Bexarano, a Muslim, lived on Calle de Santa María, alongside Canon Fernán Martínez and the Christian Luis Alonso de Toledo (see fig. 4.3, green box on Calle de Santa María between "C" and "SM"). This was not an isolated case, as on the Plaza Mayor the Muslim tailor and merchant Abraen Chicala lived next to Juan Fernández, a Christian who managed agricultural lands, and his spouse, Maria González. Juan Fernández's lease rate was a sizable 200 maravedís a year, or about two-thirds the cost of Abraen Chicala's payment.

Relationships were so close between Muslims and Christians that Abraen Chicala benefited from unusual access to special church properties. During the mid-1400s, the Muslim family of tailors, silk merchants, and purveyors of wheat and rye lived adjacent to the church and even held a license to sell its wares on the grounds of the old cemetery of the Church of Saint Steven.[149]

Like most of the city behind the medieval walls, the Muslim quarter (morería) was a residential and commercial zone for all faiths. In fact, the close proximity of Christians and Muslims was normative in Plasencia, as in the case of Abdalla Bejarano who lived next to many churchmen (see fig. 4.3, "M"). One of these churchmen was Cardinal Juan de Carvajal, who was often absent from the city when he was preaching Christian crusades against the true Muslim enemies of Spain, the Ottoman Turks (see fig. 4.3, "JdC").[150] This case of Abdalla living so close to the cardinal is intriguing because it suggests that Spanish conversos like the Carvajal–Santa María family confederation distinguished Spanish Muslims from Turkish Muslims.

What was problematic for Placentinos in the cathedral was the nonpayment of a valuable lease. In 1456, cathedral leaders found themselves lamenting their prior decision to lease an enormous property within the city walls to Abdalla Bejarano, a Muslim carpenter. On a fall day, October 9, eight church leaders, including Alonso de Salazar, dean; Alfonso Garcia de Santa María, treasurer; Dr. Juan Fernández de Betanzos; and Pedro de Carvajal, canon, met in the cathedral hoping to resolve the large annual loss of 300 maravedís (and three pairs of chickens) because Abdalla Bejarano was not paying his rent.[151] The property in question, a collection of several homes and a storehouse (*bodega*), stables, and a corral, was vast and surrounded a large portion of the eastern section of the city. It was near the Plaza Mayor and radiated out between Calle de Talavera and Calle de Sol and toward the city walls. Interestingly, it was also in front of Cardinal Juan de Carvajal's houses near Calle de Sol and next to Juan Fernández's homes on Calle de Talavera. Although Abdalla Bejarano had made two monetary payments during the year, they were insufficient and did not include the chickens.[152] With little recourse, the church leaders elected to strip Abdalla Bejarano of the valuable stables and corral and pursue a legal judgment against him and his heirs.

This situation, in spite of the negative consequences for everyone involved, demonstrates that the church was ready to grant leases on sizable properties to Muslims, provided they could pay their rents. It also indicates that the Ordinances of Valladolid of 1412 were not strictly enforced. Perhaps the presence of two church leaders, the cardinal and the doctor, living in the Muslim quarter was also perceived by Muslims as a Christian incursion into the Muslim neighborhood. The evidence is too limited to understand the entire situation in the Muslim quarter.

Plasencia was not an isolated community that the Carvajal–Santa María family confederation could mold freely into their converso image of fair treatment all faiths and peoples. As these conversos were actualizing their identity as reformed-minded administrators and promoters of a new blood lineage, the city and the region experienced unsettling times prompted by intense and violent political and economic competition among regional New Noble and Old Christian seigniorial lords. Chapter 5 explores how the family confederation reacted and responded to these challenges.

5

TURMOIL AND STRUGGLE

There was no rest for the Carvajal–Santa María confederation at the opening of the 1430s as they lurched from the challenge of creating a cohesive converso family to responding to the competition with other nobles. Just as the confederation was beginning to benefit from its dominance in the cathedral and stewardship of Plasencia's multireligious community, violent political disturbances erupted locally and kingdomwide. A regional conflict broke out between the residents of Plasencia and neighboring seigniorial lords; the New Noble Estúñiga became the secular overlords of Plasencia; and conversos battled each other and Old Christians for political survival. In effect, noble families returned to their normative competition with each other, except now many of the elite who were leading Castile were New Nobles and therefore an entirely new entity—many of them conversos.

Although all conversos were of mixed religious and blood pedigree, there were significant differences in how they conceptualized their identities. Some, such as the Carvajal and the Santa María, appeared intent on defending mixed bloodlines in Castilian society, while others, such as the Estúñiga, became ruthless competitors for secular power and predators of the surviving Spanish Jewry. They were identities at war.

The social and religious disorder of the late 1430s through 1460s was just beginning to unfold as the converso ascendency in the Kingdom of Castile and León abruptly collapsed. Although it is difficult to ascertain exactly when and why conversos' social and religious position in society deteriorated, it was likely the result of a series of mid-fifteenth-century events that began to cast them as outsiders in Castilian society. Those who considered themselves Old Christians increasingly viewed conversos as fundamentally different and referred to them disparagingly as New Christians. Old Christians targeted their wrath particularly at elite conversos, especially when King Juan II relied on this group to implement unpopular measures, such as his efforts to raise taxes to fund the war with Islamic Granada. In 1448, when the king turned to his powerful converso adviser and royal favorite, Álvaro de Luna, to oversee the collection of one million maravedís from the city of Toledo for the Andalusian war, the city's leaders and inhabitants revolted.[1] Not only did Pedro Sarmiento, the mayor of Toledo, lead the charge against de Luna's hand-selected converso tax collector, Alonso Cota, but the mayor and an "angry mob" burned down Cota's house.[2] Furthermore, from the mid- to late 1400s, new forms of societal and institutionalized discrimination focused on conversos. In the aftermath of the 1449 riots in Toledo, the local city council implemented new limpieza de sangre ordinances to exclude conversos from prominent and profitable offices.[3] These discriminatory statutes spread across Iberia, to municipalities, church institutions, and eventually the royal bureaucracy. Complicating the environment for elite conversos were the internal battle lines drawn between Constable Álvaro de Luna, who counted on the Carvajal–Santa María family confederation for support during his darkest days, and the New Noble Estúñiga clan, which was determined to see de Luna fall and grab Plasencia as their prize.

Rising to the defense of his family and other conversos during this era was Bishop Alonso de Cartagena, the brother of Gonzalo García de Santa María (former bishop of Plasencia). Alfonso was a powerful voice for the fair treatment of conversos, arguing in a letter (known as *Defensorium unitatis Christiane*, In Defense of Christian Unity) to Juan II that not only were all Jews and Christians part of a common humanity, but Jews who converted to Christianity were fully sanctified by the act of holy baptism.[4] Fernán Díaz de Toledo, a fellow converso and royal secretary, extended the line of these arguments in his 1449 letter to his friend, Lope de Barrientos, bishop of Cuenca.[5] He stated that "sacred law" dictated that conversos and Old Christians were "brothers."[6] He further argued that Castilians held misguided positions on blood purity because Old Christian and Jewish families had heavily intermarried in the preceding decades, as demonstrated within the ranks of the New Nobility. This point was vociferously articulated one hundred years later by Cardinal Francisco Mendoza y Bobadilla in *El tizón de la nobleza*, the memorial published in 1560 that indicted the nobility for its hypocrisy regarding its Jewish ancestries.[7]

Contextualizing these historical events is a complicated task, but the Sephardic historian Jane Gerber expertly explains that fifteenth-century conversos lived in a perpetual state of cultural marginality. She identified three groups of Spanish Jews that existed after 1391: "those who openly continued to practice Judaism, those who had become conversos and remained so, and those who privately renounced their forced baptisms secretly maintaining their adherence to Judaism."[8] Gerber accurately describes how, by the mid-1500s, many Old Christian Castilians viewed conversos as Jews.

By the middle of the fifteenth century, there simply was no easy answer to the
question of who was a Jew or a Christian. But for most of the population, the
conviction began to spread that Jewish ancestry or "race," not professed religious belief, defined who was a Jew [after the purity of blood statutes]. . . . The
conversos were now isolated as a new class, neither Jewish nor Christian, that
was inassimilable and could not be redeemed.[9]

Gerber's position, one that I subscribe to, exposes the troubled identities of conversos. Conversos, and for that matter moriscos, could only be described as hybrid
identities that drew from a mixture of religious, lineage, and racial identifiers. For the
Carvajal–Santa María family confederation, the Álvarez de Toledo (señores de Oropesa), and even the Estúñiga (conde de Plasencia y Béjar), their identities no longer
could be easily delineated or categorized because of the Jewish question. As a result, increasingly these conversos forcefully demonstrated their Christian identities through
overt actions and hidden activities. By the 1440s, the Carvajal–Santa María family confederation found itself moving into a defensive stance as it battled the Estúñiga clan,
which was asserting its seigniorial authority over Plasencia and harassing the cathedral of Plasencia's leadership's chapter. The family confederation tightened its bonds
not only by placing more trust and confidence in the public Old Christian persona of
the Carvajal but also by aligning its interests with Placentino Jews. As the lines of the
conflict between Pedro de Estúñiga and the family confederation became definitive,
the identities of these conversos became equally exaggerated and disparate.

JEWS, SOCIAL DISRUPTIONS, AND VIOLENCE IN PLASENCIA, 1430s

At the beginning of the 1430s, a fundamental transition within Castilian Extremadura
began to unfold—namely, a substantial increase in political unrest, violence, and economic competition. This competition reflected the continuity of medieval conflicts
between secular and religious leaders but also was colored by the role of converso elites
in society. At the heart of the dispute were the leading converso clans of the region: the
Carvajal, Santa María, and Álvarez de Toledo. What the events revealed was that conversos did not act as a unified political and cultural force in the Castilian world; rather,
they were just as likely to battle each other as to battle Old Christians.

Limitations of Authority

Although by the 1430s the Carvajal–Santa María family confederation exercised significant control over the Cathedral of Plasencia and the city council, in the previous

decade the authority of the two families was severely limited in the broader region. To a great extent, this was because of the competitive environment and interfamilial discord that characterized the leadership of the cathedral chapter, which was at the time populated by the Fernández, Estúñiga, Santa María, Carvajal, and Martínez clans. During the late 1420s, just as the Santa María and Carvajal families were gathering their collective power, the New Noble Álvarez de Toledo and the Niño (señor de Valverde) clans coordinated an attack on the traditionally recognized jurisdiction of the city council over its neighboring villages. What ensued was a fierce regional conflict over natural resources (grazing, fishing, and agricultural rights) and secular leadership in the region.

During this era, it appears that the city council and the Cathedral of Plasencia served as the de facto local authorities for resolving secular conflicts in the northeastern section of the Diocese of Plasencia. However, during the 1420s these instruments of power were insufficient to compel local lords like the Álvarez de Toledo and the Niño to comply with the will of either governing institution. As evidence for this argument, in 1431 King Juan II dispatched Judge Miguel Sánchez de Sepúlveda to the city to investigate disputes over jurisdiction and property, as well as review multiple claims of improper imprisonments and the deaths of two Placentino Jews.[10] Tragically, Christian commoners and Placentino Jews became unwilling pawns in this regional quarrel over communal access and rights to lands near the village of Jarandilla de la Vera (referred to as Jarandilla), located east of Plasencia.

In December 1431, Judge Sánchez assembled the city council of Plasencia, along with representatives from neighboring villages, to oversee a judicial investigation into a conflict between the city of Plasencia and several local lords over property rights near and around Jarandilla. Among those participating from the city council were Diego González de Carvajal (the family confederation's leading knight), Alfonso Fernández de Cabreros (a Santa María clansman) and his son by the same name, and their family ally, Alfonso Fernández de Logroño.[11] The four men shared bloodlines and enjoyed a collaborative relationship, which they employed previously to direct many of the council's actions. For instance, just three years earlier, the four councilmen and their relatives in the Cathedral of Plasencia had overseen the city council and cathedral's initiative to share portazgo (royal transit tax collections).[12]

Also gathered for the hearings, which were held in the Church of Saint Vincent, were residents from the neighboring communities of Losar, Arroyo Molinos, Jaraíz, Cuacos, Aldeanueva de la Vera, Jerete, Navaconcejo, Ojalvo, Esperilla, Gargantilla, Segura, and Tornavacas.[13] Notably absent from the meeting were García Álvarez de Toledo and Pedro Niño, both of whose interests ran counter to those from Plasencia and most other local communities. At the heart of the conflict, according to Judge Sánchez, was whether or not García Álvarez had ordered the residents of Jarandilla to take as prisoner those who fished, tended cattle, or farmed in the disputed lands.[14] However, the Fuero de Plasencia, the royal charter establishing the rights and privileges of Plasencia, granted the lands in question to the city.[15] Although King Enrique II had donated the villages of Jarandilla and Tornavacas to García Álvarez's father, Fernán Álvarez de Toledo, the territory surrounding these villages was not within the jurisdiction of the Álvarez de Toledo family.[16] To a lesser extent, the judge was also interested in Pedro Niño's efforts to appropriate lands near the village of Valverde.

Miguel Sánchez's royal charge bore a hint of the deterioration of societal affairs in the region surrounding Plasencia, which the local lords and Plasencia's leaders could not resolve. It also revealed the fractures in the converso elite and New Nobles, who were pursuing their own families' goals.

Indeed, in the years prior to the investigation, there was a significant increase in violence against persons and property in the kingdom as a result of convoluted property and jurisdictional conflicts involving the monarch, noble families, and churches.[17] Engaged in these disputes was the converso Carvajal clan. As knights, the house of Carvajal would be instrumental in holding seigniorial lords and other competitors in check. The Carvajal family's capacity for violence was a powerful deterrent that kept these competing New Noble families from politically and physically overrunning the city and the Cathedral of Plasencia. It is telling, for example, that three of the ascending members of the family received papal absolutions for their participation in violent clashes in the village of Trujillo and the surrounding region. In 1427, the Holy See granted Rodrigo de Carvajal, who would became the archdeacon of Plasencia and Béjar in the 1440s, and his cousin, Álvaro, "absolution of censure for . . . their armed intervention" in a conflict that left many persons in Trujillo injured or dead.[18] Two years later, in March 1429, the pope granted Juan de Carvajal, the brother of Rodrigo and the future bishop of Plasencia, a broader papal dispensation for his participation in a "quarrel that resulted in bloodshed" and headless bodies.[19] The Carvajal family had pursued a new identity as churchmen alongside the Santa María clan, but they clearly had not abandoned their warrior instincts. They did not fight to evict Islamic civilization from Spain, as did some of their kinsmen in the Christian military orders, but battled their fellow Christians and converso brethren.

Juan de Carvajal's crimes were so problematic to his advancement in the church that Pope Martín V absolved him of "all irregularities and infamy" that would prevent him from acquiring a religious benefice. Five months after receiving his papal dispensation, Juan was able to become canon in the Cathedral of Palencia, located to the northeast of Plasencia.[20] Thus it appears that the ecclesiastical relief that Juan and his brothers sought from the Roman Catholic Church was not linked to an isolated affair but rather to multiple regional disagreements, which ultimately required the intervention of an outside royal judge. It is no wonder the Santa María had sought out the Carvajal as their familial partners: while the earliest Santa María members reigned over institutions and bureaucracies, their Carvajal kin reigned with weapons. Administratively and militaristically, they were a lethal recombination of Jewish and Christian bloodlines.

In a 1431 letter that accompanied Judge Sánchez on his journey to Plasencia, King Juan II endowed him with broad and comprehensive authority to review the discord in the Diocese of Plasencia: "I have placed my trust in Miguel Sánchez de Sepúlveda, Bachiller of Law[,] . . . to conduct an investigation regarding any items— all of them—including . . . pleas[,] . . . allegations[,] . . . and thefts. And for half a year Miguel Sánchez can suspend the offices and powers of my local mayors and judges [to pursue this investigation]."[21] The king's decision to grant the judge such authority reveals that the confederated families lacked sufficient political sway to re- solve the regional conflicts and enforce peace in the diocese. It further suggests that the king believed he needed to subjugate all local secular powers in the region to his supreme authority. Only in this manner could the judge resolve the conflicts. This circumstance was almost certainly due to the nature of Castile's overlapping secular and ecclesiastical jurisdictions. Because the Álvarez de Toledo and the Niño were the king's vassals, only the monarch could hold them accountable in secular affairs. These señores had explicitly demonstrated that they believed the city council of Plasencia lacked any authority to impose its decisions and mandates on territories outside its city limits. In particular, García Álvarez de Toledo appeared willing to test the limits of the judge's authority outside of the villages of Jarandilla and Tornava- cas. A critical focus of the judge's investigation and findings would be on the area to the east of the city.

As all the claimants framed the conflict as a secular matter, the Carvajal–Santa María family confederation was unable to harness the authority of the Cathedral of Plasencia to resolve the issue in its favor. The line of questioning pursued by the judge focused on five issues pertaining to actions of several of the Jarandilla residents:

1. Did they occupy and take possession of the disputed lands belonging to the city council of Plasencia?
2. Did they pay the city council for these lands?
3. Had they taken anyone prisoner?
4. Had they erected a hangman's gallows in the disputed lands?
5. Did they do any of these things with the help of García Álvarez de Toledo?[22]

Judge Sánchez's questions quickly revealed critical and troubling facts about Jaran- dillans' activities as well as the obstinacy of García Álvarez and Jarandilla's village council. Not only did García Álvarez fail to present himself at the hearing, but only a few commoners from Jarandilla could be compelled to attend. It became clear that the señor had claimed the disputed properties as his own seigniorial lands. Further, he had ordered the residents of Jarandilla, who were living under his seigniorial au- thority, to enforce a fishing and herding ban in nearby areas, thereby disturbing the traditional "peace and coexistence" of the local communities.[23] Thus, if García Ál-

FIGURE 5.1. García Álvarez de Toledo's castle at Oropesa. Photo by author.

varez and the residents of Jarandilla could effectively expand the generally accepted boundaries of the village, both parties could claim new income-producing resources as their own.

The men from Jarandilla explained to Judge Sánchez that the conflict accelerated when their local village council "claimed all of the surrounding land around Jarandilla as a part of their jurisdiction and erected a hanging gallows."[24] As the questioning proceeded, the men also noted that some of their unnamed neighbors had taken three local pastoralists from the village of Losar, as well as Rabbi Abraham de Loya of Plasencia, hostage and had transported them to García Álvarez's village of Oropesa, where he held them in his formidable castle (fig. 5.1). The señor de Oropesa demonstrated that an elite converso could not only combine a warrior's stance with that of bureaucratic prowess but also could aggressively pursue his claims to these lands at the expense of other conversos such as the Carvajal–Santa María. Through his proxies in Jarandilla, who willingly used physical force, intimidation, detentions and fines, and the threat of hanging against anyone who trespassed into these disputed areas, García Álvarez was building his own group of united families.

The testimony from the men of Jarandilla also exposed the limits of what Judge Sánchez could accomplish. Ultimately he was unable to force the men to name any member of the group that had taken hostages. Moreover, the absence of García Álvarez or any his personal representatives from the proceedings highlights how little power the king had to compel the señor de Oropesa to appear and address the parties' claims in this specific investigation. Royal power was weak in this region.

Although García Álvarez did not attend the hearing, Judge Sánchez's questions revealed that he believed the city council of Plasencia was the proper local authority and owner of the disputed lands. His question, "Did the residents occupy and take possession of the disputed lands belonging to the city council of Plasencia?," makes clear his acceptance of the Placentinos' claims that the land belonged to them.[25]

Judge Sánchez's direct questioning of the residents of the village of Losar established the customarily acknowledged eastern boundary of the city, which was in direct contrast to actions of the Álvarez de Toledo and the Niño families. By securing this testimony, which occurred under the approving eyes of the Carvajal–Santa María–dominated city council of Plasencia and in a venue friendly to these clans, the Church of Saint Vincent), Judge Sánchez established the farthest eastern boundary of Plasencia (between Barco de Ávila and Candeleda). The findings were damning, as they demonstrated that Pedro Niño had encroached on Plasencia-owned lands close to the village of Losar and north toward the village of Tornavacas and the Jerete River.

Additional testimony highlighted the accepted southeastern boundaries of the jurisdiction of Plasencia. Specifically, witnesses indicated that an unknown party had tampered with and removed boundary stones marking Plasencia's southeastern limits near Campo de Arañuelo—a village under the lordship of García Álvarez.[26] These witnesses definitively noted that although the señor de Oropesa rightfully claimed the village of Jarandilla as his own secular jurisdiction, all of the territories surrounding this village fell within the City of Plasencia's authority. Thus, with the exception of Jarandilla, all of García Álvarez's seigniorial lands fell south of the Tietar River.

In addition to reinforcing the physical boundaries of Plasencia, the inquiry revealed the city's relationship with other local communities. It confirmed that the villages and inhabitants of Arroyo Molinos, Torremanga, Jaraíz, Collado, Cuacos, Aldeanueva de la Vera, Losar, Jerte, and Navaconcejo perceived themselves to be within the secular jurisdiction of the city council of Plasencia. As such, these residents likely expected Plasencia to protect them from malfeasance and the predatory behavior of García Álvarez and Pedro Niño. Interestingly, although the residents of Tornavacas were a part of García Álvarez's seigniorial jurisdiction, they too claimed to be outside his authority.

The judicial process exposed the willingness of local communities to use the royal legal process to pursue redress for a range of wrongs. For example, the Sánchez family of sheepherders added that García Álvarez incarcerated these residents, as well as other "poor men," until their families paid "great quantities of maravedís."[27] The conflict extended to lower nobles, like Martín Fernández de Toledo, when Garcia Álvarez's men took his herdsmen with their "hands bound" to Jarandilla and confiscated his cattle.[28] By presenting their claims to Judge Sánchez, it appears that these and other parties hoped to recoup lost assets and the unfair imposition of ransom for hostages.

Those least able to protect and defend themselves during this regional conflict were the Jewish residents of Plasencia. During the investigation, several imprisoned residents of Jaraiz confirmed that men from Jarandilla had not only taken Rabbi Abraham de Loya captive, but that he was singled out for especially harsh treatment and had his hands "shackled in chains," instead of being bound.[29] The prisoners noted that their captors later transported the rabbi to their village, Jarandilla, and held him captive for an extended period in an isolated house in the mountains. Although the rabbi seems to have survived the ordeal, two of his coreligionists were not as fortunate. The sheepherders Juan and Pascual Sánchez of Tornavacas reported they had seen men transporting the "bodies of Fartalo and his wife," Jews from Plasencia, to the village of Oropesa.[30] Although no one could elaborate on the circumstances of their deaths, it is possible that they were victims of Jarandilla's or García Álvarez's gallows. Although local Christians suffered during this conflict, the judge's inquiry revealed that none had lost their lives. The death of the two Jewish residents of Plasencia, and the lack of additional questioning on the matter by Judge Sánchez, revealed that Plasencia's Jews lived a precarious existence in a society that targeted them for harsh punishment and sometimes murder.

Although the archival record does not preserve the final ruling of Judge Sánchez, the thrust of his investigation demonstrated his willingness to support the claims of the city council of Plasencia over the assertions of regional lords. It was a position that was more favorable to the king because he ultimately controlled city councils, which served as valuable royal counterbalances to independently minded seigniorial lords, many of whom were among the most powerful New Noble families created by the monarchy in the late 1300s.[31]

Cumulatively, the royal inquest of 1431 demonstrated that liberty and livelihood in Plasencia were dependent on a complex interaction of political, economic, and religious factors. The nature of the investigation revealed that the Kingdom of Castile and León existed as a patchwork of royal, municipal, religious, and seigniorial jurisdictions. When local city councils and local lords could not agree on how to balance the needs of these jurisdictions, the king's supreme authority was required to settle disputes. In particular, Christian commoners and religious minorities such as Jews often found themselves trapped in the mechanics of these conflicts.

Although the Carvajal–Santa María confederation would effectively clear this jurisdictional hurdle in 1431, it would soon encounter an even more problematic situation and challenge to its local authority. García Álvarez and Pedro Niño had proved worthy adversaries of the confederated families, but they would be insignificant in comparison to the Estúñiga family, who the king made condes de Plasencia in 1441.

MANAGING CHANGE:
THE FORCEFUL ENTRY OF THE ESTÚÑIGA

The year 1441 brought the rapid expansion of the New Noble Estúñiga family into the affairs of the city of Plasencia, and, with their arrival, they planted the seeds for a forty-year conflict with the family confederation. During the remaining four years of Gonzalo García de Santa María's term as bishop of Plasencia, these united houses used their domination of the city council and cathedral chapter to thwart, albeit in modest ways, the Estúñiga clan's solidification of power in the region.

What was so significant about the Estúñiga family was not solely its aggressive expressions of secular authority, but how it diverged from other conversos in terms of its cultural approach to fellow conversos as well as the Jewish community. The Estúñiga implemented the anti-Jewish policies championed by proselytizers like Vincent Ferrer, who just a few short decades before had marched into synagogues across Iberia to preach the Christian message of redemption through the acceptance of Christ as the Messiah. These New Christians seemed intent on distancing themselves from any collective converso identity by forcefully attacking the Carvajal–Santa María and Jewish populations alike. By 1477, the Estúñiga family would begin work on the foundation of the Church of San Vicente Ferrer and later a Dominican monastery in his name within the Jewish quarter—precisely where the synagogue stood.[32] Even before it might form into a communal identity, the converso mind-set was not one but many.

The political chain reaction that initiated the animosities began in 1440 when King Juan II named Pedro de Estúñiga the new conde de Trujillo.[33] As Trujillo was one of the ancestral homes of many regional families of knights, such as the Carvajal, Orellana, and Bejarano, the community quickly demonstrated its unwillingness to accept Pedro as their new secular lord. Among the Placentinos that called Trujillo their childhood home were Dr. Garci López de Carvajal, a member of the city council of Plasencia and a royal adviser to King Juan II, and his recently deceased brother, Archdeacon Gonzalo García de Carvajal. Although these two men did not follow their father's example and become knights, their brothers, Diego García de Bejarano and Gómez González de Carvajal, had maintained the family confederation's commitment to arms and continued to live in Trujillo.

In October 1440, when Gómez González, mayor of Trujillo, received a letter from the king ordering the village to submit to Pedro de Estúñiga's authority under penalty of the "loss of life and goods," he and his brother, Diego, refused to yield.[34] Instead, the Carvajal clan rallied the village's knights, prepared the castle for battle, and vowed to resist Pedro de Estúñiga's assumption of his lordship of Trujillo. With the promised aid and support of Gutierre de Sotomayor, master of the military Order of Alcántara, a bloody military engagement between many of King Juan II's leading knights seemed all but certain. If necessary, Pedro de Estúñiga promised, "he would take the village of

Trujillo by force."[35] Pressured by the family confederation's brinkmanship and determined not to risk a war between his knights, the king preserved Trujillo as a royally administered community. In its place, he offered Pedro the city of Plasencia.[36] Pedro would henceforth be the conde de Plasencia y Béjar.

While the preservation of Trujillo as a royal city was a tactical victory for the Trujillo-based portion of the family confederation, the loss of Plasencia to the Estúñiga was a devastating and strategic setback for the Carvajal–Santa María clan in Plasencia. It had invested significant human capital and energy to garner control of the Cathedral of Plasencia—a lucrative prize that offered access to church positions and valuable church assets. Likewise, the enhanced collaboration between the cathedral and the city council from the mid-1420s to 1440 had earned the family the consistent acquiescence and approval of their fellow city councilmen. Even while the city's regional property conflict with García Álvarez and Pedro Niño in 1431 had required the intervention of a royal judge, the families had demonstrated keen management and problem-solving skills in other affairs.[37] For example, in 1428, the united family guided the city council and the cathedral chapter through a potentially crippling standoff when several churchmen had threatened city officials with excommunication over a wine tax dispute.[38]

With the arrival of Pedro de Estúñiga as their new count, the Carvajal–Santa María family confederation found its local authority minimized and political influence curtailed. In effect, it was a battle of different converso identities and values. With the consolidated authority it had amassed on the city council, the family confederation by the late 1420s had effectively transferred the control and collection of the city's portazgo to the cathedral.[39] When Pedro de Estúñiga assumed his secular position as the conde de Plasencia, which entitled him to the king's portion of the portazgo, it was highly likely he would no longer consent to this arrangement.

In December 1441, King Juan II communicated the extent of the political and financial deference he expected the Cathedral of Plasencia and the city council to extend to their new count. Not only should all noble families receive Pedro as their new lord, but his assumption of the city and its lands would include all "peripheral lands, tribute taxes, notary fees, trade taxes, rents, and all rights over the city."[40] From that point forward, the city council was required to direct the king's share of its tax collections and fees to the new conde de Plasencia, even though, in the past, the king had been inclined to share some of his proceeds with the city council.[41] Worse yet for the king's nobles on the city council was the loss of their political authority as Pedro de Estúñiga would now rule the territory as his own. Required to be "obedient" to the count, several noble families elected to abandon their homes in the city rather than live under a peer's rule.[42] These men included Rodrigo de Monroy, who retreated to his seigniorial lands in the nearby villages of Belvis and Deleitosa, and Plasencia's old foe, García Álvarez de Toledo, who abandoned his local holdings and returned to his own village of Oropesa. The Estúñiga takeover was sufficiently traumatic that the converso Álvarez de Toledo would now begin to reconcile with the Carvajal–Santa María. The reconciliation was ultimately consummated when Diego de Carvajal of Plasencia married Elvira de Toledo of Oropesa in 1469.[43]

As the city of Plasencia enjoyed the benefits of a charter granted by the king, Pedro de Estúñiga could not disband the city council; both the count and the city's nobles would live a contentious coexistence until 1488.[44] In that year, the Carvajal–Santa María confederation would eagerly eject the Estúñiga clan from the city at the request of King Ferdinand and Queen Isabel and restore the city to direct royal rule.[45] Nonetheless, in the forty years of Estúñiga governance (1441–88), it was primarily the family confederation that would regularly test the limits of the count's authority.

Sealing a Relationship with the Placentino Jews

During the final years of Bishop Santa María's term, which concluded in 1445, the family confederation used a combination of personal wealth, church authority, and church statutes to block Pedro de Estúñiga's attempt to solidify control over the region and its inhabitants. These actions revealed that these conversos were protective of their Jewish neighbors. Three months after Pedro assumed his title, the Carvajal–Santa María family used its countervailing power in the cathedral to manipulate real estate transactions and to prevent the Estúñiga clan from consolidating control of key properties in the city's Jewish quarter.

Before Pedro's arrival, the family confederation had used its authority in the city council to oversee Plasencia's Jewish population. Now, to protect themselves and some Jewish families from the Estúñiga family, the confederation transferred ownership of strategically located Jewish real estate to itself. In a transaction conducted in March 1442, Archdeacon Rodrigo de Carvajal facilitated Diego González de Carvajal's purchase of multiple Jewish homes and properties owned by Juan de Bergara, Dana de Cerjo, Alenatar de Cerjo, and Abraham Almale.[46] These collections of homes were all located in the Jewish quarter of the city, precisely where the Estúñiga family had begun to encroach and establish a presence in the 1420s. Not only were all of the domiciles and their corrals within the Jewish quarter, but two of the homes were located in La Mota—adjacent to the synagogue and the Estúñiga family's new palace.[47] Although Diego González purchased these houses, he elected to lease them back to the Jewish families.[48] Perhaps the most questionable aspect of the property transaction was that, as noted by the archdeacon, the actual sale purportedly occurred in 1430 and 1436, but the parties did not record it until 1442, after Pedro Estúñiga's arrival in the city.[49]

This event is striking in terms of how it addressed both the multilayered goals of the confederated family and the potential needs of the Jewish families. The credibility of the agreement appears dubious, especially in terms of the recorded sale date. It suggests that the parties shared a common interest—perhaps mutually agreeing to lie about the dates of the property sales—in order to prevent the Jewish families and homes from falling under the complete control of the Estúñiga clan. Similarly, it demonstrated the high level of trust between Jews and the converso Carvajal–Santa María family, as opposed to the converso Estúñiga clan. Here was an outright case of a converso-Jewish alliance that countered one of the most elite converso families in Spain.

By executing the contract under the aegis of the Cathedral of Plasencia, the family confederation reestablished competing jurisdictional oversight over some Jewish residents and partially blocked the Estúñiga family's expansion in the Jewish quarter. In essence, the Roman Catholic Church's authority was rallied to protect Jews.

If the Estúñiga clan challenged or attempted to nullify the agreement, which was likely as it was consolidating personal property in Plasencia's Jewish quarter, the cathedral chapter could threaten it with financial and religious penalties, including excommunication. Existing local church precedent, first established in 1396 and reinforced in 1410, had clarified the supremacy of the Cathedral of Plasencia over local lords and knights in affairs relating to ecclesiastical transactions and taxation.[50] In fact, before the Carvajal–Santa María family confederation had garnered control of the cathedral chapter, the church temporarily excommunicated Diego García de Bejarano (a Carvajal family knight) for failure to pay diezmos to the church for earnings produced from his lands. Thus it appears likely that any party that challenged an ecclesiastically administered transaction, such as Diego González's purchase of the Jewish homes in the Jewish quarter, would have been subject to similar church penalties. Furthermore, the Jewish residents who rented homes directly from the cathedral arguably benefited from church protections as well.[51] Since the count's jurisdiction was purely secular, this cathedral chapter action resided outside his authority.

It was not only the cathedral chapter that realized tangible benefits from the property contracts; Diego González and the Jewish sellers did as well. For Diego, a city councilman and the first cousin of the archdeacon, the transactions accomplished three goals: (1) they enhanced his family's property holdings, which were later incorporated into the entailed lands (mayorazgo) of his son; (2) they created a physical Carvajal–Santa María presence next to the Estúñiga housing compound; and (3) they provided Diego with the church's jurisdictional protection.[52]

For the Jewish parties, the property sales were more problematic and indicative of their differing perceptions of the Estúñiga and Carvajal–Santa María families. It is likely that the Estúñiga clan pressured the Jewish residents to sell their homes in La Mota. If two of the families had not done so, they likely faced eviction by the Estúñiga clan, given that the condes de Plasencia had chosen to amass and consolidate a number of properties in the area in order to create a substantial housing complex.

A royal communiqué sent by Juan II to Pedro de Estúñiga just two months before the cathedral recorded the sales provides a good indication of why the Jewish families chose to sell to the family confederation: the Estúñiga family intended to abuse its power over the Jews of Plasencia. This royal notice exposes the predacious nature of the Estúñiga clan and its likely approach to governing local Jewish residents. In January 1442, the king informed the count that he could only collect 3,500 maravedís in annual poll taxes from Placentino Jews and not the 10,200 maravedís that the count desired.[53] Although Juan II's existing agreements with the Jewish community of Plasencia entitled the king to a higher poll tax, after 1438, Juan II levied the lesser tax of 3,500 maravedís on the Jewish residents because, he noted, "there are so few of them and they are poor."[54] The king's note to Pedro revealed the count's intention to pursue as aggressively as possible the collection of substantial taxes from his Jewish subjects. Thus it seems likely that the Jewish families had much to fear from the Estúñiga clan as a potential landlord. On the other hand, Diego González de Carvajal was a well-known landlord to many Placentino Jewish families like the Zafia, Harruso, and Pando. In fact, the Carvajal–Santa María were longtime neighbors of these families. The property sale also had the blessing of the Cathedral of Plasencia, which had a proven record of providing Jews and Muslims with access to housing and income-producing lands.

The agreements reinforced the notion that the family confederation was willing to maintain a traditional relationship of healthy religious coexistence with the Placentino Jewish community. The Cathedral of Plasencia had found a novel way to intervene in the conde de Plasencia's direct rule of his Jewish subjects. Last, the Carvajal–Santa María acquired valuable territories in Plasencia, which physically constrained the Estúñiga family's consolidation of territory in the city.

Open War among Conversos

The long struggle that emerged between the Carvajal–Santa María family confederation and the Estúñiga family was at its height during the 1440s. One of the cathedral chapter's primary goals was to shield the cathedral and its administrators from the ongoing turmoil within the kingdom and the local region. The three most prominent sources of this turbulence were the growing power of Castile's new nobility and its "attempts to control and exploit the monarchy," the Castilian king Juan II's continuous political and military confrontations with the Kingdoms of Aragón and Navarra, and the rise and fall of Juan II's favorite adviser, Álvaro de Luna.[55]

These kingdom disruptions were also the backdrop for unremitting competition for economic resources between powerful secular lords and church dioceses. To be expected, property and other sources of income fostered these parties' animosity toward one another. For example, in July 1434, Pope Sixto IV named the Cathedral of Plasencia and its chapter as his "judges" in the matter of securing restitution for substantial numbers of stolen church assets.[56] The pope charged the cathedral with the responsibility of recovering the "lands, villages, castles, and other possessions" usurped from the Dioceses of Toledo, Ávila, Salamanca, and Plasencia by regional nobles and wayward ecclesiastical officials. This was a clear indication that the papacy viewed the

Carvajal–Santa María family confederation, and its administrative and religious policies, in a positive light and as capable advocates for the church's interests.

Plasencia's political environment substantially deteriorated when the Estúñiga
family began to exercise its seigniorial dominance in 1442. Like many of his predecessors, the twentieth-century historian Domingo Sánchez Loro characterized the Estúñiga clan's rule over the region as "the most ignominious and bestial event ever perpetrated in the Extremadura, that is, after taking into consideration their extensive
robbery and usurpation of church freedoms."[57] Loro's estimation of the Estúñiga
family's negative impact on the region, while strongly stated, was a widely held belief.
The charges against the clan ranged from being disobedient to the monarchs, challenging the existing rights of cities and other local lords, aggressively taxing religious
minorities, and, finally, repeatedly undermining the role of the Cathedral of Plasencia. While the hostile actions of the conde de Plasencia were not immediately visible
at the opening of the 1440s, by 1444, the Cathedral of Plasencia was able to expose
how the Estúñiga clan attacked the local church and its administrators—especially
the Carvajal–Santa María family confederation.

In March of that year, the key members of the family confederation met in the
cathedral's Chapel of Saint Catalina to discuss troubling local events with the city council.[58] Among the family members in attendance were Archdeacon Rodrigo de Carvajal,
Cantor Gonzalo Gutiérrez de Calleja (and his son, Vicar General and Canon Juan Fernández de Cabreros), Treasurer Alfonso García de Santa María, and Canon Ruy García
de Salamanca. The churchmen were apprehensive, as they had gone to the extraordinary effort of inviting members of the city council to participate and witness the chapter's efforts to record the misdeeds perpetrated against the church by "certain people,"
known to be Estúñiga partisans.[59] Giving a stark appraisal of the situation, the cathedral's notary recorded:

> We are gathered here together in the Chapel of Saint Catalina—some members
> of the city council and cathedral chapter, along with other city residents—to
> discuss . . . the conflict between this church and other persons. We must do this
> to defend the church's property and rights. Our [defense] extends to certain in-
> dividual members of the cathedral chapter and their personal entitlement to jus-
> tice and the rule of law, personal liberty, ecclesiastical immunity and privileges,
> and control over their geographic jurisdictions. . . . The conflict, hatred, and ill
> will that exist now are a sign of the great malice of our times, [especially] consid-
> ering . . . some persons have been held prisoner . . . and others cannot come into
> the city, cannot go to their personal homes, and cannot even perform their cus-
> tomary religious duties. Further, it is apparent that earlier this year when
> Archdeacon Rodrigo de Carvajal exercised his ecclesiastical authority in the de-
> fense of church properties—for some time he was forced from the city and
> physically not allowed to return. These injuries and others continue today.[60]

After hearing the churchmen's reports, those city council members who were sympathetic to Pedro de Estúñiga stated that they "did not do these things and had not prevented church officials from entering into the city."[61] However, the councilmen acknowledged that Rodrigo de Carvajal was targeted and expelled from the city and blocked from reentering for an extended period.[62] As it happened, Rodrigo was also the archdeacon of Plasencia and Béjar and thus the overlapping ecclesiastical authority who was in direct confrontation with the secular counts of Plasencia and Béjar, the Estúñiga.

The physical harassment of Rodrigo challenged the authority of the cathedral chapter and the family confederation. It suggested that the Estúñiga family had targeted the archdeacon to disrupt the confederated families' activities. After Rodrigo de Carvajal was prevented from returning to the city, he could neither perform his official duties as archdeacon nor attend regular meetings of the cathedral chapter. His lack of freedom of movement jeopardized his collection of rents and taxes in Plasencia and Béjar, prevented him from directing his church staff, and excluded him from the chapter's policy-making meetings. For the family confederation and Rodrigo, the impact of these events had even more dire consequences because it jeopardized the archdeacon's ability to reap the rewards of his ecclesiastical position. Specifically, in 1438, the cathedral chapter had implemented new residency requirements for its members.[63] If Rodrigo was not physically present and performing his duties for six months of every year, he would be ineligible to receive his salary or other forms of compensation.

The one man who had the motive and means to target the Carvajal–Santa María confederation and to deny the church its privileges was Conde Pedro de Estúñiga. The count's motives centered on his escalating regional conflict with the family and their connection and loyalty to Álvaro de Luna, a well-known enemy of the count. This consolidated house of conversos had incurred Pedro's animosity when it successfully prevented him from imposing his lordship over the village of Trujillo in 1440. The count was further provoked when the family confederation used the resources of the cathedral to facilitate the rapid purchase of Jewish homes, thus limiting Pedro's monopoly of properties in the Jewish quarter of Plasencia. In addition, the clans' domination of the local city council, as well as the autonomous authority of the Cathedral of Plasencia, posed substantial impediments to Pedro's efforts to gain control of the region. Only by weakening these local institutions and the family confederation's bases of political authority could the conde de Plasencia realize and maximize the financial benefits of the region's taxes, rents, and other resources. In addition to these local conflicts with the count, the Santa María and Carvajal clans found themselves at odds with him in broader royal affairs.

At the kingdom level, it was apparent that the family confederation's close alignment with de Luna positioned it for additional confrontation with the Estúñiga family. By the early 1440s, Álvaro considered Pedro de Estúñiga a significant threat to his personal power, even though de Luna and King Juan II needed the count's assistance during the war with Aragón and Navarra.[64] By the beginning of the next decade, in 1452, Álvaro secretly planned to capture and eliminate Pedro at his military stronghold in the village of Béjar, just north of the city of Plasencia and within the Diocese of Plasencia.[65] When Álvaro's plan collapsed and his own life was in danger, the man he turned to for physical shelter and political cover was Bishop Alonso de Cartagena, the brother of Plasencia's bishop, Gonzalo García de Santa María.[66] While Álvaro initially found asylum in the bishop's home in Burgos, royal authorities eventually forced Álvaro to surrender. In the end, a royal court convicted Álvaro of multiple crimes, including the suspected murder of Alfonso Pérez de Vivero, and the king refused to intervene on his behalf. In a startling collapse of personal power, the court executed Álvaro in 1453, after which the Santa María house experienced a steady erosion of power in royal and church affairs.[67] With Álvaro's death and the Santa María clan's decline, the elite conversos who had guided royal policies since the 1390s were now in full retreat. Thus the political loyalties that bound Álvaro de Luna to the Carvajal–Santa María confederation made them an enemy of Pedro de Estúñiga.

Although Pedro remained unnamed by the Cathedral of Plasencia, it is likely that political and economic competition motivated his harassment of the Placentino churchmen during the 1440s. Here again it is evident that converso families were pursuing different identity pathways: one directly interconnected with service in the Roman Catholic Church and religiously moderate voices in Castilian bureaucracy (such as the family confederation) and the other (the Estúñiga family) forcefully pursuing secular control over the region and influence in the kingdom.

Pedro de Estúñiga also possessed the necessary means to battle the Cathedral of Plasencia and provoke "fear" in the churchmen.[68] The count's resources included the support of large numbers of knights and men-at-arms, opulent wealth comparable to the most elite noble families, and a noteworthy political dexterity that had gained him the lordship of Plasencia and the king's reliance despite his inconsistent loyalty.[69] In short, the conde de Plasencia had the rationale and ability to attack the Carvajal–Santa María family confederation, but what he lacked was the opportunity.

The perfect opening occurred in 1445 when the churchmen were essentially defenseless due to the absence of family members who were knights. Specifically, Diego González de Carvajal, Gómez González de Carvajal, and Diego García de Bejarano were away at war fighting alongside the king, Juan II.[70] Thus, Pedro could fully exploit the military weakness of the families. He also used deception to take advantages of the cathedral's vulnerability. In addition to Rodrigo de Carvajal's expulsion from the city, other members of the cathedral chapter reported to their compatriots that they had "received letters from the king or from Conde Pedro de Estúñiga instructing them to leave the city . . . under false pretenses, persuasions, and appeals."[71] The members of the cathedral chapter and their city council associates discussed these findings and concluded that someone loyal to Pedro had sought to confuse and trick the church-men into believing their presence was required elsewhere by the king or the count.[72]

In light of this deception, the cathedral responded with a novel approach, consid-ering members' limited ability to defend themselves. Vicar General Alfonso García de Santa María proposed that the chapter should implement a temporary two-year statute that waived previously enacted residency requirements until 1446.[73] Therefore, even if the churchmen were kept out of the city by force or trickery, the cathedral would still pay them. Unfortunately, this did not resolve the underlying political siege that Pedro had effectively conducted against the Cathedral of Plasencia. Unable to protect themselves with arms and lacking the assistance of their absentee knight clans-men, the chapter's legal solution focused on the art of the possible. The churchmen's actions also demonstrated that the cathedral chapter believed it should govern itself, even in times of peril, under specific written rules and that the chapter placed a high value on the maintenance of its governing statutes.

The political attacks on the cathedral's leadership did not end in 1444. Instead, they bled into 1446 and damaged the formerly positive relationship between the cathedral and its remaining supporters on the city council. In April 1446, the canons and preben-daries gathered once again in the Chapel of Saint Catalina to discuss the difficult state of affairs, noting, "In the past two years since the Dean and cathedral chapter moved to create the statute, this great malice of our time has not stopped and it continues with no end. Now it only increases. . . . [T]here seems little calming of the situation."[74]

The church notary recorded that after the perpetrators had expelled Archdeacon Rodrigo de Carvajal from the city, in 1445 they also forced Cantor Gonzalo Gutiérrez de la Calleja (a Santa María) from Plasencia. The notary further reported on the con-dition of a third churchman: "Now Canon Ruy González is currently cast out . . . and he and others are incurring great financial expenses because they cannot return to their homes."[75] In addition, the chapter acknowledged that the "debates between the city council and cathedral chapter are now multiplying in size."[76] Because the cathe-dral chapter was unable to resolve the mistreatment of its clerical administrators, it became increasingly frustrated with the city council, which was unwilling or unable to guarantee the administrators' safe passage and residence in the city. Now that Pedro de Estúñiga was the count of the region and the principal leader on the city council, po-litical fractures were forming in this local governing body.

Once again, in 1446, the cathedral chapter elected to extend the allowable absen-teeism for its canons and prebendaries for an additional two years. In the final state-ments of the cathedral chapter on the matter, the churchmen revealed both their des-peration for divine intervention and who they believed could resolve these injustices. On these points the cathedral notary wrote, "By the mercy of God we hope that within two years God will give us peace and concord . . . and that our lords, Bishop [Santa María], Count [Pedro de Estúñiga], and the Countess will return to the city . . . so hopefully this conflict will end."[77]

Only secular and ecclesiastical lords could negotiate the necessary solution to the matter. Even though they believed Pedro had instigated the attacks on the church's privileges, the churchmen understood that it would require the bishop and the count to bring them to an end. By 1448, the attacks on the Cathedral of Plasencia presumably ended, as the chapter did not renew its absenteeism statute. Likewise, no other forced expulsions of church members were recorded. Cumulatively, the cathedral's governing initiatives, both those regarding ecclesiastical residencies and those demanding secrecy, indicate the Carvajal–Santa María family confederation would not readily concede its positions and authority to the Estúñiga clan. Rather, the family remained vigilant and devoted to protecting and advancing its interests, as well as those of the Cathedral of Plasencia.

Troubled Times for Jews and Conversos

From the 1440s through the 1460s, life for the Carvajal and Santa María in Plasencia proceeded at a steady pace even though the bishop's miter passed from the Santa María to the Carvajal clan. In 1446, the elderly Gonzalo García de Santa María stepped down as the bishop of Plasencia and completed the remaining years of his ecclesiastical service as the bishop of Sigüenza.[78] King Juan II nominated Juan de Carvajal to take his place. At the time, Juan was heavily involved in papal affairs, serving as the legal auditor on the Vatican's Roman Rota, the governor of Vatican City, and a papal legate to many regions in Europe.[79] These responsibilities, along with his appointment by Pope Eugene IV to the Council of Cardinals, prevented him from actively governing the Diocese of Plasencia.[80] Instead, he left the administration of the bishopric to the cathedral chapter, which the family confederation managed exclusively throughout his tenure.

Rather than disrupt the smooth functioning of the cathedral and its leadership chapter, Juan de Carvajal continued to support the involvement of his extended clan, the Santa María, throughout his administration (1446–69). While the cardinal's brother, Rodrigo de Carvajal, served as the archdeacon of Plasencia and Béjar from the 1440s until 1470, the Santa María family continued to occupy a significant number of chapter posts.[81] During the late 1440s and 1450s, these members of the Santa María clan included Cantor Ruy García de Salamanca, Archdeacon Pedro González de Illescas, Treasurer Alfonso García de Santa María, and Canon and Vicar General Dr. Juan Fernández de Cabreros.[82] Cardinal Carvajal's comfort with and support of the family was evident through his retention of Juan Fernández, a Santa María clansman, as his personal representative on the chapter. However, undermining the family confederation's stability within the cathedral was its ongoing conflict with the Estúñiga clan.

During this era, the Estúñiga family remained a thorn in the side of the Carvajal–Santa María family confederation. In 1454, the Cathedral of Plasencia and Conde Álvaro de Estúñiga, the son of Pedro (d. 1453), renewed family hostilities and engaged in a legal battle over control of the city's portazgo.[83] As the secular lord of Plasencia,

Álvaro successfully enforced his right to control these levies and leased their collection to a new party, Yuça "the Muslim," who now found himself aligned with the count. Defying easy explanation, an odd sort of convivencia had reseeded itself in Plasencia. Now the converso count and a Muslim were aligned against the converso family confederation and the local Jewish population.

While the city and cathedral could not prevent the count from taking these tax collections, the family confederation continued to antagonize Álvaro in other ways. Repeatedly, from 1461 to 1465, he appeared before the city council claiming, "With great injury to me—you, the members of this council—do not obey my ordinances . . . as is customary for one's vassals."[84] Yet his protests often fell on deaf ears as family confederation council members such as Fernándo de Carvajal, Juan Fernández de Cabreros, Francisco de Carvajal, and García de Carvajal repeatedly refused to appear at the council meetings.[85] Left with few alternatives, Álvaro could only order his personal notary to take temporary possession of the city council's Book of Acts (Libro de actas) and record his protests and orders, which he had read in the Plaza Mayor.[86] Carrying on their duel via notaries, the council would respond and confront Álvaro's claims in the Book of Acts and argue that council members were not bound to the count since they maintained their position as noblemen (hijos de algo), not by his authority, but "by the grace of their king."[87] The confederated family would not back down.

The family was likely emboldened by Cardinal Carvajal's high profile in the kingdom and papal affairs, as well as its family's local success in transitioning their younger men into new leadership roles in the cathedral when its representatives on the cathedral chapter retired. For instance, Diego de Carvajal ascended the ecclesiastical ladder in the Cathedral of Plasencia when the chapter named him a prebendary in the 1460s and later promoted him to archdeacon of Coria in the 1470s.[88] Likewise, after the cardinal's brother, Rodrigo, stepped down as archdeacon of Plasencia and Béjar in the late 1460s, the cathedral replaced him with Sancho de Carvajal.[89] In this manner, a third generation of the house of Carvajal, all descended from the caballero Diego González de Carvajal y Vargas and Sevilla López de Villalobos, assumed the reins of the cathedral chapter. Similarly, the Santa María side of the family promoted its junior members within the chapter. Ruy García assumed the archdeaconship of Trujillo and Medellín in the 1460s and held this post into the 1470s.

Although both families effectively promoted their relatives into new local ecclesiastical positions, the 1470s were a watershed decade for the confederation, as the Carvajal became the dominant clan. After Cardinal Juan de Carvajal retired as Plasencia bishop in 1469, the king and the pope replaced him with Rodrigo de Ávila (1470–96). Because Rodrigo was not a member of the family confederation, it understood its local authority in the Cathedral of Plasencia was at risk.[90]

In fact, a review of the key leadership positions in the cathedral reveals many critical church roles began to shift from the Santa María to the Carvajal clan during the 1470s (table 5.1).[91] From the 1420s through the late 1460s the Santa María family had occupied almost every significant position in the cathedral chapter, whereas the Carvajal clan controlled only the archdeaconship of Plasencia and Béjar.[92] However, in the late 1460s and early 1470s, a major rebalancing of these cathedral posts occurred. While Sancho de Carvajal continued to hold the title of archdeacon of Plasencia and Béjar, Álvaro de Carvajal assumed the role of treasurer, and the churchmen named Diego de Carvajal archdeacon of Coria.

What appeared to be a significant departure from the pattern of the previous forty years, in which the Santa María claimed most positions, was in fact the perceived need by the family confederation to promote the Carvajal family lineage (presumed by others to be Old Christian) in light of increasing attacks on well-known conversos like the Santa María. In reality, the family confederation was now entering a historical era that required careful Old Christian laundering of perceived Jewish ancestry names. By the late 1470s, the only Santa María–named churchman retaining a senior post on the cathedral chapter was Ruy García. Instead, the family confederation promoted those with either Old Christian surnames (Carvajal) or surnames of unknown religious ancestry (Cabrero, Villalva).[93]

In countless ways, the 1460s–70s would represent a fundamental turning point for the Carvajal–Santa María family confederation because of the dire cultural and political straits in which conversos found themselves in Iberia. As discussed earlier, it is difficult to know exactly when and why the position of conversos in Castilian society rapidly deteriorated.[94] Old Christians (*cristianos viejos*) viewed conversos as fundamentally different from themselves and disparagingly referred to them as New Christians (*cristianos nuevos*), but this position had not affected royal policies. Ultimately, conversos' treatment was tied to institutionalization of anti-Semitism.

After the Old Christian riots in 1449 against conversos and Jews in Toledo, this dangerous religious fuel was ignited in other communities.[95] What started as conflict over royal taxes devolved into physical violence against conversos. Furthermore, from the mid- to late 1400s, conversos became the focus of new forms of societal and institutionalized discrimination. In the aftermath of the Toledo riots, the local city council implemented new limpieza de sangre ordinances to exclude conversos from prominent and profitable offices.[96] These blood purity ordinances, such as those passed in Toledo in 1449, stated:

> We declare the so-called conversos, offspring of perverse Jewish ancestors, must be held by law to be infamous and ignominious, unfit, and unworthy to hold any public office or benefice within the city of Toledo, or land within its jurisdiction, or to be commissioners for oaths or notaries, or have any authority over the true Christians of the Holy Catholic Church.[97]

Although Pope Nicolas V stated that these statutes violated the spirit of the Christian community, they were nonetheless broadly institutionalized across Castile

Table 5.1. Carvajal–Santa María Family Confederation Leaders in the Cathedral of Plasencia, 1420s–1470s

(*All color-coded cells are confederation members.*)

Decade	Bishop	Archdeacon of Plasencia and Béjar	Archdeacon of Trujillo and Medellín	Archdeacon of Coria	Cantor	Treasurer	Vicar General (appointed by bishop)
1420s	Santa María	Carvajal	Other Family	Maluenda	Other Family	Gutiérrez	Other Family
1430s	Santa María	Carvajal	Santa María	Maluenda	Gutiérrez	Gutiérrez Carvajal	Fernández de Cabreros Gutiérrez Maluenda
1440s	Santa María Carvajal	Carvajal Carvajal	Santa María	Maluenda	Gutiérrez Salamanca	Gutiérrez Fernández de Cabreros Santa María	Fernández de Cabreros
1450s	Juan de Carvajal	Rodrigo de Carvajal	Alfonso García de Santa María Pedro González de Illescas	No information available	Ruy García de Salamanca	Alfonso García de Santa María	Juan Fernández de Cabreros
1460s	Juan de Carvajal	Rodrigo de Carvajal Sancho de Carvajal	Ruy García de Salamanca	No information available	Ruy García de Salamanca	Alfonso García de Santa María Álvaro de Carvajal	Position vacant
1470s	Other Family	Sancho de Carvajal	Ruy García de Salamanca	Diego de Carvajal	Ruy García de Salamanca	Álvaro de Carvajal	Other Family

and Aragón by 1451.[98] By 1453, the Carvajal–Santa María family confederation's greatest ally—the converso royal adviser Álvaro de Luna—was dead. In 1460, the religious frenzy infiltrated the Aragonese King Ferdinand's orbit when his confessor, Friar Alonso de Espina, "used his position to stir up hatred against Jews and conversos" in his work *Fortalitium fidei contra judeos* (Fortress of Faith against Jews).[99] With the approach of the royal marriage of Queen Isabel of the Kingdom of Castile and León and King Ferdinand of Aragón and Catalonia in 1469, this anticonverso trend was on the ascent across the Iberian Peninsula. By the early 1470s, violence against conversos spread to Valladolid and Córdoba (1473) and Segovia (1474).[100] The final collapse of overt converso influence in Iberia occurred with the creation of the Holy Office of the Inquisition in 1478, which was initiated to rout Jewish heresy from within Christian ranks.

Changing Names, Concealing Identities

After the 1470s, the royal and political influence of the Santa María portion of the Carvajal–Santa María family confederation began to wane in this highly charged environment. However, the collective family did not abandon its extended clan but began a process of hiding the remaining portions of the Santa María clan under the public Old Christian surname Carvajal and adopting new surnames of uncertain religious origin. In essence, the entire converso family confederation began to conceal Jewish aspects of its identity and ancestry.

As was noted, by the late 1390s, the Old Christian Carvajal and converso Santa María shared extended family relations via the Almaraz and Sánchez clans (see ch. 3). Through these documented associations, we know that the two families genealogically became a converso one in the early 1400s. No later than 1470, the once separate clans became publicly related through the marriage of Mariana Gutiérrez de Álvarez and Juan de Carvajal (fig. 5.2). During the 1480s, both families were also intermarried through their descendants, Estefanía de Trejo Carvajal and Christóval de Villalva. Last, in the 1530s, such a well-known person as Miguel de Carvajal, the Golden Age playwright, was exposing the Jewish lineage of Carvajal–Santa María ancestry in his *Tragedia Josefina*. Thus, through the renaming process, many arms of the Santa María clan were mixed into the Carvajal surname in order to be properly cleansed of their Jewish genealogies. In most cases, their descendants tended to prefer their Carvajal surname to others that were known to be of Jewish ancestry.

On the other hand, those family confederation members who carried potentially damaging Santa María–related surnames such as Gutiérrez simply abandoned them (see fig. 5.2). For example, the most prominent lineage of the local Santa María in Plasencia descended from Gonzalo Gutiérrez de la Calleja, who served as canon, treasurer, and cantor in the Cathedral of Plasencia. This family line routinely shed both

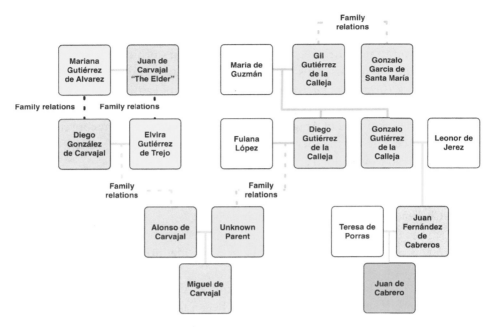

FIGURE 5.2. Adopting the Carvajal surname and choosing new surnames.

surnames in each generation.[101] Gonzalo's wife was Leonor de Jerez. Yet the couple did not bestow either the "de la Calleja" or "Jerez" family names on their son, Juan Fernández de Cabreros. The origin of the Fernández and Cabreros lineages are not entirely evident but may have a connection to the well-known converso Andres de Cabrera, a royal official in King Ferdinand and Queen Isabel's royal court, who also shared converso family relations with Lorenzo Galindez de Carvajal of Plasencia and the Álvarez de Toledo family.[102]

Juan Fernández also participated in the cathedral as a notary. When he served in the church, he often dropped the "Cabreros" surname and substituted "Betanzos." Betanzos also was not a known surname in the family. Likewise, when Juan had his own son with Teresa de Porras, he named him "Juan de Cabrero," dropping the *s*. Thus, by 1500, the time of Juan de Cabrero's generation, the Santa María clan had effectively obscured its surname.[103] It appears that the Gutiérrez de la Calleja family, like many conversos concerned about the limpieza de sangre prohibition, renamed themselves to hide their identities and their link to the Santa María lineage.[104]

Hitching Their Wagon to a Carvajal Star, 1420s–1460s

At the opening of the 1440s, after more than twenty years of royal service, Garci López de Carvajal was the family's leader in royal affairs. Not only had he served as one of

Juan II's judges in Valladolid, but the king also named him to simultaneous posts as a corregidor in the cities of Plasencia and Valladolid.[105]

When he was not attending to legal affairs in Valladolid, Garci López performed a variety of administrative and diplomatic services for the king. For instance, during the 1420s, the king ordered the doctor to supervise the removal of old city walls near Valladolid's castle.[106] By the early 1440s, the monarch entrusted Garci López with more important affairs. He was a member of an elite group of royal advisers (including Bishop Alonso de Cartagena) that the king dispatched as his peace emissaries to the Kingdom of Navarra.[107] While at the pinnacle of his career within the royal administrative service, Garci López witnessed the rise of another family confederation member who would eventually surpass his achievements. For the next three decades, Garci López's cousin, Cardinal Juan de Carvajal, would expand the clan's influence well beyond Spain and would come to embody its noble and religious ideals. (Chapter 6 discusses how and why the family confederation crafted the public memory of Juan de Carvajal to promote the clan's religiosity.)

Juan de Carvajal was the first of the family's new ecclesiastical lineage to traverse a path that led beyond the protected sanctuary of the Cathedral of Plasencia and into the arena of papal affairs.[108] More important, his family carefully managed his ascent in the Roman Catholic Church and used its political power to eliminate defects in his background that might hamper him. Like Garci López, he embodied the fusion of Santa María churchmen and Carvajal knights. He was likely born in the first decade of the 1400s, just as the Carvajal–Santa María family confederation began its collective efforts to model a new converso identity.[109] Like his extended family, he benefited from noble birth: he was the son of Juan de Tamayo, a nobleman from Bonilla de la Sierra, and Sara de Carvajal, the daughter of a Placentino knight, Diego González de Carvajal (fig. 5.3).[110]

Among his five siblings, his brother, Rodrigo, and sister, Sancha, also had a close relationship with the Catholic Church. While Rodrigo served in an official capacity as the archdeacon of Plasencia and Béjar from the mid-1440s to the mid-1460s, Sancha lived a devout life. As discussed in the following chapter, although she never took the vows of a nun, in her final years she was a generous benefactor of churches in Plasencia and Bonilla de la Sierra and a prominent leader in the family's casting itself as devote, pious Christians.

A close inspection of Juan's ascension in the Catholic Church hierarchy reveals not only how church officials manipulated the advancement process but also the extent to which he was transitioning from a family of warriors to the world of ecclesiastical leaders. After completing most of his academic training for his bachelor's degree in law at the University of Salamanca during the 1420s, in one short decade he would graduate from serving as a canon in the Cathedral of Toledo to the position of a legal administrator in the Roman Rota in Vatican City.[111]

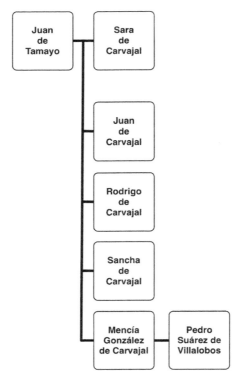

FIGURE 5.3. Immediate family of Juan de Carvajal.

Juan did not achieve his rapid progression from local church affairs in Spain to papal matters in Rome by his merits alone. Rather, intervention by Pope Martín V and King Juan II made his rapid journey possible, even when Juan's background and training fell short of what was expected. For example, in 1429, when Pope Martín V bestowed on Juan a canonship in the Cathedral of Toledo, he also granted him an extensive papal dispensation forgiving his participation in a "quarrel that resulted in bloodshed."[112] The papacy's intervention proved helpful, possibly necessary, because five months after receiving his papal dispensation, Juan's acquisition of church posts accelerated. He subsequently accepted another canon's position, this time in the Cathedral of Palencia, another key religious center in the Castilian heartland.[113]

By 1430, it appears that Juan's superiors in Toledo or Palencia expected him to join a religious order—a responsibility that might have slowed his progress in joining the church's elite administrative class. However, once again, the family confederation used its sway with Pope Martín V and had the pope intervene on Juan's behalf. The pontiff ordered that no one could compel Juan to join a religious order while he was pursuing his studies at the University of Salamanca because he desired that Juan be prepared fully for his "journey" to the Roman Curia.[114] Furthermore, the pope noted that Juan already had sufficient church responsibilities, given his position in Palencia and another post provided by his relatives in the Cathedral of Plasencia.[115] With respect to the latter, Juan collected a salary generated from two annual memorial masses said by the clergy in the Church of Holy Mary in the village of Trujillo.[116]

During the remainder of the 1430s, church leaders ushered Juan through a series of church appointments intended to prepare him for service in the Vatican. In 1432, he received another canon's position in the Cathedral of Zamora but then quickly transferred to the Diocese of Astorga where he became the dean of the cathedral chapter.[117] In this role, Juan gathered valuable administrative experience working with archdeacons and a staff of canons. His family member, Bishop Gonzalo García de Santa María of Plasencia, likely made Juan's move to Astorga possible as Gonzalo had served as Astorga's bishop less than ten years earlier.[118] However, just as Juan was becoming accustomed to leaving behind the violent past of his family, in 1433, he found himself seeking and receiving another papal absolution. On this occasion, he had participated in a conflict that ended in the deaths of several men, as well as the "mutilation" of their headless bodies.[119] The pope's willingness to approve this dispensation, as well as the prior one in 1429, indicates that Juan had powerful family members, like his Santa María cousins who were bishops, who were willing to clear his path of any obstructions that might impede his advancement.

In the final years of his preparation for service at the Vatican, Juan de Carvajal continued to benefit from papal leniency. In 1433, the pontiff granted him another benefice, this time in the Church of Holy Mary of Écija.[120] Even though his academic studies were faltering, he received a promotion in the church hierarchy. In spite of these shortcomings, the church granted Juan yet another source of income in addition to the income he received from the Dioceses of Astorga, Zamora, Plasencia, and Palencia.[121]

Not surprisingly, Juan secured the benefice in Écija by way of family connections—a traditional appointment mechanism. He received the position vacated by the death of his extended family member, Alfonso de Cabreros, who was also a relative of Cardinal Juan Cervantes of Sevilla.[122]

In 1436, Juan de Carvajal secured one last position with the aid of King Juan II and his adviser, Álvaro de Luna, who had consistently relied on the Carvajal–Santa María family confederation for loyalty and aid.[123] In that year, Pope Eugene IV made Juan the abbot of Holy Mary of Husillos (abadía de Santa María de Husillos), which was located on the periphery of Palencia.[124] Although another church official, Juan de Quiñones, tried to block his appointment, the king and de Luna wrote to the pope asking him to intervene on behalf of Juan de Carvajal.[125] Understanding that "King Juan II expressed his concern and preference for Carvajal," the pope ordered Quiñones to cease his actions and to "no longer oppose the rights of who he had named."[126] As mentioned earlier, at this critical juncture in Juan de Carvajal's ecclesiastical progression and accumulation of benefices, both Bishop Santa María and Garci López served as royal advisers and were also associates of de Luna. Álvaro de Luna's involvement in Juan's promotion also indicates that the Carvajal–Santa María family confederation was part of the converso de Luna faction that circulated in the Castilian royal court.

While he was the abbot of Holy Mary of Husillos, Juan de Carvajal had his first taste of papal service: between 1438 and 1440, Pope Eugene IV dispatched him—no less than twenty-two times—to attend the schismatic Council of Basel (1431–49).[127] Perhaps due to his effectiveness at the council, as well as the loyalty he demonstrated to the papacy, in 1439, Juan entered full-time service as an auditor of the Roman Rota.[128] In this position, he was responsible for assisting in the preparation of papal judgments for legal cases that flowed in from all areas of the Catholic world.[129] These included all issues concerning the Holy See, such as "rites and procedures pertaining to beatifications and canonization," as well as "special cases of civil and canon law, such as annulling marriages."[130] Likely one of a dozen such auditors, Juan occupied the seat typically reserved for a Castilian.[131] Within the Vatican, only the ambassadors from the Christian kingdoms had more influence than the auditors.[132]

As in other cases involving Juan's promotion in the Catholic Church, his assumption of the duties and title of auditor came with a specially crafted papal concession. Although he had attended the University of Salamanca to pursue a degree in canon and civil law, it is likely he never completed these studies.[133] Pope Eugene IV had to certify that Juan could assume his new legal post without providing proof of either his academic degrees or his church ordination.[134]

After three years of service on the Rota, in 1441 Juan entered the pope's foreign service, where he began a thirty-three-year career in Rome.[135] From 1441 to 1448, he was a papal legate and emissary to the German princes who had allied themselves against Pope Eugene IV. In 1446, he reached the pinnacle of his career, when the crown and pontiff made him bishop of Plasencia and cardinal of San Angel in Rome. Later, in 1455, he demonstrated his Christian zeal when he publicly advocated a holy crusade in Hungary to rally support behind efforts to counter the Ottoman Turks.[136]

Because Juan de Carvajal spent so much of his life outside of Plasencia, it appears that he held his title as bishop in absentia. Although the *Actas capitulares* speak of him as the bishop and "perpetual administrator of the Bishopric of Plasencia," he was not present at any recorded meetings of the cathedral chapter.[137] Although absent physically from the diocese, he did implement several local church initiatives. For instance, in 1468, Juan founded the Cathedral Grammar School (Escuela de gramática) in Plasencia to address what he considered the "ignorance" of local clergy and to revive the study of philosophy, Latin, and theology.[138] To serve as the first chair of the school, Juan selected his relative, the prebendary Dr. Gil Fernández de Carvajal.[139] Perhaps this focus on local educational training was a recognition of his own educational inadequacies that had become apparent more than thirty years earlier when Pope Eugene IV granted him a special exemption pertaining to his legal training.

In the final years of Juan de Carvajal's term as cardinal and bishop of Plasencia, his extended family embarked on several critical family memorial projects. Unlike its previous endeavors, which had primarily focused on building the power of the family confederation in the cathedral, these new initiatives aimed to lionize the Carvajal clan's noble and religious status in light of the backlash against conversos. As individuals, as well as through intensively planned collective actions, the Carvajal–Santa María family confederation dedicated the next twenty years to the foundation of a broad array of religious endowments that simultaneously promoted piety as well as its social stature.

In sum, the conversos in the Cathedral of Plasencia had managed the successful transition from a Santa María leadership to a Carvajal future. The struggle had been a success.

6

MEMORY AND RELIGION

During the mid-fifteenth century, the Carvajal–Santa María family confederation implemented an extensive program to memorialize their lineage and religiosity. This initiative was the single most important endeavor they pursued in blood-obsessed Christian Spain, and it explains why and how conversos created family memory for the purposes of public consumption and privately held knowledge. Further, their publicly performed religious rituals and practices reveal elements of their converso faith.

At the beginning of the century, conversos accelerated their social and religious efforts to demonstrate their Christian worthiness to a skeptical Castilian public. These New Christians labored aggressively to counter the belief that their Jewish ancestry forever tainted their Christian credentials. What began as initial steps to bolster New Christian social status and piety escalated into an intensive and vital program of creating a collective public and hidden private memory of the Carvajal–Santa María family confederation. It reflected what scholars, such as George Mariscal, David Nirenberg, Norman Roth, and Ann Laura Stoler, identified as an increasing fifteenth-century Castilian interest in weighing Christians' virtue based on their limpieza de sangre— namely, whether or not they were tainted by Jewish or Muslim ancestries.

Memory, as I use it in this text, describes the acts of both creation and recollection. Creation begins with the occurrence of real and imagined personages, places, events and practices, objects, ideas, and beliefs. Recollection involves persons building physical spaces and structures, writing textual and spoken narratives, and performing specific actions, behaviors, and rituals. In the context of the family confederation, specific "creations" for "recollection" were selected for the purposes of communicating who they were to a broad audience that included local community members, noble and social peers in Spain, and the broader European and American worlds. From these creations, a converso religion can be described as a Marianist and ancestry cult. However, there was a covert memory as well that was communicated privately among family members that acknowledged and remembered their blended Jewish-Catholic origins. At times, these private recollections were hidden in public memorials. This private memory was also a contested one within the extended clan because it presented the risk of exposing and undermining their public personae as Old Christians.

Castilian societal attitudes toward elite conversos began to change fundamentally by the mid-1400s. Increasingly, Old Christians, those who claimed an ancient Christian pedigree, perceived conversos as insincere converts to Christianity. They also believed that these New Christians had amassed too much influence in royal affairs and over the Trastámaran dynasty that began under King Enrique II now continued under Juan II and Enrique IV. Unfortunately for all conversos, these hardening attitudes found footing in some of Castile's most important cities, such as Toledo, where Old Christians rioted and attacked their kinsmen of newer origin and Old Christians formulated new limpieza de sangre statutes to exclude conversos from public office.

In this chapter, I present the Carvajal–Santa María confederation's aggressive creation of its Christian identity that could be used as public memory to safeguard their religious and social station in Castile. This included the actions of individual family members, such as Bishop Gonzalo García de Santa María, who instituted annual church memorial services to honor themselves as well as their ancestors. Ladies, such as Sevilla López de Carvajal and Sancha de Carvajal, pursued complementary efforts by establishing sizable religious foundations and endowments that funded the creation of a convent and other religious programs. Most important, religious institutions like the Cathedral of Plasencia and Cardinal Juan de Carvajal implemented a comprehensive program to integrate the Carvajal family's perpetual presence into the diocese's religious practices, architecture, and public works.

HISTORIOGRAPHICAL NOTES: THE ROLE OF "BLOOD" IN IDENTIFYING CONVERSOS

In many respects, the mid-fifteenth century was the start, in the early modern era, of an emphasis on bloodlines to identify conversos, and, to some extent, this position is related to conceptions of race. Several scholars have articulated this point, and their opinions are highly relevant to the Carvajal–Santa María family confederation's memorialization activities because they help explain the clan's rationale for overt Christian protests of piety. Stoler, a scholar of identities, argues that racial selves are constructed in two manners: "In one, the 'truth' of race is understood as grounded in somatically observable, dependable differences; in the other, the 'truth' of racial membership is not visually secured at all . . . [but] is dependent on . . . hidden properties."[1] Thus conversos epitomized a form of race that was difficult to observe because of "unseen" characteristics, including "affective sensibilities" (feelings, attitudes) and biological elements (eye color, skin tone, blood and tissue).[2]

Likewise, Mariscal notes that by the fifteenth century, "the language of religious difference is clearly dominant, yet pseudobiological concerns are already visible in mid-fifteenth texts such as Alonso de Cartagena's *Defense of Christian Unity*."[3] Mariscal sees a Castilian world wrestling with the tensions of race and religion. To bolster this position, he interprets Cartagena's treatise as an attempt to use "the biblical story of Ruth to argue for the primacy of faith over blood" in order to defend conversos from Christian attacks focused on their "enemy blood."[4] As Alonso was the brother of Bishop Santa María, it appears that this specific family confederation was deeply troubled by its inability to prove its Christian worthiness because of its blood defect.

Nirenberg also argues that blood lineage was a determinant of identity by the mid-fifteenth century.[5] He notes that Old Christians used "lineage as one means of re-establishing the integrity of religious categories of identity," because of the obscuring Jewish and Christian fusion of blood and cultures.[6] Roth also arrived at similar conclusions. He states that "the pernicious doctrine of 'racial impurity' was invented . . . to discriminate against them [conversos] on the grounds of their Jewish racial heritage," which thereby further defined the conversos as a new and unique community.[7] These perceptions of blood dictating identity also traveled to colonial Spanish America, as María Elena Martínez has demonstrated in colonial Mexico.[8]

To counter these blood purity attacks, the converso Carvajal–Santa María family confederation in Plasencia embarked on an ambitious plan to secure a memory that portrayed them as among the chosen Christians. These initial efforts began with the Santa María family, but subsequently it was the Carvajal lineage that mastered this endeavor.

INDIVIDUAL EFFORTS TO MEMORIALIZE THE FAMILY CONFEDERATION

Recentering the Memory of a Family Because of Blood Purity Concerns

Across Europe during the fifteenth century, both wealthy and modestly financially endowed noble houses highly valued the social currency they could accumulate by making personal donations to the church.[9] If this religious identity was prized throughout Europe, then Castilian conversos seemed to place a premium on it, given the extent of their Christian memorialization efforts. In particular, converso families exploited religious memorial services to celebrate distinct clan lineages perceived by others to be Old Christian while limiting the visibility of surnames that were well-known New Christian ones.[10]

The Carvajal clan was a celebrated but minor noble family that persisted into the fifteenth century as Christian knights. As introduced in earlier chapters, Spanish nobility genealogies celebrate the Carvajal family of Plasencia as one descended from the line of King Bermudo II of León (982–99), and through these noble origins they entered into knightly service.[11] Thus they were among those Christians of ancient roots— Old Christians. The earliest tangible evidence connecting the Carvajal clan to Plasencia is a blend of narrative and physical evidence. According to Friar Alonso Fernández, a sixteenth-century historian of Plasencia, Diego González de Carvajal and his father resided in Plasencia and were in the service of King Ferdinand III (1217–52). The two men participated in the king's military campaigns against the Islamic al-Andalus and were attendants to the king's mother, Doña Berenguela, as her personal stewards, or mayordomos.[12] After the Castilian reconquest of Sevilla in 1248, Diego González and his father retired to Plasencia.[13] Friar Fernández also indicated that Diego González gave a founding donation to the nuns of the Monastery of Saint Mark of Plasencia, which allowed them to establish their order in Plasencia in the 1230s.[14] In the monastery's church, and at its main altar, an inscription on a sepulcher reportedly read, "Diego González de Carvajal, family founder."[15] The friar added, "From these words recorded on the epitaph, we know that Diego González de Carvajal was the progenitor and propagator of the Carvajal family in Plasencia."[16] What was unknown in the public arena was the extent to which the Santa María and Carvajal families had intermarried at the opening of the fifteenth century, especially through the Sánchez, Ulloa, Almaraz, Trejo, Fernández, Cabreros, Villalva, and Gutiérrez.[17] This hidden connection was crucial to the converso family confederation's survival and efforts to mask themselves with an Old Christian identity.

Precisely because of the family confederation's caution during the period's anti-converso hysteria, it appears that the Carvajal and Santa María families labored to conceal their intimate relations.[18] By the mid- to late fifteenth century, many noble families began a systematic process of hiding and destroying evidence of their converso ancestries. For example, in the archive of the Cathedral of Plasencia, not one single last will and testament, dowry letter, or religious foundation document can be found for a Santa María–surnamed family member. On the other hand, there are dozens upon dozens for the Carvajal and fewer than ten for interlinking clans such as the Fernández, Cabreros, Gutiérrez, and Villalva.

With little doubt, some agent or individuals tampered with the Placentino archival record and methodically removed or destroyed these records, as confirmed by the disappearance of critical institutional documents as well as personal ones. For example, the lost Book 2 of the *Actas capitulares* of the Cathedral of Plasencia corresponds to the first half of the fifteenth century when the Placentino clans were inter-marrying and during the administration of Bishop Santa María. As previously dis-cussed, Alonso de Cartagena's *Defense of Christian Unity* included the cathedral's un-usual 1437 church statute that held Archdeacon Gonzalo García de Carvajal, Canon Gonzalo Gutiérrez de la Calleja, Archdeacon Alfonso García de Santa María, and other church family members "never to reveal their secret discussions to any person" and that if one should violate this statute, "[he] would face penalties imposed by the chap-ter that could not be reduced."[19] Secrecy and concealment were already on the minds of the family confederation during the 1430s, and it was materially enacted by the de-struction and elimination of important institutional records in later years.

Similarly, the wholesale removal of Santa María–surnamed testaments, marriage contracts, and individual clan religious endowments from the archive of the cathedral can be inferred based on corollary documentation. Specifically, the Calendar, or Book of Anniversary Masses, for the Holy Church of Plasencia provides minute details from these lost documents.[20] The Book of Masses, a fifteenth-century text that was consid-ered lost until the mid-2000s, is a record of all the memorial masses sung in the name of deceased churchmen and parishioners. It appears to have been created in 1433, based on the first masses recorded. Because approximately thirty confederation mem-bers are named in the Book of Masses, we know that individual memorial documents (often naming extended family and benefactors) existed for the Santa María, Gutié-rrez, Camargo, and other interrelated families, yet these manuscripts are missing from the archive and were never cataloged. This is in direct contrast to the many dozens of memorial documents, many in excess of thirty pages in length, for the Carvajal-surnamed clan.

There was good reason for the family confederation to eliminate these documents, because blood purity statutes banned all New Christians from lucrative positions in the church and royal administration. In fact, it was not until the early seventeenth century that the descendants of the Santa María family received a special papal dispensation from Pope Clement VIII (1592–1605) granting them blood purity, which exempted them from these discriminatory practices.[21]

Creating Memory, Practicing Religion: The Virgin Mary

In the early fifteenth century, the Santa María side of the family initially pursued efforts to preserve the memory of its most prominent clansmen such as Bishop Santa María. However, by the mid-fifteenth century, its claims of Christian piety had been replaced by promoting the Carvajal name. Simply possessing attributes of Christian piety and charity was socially irrelevant unless a clan could publicly display them in high-profile settings, such as the Cathedral of Plasencia and other local parishes in the city. Even though the family confederation customarily established memorial services in its local parish churches, these efforts provided little public exposure for the family's lineage.[22] However, the Santa María extended clan in Burgos pursued similar efforts in the Cathedral of Burgos's Chapel of the Visitation to remind the community of their piety.

Via the Book of Masses, as well as other records left behind by the Placentino churchmen, we learn that, like the deceased family patriarch Pablo de Santa María (aka Solomon ha-Levi), the family had instituted Saturday as their day of worship devoted to the Virgin Mary.[23] As is evident by their surname—Santa María, or Holy Mary—the family of Jewish converts to Christianity expressed an intense attachment to Mary because of Pablo's conversion-inspiring vision of the Virgin in the late 1300s. When Bishop Pablo died in 1435, to honor him, his sons, Bishop Gonzalo García de Santa María and Alonso de Cartagena, who replaced his father as bishop of Burgos, endowed in the Cathedral of Burgos a perpetual Saturday Mass to be said in the name of the Virgin Mary.[24] In many respects, this was the initiating moment for the family confederation's special devotion to the Virgin Mary, which created a middle way of converso worship and life—recentering its spiritual existence from the traditional Christian Sunday to Saturday.

In 1451, Bishop Gonzalo García de Santa María initiated this practice in Plasencia when he donated a considerable sum to the cathedral to have similar Masses said on his behalf and in the name of the Virgin Mary every Saturday.[25] Thereafter, the Virgin Mary became the idealized way for the Santa María, Carvajal, and other members of the converso clan to express their Christian faith. The masses that the bishop initiated, furthermore, were to be sung over his sepulcher located in the floor of the main altar (*altar mayor*) of the Cathedral of Plasencia, at the head of the congregation.

In order for Bishop Santa María's endowment to be self-sustaining, it required the cathedral chapter to utilize his gift of 200,000 maravedís to purchase income-generating lands.[26] Once again, the Carvajal element of the family confederation aided Bishop Santa María by selling multiple pieces of property to the cathedral in return for these funds. In essence, the Santa María side of the family transferred its liquid wealth to the Carvajal side. In four separate transactions conducted between September 1451 and March 1452, the cathedral chapter used the bishop's monies to purchase lands from Gómez Gónzalez de Carvajal, Garci López de Carvajal, Sevilla López de Carvajal, and Sevilla's husband, Luis de Trejo.[27] Gómez and Garci López were brothers, and Sevilla López was their first cousin.[28] The real estate purchased with Bishop Santa María's donation consisted of the Heredad de Valsagrado and one-fifth of the Heredad de Carrascals, Gorjadas, and Las Mazas.

Although the record is unclear on the issue, it appears that before his death the bishop directed the cathedral to use his monetary donations to purchase these specific properties from the Carvajal clan. If the bishop had not made his intentions clear, the family confederation would most likely have used the more customary approach of sharing church spoils—allowing all chapter families to sell properties to the cathedral so that each could extract a portion of the bishop's recently deposited money. Instead, the Carvajal–Santa María confederation made these new devotional services in honor of the Virgin Mary possible through its collective efforts.

Sustaining Memory and Religion into the Next Century and Beyond

Thereafter the combined converso houses focused on making new investments in church institutions. Before this era, the family confederation made only modest contributions to local parish churches and had no history of gifting monies to the Cathedral of Plasencia. Individuals customarily arranged donations to local churches in their last testaments.[29] The most common gifts involved the granting of money or property to a local parish or the cathedral so that the clergy would say memorial masses for their relatives, as well as for themselves. Typically, a prosperous knight, widow, or church official would will to the cathedral 200 to 300 maravedís for a single one-time funerary service.[30] For masses that were more elaborate, often donors would gift real estate or commit family members to providing continuous yearly payments to the church.[31]

A review of the Book of Masses and additional individual manuscripts shows that before the 1440s the family confederation had not established any cathedral memorial services for its members.[32] However, from the 1440s through the 1550s, the clan's purchase of such services proliferated in this diverse and prosperous community of Old and New Christians. Ten percent of all the people (approximately 30 of 300) named in the Book of Masses were Carvajal–Santa María family members.[33] Although it represented a small portion of the several thousand inhabitants of the Diocese of Plasencia, the family confederation was a dominant presence in memorial masses said every day at the cathedral (tables 6.1, 6.2).

The bulk of individual memorial masses recorded in the Book of Masses are for the period 1440–80, exactly when the limpieza de sangre mania of Old Christians was increasing in Castile. Although many personal documents creating these memorial masses no longer exist, the Book of Masses presents a robust plan of action initiated by Bishop Santa María and followed by family churchmen, knights, noblemen, and ladies alike. For example, church leaders from every component of the family confederation were represented, including Alfonso García de Santa María, Pedro García de Illescas, Gonzalo García de Carvajal, Gonzalo Gutiérrez de la Calleja, Rodrigo de Carvajal, Ruy García de Salamanca, Juan Fernández de Betanzos (aka Cabreros), Pedro de Villalva, Diego de Carvajal, Sancho de Carvajal, and Francisco de Carvajal. One limitation of these memorialization efforts was that after the mid-fifteenth century the Santa María surname was too well known as a converso one. As a result, the family confederation abandoned the use of the surname after the 1460s so as to distance themselves from this stained Jewish ancestry; all Santa María descendants changed their surnames and adopted the Fernández, Cabreros, Villalva, Camargo, and Carvajal surnames. The

Table 6.1. Calendar of Memorial Masses Sung for the Carvajal–Santa María Family Confederation, 1400–1600

Total for Each Month	*Memorial Mass for Family Member (Days of Week)*
JANUARY *17 said in honor of a family member on 14 of 31 calendar days.	• Juan Fernández de Betanzos (aka Cabreros), canon (January 2) • Juan Ruiz de Camargo (January 9) • Gonzalo Gutiérrez de la Calleja, cantor (January 11 or 18) • Alfonso García de Santa María, archdeacon (January 12) • Sara de Carvajal (SC), mother of Cardinal Juan de Carvajal (January 16) • Rodrigo de Carvajal (RC), archdeacon (January 16 and 26) • Gonzalo García de Carvajal (GGC), archdeacon (January 16 and 26) • Diego González de Carvajal (DGC) (January 16 and 26) • Gonzalo García de Santa María (GGSM), bishop (January 24 and every Saturday) • Pedro García de Illescas, archdeacon (unspecified date) • Ruy García de Salamanca, cantor (unspecified date)
FEBRUARY *13 said in honor of a family member on 7 of 28 calendar days.	• GGSM (every Saturday) • Alonso Ruiz de Camargo (ARC) (February 10) • SC, RC, GGC, and DGC (February 16) • Diego de Carvajal, archdeacon (February 16) • RC, GGC, and DGC (February 26)
MARCH *16 said in honor of a family member on 9 of 31 calendar days.	• GGSM (every Saturday) • Pedro de Villalva, cathedral accountant (March 7) • ARC (March 10) • SC, RC, GGC, and DGC (March 16) • "Solemn processions ordered by Bishop Santa María" (March 16) • Sara de Carvajal, daughter of Archdeacon Rodrigo de Carvajal (March 17) • Sancho de Carvajal, archdeacon (March 26) • RC, GGC, and DGC (March 26)
APRIL *13 said in honor of a family member on 8 of 30 calendar days.	• GGSM (every Saturday) • ARC (April 10) • Martín de Camargo (April 11) • SC, RC, GGC, and DGC (April 16) • RC, GGC, and DGC (April 26)
MAY *14 said in honor of a family member on 9 of 31 calendar days.	• GGSM (every Saturday) • Beatriz Fernández (de Betanzos) (May 9) • ARC (May 10) • SC, RC, GGC, and DGC (May 16) • Bernardino López de Carvajal, cardinal (May 20) • RC, GGC, and DGC (May 26)

Table 6.1. Calendar of Memorial Masses Sung for the Carvajal–Santa María Family Confederation, 1400–1600 (*cont.*)

JUNE *13 said in honor of a family member on 8 of 30 calendar days.	• GGSM (every Saturday) • ARC (June 10) • SC, RC, GGC, and DGC (June 16) • Velasco Gómez de Almaraz (June 17 and five other dates in the year) • RC, GGC, and DGC (June 26)
JULY *13 said in honor of a family member on 8 of 31 calendar days.	• GGSM (every Saturday) • ARC (July 10) • SC, RC, GGC, and DGC (July 16) • RC, GGC, and DGC (July 26) • Bernardino de Carvajal, canon (July 31)
AUGUST *17 said in honor of a family member on 10 of 31 calendar days.	• Martín González de Carvajal, canon (August 6) • GGSM (every Saturday plus August 11) • Ruy García de Salamanca (August 11) • SC, RC, GGC, and DGC (August 16) • Juan Alfonso de Almaraz (August 16) • Gonzalo Gutiérrez de la Calleja (August 24) • RC, GGC, and DGC (August 26) • Pedro de Carvajal, canon (August 28)
SEPTEMBER *12 said in honor of a family member on 7 of 30 calendar days.	• GGSM (every Saturday) • Diego de Carvajal (September 4) • SC, RC, GGC, and DGC (September 16) • RC, GGC, and DGC (September 26)
OCTOBER *13 said in honor of a family member on 8 of 31 calendar days.	• GGSM (every Saturday) • Francisco de Carvajal, archdeacon of Plasencia and Béjar (October 4) • Francisco de Carvajal, archdeacon of Medellin (October 5) • SC, RC, GGC, and DGC (October 16) • RC, GGC, and DGC (October 26)
NOVEMBER *12 said in honor of a family member on 7 of 30 calendar days.	• GGSM (every Saturday) • Hernando de Villalva (November 10) • SC, RC, GGC, and DGC (November 16) • RC, GGC, and DGC (November 26)
DECEMBER *13 said in honor of a family member on 7 of 31 calendar days.	• GGSM (every Saturday) • SC, RC, GGC, and DGC (December 16) • RC, GGC, and DGC (December 26) • Juan Alonso de Almaraz (unspecified date)

Source: ACP, *Calendario o libro de aniversarios de la Santa Iglesia placentina.*

Table 6.2. Selection of Family Confederation Donations for Memorial Masses in the Cathedral of Plasencia, 1440s–1570s

Year/Decade	Family Member	Type of Memorial and Donation
1448	Gonzalo Gutiérrez de la Calleja, cantor	• Procession and 1 annual requiem mass. • Donation: 50 maravedís
1460s	Sara de Carvajal (mother of Cardinal Juan de Carvajal)	• 12 annual masses, 12 annual vigil masses, and 12 annual requiem masses • Donation: 100 maravedís and additional monies given to purchase six parts of the Heredad de Almendral
1468	Ruy García de Salamanca, cantor	• Procession and one annual requiem mass and all responses in honor of Virgin Mary • Donation: properties located at Guaco, 600 maravedís, three houses on Calle de Trujillo, and an additional 200 maravedís to be paid annually
1474	Francisco de Carvajal, archdeacon	• 1 annual vigil mass • Donation: 1,200 maravedís generated from the Dehesa de las Cabezas property and an additional 40,000 maravedís
1477	Sara de Carvajal (daughter of archdeacon Rodrigo de Carvajal)	• 1 annual mass and 1 annual vigil mass
1478	Sara de Carvajal and Juan de Tamayo (parents of Cardinal Juan de Carvajal and Sancha de Carvajal) and Diego Gónzalez de Carvajal y Vargas and Sevilla López de Villalobos (grandparents of Juan and Sancha)	• 1 annual mass • Donation: 1 property at the periphery of the city of Plasencia
1478	Juan Ruiz de Camargo	• 1 annual mass and 1 annual vigil mass • Donation: 200 maravedís and 6,000 maravedís generated from the Heredad de los Arenalejos
1479	Pedro de Carvajal, archdeacon of Cáceres (son of regidor Ruy Díaz de Buezo)	• 1 annual mass and 1 annual vigil mass • Donation: 300 maravedís of annual income from the Heredad de Picarroso

Table 6.2. Selection of Family Confederation Donations for Memorial Masses in the Cathedral of Plasencia, 1440s–1570s (*cont.*)

Year/Decade	Family Member	Type of Memorial and Donation
1470s	Rodrigo de Carvajal, archdeacon of Plasencia and Béjar; Gonzalo García de Carvajal, former archdeacon of Plasencia and Béjar; and Diego González de Carvajal.	• 24 annual masses for each family member • Donation: 1,500 maravedís and one-eighth part of the Heredad de Cabeza Pardas
1490s	Sancho de Carvajal, archdeacon of Plasencia	• 6 annual masses and 6 annual vigil masses • Donation: 3,000 maravedís
1508	Diego de Carvajal, archdeacon of Coria (son of Dr. García López de Carvajal)	• 1 annual mass and 1 annual vigil mass • Donation: houses on Calle de Santa María
1510s–1520s	Francisco de Carvajal, archdeacon of Medellín	• 1 annual mass and 1 annual vigil mass • Donation: 1,500 maravedís
1520s	Bernardino López de Carvajal, cardinal and bishop of Plasencia	• 1 annual vigil mass • Donation: 1,000 maravedís of annual income from the Dehesa de las Cabezas property
1546	Dr. Bernardino de Carvajal, canon	• 1 annual mass and 1 annual vigil mass • Donation: 1,200 maravedís of annual income from a house and corral on Calle de Santa Maria
1550s	Francisco de Carvajal, archdeacon of Plasencia and Béjar	• 1 annual mass and 1 annual vigil mass • Donation: 1,200 maravedis of annual income from the Dehesa de las Cabezas property
1578	Martín González de Carvajal, canon	• Chapel in new cathedral • Donation: Unavailable

Source: ACP, *Calendario o libro de aniversarios de la Santa Iglesia placentina.*

most prominent and most commonly used was the highly recognizable Old Christian Carvajal surname. Noblemen and family knights such as Juan Ruiz de Camargo, Martín de Camargo, Velasco Gómez de Almaraz, Juan Alfonso de Almaraz, and Hernando de Villalva were also represented in this memorial mass practice, as well as noblewomen like Sara de Carvajal and Beatriz Fernández de Betanzos.

Another aspect of these memorialization efforts was the manner in which they ritualized the family confederation's spatial and physical connection to the cathedral. For example, Chantre Gonzalo Gutiérrez de la Calleja's 1448 donation required the family's cathedral dignitaries (archdeacons, canons, prebendaries, etc.) to gather at the cathedral in black silk capes and walk in procession to the choir where Gonzalo Gutiérrez was buried. Over his grave they would sing responsorial psalms for his soul and then proceed to the altar mayor for a requiem mass. In 1468, Cantor Ruy García de Salamanca initiated a similar memorial effort that began with church dignitaries, again in black silk capes, gathering in the vicinity of the cathedral's water fountain bearing the heraldic family and ecclesiastical crest of Cardinal Juan de Carvajal. (The creation of this fountain will be discussed shortly.) From this location, the churchmen would walk in procession into the cathedral and sing a requiem mass in honor of the Virgin Mary, presumably at the altar mayor. Finally, they completed their memorial with chanted prayers for "the soul of our lord bishop, Gonzalo García de Santa María."[34]

The collective result of this intensive plan of action was a vivid, robust, and highly public demonstration of Christian piety that dominated the Cathedral of Plasencia's schedule of masses. First, parishioners would hear a mass for a Carvajal–Santa María family member on every Saturday and the sixteenth and twenty-sixth of each calendar month. Saturdays would always hold special significance as well because of Bishop Santa María's emphasis on devotion to the Virgin Mary. Second, in any given month of the year, parishioners would hear twelve to seventeen masses said on behalf of the family. This translated into such a busy mass schedule that on every third day in the cathedral the names of deceased family confederation members were publicly remembered as good Christians.

Although the Santa María surname would ultimately fall out of favor because of blood purity concerns, the church calendar remained a demonstration of the family confederation's Christian worthiness well into the mid-sixteenth century. Mapping the memorial days onto the monthly calendar for the year 1550, it is evident that masses in memory of those with Old Christian surnames (every name except Santa María) filled almost every week of the year. Interestingly, the severest winter month, January, and summer month, August, offered a bonanza of untimely deaths and Christian opportunity.

No other clan in Plasencia, either in the past or in the future, would make such extensive and elaborate plans for preserving the memory of their families. For almost two centuries, as detailed in the Book of Masses, the family confederation monopolized the cathedral's schedule of funerary masses. In this manner, the family fully harnessed the church's religious authority and rituals to memorialize the religious devotion of its lineage.

Women's Special Religious Efforts

Among the most prominent of the family confederation's religious donors were Sevilla López de Carvajal and Sancha de Carvajal. Like other Castilian women during this era, such as those in the nearby city of Ávila, Sevilla and Sancha chose to direct substantial amounts of their personal wealth to religious memorials, endowments, and charity.[35] Their personal initiatives, which their surviving family members attended to after their deaths, indicate that this converso clan highly valued striking displays of religiosity. It further demonstrates one of the ways women exercised social power in the Castilian world.

In 1467, Sevilla López conceived of the most ambitious of the family confederation's religious projects when she provided in her last testament for the founding of the Church and Convent of Saint Clare.[36] The large scope of her endeavor was the first of its kind for any family member in the greater diocese or in Extremadura. Sevilla was the daughter of Diego Rodríguez de Carvajal and the wife of Alonso Ruiz de Camargo and thus a part of the Carvajal–Santa María union of families.[37] Her cousins, among others, included Cardinal Juan de Carvajal and the royal adviser, Garci López de Carvajal.[38] By the 1460s, Sevilla and her cousins had intermarried with the Trejo, Buezo, Camargo, and Villalva clans.[39] The Carvajal family's relationship to the Villalva is particularly intriguing because the Villalva clan was also kin of Bishop Santa María (see ch. 2).[40]

Sevilla's will provided sufficient funds to support twelve to fifteen nuns and a resident abbess, as well as two dedicated chaplains.[41] To house the "Poor Clares," she ordered the construction of a new convent, with its own church, on the grounds of her residence on Calle del Rey. However, Sevilla's spouse, Alonso, delayed construction of the convent until 1474 and chose to site it closer to the Cathedral of Plasencia on Calle de Santa María, which the city subsequently renamed Calle de las Claras, and one block from both Cardinal Carvajal's new cathedral Grammar School and the homes owned by Garci López de Carvajal.[42] During the 1470s, this section of the city increasingly became a family stronghold.

In her will, Sevilla placed great emphasis on the proper provisioning of the convent and thus revealed her appreciation of the details of worship and a cloistered life. Among the most noteworthy gifts that she gave to the nuns were those directly tied to the observance of daily mass.[43] First, she specified that the nuns should celebrate Holy Communion with her gifts of a silver chalice, a paten, and two wine ampoules. To adorn the convent's church altar, she gave the sisters two silver candleholders and two silk altar cloths. To support the chaplains' and nuns' proper performance of mass, Sevilla paid for "the necessary books for the altar and choir."[44] Last, wishing to attire her nuns suitably, she provided instructions to give each of them "a chasuble, two dalmatics, and a black silk cloak (similar to those used by the dignitaries in the cathedral)."[45]

To endow the convent with sufficient operational funds, Sevilla granted a mixture of monies and agricultural lands and resources, as well as other real estate. The most substantial of these provisions included an annual income of 15,000 maravedís from her collection of inherited properties as well as from two mills. By guaranteeing a continuous income for the convent, Sevilla ensured that the institution could support itself.

For all of these gifts, Sevilla López requested and expected the Convent of Saint Clare to memorialize her piety in a meaningful manner. After the convent was constructed, she instructed that her grave be moved from the Church of Saint Martin to the convent's church and reinterred in a "well-made sepulcher of stone and alabaster."[46] At her new grave, near the convent's church altar, she mandated the following:

> The chaplain is obligated to sing four [memorial] masses—on Sunday, Wednesday, Friday, and Saturday—every week for me. Also, on every day he sings a regular mass he is to say the responsorial psalms in front of my grave. He is to do this in a clear voice and in a manner such that the nuns in the choir can hear them as well.[47]

In this manner, Sevilla guaranteed that she would remain a constant presence in every mass said at the convent. Mirroring the memorial events occurring inside the convent, she similarly communicated her family's devotion in the world outside the cloister. Specifically, her family would later integrate the Carvajal and Camargo coats of arms into the front facade of the Convent of Saint Clare (fig. 6.1).[48] Within the convent, the physical presence of Sevilla was a constant, as a gold-leaf Carvajal heraldic shield was integrated into wood ceiling beams and other locations (fig. 6.2).

Before the Carvajal and Camargo families could secure a papal bull for the convent's foundation, they first had to confront their local rivals, the Estúñiga, who in 1472 were in the process of establishing a competing religious institution, the Convent of Ildefonso.[49] In his work, *El convento placentino de San Ildefonso*, Domingo Sánchez Loro discusses how the New Nobles Álvaro de Estúñiga and Leonor Pimentel, the count and countess of Plasencia and Béjar, actively labored "in bad faith" to take possession of Sevilla López's estate so that her convent would not be built or completed.[50] During the 1470s, the Estúñiga clan attempted to halt her project by convincing Alonso Ruiz de Camargo's second wife, Beatriz de Monroy, to intervene. As Beatriz and Leonor shared an "intimate friendship," Beatriz was amenable to preventing the wishes of her husband's first wife from coming to fruition.[51] Although Beatriz could not convince Alonso to abandon his promise to create the convent, she was able to "distort" the foundation of the Convent of Saint Clare.[52] Thus, in their battle of Christian identities, these two

FIGURE 6.1. Carvajal-Camargo family heraldry on the facade of the Convent of Saint Clare. Carvajal coat of arms (left) and Camargo coat of arms (right). Photo by author.

FIGURE 6.2. Convent of Saint Clare's third-floor ceiling beams with Carvajal heraldry. Photo by author.

converso families, the Estúñiga and the Carvajal–Santa María, pursued every path to make their Christian piety more ostentatious than the other.

In 1479, Beatriz secured her husband's agreement to accept a papal bull that founded the Convent of Saint Clare but with the provision that it would house, in the short term, the nuns of the Estúñiga Convent of Ildefonso, who were waiting for their convent quarters to be constructed.[53] By temporarily housing the Ildefonso nuns in the Convent of Saint Clare, the Estúñiga clan hoped to use them as a tool to incorporate Sevilla's convent into the Convent of Ildefonso.[54] However, the Estúñiga family's plan did not come to fruition. Rather, when the Ildefonso nuns' permanent convent was completed, they refused to abandon the Convent of Saint Clare.[55] In 1484, after the Estúñiga clan's efforts to subvert the Carvajal–Santa María family confederation's wishes had collapsed, Pope Innocent VIII approved the constitution of the Convent of Saint Clare and confirmed its first abbess.[56] Thus, the foundation of the convent not only contributed to public perceptions of the family confederation's piety but also was another facet of the multilayered religious and political rivalry between the conversos in Plasencia.

By the late 1480s, the competition between the New Noble Estúñiga and the converso Carvajal–Santa María would enter its final phase. In 1488, two significant events occurred. First, after four decades of seigniorial control by the Estúñiga clan, the family confederation finally defeated it politically when the clan's knights restored the city of Plasencia to direct royal rule. Second, the Catholic monarchs overtly recognized the Carvajal family for its continuing royal service by patronizing the clan's religious institutions. Specifically, when King Ferdinand traveled through Plasencia that year, he visited the nuns of the Convent of Saint Clare and presented them with a gift of 17,000 maravedís.[57] In this manner, the family confederation ensured the Carvajal-surnamed lineage could repeatedly claim its Old Christian heritage in spite of hidden Jewish bloodlines.

A cousin of Sevilla López de Carvajal followed her actions with additional religious endowments. Sancha de Carvajal directed her efforts to advancing the family's pious religious persona. Sancha, an unmarried sibling of Cardinal Juan de Carvajal, demonstrated a keen interest in the church, which was manifested through the foundation of multiple memorial masses, the construction of a church chapel, and gifts for the less fortunate. While Sancha did not become a nun or work in the church like her brothers, Juan and Archdeacon Rodrigo de Carvajal, she gave a sizable portion of her wealth to the church. Her testament, taken on Christmas Eve of 1478, provides a strong sense of her religiosity and her faithful commitment to preserving the memory of the family at the Church of Saint Martin.[58] While Sancha lived most of her adult life in Bonilla de la Sierra, her father's ancestral city, she maintained property and family connections in her mother's birth city of Plasencia.

Just as her converso relatives Pablo de Santa María, Gonzalo de Santa María, and Ruy García de Salamanca had done many years before her, Sancha viewed the Virgin

Mary as her personal redeemer. She expressed this profound belief in the Virgin in her last testament.

> In the name of God. Amen. . . . I Doña Sancha de Carvajal . . . understand that death naturally calls upon all of us and none of us can escape it. I firmly and reverently believe in the Holy Trinity that is God the Father, God the Son, and God the Holy Spirit and that the three are one. That there is only one true God who lives and reigns forever. I will that this, my testament, is taken of my own free volition and in the service of God. And I have as my advocate and lady on the celestial court, the very blessed virgin, Holy Mary.[59]

Sancha's devotion to Christ's mother was an innovation for the women of the family confederation. In their wills, Sevilla López de Carvajal and Catalina González de Carvajal called on the Holy Trinity to intercede on their behalf when they died.[60] Like her brother, Cardinal Juan de Carvajal, Sancha deliberately and forcefully claimed Mary as her idealized vision of piety.[61]

To sanctify her life and death, Sancha set out specific memorial requirements that spoke to her detailed-oriented character, as well as her knowledge and appreciation of religious rituals. She instructed the church to place her remains in a specific location in the Church of Saint Martin. She ordered the churchmen to inter her "inside of its choir on the right-hand side and inside of one of the lead vessels, the better of all the vessels, which are in the wall."[62] Likewise, she had an intimate understanding of what types of local masses the clergy said for deceased monks and nuns. Perceiving herself worthy of such services, Sancha requested the chaplains to sing a novena for her on her death. With this request came additional yet modest gifts for locally cloistered nuns and monks. She bequeathed each of them five maravedís.

Like most of the members of her converso house, Sancha wished the local clergy to sing a trinitary of masses (*trinitario*) for her soul.[63] Typical of her intense interest in religious ritual, she asked that the church sing four, not just the traditional one trinitary, in her memory.[64] Thus Sancha asked the community to remember her as a devout sister of the church and to perform those traditional funerary services normally reserved for wealthy noble families. Finally, and different from other family wills that typically granted funds for a few meals for the poor, Sancha provided the local Hospital de Santa María with a greater abundance of gifts. To ensure that the hospital could more adequately care for the poor, she gave useful items such as household furniture, livestock, forty-eight chickens, and twenty-five casks of wheat.[65]

Sancha's most important gifts were those she formulated to preserve not only her memory but also that of her family. These bequests included the endowment of recurring memorial services as well as a family chapel structure that future generations would patronize for years to come. Throughout Western Europe during the fifteenth century, it was common for noble and wealthy families to establish family chapels, which could entail either constructing a physical chapel within a church or simply having a daily mass said there by a dedicated clergy member.[66] It was even more important for conversos like Sancha to do so, given the intensity of the animosity directed at New Christians during this era in Spain. To this end of creating a physical structure, her will stated:

> Likewise, I establish . . . a chapel and daily memorial mass in the said Church of Saint Martin for which I donate five vineyards, an irrigated plain, the property of Heredad de Arenabillo, the Heredad de San Ximénez near Congosto bridge, and my houses of Pedrahita and all that it contains. Also, Benito Martín, my servant, is requested to bring to these memorial masses the fruits that I have donated for the church . . . and place them next to my sepulcher in the said church. Also, I will that Álvaro de Carvajal, my nephew, and those persons who come after him assume the responsibility of maintaining the chapel and memorial services. . . . [Last,] to the Church of Saint Martin, I will twelve silver marks for church works . . . and an additional 36,000 maravedís for the chapel and memorial services.[67]

With this substantial donation, Sancha purchased her perpetual sanctity and that of the family confederation. With the appointment of Álvaro, her nephew and the first patron of the chapel, Sancha de Carvajal also ensured that the church would receive a continuous stream of donations well into the future. In the latter part of her will, she supplemented her donation to the local clergy in Bonilla de la Sierra with additional bequests pertaining to her deceased parents. Here she instructed, "And I give my inherited property of Navalmaillo, which is in Pedrahita, to the Friars of Santo Domingo de Pedrahita . . . for my soul and the souls of my parents."[68]

At the Cathedral of Plasencia, she established services to honor the memory of her parents, Sara de Carvajal and Juan de Tamayo, and her grandparents, Diego González de Carvajal y Vargas and Sevilla López de Villalobos.

> And I will, from my inherited properties that I own at the entrance into the City of Plasencia, a memorial service for the sanctification of Holy Mary. That a mass and responsorial be said for her every day for my soul and for my parents and grandparents.[69]

Taken together, both Sevilla López de Carvajal's endowment of the Convent of Saint Clare and Sancha de Carvajal's initiation of memorial masses and chapel foundations, demonstrate that individual women within the family confederation led key efforts to promote a public Old Christian image of the family that emphasized generosity and religious devotion. Furthermore, their actions fit into a grander, more ambitious family memorial project that emanated from Sancha's brother, Juan de Carvajal.

THE CULMINATION OF FAMILY MEMORY: INVENTING CARDINAL JUAN DE CARVAJAL

Although Cardinal and Bishop Juan de Carvajal was initially shaped by a violent past and was inadequately educated, the converso Carvajal–Santa María family confederation found in him a proactive leader willing to become their idealized Christian vision. As discussed in chapter 5, Juan had spent almost his entire religious career outside the Diocese of Plasencia and when he replaced Gonzalo García de Santa María as the cathedral's new bishop in 1446, instead of attempting to transform the Carvajal–Santa María family confederation, he instead maintained its long-standing partnership. Even if the once ascendant Santa María side of the clan could not overcome discriminatory blood purity laws and increasingly harsh attitudes toward New Christians, the Carvajal lineage could propel and save the extended family with extravagant Christian works.

As the years passed, and certainly by the late 1460s, Cardinal Carvajal and the family members dominating the Cathedral of Plasencia began to plan for the end of his term as bishop. The uncertainty generated by who would replace him, which might have had negative religious and political consequences for the family's control of the cathedral, prompted the clans to develop a concerted plan to promote the image of the Carvajal clan as a noble, devout, and learned Old Christian family. Their plan entailed blending the church's religious practices with an idealized memory of the family. They would utilize religious rituals, church architecture, sacred objects, regional public works projects, and church improvements to lionize Juan de Carvajal.

It appears Juan only contributed a small portion of his personal funds to these initiatives.[70] A potential funding source for these projects may have been the cathedral's collection of diezmos, which the cathedral chapter did not account for in its financial records during the 1460s and 1470s.[71] The family confederation's rationale for this plan was straightforward: a well-respected and admired Carvajal family would represent its best opportunity to maintain control of the cathedral's leadership and to project its unquestionable Christian identity. It would appear this initiative was partially successful given that the family confederation continued to dominate the cathedral chapter deep into the sixteenth century, in spite of its loss of the bishop's position from the 1470s until the 1520s.

Blending Religious Practices with the Family Legacy

In the last years of Cardinal Juan de Carvajal's role as bishop of Plasencia, he and the cathedral chapter went to great lengths to establish new daily religious practices that would communicate to future generations the honor and religious fidelity of the family confederation. Their efforts fit neatly into a sustained program of religious contributions and church endowments, which began in 1395 when Gonzalo Lorenzo de Espadero, the Carvajal clan's ancestor, founded memorial masses for Don Vidal in Cáceres.[72] However, as discussed earlier, the size of the family's religious endowments

FIGURE 6.3. Altar mayor of the Old Cathedral of Plasencia. Photo by author.

did not substantially increase until the 1460s and 1470s, as demonstrated by the donations of Sevilla López and Sancha de Carvajal.

All of these devotional initiatives—memorial services, the construction of a chapel, the establishment of the Convent of Saint Clare, and the cardinal's new religious services—were based on a belief that families could enhance their social position and validate their nobility through religious devotion and contributions.[73] Key to bolstering family honor was the inauguration in the Cathedral of Plasencia of new masses that overtly blended religious practice and devotion with the clan's lineage.

The first of these new family initiatives occurred in October 1468, when the cathedral chapter assembled in the Chapel of Saint Paul to institute one of Cardinal Carvajal's proposals.[74] Álvaro de Carvajal, the nominal head of the chapter, along with Alfonso Fernández de Cabreros (a Santa María clansman) and other members of the chapter, enacted a statute that committed the clergy to the singing of a trinity of masses on a daily basis. Each morning the chaplain, deacons, and subdeacons would first chant a daily mass for the forgiveness of sins (*misa del perdón*), with its responsorial psalms, over the tomb of the cardinal's mother, Sara de Carvajal, which was located at the main altar. Alongside Sara's grave, but not recorded in these documents, was that of Bishop Santa María. Thus even in death the Carvajal and Santa María remained united as one family (fig. 6.3).

The officiates would celebrate a second regular mass at this same altar, which had an altar screen (*retablo*) that bore the Carvajal coat of arms (fig. 6.4).[75] The clergy's

FIGURE 6.4. Retablo mayor in the Old Cathedral of Plasencia, Virgin of the Tabernacle. Photo by author.

morning duties concluded after they walked from the main altar and through the cathedral's central aisle (adorned with Carvajal emblems on its pillars) and celebrated a third mass in the Chapel of the Doctors (Capilla de los Doctores).[76] The third service most likely served as tribute to and thanksgiving for scholarly churchmen who had made meaningful contributions to the cathedral, such as the cardinal's deceased first cousin, Garci López de Carvajal. Both men shared a great admiration of each other. In his later years, Garci López expressed his high regard for his cousin in a ten-line couplet that he sent to the cathedral:

> You, Don Juan de Carvajal,
> of grand virtue and knowledge,
> we saw you become cardinal,
> carrying the title of Angel,
> and prelate of Plasencia,
> through this door you arrived,
> and when the Turks came,
> to this royal bridge you headed,
> because you believed by crossing it,
> with heaven you would be rewarded.[77]

The poem communicated key character traits that the family confederation wished to preserve, namely, the cardinal's learnedness, his position as a prince within the church, his identity as a Plasencia Carvajal, and his intense Christian faith that propelled his crusading sermons in Western Europe.

Unlike traditional memorials and other masses, the chapter placed such a high priority on the cardinal's new religious services that it established considerable penalties if the clergy did not regularly attend to them. If the chaplain failed to conduct a mass for the cardinal's mother, the cathedral chapter would fine him 20 maravedís.[78] The deacons and subdeacons similarly faced a penalty of 4 maravedís and 3 maravedís, respectively, if they neglected to provide the services. Failure to officiate the second mass at the main altar also carried the penalty of fines.

The Carvajal–Santa María-dominated cathedral chapter chose to fund the three services primarily with church resources and not the cardinal's personal wealth. Although the cardinal was the impetus for these initiatives, and his deceased mother a primary beneficiary of the repentance masses, the cathedral chapter did not expect its ecclesiastical leader to shoulder the entire cost. Rather, Dean Álvaro de Carvajal, the cardinal's first cousin, and Chantre Ruy García de Salamanca, another Santa María family member, secured the approval of the chapter to share the expenses with their bishop.[79] Chapter officials contributed 4,000 maravedís from their individual church budgets, as well as an additional 3,000 maravedís from church funds usually reserved for the direct "works of the church."[80] Cardinal Juan de Carvajal matched these funds with 1,000 maravedís in personal monies. The cathedral chapter's decision to bear over 87 percent of the costs highlights the extent to which the family confederation could marshal church resources for the projection of its pious Christian identity.

The masses' emphasis on the Carvajal family positioned it as a primary community intermediary with the Christian God. The focus on Sara de Carvajal, a female intercessor, appears to be closely related to the Santa María clan's prior attention to another woman—the Virgin Mary. The daily repentance mass presented Sara not only as an honorable woman worthy of the cathedral's intercession, but as a communal representative to God for all Christians seeking atonement and forgiveness for their sins. As penance and repentance were key elements of the Christian faith, on any given day some parishioners likely would need to undertake religious acts for the forgiveness of their sins. While confession, fasting, prostrations, donations to the church, and other acts could be performed as acts of contrition, one of the more favorable options was to attend mass, especially those in which the psalms were repeated.[81] The daily morning misa del perdón said for Sara de Carvajal served two functions in this respect: it provided a communal avenue for penitential requirements, and it presented the Carvajal family as a facilitator of repentance.

Both the mass and the service conducted in the Chapel of the Doctors reaffirmed the bonds between Plasencia's living and deceased. During the later Middle Ages, Christians conceived of themselves as a community of the living and the dead who were brought together through the service of the mass.[82] Therefore, it seems plausible that the Carvajal clan intended to reinforce the notion that both the living family members (Archdeacon Rodrigo de Carvajal and Ruy García de Salamanca) and the deceased (Sara de Carvajal, Garci López, Bishop Santa María, and Gonzalo Gutiérrez de la Calleja) were actively leading their respective congregations during devotional services.

In the year after these services began, other community members such as the councilman Gómez de Soria perceived the repentance mass as a new avenue to remember deceased loved ones.[83] Rather than establish a separate memorial mass for his spouse, as was the customary practice for wealthier individuals, Gómez donated 500 maravedís to the cathedral to have his deceased wife's soul spoken for each morning. Possibly he viewed this option as more prestigious because of its connection to the cardinal's three-mass initiative. Likewise, it offered a daily Mass for his wife, as opposed to a single one-time memorial service, which typically cost 200 to 300 maravedís.[84]

Gómez's action suggests that other Placentino families wished to participate in, and possibly emulate, the converso family's public display of piety. In effect, the family confederation had successfully convinced the public that the Carvajal family was indeed Old Christian, not converso. From the family confederation's perspective, this donation from Gómez was ideal because the chapter had already created an endowment for the cardinal's ceremonies, and thus Gómez's bequest created another opportunity for the chapter to reap new financial benefits and to project its Christian identity. Rather than save Gómez's contribution for other church works, the chapter awarded it to its youngest servants and its future leaders—the thirteen boys and young men in the choir.[85] Among the beneficiaries of this reward was yet another generation of family members,[86] including Archdeacon Pedro de Carvajal's son, Gómez de Carvajal, who would join the chapter in 1469 as a canon, and Alfonso Fernández de Cabreros.[87]

As had become the religious custom of the Carvajal–Santa María family confederation, these conversos once again expanded the prayers said on behalf of the Virgin. At the direction of Cardinal Carvajal, in the late 1460s, the cathedral chapter enacted a governing statute that required the chaplains and choir to chant the "Hail, Holy Queen" (Salve Regina) prayer every day "just before nightfall" in the cathedral.[88] During the later Middle Ages, devotion to Mary was particularly popular as she was viewed as both "model and guide" to women.[89] By the opening of the sixteenth century, the singing of the Salve Regina became fashionable across Europe. Often, local parishioners supported these services with church endowments, as was the case in the Church of Saint Lorenz in Nuremberg.[90] In Plasencia, Cardinal Carvajal assumed the role of primary benefactor for the Salve Regina. Again, this act, like the other new religious services, bolstered the community's perception of Cardinal Carvajal as a patron of the church, especially its Holy Mother.

When chanting the Salve Regina, the cathedral's chaplains and choir would sing the verses while kneeling at the main altar. An English translation of the Latin prayer reads:

Hail Holy Queen, Mother of mercy, our life, our sweetness, and our hope! To you do we cry, poor banished children of Eve! To you do we send up our sighs, mourning and weeping in this vale of tears. Turn then, most gracious advocate, your eyes of mercy toward us; and, after this our exile, show us the blessed fruit of your womb, Jesus![91]

Within this plea for help and mercy, the plight of this converso family confederation was fully recognizable. As New Christians they were being forced into a form of spiritual exile thrust upon them by Old Christians. Only through Mary, "the gracious advocate," could they hope to find spiritual salvation.

Projecting Piety through Material Culture

Cardinal Carvajal also commissioned new architectural and altar improvements in the Cathedral of Plasencia. Among the more prominent efforts implemented by the cardinal and the cathedral was the commissioning of a modified *retablo mayor* (main altarpiece).[92] It should be noted that the early twentieth-century historian and churchman José Benavides Checa explained that this specific main altarpiece occupied the main chapel since at least the sixteenth century. However, in the early 1500s, as a new Cathedral of Plasencia was being constructed, several modifications were made to the exist-

FIGURE 6.5. Virgin of the Tabernacle. This portrait of Mary with Christ is heavily damaged as it was carried in outdoor processions in the sixteenth through eighteenth centuries. However, most of the damage to the painting is the result of heavy-handed cleaning with hot water and soap in 1892, which destroyed the portrait's finish, removed much of its detail, and may have required repair. Source: Benavides, *Prelados placentinos.* Photo by author.

ing cathedral's structure and decorative elements.[93] With the addition of Cardinal Carvajal's retablo mayor, the family members would position themselves at the cathedral's spiritual center. Like the cardinal's Salve Regina prayers, this two-panel gilded altarpiece concentrated the parishioners' attention on a unique depiction of Mary with Christ. The retablo's upper panel frames a traditional depiction of the Virgin of the Tabernacle (Virgen del Sagrario), which shows a childlike Christ figure seated on the lap of the primary subject of the painting, the Virgin Mary (fig. 6.5) The retablo's lower panel integrates a baldachin, or domelike four-column canopy, over a praying female statue (fig. 6.6).[94]

It seems likely that Cardinal Carvajal ordered the alteration of the cathedral's existing altarpiece, as this screen appears to be a mixture of late Romanesque and Gothic elements. A comparison with contemporary fifteenth-century altarpieces in Western Europe indicates that Plasencia's altarpiece has several decorative and motif commonalities.[95]

Whereas the lower panel of the Plasencia retablo indicates the period in which the altarpiece was created, the upper panel communicates information about its later patrons. The upper panel of the retablo, the portrait of Mary with the Christ child, is particularly revealing as its composition appears attuned to the Carvajal–Santa María family confederation's interest in the Virgin Mary. In this depiction of the Virgin of the

FIGURE 6.6. Lower panel with baldachin and praying statue. Photo by author.

Tabernacle, Mary wears a traditional gold-trimmed blue cloak over a scarlet dress.[96] This image of Mary reveals her divine majesty, which is signified by the presence of a heavenly angel and twelve stars that form a halo around her head. The latter elements perhaps represent the twelve apostles. This use of numerical symbolism, found also in Petrus Christus's *Virgin of the Dry Tree* (ca. 1465), was common in religious art.[97] For example, in the latter, Mary and the Christ child are encompassed by fifteen letter *A*'s hanging from dry tree branches.[98] The gilded letters signify "the first letter of the Ave María; their number, fifteen, has been related to the Mysteries of the Rosary."[99]

Reinforcing the prominent position of the Placentino Virgin of the Tabernacle was the painter's decision to place the divine orb, which represents the power and authority of Christ, in her right hand, while he positioned the Virgin's left arm gently around the Christ child.[100] This powerful symbolism communicates not only the interceding authority of Mary, but her physical ability to encompass God the Father's divine will, as well as his instrument, Christ. Typically, in other paintings depicting Mary and the Christ child during this period, if an orb is present, it is Christ who is holding it.[101] Thus the Mary depicted in Plasencia's altarpiece appears to be acting as the primary intermediary between the parish and the Christian God, which was a motif the Santa María and Carvajal families continuously reinforced in local church affairs through memorial masses, especially on Saturdays.

In addition to the symbolism of the orb, perhaps the most fascinating element of the Virgin of the Tabernacle is the direction of Mary's and the Christ child's gaze: both are looking down and to the left into the main altar space. Although there is substantial variation in fourteenth- and fifteenth-century illustrations of Mary and the Christ child, often one is gazing upon or at the other. These types of depictions occur in Della Francesca's *Polyptych of St. Anthony*, da Negroponte's *Madonna and Child Enthroned with Angels*, Antonio Vivarini and Giovanni D'Alemagna's *Triptych of Madonna Enthroned*, and Rogier Van Der Weyden's *The Virgin and Child Enthroned* (ca. 1433).[102] In contrast to these works, Plasencia's Virgin and Christ child gaze downward at the altar floor, which was the location of the grave of the cardinal's mother, Sara de Carvajal.[103] This evidence further suggests that this panel of the retablo mayor engaged in a direct and unique relationship with its surroundings and focused the community's eyes, once again, on the Carvajal and Santa María families.

The religious significance of the Virgin Mary and Christ looking out of the portrait and to the floor where Sara de Carvajal and Bishop Gonzalo García de Santa María are buried in a face-up position is astonishing because of the intense relationship it communicated between the parties. With mercy and comfort, the divine personages looked after the souls of these conversos, and they, in return, gazed upward toward them. Both woman and man were perfectly balanced above and below. The family confederation had constructed the perfect familial devotion to Christianity.

In concert with the portrait's relationship with Sara de Carvajal, another decorative element that conveyed Cardinal Carvajal's patronage of and constant presence in the cathedral was the prominent positioning of his ecclesiastical heraldry at the top of the main altarpiece.[104] The cardinal's heraldry incorporated a *galero* (wide-brimmed, red pilgrim's hat with twelve tassels) placed over the Carvajal family coat of arms (a sable bend on a gold shield).[105] (A contemporary fifteenth-century version of this heraldry is shown in fig. 6.8b later in this chapter.) During the late 1490s, when the family confederation lost its dominance in the cathedral, New Noble and converso Bishop Gutierre de Toledo had the Carvajal emblem removed from the retablo, "without any good explanation, other than it pleased him to do so."[106] In this manner, converso families like the de Toledo, Carvajal, and Estúñiga competed with each other when they attempted to claim religious structures and material culture for their own family benefit.

Although the Carvajal coat of arms was removed from the retablo mayor, other altarpieces in the Cathedral of Plasencia display how the heraldry of other patrons were incorporated into chapel altarpieces. For example, at the top of the retablo mayor in the new cathedral is Bishop Pedro González de Acevedo's ecclesiastical heraldry, a green galero over a shield with a holly tree.[107] The bishop had his family's emblems integrated into the altarpiece upon its completion in the 1590s in return for a donation of 20,300 ducats.[108] Similar family heraldry for the Herrera and Almaraz clans is incorporated into the Retablo de la Crucifijo in the old cathedral.

Bishop Álvarez de Toledo's decision to remove the Carvajal heraldic device was likely the result of the tensions that existed between his office and the cathedral chapter, which remained a locus of the family confederation's ecclesiastical power.[109] In the 1490s, Bishop Gutierre de Toledo began efforts to immortalize his own family, the powerful and wealthy counts of Alba, by beginning the construction of a new cathedral that was attached to the old structure.[110] Put simply, the old Cathedral of Plasencia, with its extensive Carvajal heraldry, was competition that he would do well to minimize. During this period, the cathedral chapter and the bishop were also at odds over his demands that the cathedral sell him its properties and rights in the village of Jaraicejo. This demand was a partly successful strong-arm attempt to secure new lands and properties for his family. It harkened back to the bitter regional war of 1431 between the Cathedral of Plasencia and the Álvarez de Toledo family. On this matter, the chapter bitterly complained:

> Bishop de Toledo has caused great harm to and acted against the will of the cathedral chapter when he took possession of the diocese's fortress and *señorio* of [Jaraicejo]. . . . We do not give it freely. Nor do we grant half of the *señorio*, its property, and its fruits as the donator [Gutierre de Toledo] demands. [However,] now we authorize the Dean to conclude this agreement with the bishop.[111]

Before Bishop de Toledo removed the Carvajal clan's coat of arms from the retablo mayor, the Carvajal–Santa María family confederation added other architectural and structural elements to the cathedral that conveyed their honor and status. While the replacement of the church's floor with new stone slabs or paving (*losado*) was a functional improvement, the addition of new stone pillars with the Carvajal shield was a point of family pride.[112] However, like the altar screen, Bishop de Toledo removed the family's heraldry from the stone pillars during his administration of the diocese. Even though the family confederation was successful in securing royal support for the restoration of its heraldry on the pillars, the bishop had the stones destroyed before the clan could replace them.[113] Prior to its destruction, it is likely that the Carvajal and Santa María heraldry was extensively incorporated into the old cathedral's pillars in the central nave (fig. 6.7a). Only a few examples of the Santa María emblem, the flores de lilio, remained intact in the cathedral's cloister (fig. 6.7b). The converso Santa María family's use of the flores de lilio dated back to at least the mid-fourteenth century when the family was still Jewish and known as the ha-Levi; the Castilian treasurer Samuel Levi was granted the privilege of incorporating his genealogical crest, the flores de lilio, into the commemorative stucco plaque of El Tránsito Synagogue in Toledo (see ch. 2, fig. 2.1).

FIGURE 6.7A. Old Cathedral central nave. Photo by author; 6.7B. Cloister heraldic detail. Santa María heraldry (flores del lilio) incorporated into the cathedral's cloister. Photo by author.

FIGURE 6.8A. Cardinal Juan de Carvajal's cloister fountain. Photos by author.

One of Cardinal Carvajal's most striking architectural additions to the cathedral, which symbolically expressed fundamental Christian tenets relating to life, death, and resurrection, was a Gothic water fountain placed in the center of the cathedral's enclosed courtyard (fig. 6.8a).[114] (This was the same fountain where the memorial procession for his extended family member, Ruy García de Salamanca, began.) The carved stone fountain, in the shape of a dodecagon, displayed Juan de Carvajal's ecclesiastical shield on one of its decorative faces (fig. 6.8b). Perhaps intentionally, the twelve-sided geometry of the structure corresponds to the stone-carved representation of the cardinal's galero, which has twelve tassels. This fountain, in the Patio of the Oranges (Patio de las Naranjas), is one of the few physical enhancements to the cathedral spared from Bishop de Toledo's later defacements of the Carvajal family's heraldry.

The fountain was exceptionally expressive in terms of Christian symbolism for conversos, whom the church accepted through the act of baptism. According to Gerhart B. Ladner, during the Middle Ages Christians viewed symbols as "objects or events which have a wider meaning that reaches beyond stories and their structures."[115] To strengthen this position, Ladner quotes Hugh St. Victor's twelfth-century commentary on the *Areopagite*. St. Victor wrote, "A symbol is a collecting of visible forms for the demonstration of invisible things."[116] In Europe, especially within the surrounding context of a church, water was the dominant symbolism of Christian baptism.[117]

Resurrection through immersion in water was considered a shared experience with Christ as well.[118] Likewise, in Carolingian France, the baptismal font was "equated with . . . fountains of water."[119] The trees around the cardinal's fountain tie into Judeo-Christian and Islamic visions of the Tree of Life and a garden paradise.[120] In particular,

FIGURE 6.8B. Fountain detail, Cardinal Juan de Carvajal's ecclesiastical shield.

Christians associated orange trees with the Tree of Life.[121] Thus, when viewing Cardinal Carvajal's fountain in this setting, parishioners would likely have contemplated Christian baptism, life, death, and resurrection. In this way, once again, the cardinal and the cathedral chapter integrated the family confederation's presence into religious life in Plasencia.

The artifact that most completely represents the Carvajal–Santa María clan's integration into the cathedral's practices was the Gothic monstrance (*custodia*) given by Cardinal Carvajal (fig. 6.9).[122] A monstrance is a vessel used to display the Eucharist during the Benediction of the Blessed Sacrament, a religious service in which the priest blesses the Eucharist and places it inside the vessel's glass tabernacle.[123] This ritual is usually held after vespers, compline, or the Stations of the Cross, and involves parishioners kneeling and venerating the Eucharist.[124] A typical Benediction of the Blessed Sacrament ceremony includes the praying of the Litany of Loreto and the singing of popular hymns devoted to Mary.[125] In particular, the Litany of Loreto emphasizes Mary as the intercessor of the faithful congregation and cites her divine qualities through a series of invocations.[126] During the late fifteenth and early sixteenth centuries, the cathedral's churchmen carried this monstrance containing the Eucharist during the community's Feast of Corpus Christi processions.[127] Like the cardinal's altarpiece and Salve Regina services (all of which tied into the Santa María's initial dedication to Christ's mother), this monstrance was evidence of the family confederation's explicit devotion to the Virgin Mary.

FIGURE 6.9. Cardinal Juan de Carvajal monstrance. Photo by author.

Reportedly, Juan de Carvajal commissioned the silver-gilt vessel during his long absence from the diocese and later sent it as a gift to the cathedral.[128] The vessel is divided into five primary sections. Viewed from top to bottom, the sections are a crucifix, an enclosed octagonal chapel, an open octagonal chapel enclosed with glass (the tabernacle), a three-tiered church structure, and a four-petal base.[129] Although it is difficult to ascertain the monstrance's exact origin, it is likely that the cardinal selected a craftsman from one of the many European regions he visited during the 1440s and 1450s. Juan routinely traveled as Pope Nicolas V's papal legate from 1447 through 1455 to Bohemia, Hungary, Florence, Venice, and Milan.[130] Later, from 1456 to 1458, he performed similar services for Pope Calixto III, traveling to Germany, Hungary, and Bosnia to preach a crusade against Muhammad II, who captured Christian Constantinople in 1453.[131]

Although the cardinal's monstrance shares commonalities with five others produced during the fifteenth century in Germany and Bohemia (i.e., ornamental spires with crockets, ornamental foliated cresting, chapel structures, human figurines placed around the tabernacle, and a petal-shaped base), this object was unique to Plasencia and includes references to distinctive architectural feature of the cathedral.[132] In comparison to the other monstrances produced during this period, the use of an eight-sided tabernacle appears to be a defining characteristic of the Carvajal piece. Other similar fifteenth-century German and Bohemian vessels utilized either circular or square tabernacles to enclose the Eucharist. For example, Jan van Eyck's painting of the Ghent Altarpiece (1390–1440) and another vessel designed by Wenzel von Olmutz (ca. 1481–1500) show the Eucharist enclosed in a square tabernacle. Three other monstrances from this era used minimalistic circular glass tubes to display the Eucharist within the tabernacle. Among these were a design for a monstrance by Alart du Hamel (ca. 1450–1516), a German monstrance with the *Paten of Saint Bernwald* (ca. 1413–95), and a Bohemian monstrance (ca. 1400–1410). These findings suggest that Cardinal Carvajal tailored his gift to a specific audience, namely, the Diocese of Plasencia. His commissioning of a monstrance that architecturally paralleled the Cathedral of Plasencia explicitly and materially bonded the family confederation to the Placentino religious community.

The monstrance's dominant architectural reference is to the Chapel of Saint Paul, which is where the cathedral chapter would routinely meet to conduct church affairs. Situated along the enclosed cloister walkway, the octagonal chapel is one of the oldest structures in the cathedral's complex of buildings and by far the most important in terms of ecclesiastical governance (see ch. 1, fig. 1.8, for the location of the Chapel of Saint Paul). Both of the vessel's chapel structures utilize the octagonal form and thus suggest that Cardinal Carvajal had a role in dictating the structure of the monstrance. The octagonal chapel roof is composed of sixteen individual vaults. Thus, for each wall of the chapel there are two ceiling vaults that are separated by three ceiling ribs (see fig. 6.10). This exact configuration is repeated in the exterior and interior of the cathedral's Chapel of Saint Paul—eight walls and sixteen vaults. Likewise, the monstrance's tabernacle, the receptacle of the Eucharist, matches this roof and wall layout.

Similarly, a shared language of ornamentation integrates the monstrance's chapel and tabernacle and the Chapel of Saint Paul. All three structures utilize hip knobs (circular and spiked) along their exterior roof ribs. The monstrance tabernacle and the chapel both display multiple spires with crockets. Last, the tabernacle and cathedral chapel incorporate quatrefoils, or four-lobed, windowlike openings. These convergences of geometry and ornamentation may indicate that the family confederation perceived the chapel and its cathedral chapter as symbolic corollaries of the monstrance tabernacle and the Eucharist. Put simply, just as the tabernacle housed the Eucharist, so did the Chapel of Saint Paul hold the cathedral chapter and its members. Thus in the Diocese of Plasencia, the dean, archdeacons, canons, and prebendaries represented the physical body of Christ (the Eucharist) and, as such, embodied the Christian God's authority and leadership.

Like the architectural similarities that link the Carvajal monstrance to the Cathedral of Plasencia, the vessel's petal-like base and tabernacle reveal the identity of its

FIGURE 6.10. Portion of Chapel of Saint Paul, with quatrefoil opening at the top of the peaked arch. Photo by author.

patron and associate the cardinal with a learned religious past. On each of the four metallic petals of the base there is a finely etched badge (fig. 6.11). Two of these discs, placed on opposites sides, present the cardinal's ecclesiastical heraldry—the galero and the Carvajal coat of arms.

The iconography on the other two badges of the base appears to be two different Christian saints. On one badge a bearded man wearing a bishop's miter holds a book in his right hand and a quill in his left. The other image is of a different bearded man who also holds a book and quill. Similar to these badges on the foot of the monstrance, the tabernacle also holds several discs, only one of which is clear enough to identify. This badge shows a third unique depiction of a bearded man with a book and quill. Because the monstrance adheres to strict geometries and symmetries, it seems likely that the tabernacle has two badges with images of saintlike men.[133]

Although none of the saints on the silver-gilt badges are clearly identifiable, their distinctive individual depictions indicate that Cardinal Carvajal wished to reference several learned Christian leaders commonly associated with books and the quill at this time. Perhaps, as four saints are depicted on the monstrance, two on the tabernacle and two on the base, these are the four fathers of the Latin Church—Saints Ambrose, Augustine, Gregory, and Jerome.[134] Augustine and Ambrose were two of the

FIGURE 6.11. Carvajal monstrance base. Photo by author.

more prominent saints identified with book and quill symbols. Augustine of Hippo (ca. 354–430), a North African convert from Arianism to orthodox Catholicism, was a renowned scholar and philosopher.[135] In his most important works, *City of God against Pagans* and *Confessions,* he defended Christianity and discussed his conversion for the purpose of evangelization.[136] During the Middle Ages, Augustine was so well known that his writings "were second only to the Bible in popularity, particularly among the learned."[137] The man who brought Augustine into the orthodox Catholic Church was none other than Ambrose, who personally baptized Augustine and advocated a tolerant approach toward the Arians.[138]

These saints epitomized the key religious counterweights of fervent piety and tolerance of converts—both pressing issues in late fifteenth-century Catholic Castile. The craftsman's decision to use the symbols of the book and quill on the monstrance's badges seems part of his strategy to reference other contemporary artistic works that contained images of Augustine and Ambrose. In Benozzo Gozzoli's 1460s' frescos depicting the life of Saint Augustine in the Church of Sant'Agostino (San Gimignano, Italy), the artist presents the bearded saint with his miter placed on his worktable, a book in its stand, and a quill in the saint's hand.[139] Similarly, in other artworks of the period, a bearded Ambrose appears with a book and quill.[140]

Although it was created approximately one hundred years after the Carvajal–Santa María family confederation's efforts to celebrate the religiosity and worthiness of Cardinal Carvajal, one last religious endowment must be brought to light. In the last decade of the 1500s, well after the religious hysteria of *limpieza de sangre* had passed in Spain (but legal prohibitions remained in effect), the Carvajal clan commissioned and dedicated a family chapel to Canon Martín González de Carvajal (d. 1580) (figs. 6.12a–d).[141] The chapel, erected on one side of the new Cathedral of Plasencia's choir, restated the family confederation's long-term affinity for Ambrose and

FIGURE 6.12A. Chapel of Canon Martín González de Carvajal. Photos by author. **6.12B.** Chapel detail, upper view with statues and heraldry; **6.12C.** Chapel detail, exterior coat of arms; **6.12D.** Chapel detail, interior coat of arms.

Augustine with the placement of statues in the front facade of the chapel. More intriguingly, the family elected to incorporate heraldic devices on an interior vaulted ceiling above the grave of Martín González and the small built-in altar. These painted symbols are distressingly difficult to interpret if one does not understand the extent to which the family confederation had labored to hide its Santa María lineage. The coats of arms revealed in the vaulted ceiling are a black bend (a diagonal band) on a gold shield and, intriguingly, a gold flores de lilio on a blue shield. The first is unmistakably the Carvajal heraldry.

The presence of the flores de lilio elicits an intriguing question: was this the Santa María's heraldry or, as one church historian suggested, a lesser-known coat of arms of the González clan? In the recorded material and documentary history of the Placentino Carvajal clan, which began with the thirteenth-century appearance of the knight Diego González de Carvajal and his father, the family had exclusively used the sable bend on a gold shield. However, the flores de lilio had been associated with the ha-Levi and Santa María since the mid-fourteenth century in Toledo, Burgos, and Plasencia. In the most unequivocal terms, this chapel appears to be a coded message to the public and to the family confederation.

Publicly, the chapel communicated to the Placentino community that the Carvajal were an Old Christian family of deep religious devotion, as evidenced by its distinguished past of learned churchmen. Under this interpretation, the flores de lilio was an unusual choice but offers a plausible explanation for the never-used González coat of arms.

Privately, for the Carvajal–Santa María family confederation the chapel whispered a more convoluted creation story that acknowledges an Old Christian knightly ancestry blended with the New Christian Santa María. The family confederation's focus on tolerant Ambrose and fervent Augustine was the epitome of its convoluted identity—one that acknowledged the need for wholehearted acceptance of converts because of their many gifts but also of unwavering Christian fidelity, shaped by a distinct devotion to the Virgin Mary. Although blood purity laws had eradicated the Santa María–surnamed lineage, it lived on in the collective memory of those Carvajal clan members who were aware of their blood ancestry.

7

SUCCESS AND LOYALTY

The long turn of the century, from the 1480s to the 1530s, was a momentous period in the emergence of early modern Spain, Europe, and the Americas. Contentious religious issues, political intrigue, and encounters with old and new peoples characterized the era. It reflected the successes that now unfolded for the Carvajal–Santa María family confederation, which had successfully integrated Jewish ancestry into a prominent Old Christian one. After the Castilian princess Isabel's 1469 elopement with Ferdinand of Aragón and her successful effort to spoil the claims of her cousin Juana "la Beltraneja" to the Castilian crown, a united Spanish future was secured. Any confusion about Spain's future rulers ended with the conclusion of the Castilian succession crisis in 1479.[1] Queen Isabel and King Ferdinand would thereafter rule the united Kingdom of Castile and León and the Kingdom of Aragón.

Among their many efforts to solidify an integrated and culturally homogeneous Spain, the monarchs sought to enforce and imprint a strict Christian identity on all of their subjects—Christians, Jews, and Muslims. Unfortunately for Jews and Muslims, this meant conversion to Christianity or expulsion. Those who adopted Christianity were, as had been the case since the 1450s, subjected to tests of their religious purity. In Plasencia, the family confederation attempted to maintain a supportive cocoon for the Jewish community, especially after the Estúñiga evicted Jews from their synagogue. However, intolerance not only targeted the Sephardic people, but now forced conversos such as the Carvajal–Santa María to bury their Jewish past even deeper.

In 1478, via a papal bull, the Spanish monarchs secured the establishment of the Holy Office of the Inquisition, and, just two years later, in 1480, it began its efforts to uncover suspected heretics, especially Judaizers, within the Christian flock. Caught in this machinery were conversos of all stripes—Jewish commoners and merchants turned Christians, lower nobles and clerical leaders like the Carvajal and Santa María clan members, and even elites like the New Nobles, the Estúñiga and Álvarez de Toledo. As I discuss in this chapter, the family confederation, in particular, stood to both benefit and lose the most in this era of identity shifting. If the family could successfully mask their Jewish ancestry and serve the emergent imperial Spain, they might enjoy the fruits of their past one hundred years of transformation from rabbis and knights into members of the royal court and the Roman Catholic Church. If they failed to mask their former identities and promote a pure Christian one, all could be lost through the constant probing of the Inquisition and Old Christians, who might challenge their religious purity.

By 1492, the march of history claimed its Christian victories and Muslim, Jewish, and Native American losses. After a ten-year war to reclaim Islamic Nasrid Granada, the Spanish monarchs took up residence in the luxuriously ornate Alhambra palace (January 1), the remaining 250,000 to 300,000 Jews were exiled from Spain (July 31), and Cristóbal Colón and his crew landed on Hispanola in the Americas (December 25).[2] Witnesses and participants in this history, the Carvajal–Santa María family confederation must have understood their unique and privileged position in the making of what would become the early modern period. As cardinals, bureaucrats, and, in a few cases, knights, they participated in almost every monumental affair in Spanish history from the 1480s to the 1530s.

While Europe was simultaneously inflamed with political and religious challenges, Spain appeared to benefit at every step of the way. In the same year that the Catholic monarchs occupied the Alhambra, Pope Innocent VIII died and a Spaniard, Rodrigo Lanzol y de Borja, was elected as Pope Alexander VI.[3] A great patron of the Carvajal–Santa María, the Spanish pope sought to secure a prosperous future for Spain and for them. At the direction of Ferdinand and Isabel, the confederation's ambassador in Rome, Cardinal Bernardino López de Carvajal, sought and obtained Pope Alexander VI's blessing of the Spanish claims in the Americas via the May 3 and 4 *Inter caetera* (Among other [works]) papal bull.[4] The cardinal, now at the forefront of international affairs, routinely shared correspondence with many noteworthy personages—the future emperors Maximilian I and Carlos V, the French kings Charles VIII and Louis XII, the politically astute and treacherous Machiavelli, and, of course, Ferdinand and Isabel.

At the end of the 1490s, just when international affairs should have settled down, as the Spanish and Portuguese concluded their mutually agreeable partitioning of their American claims with the Treaty of Tordesillas (1494), a violent and alliance-shifting confrontation was escalating between France's Charles VIII, Austria's Holy Roman Emperor Maximilian, Naples, and the papacy.[5] The early 1500s brought no reprieve as both tumultuous and celebrated events guided Spain into imperialism. This was especially the case when Queen Isabel died in 1504 and Ferdinand ruled a united

Spain as king of Aragón and regent of the Kingdom of Castile and León until his death in 1516.[6] Ferdinand's role as caretaker of Castile, León, and the Americas was necessary due to the royal dynastic determination that Princess Juana, the couple's daughter and heir, was "mad" and unfit to rule. Before Ferdinand would leave this world, he contended with one last European conflict that shook the Carvajal–Santa María family confederation to its foundation and relegated it to a lesser noble family, which would achieve only limited international fame and power. In 1511, when a new pope, Julius II, and the same European parties engaged in a new phase of political and religious conflict over the political future of Venice, Cardinal Carvajal sought the pontifical tiara at the schismatic Council of Pisa.[7] Carvajal failed, undercut by King Ferdinand and Emperor Maximilian I and with insufficient support from Louis XII, and was excommunicated by Pope Julius II. Although Pope Leo X later reconciled Cardinal Carvajal with the church, he and the family learned that their final place in the early modern world would be limited to serving as loyal retainers of the Spanish monarchy. As such, they benefited greatly in terms of political opportunities and social status, but the family always understood their station was tied to duty.

Imperial Spain found formidable footing in 1519. In that year, Carlos V, grandson of Isabel and Ferdinand, assumed the mantles of king of Spain and Holy Roman Emperor, and the Spanish conquistador Hernán Cortés conquered the Aztecs in Mexico.[8] After Carlos V and his noble supporters suppressed the Comuneros Revolt (1519–21), a native effort of Spanish nobles opposed to the emperor's overly Flemish court, Spain's rise seemed assured when it effectively confronted and held off the Ottoman Turks at the Siege of Vienna (1529) and the Spanish Extremaduran Francisco Pizarro and his Placentino Carvajal family defeated the Peruvian Inca Empire (1532–33).[9]

It is in this earthshaking Spanish, European, and American historical context that the Carvajal–Santa María family confederation entered into the terminal stage of its transition into early modern identities. Since the end of the 1300s, its transformation was characterized by a progressive, positive sense of change that required a public repudiation of Judaism as a religion. The ha-Levi rabbinic family that had turned into the converso Santa María churchmen and the Old Christian knightly Carvajal clan that had morphed into converso ecclesiastical and royal bureaucrats appeared to believe they could create and mold their own future from bewildering times. Yet this was not to be the case if they could not successfully mask their mixed heritage. The shift into the sixteenth century brought with it intransigent Spanish Christian—and Jewish—beliefs that saw conversos like the family confederation as dangerous hybrids that would not be tolerated by either community. Purity was essential to the survival of Jews and Christians. With the arrival of the sixteenth century, the Carvajal–Santa María family confederation pushed forward as Spaniards and Christians. They labored to forget their Jewish past and, in doing so, assisted the Spanish monarchy and its nobility in disavowing their hybrid religious pedigree.

PLASENCIA'S JEWISH COMMUNITY, 1477–1492

Within the highly charged religious and cultural environment, created as early as the anti-Jewish pogroms of the 1390s and the blood purity laws of the 1450s, Plasencia's Jewish community was in full retreat by the 1470s. In the course of fifteen years, the judería would find itself increasingly on the defensive as the Estúñiga asserted their authority over Jewish properties (even the synagogue) and King Ferdinand and Queen Isabel prepared to expel them in 1492. Faithful to the end to a more pluralistic community, the Carvajal–Santa María family confederation attempted to mitigate this slow-moving religious and cultural disaster by lending moral and physical aid to Placentino Jews. While promoting an overt but farcical Old Christian pedigree with the construction of the Convento de San Vicente Ferrer, the Estúñiga clan exerted the greatest pressure on Jews by casting them from their synagogue and homes At the same time, the family confederation made room for the Jewish community near their homes and incorporated a synagogue within the tight cluster of Carvajal and Santa María residences that centered on the Plazuela de Don Marcos. Unfortunately, the path to move forward with better Christian-Jewish relations in Plasencia and Spain was both narrow and, ultimately, a dead end due to the expulsion of Jews in 1492.

In a donation recorded in the Registro del Sello de Corte of the Kingdom of Castile and León, on July 22, 1477, Álvaro de Estúñiga, count of Plasencia and Béjar, turned over the Jewish neighborhood of La Mota and the synagogue to the Dominicans to construct a convent in the name of the most voracious of Christian proselytizers, Vicente Ferrer.[10] By virtue of his "seigniorial privilege and ownership and possession of the Jews and the Jewish community," Álvaro gave the synagogue, "those houses that belonged to Rabbi Abrahan," and other structures to the religious order charged with protecting the Christian faith from heretics. Intriguingly, the count did not enact this donation in Plasencia but rather from his stronghold just to the north, in the smaller city of Béjar, and in the presence of its mayor and local nobility. There was little the Placentino Carvajal–Santa María family members in the cathedral or on the city council—or their Jewish allies—could do to counter this action; it was a fait accompli (fig. 7.1, Estúñiga Zone of Control).[11]

In the letter of donation, Álvaro and his spouse, Leonor de Pimentel, stated they gave these properties to the Order of the Dominicans, "with the hope that [Ferrer's] many good and chasten examples would inspire faithful Christians in this city" and so that "our sins and errors can be forgiven so that we are brought to your [God's] holy and infinite glory."[12] The count and his wife thus hoped to secure their Christian credentials and counter any future accusations that they were not good Christians even if they were members of the converso new nobility.

With the creation of the convent and the eviction of Jewish residents from the neighborhood of La Mota, the count of Plasencia and Béjar effectively created a mas-

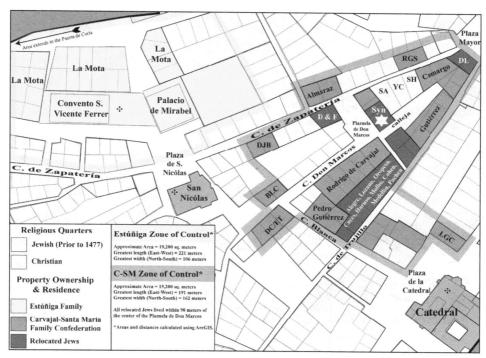

FIGURE 7.1. Displacement and relocation of synagogue and Jewish community, 1477–1492.

sive zone of control in the southwestern portion of the judería that radiated out from his Palacio de Mirabel (Palace of Mirabel) (figs. 7.2, 7.3). From this locus of power, the Estúñiga family owned and controlled over 19,200 square meters of the city, or roughly 4.75 acres within the city walls, and their properties represented the largest contiguous family zone in all of Plasencia.[13] This was the most brazen of all the count's and his supporters' actions, which turned out to be short-lived.

The response of the Carvajal–Santa María family confederation was remarkable as it demonstrated that not all conversos were committed to the elimination of the Jewish community; rather they stood steadfast and ready to integrate the displaced Jews and synagogue in their immediate neighborhood in Plasencia (see fig. 7.1, Carvajal–Santa María Zone of Control). Within eight days of the count's actions, on July 30, 1477, Rodrigo de Carvajal sold a large complex of his homes on Calle de Zapatería to the Jews Saul Daça and Yuda Fidauque for 25,000 maravedís for "forever after," rather than just leasing (see fig. 7.1, D & F).[14] Rodrigo himself lived in a large housing complex in the immediate vicinity and on the connecting Plazuela de Don Marcos. This son of the knight Diego González de Carvajal, who had lived his entire life adjacent to Jews and Muslims on the Plaza Mayor, had elected to welcome Saul and Yuda as his permanent neighbors.

FIGURE 7.2. Palacio de Mirabel (Palace of Mirabel) (home of count of Plasencia and Béjar). Photo by author.

FIGURE 7.3. Palacio de Mirabel (Palace of Mirabel) (right section of structures) and the former Synagogue of Plasencia/Convent of San Vicente Ferrer (left section). Photo by author.

In a reversal of what had been done in La Mota over sixty years earlier, Jews took possession of Christian homes. Saul and Yuda did so by "entering into them and walking through them, and to signal their possession of them, in the presence of everyone that was there, they closed the houses' doors while they remained inside."[15] Witnessing the transaction were several members of the family confederation who ensured the enduring relationship of intertwined clans, albeit with the Santa María surname. Among them were Gonzalo de Carvajal, who was the son of Alfonso Fernández (one of the original lines of the Santa María), Luis de Carvajal, and Alfonso Gutiérrez.[16]

Thus, this converso family, most of whose members resided in this area and had worked over the course of eighty years to maintain a peaceful coexistence in Plasencia, was in agreement that Plasencia's Jews needed a protective and defensive cocoon of housing. However, there may have been some discomfort with this cozying up to Jewish neighbors. One family member present at the transaction was already marching toward a more religiously pure and Christian identity and had rejected the family's Jewish past. Luis de Carvajal, a witness to these events and with deep knowledge of the family's Jewish bloodlines, was the same church official who later put pressure on the entire family to reject its Jewish past through his actions as a member of the Holy Office of the Inquisition.

The boundary of the family confederation's 15,200-square-meter (3.75-acre) zone of control in Plasencia was created with houses serving as anchor points in which resided Rodrigo de Carvajal, Diego Jiménez de Burgos (fig. 7.1, DJB), Bernardino López de Carvajal (BLC), Diego de Carvajal and Elvira de Toledo (DC/ET), the family of Lorenzo Galíndez de Carvajal (LGC), Pedro Gutiérrez, the Camargo clan, Ruy García de Salamanca (RGS), and the Almaraz family. From the zone of control's central point, located in the Plazuela de Don Marcos and precisely where a new synagogue was founded (Syn), all relocated Jews resided within 90 meters (100 yards).

In order for Plasencia's Jewish community to have a proper synagogue, as well as an attached women's section, the Carvajal side of the family confederation sold multiple properties so that it could be constructed on the Plazuela de Don Marcos.[17] In sum, the family confederation's approach to this neighborhood implied an intense interest in protecting its Jewish neighbors and itself should events proceed on a more destructive path with the Estúñiga clan.

In particular, Diego's and Rodrigo's homes offered substantial, fortified castlelike structures that would be used to shelter the family confederation and Jewish community when a bloody hand-to-hand war broke out between the Estúñiga clan and the confederation in 1488. As previously discussed, in 1469, the converso New Noble Álvarez de Toledo (señores de Oropesa) and the Placentino Carvajal had reconciled and secured a family alliance through the marriage of Diego de Carvajal, by then a regidor in the town of Talavera de la Reina, and Elvira de Toledo.[18] Elvira not only brought an enormous dowry to the partnership but also ownership of the family castle in the

FIGURE 7.4. Casa de Dos Torres. Photo by author.

village of Oropesa as well as Plasencia's Casa de Dos Torres (House of Two Towers) situated at the corner of Calle Blanca and Calle Don Marcos (fig. 7.4; see also ch. 5, fig. 5.1). The Casa de Dos Torres and Rodrigo's large housing complex allowed for improved family protection and revealed an overt converso fraternity with the surviving members of the Jewish community.

　　Between 1477 and 1485, the family confederation acted decisively, integrating as many as a dozen Jewish families into their immediate neighborhood. First, Saul Daça sold several houses to his coreligionist, Yuce Caçes.[19] These houses were next to those of Simuel Harañon, the Jewish chainmail maker who rented a residence from the church, and the wife of Salamon Abenhibibe, who owned a home in the immediate vicinity (see fig. 7.1, "YC," SH," and "SA" in light blue on Calle de Zapatería). Subsequently, Rodrigo de Carvajal and his sister, Estefanía González de Carvajal, executed a large array of property agreements (perpetual leases, short-term leases, and sales contracts) that settled Jewish families along Calle de Trujillo (from Calle Blanca up to the alleyway behind Rodrigo's housing complex). These property arrangements allowed Rabbi Mose Caçes, Yuda Alegre, Simuel Alegre, Jacob Lozano, Abrahan Lozano, Levi

Alegre, Pedro Alegre, Isay de Oropesa, Ysay Pachen, Yuda Caçes, Yuce Haruso, Yuce Molho, Habine Molho, Albrana Cohen, and Yuce de Medellín to relocate and, in some cases, build new homes.[20] At the same time, the Carvajal family also leased a massive house on Calle Blanca to their extended family member, Pedro Gutiérrez, thus further consolidating the presence of the family confederation in the immediate area.[21]

Just a few short years after the formation of this new Jewish neighborhood, on March 31, 1492, Queen Isabel and King Ferdinand issued the Alhambra Decree, which required the remaining 250,000 to 300,000 Jews in Spain to convert to Christianity or leave Spain by July 31, 1492—within four months.[22] This Edict of Expulsion served as the terminal point for Plasencia's Jews. Likewise, since 1480, the Holy Office of the Inquisition had been busy investigating conversos suspected of falsely converting to Christianity. For all intents and purposes, the Carvajal–Santa María family confederation of Plasencia was largely left untouched by the Inquisition; after all, it claimed great churchmen as its stewards. Other conversos were less fortunate, as in the 1487 case of Cristóbal Manrique, who was sentenced to death and burned alive in Plasencia after inquisitors found him guilty of heresy.[23]

Also in 1492, the new synagogue of Plasencia was shuttered and became royal property; on May 21, the Jewish community sold the Jewish cemetery, and in particular its headstones, to Diego de Jerez, then dean of the Cathedral of Plasencia, for 400 reales.[24] The transaction was conducted on behalf of the Jewish community by Yuce Castaño and witnessed by Yuce Caçes, Ysay Pachen, Abrahan Haruzo, Mayr Cohen, Yuce Abenhabibe, Rabbi Abraham, and others. Diego de Jerez's relations with the Carvajal–Santa María family confederation were tense because he was in the service of and loyal to Álvaro de Estúñiga and Leonor de Pimentel.[25] While in the past the Cathedral of Plasencia had been the exclusive domain of the Carvajal–Santa María family confederation, by the 1490s, it only retained a few seats on the governing chapter of the cathedral. More important, since 1470, Bishop Rodrigo de Ávila had complicated local family power in the cathedral because he was allied with the Estúñiga family as well as the Carvajal clan via intermarriage.[26] It seems likely that the converso Carvajal and Santa María clans would have regarded Diego de Jerez with contempt because of his loyalty to the Estúñiga family and his purchase of Jewish graves.

The Alhambra Decree expressly prohibited Spanish Jews from leaving Spain with any precious metals (gold, silver) or currency; Jews were forced to sell homes, property, and household goods for a pittance. According to Gerber, "The contemporary priest Andres Bernáldez describes how most possessions went for a pittance: a vineyard for the price of a handkerchief, a house for a donkey, a workshop for a piece of linen or a loaf of bread."[27] In spite of its royal and ecclesiastical positions in the Spanish monarchy and church, the family confederation was powerless and unable to prevent these wretched terms for their Jewish neighbors. However, they attempted to mitigate their impact.

Less than a year after Placentino Jews' departure from Spain, it became apparent that some had left with substantial caches of gold and silver funds, with the explicit assistance of the Carvajal–Santa María family confederation. Using an elaborate scheme, multiple members of the family served as "fronts" for financial transactions so that substantial funds could be transferred to the departing Jews. In multiple claims starting in March and continuing through June 1493, Juan Pérez Coronel in Segovia, a converso related to the family confederation via the Villalva family, claimed he was owed debts by the Cohen family of Plasencia.[28] Using the same royal institutions and courts that had exiled Jews, Juan Pérez requested and received payments from Garci López de Carvajal, Pedro de Villalobos, Juan Fernández, and Gonzalo de Carvajal to pay these debts on the grounds that they had purchased equally valuable property from the Placentino Cohens. In total, these collective family members were liable for 178,000 maravedís. Only after the fact of the transactions did it become apparent that Juan Pérez had given the Jewish Cohens a presumably large amount of liquid funds as they left Spain, which he in turn recovered via payments from the Placentino family confederation, which had assumed ownership of the Cohens' local property. In this manner, these conversos demonstrated uncharacteristic devotion to many Jews who may have been, at minimum, longtime friends and neighbors or even extended family relations who had retained their Jewish faith. Interestingly, when the Cohens left Plasencia, they adopted the converso surname Gutiérrez, perhaps indicating a family connection to the Carvajal–Santa María family confederation.

These dramatic shifts in social and religious fortune felt by Plasencia's Jewish community were not equally shared by the converso Carvajal–Santa María family confederation. Rather, at the opening of the 1490s, the Carvajal-surnamed clan found itself in Spanish leadership circles and would participate as notable actors in pressing European and early American affairs. Likewise, the Santa María name was mostly whitewashed by family members taking other surnames.

CONVERSO IDENTITIES IN THE EARLY MODERN PERIOD

For turn-of-the-sixteenth-century conversos like the Carvajal–Santa María, a rich historiography invites a discussion surrounding the perplexing cultural and religious beliefs of the period. In essence, conversos constituted a transgressive identity that could not be easily or satisfyingly recognized by Spanish Christians and Jews, and as such required the formulation of careful delineations and definitions of who was a "Christian" and who was a "Jew." Early modern Spaniards as well as contemporary scholars of Christian and Sephardic Spain continuously enforce these boundaries. These two historiographies—Jewish and Spanish—prefer to argue *at* each other and not *with* each other. Until the late twentieth century there was little room for complex explanations and identities.

It is in this environment that the Carvajal–Santa María family's actions need to be evaluated, because they did not live in a cultural or religious vacuum. Rather they attempted to chart a path that clarified their religious identity and that required overt public dedication to Christianity. When there was a chink in their religious armor, the family confederation was exposed to real religious and political danger. As I discuss in this chapter and the next, they met these challenges forcefully and unequivocally, even if it meant silencing extended family members by humiliation or, worse yet, execution.

During the sixteenth century, elite converso families, New Christians, used Jewish ancestry as a blunt political and religious weapon to limit their competitors' aspirations. This was especially evident in the case of Cardinal Francisco Mendoza y Bobadilla. After learning that his nephew would not be admitted into any of the three leading Christian military orders (Calatrava, Santiago, Alcántara) because of his Jewish lineage, the cardinal wrote a denunciation of the hypocrisy of the nobility's humble and Jewish origins, *El tizón de la nobleza*, a memorial published in 1560 that amounted to an attack on most of his fellow conversos. Speaking to King Philip II, Cardinal Mendoza asserted, "The knights, dukes, counts and marquises of the republic, those that illuminate the republic and who are the petals of the rose that all can see[,] . . . in these noble hearts there is infamy and backbiting and scandal that separates them from the people."[29]

The "ignobility" that separated the nobility from the commoners was the pollution of most of the nobility with Muslim and Jewish ancestors. Accordingly, and now as the "sworn enemy until death" of those who deprived his nephew of future opportunities, the cardinal named countless lineages that descended from Jewish and Muslim bloodlines.[30] Among them were Extremaduran New Noble counts of Plasencia and Béjar (the Estúñiga family), the perpetual competitors of the Carvajal–Santa María family confederation, and the New Noble counts of Oropesa (the Álvarez de Toledo), a lineage that the Carvajal clan intermarried with during the 1460s.[31] No noble lineage escaped the cardinal's written wrath as he systematically named most living high and minor nobles, adding particularly provocative commentary that attacked every aspect of their status with entries such as, "The descendants of Inés Hernández Estévez, the daughter of a Jewish convert and shoemaker."[32] The cardinal exposed every noble converso and morisco clan that he could but excluded his owned extended relatives—the Carvajal–Santa María family confederation.

The scholarly discussion of Jewish and converso identities in the late 1400s began in earnest with Juan Antonio Llorente's monumental work, *Historia crítica de la inquisición en España*, first published in French in 1870. He argues that persecution of conversos, officially and socially, through the end of the fifteenth century created "an eerie silence" and lack of criticism from the most elite segments of society.[33] This behavior by elites suggests the extent to which New Nobles, many of them conversos, kept quiet in order to protect themselves. However, some contemporary historians of the period, such as Fernando del Pulgar, did voice an opposition to the societal problems created by the attack on conversos. Pulgar argued that the Inquisition had taken on more rigor than anyone intended and that the "crime of heresy should not be penalized with capital punishment."[34] Yet that is precisely what occurred. Llorente records that during the eighteen-year administration (1481–98) of Tomás de Torquemada, himself a converso, the Inquisition dealt harshly with New Christians convicted of returning to Judaism. Over 10,220 were burned at the stake, 6,680 were burned in effigy (because they had fled and could not be located), and 7,321 received punishment in the form of penance.[35] Llorente's contribution is noteworthy as he documented how traditional Christianity, a faith built on evangelization and conversion, would no longer apply to many Spanish Jews who converted to Catholicism or their descendants, regardless of their mixed pedigrees or actions. Implicitly, Llorente argued, there were three well-defined religious identities (Judaism, Catholicism, and Islam) and a fourth emergent one that captured the experience of conversos as well as moriscos, Muslim converts to Christianity.

Approximately seventy-five years after Llorente's critical text on the Spanish Inquisition, Henry Charles Lea, a North American author, returned to the topic of Jewish-Christian relations in his polemical work on the Spanish Inquisition. In 1901, Lea's *History of the Inquisition of Spain* served as the first academic indictment of all Spanish cultural, political, and spiritual organizations for their complicity in creating the Inquisition. Lea claimed all of these institutions were debased and that the historical record proved that no good came from them. He contextualized the Inquisition in light of the 1470s War of Spanish Succession and Queen Isabel's quick efforts to address the chaos of the period with vigorous, unbending use of a reformed legal system.[36] It was from this litigious environment that the Inquisition arose. According to Lea, the Inquisition served as a useful tool to enhance royal power over feudal systems.[37] Lea painted Spanish Jews as a desperate community fighting for survival. Moreover, the Christian attack on Jews was derived from the position that Jews had always been detested in Europe as a debased race with no natural rights.[38]

Lea decisively bifurcated the identities of conversos: those who converted out of necessity of survival, the *anusim*, and those who willingly converted, the *meshuhamdin*. The anusim existed as a unique religious identity and group still recognized as part of the Jewish community. Those Jews who converted willingly were no longer acceptable to the Jewish community, Lea adds, because they were cultural turncoats and

> were thenceforward to become the deadliest opponents of their former brethren. Many chiefs of the synagogue, learned rabbis and leaders of their people, had cowered before the storm and had embraced Christianity. Whether their conversion was sincere or not, they had broken with the past and, with the keen intelligence of their race, they could see that a new career was open to them in which energy and capacity could gratify ambition, unfettered by the limitations surrounding them in Judaism.[39]

For Lea, then, the descendants of the Carvajal–Santa María family confederation could not be considered Jewish from an internal Jewish standpoint. On the other hand, he argues that the anusim

> might have brought up their children as Christians and the grandchildren might have outgrown the old customs, but the conversos could not be earnest converts, and the sacred traditions, handed down, by father to son from the days of the Sanhedrin, were too precious to be set aside. The *Anusim*, as they were known to their Hebrew brethren, thus were unwilling Christians, practising what Jewish rites they dared, and it was held to be the duty of all Jews to bring them back to the true faith.[40]

Lea's inability to account for diversity and hybridity within the ranks of the conversos undermines any attempt to appreciate the predicament and the range of agency of individual conversos. While his research and findings are exceptional, they characterize converso life in unhelpful monochromatic shades.

By the late twentieth century, scholarly inquiry began to experiment with more granular explanations of New Christian identities. One particularly noticeable trend in scholarship was attention to conversos who acculturated and succeeded in Catholic Spain. For example, Thomas Glick posited that New Christians readily adapted to Christianity but still retained elements of Jewish identities. He states, "Elements of Jewish religion and religious practice were the last redoubt of cultural distinctiveness."[41] Arguing for this movement toward accepting Christianity are other scholars who study noble New Christian families. In her doctoral dissertation, "Los Judeoconversos en la corte y en la época de los reyes católicos," Rábade Obradó discusses elite New Christian families that were closely associated or intermarried with the Carvajal–Santa María— namely, the Álvarez de Toledo, Cabrera(os), Talavera, and Coronel clans.[42] Stafford Poole similarly wrote about Juan de Ovando, a converso *letrado*, or professional administrator, during the rule of King Felipe II.[43] As elites, all of these clans very much tend to create identities that were overtly Christian while also obscuring Jewish ancestries and therefore retained little "Jewishness" from an internal Jewish perspective.

Where these other scholars were content to allow flexibility in deciding if the conversos retained Jewish sympathies, Benzion Netanyahu, in *The Marranos of Spain*, was not. The central question that the author posed was, how Jewish were the *marranos* (conversos)? Netanyahu argued that the Inquisition assumed the conversos were Jews.[44] That is, Jewishness, from a Christian perspective, was just as predicated on faith and practice as it was on blood lineage. Netanyahu rejected this opinion and even took issue with other Jewish scholars, including I. F. Baer, who considered that "the majority of the conversos were real Jews. . . . *Conversos* and Jews were one people, bound together, by ties of religion, and fate, and messianic hope."[45] These complications of faith, lineage, and identity were unacceptable to Netanyahu. In his revised text, published in 1999, he reiterated his 1966 positions and reaffirmed that (1) "the overwhelming majority of the Marranos" at the time of the establishment of the Inquisition were not Jews but "detached from Judaism," or rather, to put it more clearly, Christians; (2) that "in seeking to identify the whole Marrano group with a secret Jewish heresy, the Spanish Inquisition was operating with a fiction"; and (3) that "it was driven to this operation by racial hatred and political considerations rather than by religious zeal."[46]

There is no resolution to this difference of perspectives, both past and present, and it finds the same destination: overall, there was no place for conversos in either a Jewish or Christian world after the fifteenth century.

Scholars such as David Graizbord champion another strain of thinking, one that focused on the uncertain social position of New Christians and that rejected dualistic views of conversos. His expert treatment of the converso experience in *Souls in Dispute*, speaks to the issue of religious hybridity in early modern Spain. No other academic of the early twenty-first century has captured the essence of the complications of Jewish-converso historiography better than has Graizbord. Astutely, he argues:

> Studies that focus on Judeoconversos . . . do not represent a unitary field of research but a somewhat eclectic subfield of various branches of scholarship. Chief among the latter are Jewish history and literature (especially Sephardi studies and the history of anti-Judaism), Spanish history and literature (especially the history of the Inquisition), Portuguese history, the history of the Netherlands, the economic history of the early modern Levant, the history of European religion(s), and the history of philosophy (especially skepticism and rationalism). The fact the problem of conversos covers so much academic ground bears witness not only to the geographic mobility of New Christians, but also to their multifaceted cultural and social profile.[47]

Because the study of Spanish Jews and their descendants is so fragmented, so also is academicians' understanding of early modern Spanish identities and what it meant to identify as a converso. As yet, no scholar has amassed the breadth of knowledge, collection of manuscripts, and knowledge of the source languages to comprehend conversos' world. Graizbord's unique gift to the field is a stimulating pivot on Jewish and Christian perceptions of conversos' religious purity. He postulates that not only did the "so-called Old Christians" suspect the New Christians of continuing to practice their Jewish faith and cultural practices, but rabbinic Judaism spurned conversos as intolerable cultural "renegades" who existed in the "anomalous condition" of "cultural liminality."[48]

Other scholars with positions similar to Graizbord's have advanced the idea that conversos could never live comfortably in Spain. Yirmiyahu Yovel explores how conversos embodied "split identities" that "were considered illicit and illegal, a grave social and metaphysical sin."[49] Nathan Wachtel's work argues that these split identities are reflective of modernity, adding that New Christians were "mutations and creations of the modern West" developed from notions of race, biology, and anti-Semitism.[50]

By the early twenty-first century, scholarly texts finally engaged with the messiness of converso lives. Within Spain, converso identities seem to have varied widely in terms of conversos' ability to adapt to an overtly Christian environment. Among the most valuable contributions is Renée Levine Melammed's *A Question of Identity*, which documents the diversity in the Spanish, Portuguese, Dutch, and French converso communities. Melammed succeeds in exposing the full sphere of identities—Spanish assimilators and returnees to Judaism, Portuguese "members of the Nation" who retained ethnic and cultural Jewish ties, Iberian Jewish émigrés to Protestant Holland, and "fuzzy Jews" and cultural commuters in France.[51]

Gretchen D. Starr-LeBeau, who expertly explored the sixteenth-century ecclesiastical community of Guadalupe, Spain, offered a groundbreaking text that explains how Old and New Christians used the same rituals for their own unique purposes of identity. Therefore, her book is among the most useful for understanding the Carvajal–Santa María family confederation that blended Christian and Jewish lineages. She argues that rituals could serve both Christian and Jewish masters.

> All Guadalupenses—both Old and New Christian—marked each stage of their lives by ritual acts. . . . For each resident of the Virgin's town, those rites could reaffirm a link to ancestors and the past, connections particularly dangerous for *New Christians*. While all conversos celebrated, with greater or less enthusiasm, at least some of the rites of their Christian faith, others also chose to unite with some family members and with the family's former faith through unbaptisms, circumcisions, and traditional burials. At the same time, those New Christians affirmed, to some extent, a separate identity from their Old Christian neighbors, a distinct sense of religious community that compelled them to act in ways undeniably dangerous to themselves if discovered.[52]

Starr-LeBeau's observations demonstrate that conversos' Jewish notions of self could survive even in one of the most important Christian communities in Spain and the home of the royally patronized Monastery of Santa María de Guadalupe. She adds that some conversos "developed their own alternative religious identities, organized around secret observances of some of the primary Jewish holidays, including Yom Kippur and Sukkoth."[53] The Placentino family confederation's mid-fifteenth-century observances of Saturday rituals and devotions to the Virgin Mary seem to be early indications of what Starr-LeBeau discovered in sixteenth-century Guadalupe. Conversos did not necessarily discontinue meaningful practices; rather their identities dictated a need to blend and perpetuate elements of their former lives.

Other sixteenth-century conversos, especially elite families in Toledo, enjoyed societal accomplishments as they carefully constructed their Christian identities while limiting public knowledge about their Jewish ancestors, just as the Placentinos had done. Linda Martz's *A Network of Converso Families in Early Modern Toledo* argues for three types of conversos: assimilators, integrators, and exclusionaries.[54] Those willing to assimilate took on the "mannerisms" of Old Christians, which included expensive marriages to Old Christian Castilian families, not revealing their ancestry, abandoning problematic surnames, and avoiding controversial positions relating to blood purity laws.[55] Martz advances the idea, as I do for the Carvajal–Santa María family confederation, that Toledan converso families "hardly seem to be withdrawn or suffer exclusion from the larger community. They are present in all facets of local affairs, and it is not easy to pinpoint any local institution that does not include conversos, despite statutes dedicated to keeping them out."[56] Overall, Martz concludes that conversos' "status and acceptance is uncertain and complex," because "wealth and good connections" could be used to outmaneuver blood purity sanctions at times.[57] She also argues that blood purity was more of "a state of mind, a willingness to adopt, or at least do lip service to, the doctrine and values."[58]

Collectively, Martz, Starr-LeBeau, and I have identified Toledo, Guadalupe, and Plasencia as communities where converso identities were carefully managed and constructed ones that drew from Jewish religious and cultural roots but ultimately were states of mind that adopted public Christian attitudes and actions to hide their blood lineages. This begs the question, were these experiences exceptional or normative in early modern Spain? Increasingly it appears that many conversos were true hybrids who fell into an uncomfortable middle way of life that Old Christians and Jews did not understand or refused to accept. In this respect, converso identities are a hallmark of the early modern period because they facilitated unusual fluidity, and conversos existed as their own multiverse of self and group perception.

HEIRS OF THE CARVAJAL–SANTA MARÍA FAMILY CONFEDERATION, 1470s–1480s

In 1472, two of the family confederation's most impressive leaders—Cardinal Bernardino López de Carvajal and Dr. Lorenzo Galíndez de Carvajal—made their first appearances in the Castilian world. Bernardino López completed his bachelor's degree in theology and began to serve as professor at the university at the Cathedral of Salamanca,[59] and Archdeacon Diego de Carvajal fathered and Juana de Galíndez gave birth to Lorenzo. Although Lorenzo was born out of wedlock, he ascended to the highly coveted position of judge on the Royal Chancellery of Valladolid (Real Chancillería de Valladolid) and the first *correo mayor*, or primary administrator, of the Council of the Indies (Consejo de Indias), the Spanish American government based in Sevilla, Spain.[60] During the 1480s and 1490s, these two men circulated in Spain's most desirable royal administrative and ecclesiastical circles and epitomized the successful converso identity that was born from and tainted by a hybrid Christian-Jewish lineage. While blood ties did not impede their personal initiatives, it remained a taint that limited the family confederation's next generation of leaders, who would never soar as high as these two men.

The university at the Cathedral of Salamanca (hereafter referred to as the University of Salamanca) was among the most critical institutions to shape the professional futures of Bernardino López and Lorenzo Galíndez. According to Isodoro L. Lapuya, Castile's King Alfonso X "the Wise" (r. 1252–84) established the university during the Iberian Peninsula's age of "warriors and wars."[61] One of the outcomes of the Reconquest, the Christian kingdom's political and military initiative to retake Iberia from the Muslims, was the recapturing of lands governed by different Christian, Islamic, and Jewish legal traditions. Recognizing that this patchwork of laws was problematic, Alfonso X elected to overhaul Castile's existing use of the Visigothic legal code, as well as address the novel situations generated by the commingling of Jews, Christians, and Muslims in the Kingdom of Castile, through the creation of his own legal code, Las Siete Partidas.[62]

Embedded in the code were the foundational components for the University of Salamanca. Before the university was established,, Castilian students had to pursue legal and scholarly studies outside of Spain, particularly in Bologna, because there was no equivalent Castilian institution.[63] After the implementation of the Siete Partidas, which the crafters completed in 1268, Castile recognized it could no longer do without its own comparable educational institution. To properly maintain and implement the king's new legal code, Castile needed to produce its own legal scholars and jurists.

Although by 1143 a rudimentary Castilian university existed in the city of Plasencia, the church later moved its primary activities to Salamanca but did not establish the University of Salamanca until 1200.[64] However, the new university did not offer sufficiently rigorous legal training to properly prepare jurists until 1254, the year Alfonso X granted the university a new charter. This was just fourteen years before the completion of Las Siete Partidas. The charter established that the enhanced university would consist of "two professors of law, three of canon law, two of logic, two of grammar, and two of physics."[65] The Siete Partidas also contained several sections relating to the administration of the University of Salamanca.[66] Title 31 of the second part of the legal code is devoted to the operation of universities, including Salamanca, and defines the nature of general academic studies, the qualifications of professors (*maestros*), and the regulation of students and their examinations.[67]

Among the most crucial elements of the legal code was Law Eight, which pertained to the rights of "doctor of law" graduates.[68] These privileges established doctors as an elite cadre of men, and by the late 1400s, the Castilian monarchs would promote these individuals in their royal administration and judiciary. Not only did doctors enjoy preferential titles, compensation, and exemption from royal taxes and military service, but the legal code also ensured they had preferential access to the king.[69]

Law Eight specified that "the doorkeepers of emperors, kings, and princes must allow the doctor to enter into the presence of the ruler at any time except when affairs of great secrecy are being discussed, and even then, his call must be announced."[70] Thus when Bernardino López completed his studies at the University of Salamanca in the 1470s and became a member of its faculty and administration, he became part of an institution and profession that would radically remake the Castilian royal administrative world in the 1480s. Likewise, his cousin Lorenzo Galíndez would directly benefit from the ascent of elite, educated men who would dominate King Ferdinand and Queen Isabel's royal bureaucratic service by the end of the fifteenth century. The two men represented the ultimate combination of skill, expertise, and well-hidden problematic family lineages.

Inside the University of Salamanca, Bernardino built an ecclesiastical career based on superior academic performance and the assistance of well-placed patrons. At the age of twenty-five, he secured his first opportunity to demonstrate his intellectual talents. In the spring of 1475, university schoolmaster, Juan Ruiz de Camargo, appointed him to temporarily teach a theology course.[71] Although Bernardino was qualified to do so, it seems highly likely that the schoolmaster selected him because the Camargo, Santa María, and Carvajal families of Plasencia were intermarried and part of the same church patronage network.[72] In fact, Juan Ruiz was such a trusted member of the Carvajal–Santa María family confederation that, in 1465, Cardinal Juan de Carvajal named him conservator in his will and made him responsible for the disposition of his assets and possessions.[73] Thus Bernardino López's converso family connections most likely played a key role in this critical ecclesiastical opportunity.

Over the course of the late 1470s, Bernardino circulated among Spain's emerging intellectual elite and continued to climb the university's academic ladder. After securing his temporary professorship, he served on the university's leadership council, the Cloister (Claustro). As a member of this body, he participated in the oversight of the university, along with his relatives, Dr. Martín de Ávila, who was both a professor at the university and the bishop of Ávila; the schoolmaster Camargo; and the converso humanist Antonio de Nebrija.[74] Each of these men had mixed Jewish-Christian pedigrees, so it seems likely that they believed there was a future for conversos. In spite of hardening societal attitudes about Christian descendants of Jews, even well-known New Christians such as Nebrija could be among Spain's elite.

Bernardino represented the development of humanism in Spain and was one of its active leaders in Salamanca and Plasencia. The University of Salamanca; the church leaders of the Dioceses of Plasencia, Ávila, and Salamanca; the Hieronymite Monastery at Guadalupe; and the military Order of Alcántara—all were responsible for the development of Spanish humanism, the revival of the study of classical philosophy, science, art, and poetry, as well as for the corollary preservation of "Hispano-Judaic culture."[75] Bernardino secured a series of eight teaching positions between 1475 and 1479 and was able to assume increasingly well-respected roles in the Salamancan church.[76] By 1479, he was a prior, or a monastic leader, in the Convent of Saint Steven, and in the following year his colleagues named him rector of the university.[77]

In the same year that Bernardino became the university's rector, King Ferdinand and Queen Isabel instituted a significant shift in the Castilian royal government that would ultimately favor university graduates. In 1480, they altered the membership of their most important advisory council, the Consejo Real (Royal Council). Before this period, aristocratic families of knights occupied a majority of the seats on the Royal Council.[78] After the king and queen's reforms, the reconstituted council reserved seven of its twelve seats for a new class of administrative elites in Spain—the university-educated letrados—thereby disenfranchising noble families like the Mendoza.[79] Helen Nader, in *The Mendoza Family in the Spanish Renaissance 1350–1550*, writes:

> The *letrados* in the royal council of Fernándo and Isabel brought to their positions a coherent and rational concept of the goals of the government and of their role in it, the concept developed by don Alfonso de Cartagena [the brother of Bishop Gonzalo García de Santa María of Plasencia] and his students long before the reign of the Catholic Monarchs. This *letrado* concept of the history and nature of the Spanish monarchy, based on medieval scholastic political theory and Roman law, formed a sharp contrast to the assumptions of previous royal councils.[80]

Thus this new professional class of letrados, populated by conversos like the Carvajal–Santa María, would play a crucial role in the Spanish royal government after the 1480s. In addition, the favoritism the monarchs showed university-educated men occurred in concert with improvements at the University of Salamanca.

Over the course of two years (1480–81), Rector Bernardino López served as a powerful catalyst in readying the university to produce Spain's new bureaucratic elite. For example, he tightened regulations relating to students' education and graduation.[81] Of concern was the practice of allowing students to complete their education with external faculty or at other universities. Rather than allow this to continue and thus "open the door to the chance that no one would ever graduate from here [the University of Salamanca]," the Cloister elected to require students to matriculate at Salamanca.[82] This measure ensured that all students met the university's requirements for graduation, and it positioned the university to compete against other emerging Spanish educational institutions. A likely beneficiary of Bernardino López's efforts was his younger cousin, Lorenzo Galíndez, who in less than ten years would arrive on campus to pursue his doctorate in law. In addition to his work on university regulations, when the university

faced an acute shortage of qualified instructors of theology in December 1480, Bernardino López agreed to teach these required classes.[83] Because this teaching duty was
in addition to his responsibilities as the university rector, the Cloister handsomely compensated Bernardino with a supplemental salary of 25,000 maravedís.[84]

Bernardino's role in the expanding university was an important one. As rector, he
was the keeper of one of the five keys needed to open the university's strongbox holding its deposits of gold and silver ducados, reales, and maravedís.[85] Bernardino was not
only trusted with access to the university's actual monies, but also with the responsibility of negotiating with the Cathedral of Salamanca regarding the university's funding. As the university was a component of the local church, it was dependent on the
church for a portion of its financial support. Working with others, Bernardino routinely concluded agreements such as a financial settlement concerning the sharing
of diezmos revenues between the cathedral and the university.[86] Simultaneously, in
December 1480, the University of Salamanca Cloister dispatched Bernardino to lobby
his ecclesiastical patron, Cardinal Pedro González de Mendoza, to found a college at
the university.[87] Although the Cloister had sent a letter to Cardinal Mendoza in 1479
communicating its unanimous support of his interest in endowing a new college and
providing several scholarships, the Cloister had not received an affirmative reply.[88] Unfortunately, Bernardino was unable to convince Mendoza, who instead elected to install
his College of the Holy Cross (Colegio de Santa Cruz) at the University of Valladolid.[89]
Although Bernardino's mission proved fruitless for the university, he likely used his
time with Mendoza to further his own interests. Only two years later, Mendoza, then
bishop of Sevilla, granted Bernardino a canonship in the Cathedral of Sevilla.[90]

During the remainder of the 1480s and into the 1490s, the Carvajal family's involvement in the University of Salamanca's administration declined. Rather than invest
all of their vital energies in the development and growth of the institution, the family
used the university as a stepping-stone to better ecclesiastical and royal bureaucratic
opportunities. After several years of service to the university, Bernardino took a series of
increasingly important church appointments and papal positions. Each step of the way,
he was ascending the Christian hierarchy and demonstrating that his family confederation's identity was tied to service in the church, as well as to the Catholic monarchs.

In 1484, Bernardino launched his career in the Vatican when he delivered an
erudite and passionate sermon to Pope Sixtus IV, a Franciscan, and the College of
Cardinals on the relationship between the Passion of Christ and the circumcision of
Christ.[91] On this point, Bernardino argued, "Truly . . . the human flesh of Christ has
been most fully demonstrated by his circumcision."[92] It seems likely that Bernardino
selected this theological topic emphasizing the humanity of Christ, a belief strongly
held by Franciscans, so that he could play to his primary audience, the pope.[93] Catholic
leaders were so impressed with his oratory that, shortly after his sermon, the subsequent pope, Innocent VIII, named Bernardino a papal nuncio to Naples in 1486. Later,
in 1487, the pope appointed him papal nuncio ambassador to Spain.[94]

Much like his ancestor, Bishop Pablo de Santa María, Bernardino found himself at the center of affairs of the papal and Spanish royal court, and he owed everything, just as did Pablo, to his loyalty to the faith and the state. Bernardino followed in the likeness and footsteps of his early clansmen Alonso de Cartagena, Gonzalo García de Santa María, and Juan de Carvajal with his appointment as a bishop. His first high-level Spanish post was bishop of Astorga in 1488, which was followed by his appointment as bishop of Cartagena in 1489.[95] Both bishoprics had been seats that his family confederation predecessors had occupied, but for Bernardino there were no apparent public impediments to even greater heights.

RESOLVING AFFAIRS WITH THE ESTÚÑIGA FAMILY IN PLASENCIA, 1488

The religious and political ascent of the Carvajal–Santa María family confederation came with royal obligations, as well as rewarding opportunities to settle scores with New Christian competitors. From the perspective of the converso nobility, Jewish bloodlines did not unite them into a common identity and in collective action. Although the late fourteenth-century king Enrique II's testamentary acts had created a New Nobility from the ashes of the civil war and the integration of Jewish and Old Christian families, there was no shared identity that promoted mutual initiatives. Conversos were perfectly willing to engage each other, in the most violent of traditions, in open warfare. New Christians were a fragmented community, where family, faith, and lineage commingled into unexpected alliances, as was demonstrated by the reconciliation of the Carvajal–Santa María family confederation with the New Noble Álvarez de Toledo, señores de Oropesa. While they tended toward extreme loyalty to extended clan relations, their shared Jewish-Christian ancestries was also their Achilles' heel. As the by-product of the late fourteenth-century transformation of the Castilian nobility via Jewish conversion and intermarriage with Old Christian families, elite conversos' blood ancestry was viewed with contempt by late fifteenth-century Old Christians, who voiced and advanced anti-Jewish and anticonverso public norms and laws. It was within this perplexed tangle of identities, relationships, and thirst for superiority that the Carvajal–Santa María family confederation confronted the Estúñiga clan, condes de Béjar y Plasencia.

In 1488, precisely the same year that the Spanish monarchs and Pope Innocent VIII made Bernardino López bishop of Astorga, the Placentino family confederation settled tense familial and royal affairs with the Estúñiga. In an act of deep loyalty to King Ferdinand and Queen Isabel, the Carvajal–Santa María clan served as the monarchs' weapon to relieve the Estúñiga family of its title and seigniorial hold on Plasencia. The family confederation's actions demonstrate both how the Spanish monarchy utilized its noble converso families against one another and the rewards the crown was willing to bestow on its most loyal servants.

Since King Juan II had granted the Estúñiga family the city of Plasencia in 1441 as a portion of its seigniorial lands, Placentinos had aggressively disputed the counts' secular rule. Throughout the mid- to late 1400s, the Carvajal–Santa María confederation had routinely intervened in the Estúñiga family's rule of the city by using the confederation's authority in the cathedral, as well as its seats on the municipal council. In addition, in 1472, the Carvajal and Santa María clans engaged the Estúñiga family in a judicial battle over local and regional property claims.[96] The political deadlock between the competing converso nobles reached its conclusion in 1488 when the king and queen instructed Bernardino López's father, Francisco de Carvajal, to terminate Estúñiga rule in Plasencia.[97] As the Estúñiga were in a weakened state due to the death of Count Álvaro de Estúñiga in June 1488, the monarchs exploited this opportunity to act quickly against the count's inexperienced grandson, also named Álvaro de Estúñiga.[98]

The family confederation's plan for the demise of the Estúñiga clan concentrated on the efforts of Francisco, his brother Gutierre de Carvajal, who "had it in" for the Estúñiga family, and their relative, Hernando de Carvajal.[99] Francisco would lead the principal military effort to eliminate the Estúñiga hold on Plasencia. As Hernando lived in the first house adjacent to the Plasencia city gate known as the Puerta de Berrozanas, the family confederation would also lead a secondary effort to funnel warriors into the city at the appointed time. (See fig. 1.3 for an overview of the locations described in this section.)

According to the early seventeenth-century historian of Plasencia, Friar Alonso de Fernández, the royalist forces had devised a plan to fight two fronts because Count Estúñiga ordered all city gates locked before nightfall each day.[100] The Plasencia family confederation, which lacked a sufficient number of armed men as a result of their transition into learned careers, called on roughly fifty extended family members who had remained knights, and allies from Cáceres to support its armed operation to evict the Estúñiga family.[101] In early October 1488, the Cáceres contingent, led by Francisco's son, Juan de Sande Carvajal, rode to a meeting point outside the city known as the Heredad de Carrascal. At this location, they joined Francisco and twenty laborers armed with axes who would hack through the Puerta de Trujillo so that the mounted knights could enter the city.[102]

The king and queen, eager to ensure victory, also called on knights and men-at-arms from Zamora, Toro, Ciudad Rodrigo, Trujillo, and Badajoz to participate in an elaborate ruse to deceive the Estúñiga family.[103] King Ferdinand reportedly summoned these nobles to Plasencia to aid—in a peaceful manner—with smoothing over disagreements with the Estúñiga clan. The trickery involved using the knights not as parties to a negotiated agreement but instead as elements of a military operation. As Álvaro anticipated an attack by the royalist knights, he and his men secured the city's gates, while his uncle, Juan de Estúñiga, master of the Order of Alcántara, fortified the city's castle.[104]

The ensuing bloody clash split the loyalties of the Order of Alcántara. While the Estúñiga clan claimed membership in this religious brotherhood of knights who were committed to the Spanish Reconquista, so did the family confederation, whose leaders in the order included the Segovian Alonso de Almaraz (master of Castilnovo and head of the order); the Cáceran Juan de Ulloa (master of Benquerencia), and Gonzalo de Carvajal (master of Las Elges).[105]

On the night of October 17, 1488, Francisco de Carvajal and his son, Juan de Sande, led royalist knights and soldiers to the city's barricaded Puerta de Trujillo. Swinging hatchets and axes, the laborers made quick work of the wooden city gate. Mounted warriors burst into the walled city. As they galloped in on Calle de Trujillo, the men yelled, "Plasencia! Plasencia! For King Ferdinand and Queen Isabel!," and entered into hand-to-hand skirmishing with the Estúñiga forces.[106] Not deterred, the battle-hardened defenders returned the king's challenge with the call, "Plasencia! Plasencia! For our duke, Lord Álvaro de Estúñiga!" With Francisco's forces now flooding in through the Puerta de Trujillo, as well as those passing through the Puerta de Berrozanas controlled by Hernando de Carvajal, a "bloody battle in the streets and plaza" lasted three days.[107] Reportedly, as many one thousand armed combatants fought this carryover of feudal war.

The second full day of fighting was centered in the Plaza Mayor—where the battle would be decided—not only by the wielding of swords but also through the intervention of cathedral cantor Diego de Lobera. Nothing less than a miracle reportedly transpired. Employing the "tradition of the Eucharist," Diego and other members of the cathedral, who must not have been involved in the conflict as deeply as the Carvajal–Santa María family confederation, intervened with the intention of ending the bloodshed. A first-person account related what ensued:

> As the parties of the duke and the parties of the monarchs fought . . . Diego de Lobera went to Santa María [the Cathedral of Plasencia] in the company of many devoted souls, especially women. There, they placed the Holy Sacrament in the monstrance that Cardinal Juan de Carvajal had given to the cathedral and organized a Eucharistic procession. [As the procession marched into the Plaza Mayor], "those of one party and those of other party," in the words of Lord Jose Benito, "undulated as if forced by a gale of wind that moved them in a terrifying zigzagging of motion." The gust went to the dead and gave them aid. The moment was supreme, providential, and in this instance, decisive. Jesús Sacramentado entered the plaza. His sacramental robes, white and shining, contrasted with the blood-covered feet of the combatants. The procession, which had been advancing silently and gravely, appeared to stop in amazement and awe. The clash had not diminished; you could hear crashing of swords; you could hear the cries of the seriously injured. The procession continued its

march; the voice of Lord Diego de Lobera, full and prevailing, stood out from the thousand of voices of those still fighting. Lifting in his hands, he raised the Holy Host to the sky. At this moment, one hundred knights encircled him. Hundreds of lances served as his escort. Windows and balcony doors burst open and lamps ignited as God blessed all men of good will, and a silence of amazement, an enormous silence of stupefaction sealed their lips and opened their souls. Jesus had triumphed. Lord Diego de Lobera turned and presented the Divine Host to the heroes of both parties and they lowered their lances in a sign of respect and compliance. "Peace be with all of you," he exclaimed . . . and calm entered the city . . . until [others, not witness to this event,] came into the plaza via the Calle de Sol and chanted, "Plasencia! Plasencia! For King Ferdinand and Queen Isabel!" . . . [B]ut before its echoes could continue . . . from a thousand mouths, and with true heart-felt sentiment of thousands of hearts, resoundingly, triumphantly, and decisively, a new yell came: "Plasencia for Jesús Sacramentado."[108]

The family confederation's restoration of the city to royal rule demonstrated its fidelity to the Spanish monarchs, and the king and queen compensated the family confederation for its service. In October 1488, when King Ferdinand traveled to Plasencia to commemorate the victory, he passed through the Puerta de Trujillo, where he ordered the city to carve the royal coat of arms, as well as the Carvajal heraldic shield, into the gate's stone facade (fig. 7.5).[109] As a reward for their leadership and their engagement of the Estúñiga, the Carvajal family received their first seigniorial title, that of señores de Torrejón.[110] In addition, the king applied the title retroactively so that Francisco de Carvajal was to be known as the second señor de Torrejón and as "the Subduer of Plasencia."[111] Francisco's father, Garci López de Carvajal (the royal judge), would now be remembered as the first señor.

Significantly, the community leaders serving as witnesses to the king's pronouncement in Plasencia were not the knights from Cáceres but the Plasencia churchmen and royal administrators, the source of the clan's growing local and kingdomwide authority. Among them were Garci López de Carvajal y Sande, a Spanish royal ambassador; Sancho de Carvajal, the archdeacon of Plasencia and Béjar; and Juan Fernández de Cabreros, a cathedral notary.[112] Although it was their Cáceres clansmen who provided the majority of the armed forces that took the city from the Estúñiga, the Plasencia family confederation received the royal rewards of patronage and honorific titles.

The battle for political control of the city of Plasencia also resolved the Carvajal–Santa María family confederation's jurisdictional contests with the Estúñiga clan: namely, the churchmen in the Cathedral of Plasencia would once again strengthen their hold on the city. Remarkably, the family confederation remained robust inside the Cathedral of Plasencia, in spite of its loss of the bishop's position for most of the pe-

FIGURE 7.5. Puerta de Trujillo. Photo by author.

riod from 1480 to 1530. The resilience of its efforts was no doubt because of its fruitful identity shifting that framed Carvajal-surnamed clansmen as the most prominent leaders of the family while preserving the remainder of its interrelated lineages within the Sande, Fernández, Cabreros, and Villalva families.[113] With few exceptions, local cathedral offices—archdeacon, cantor, and treasurer—were continuously occupied by the extended family (table 7.1). By the 1520s continuous family control of the diocese returned when Cardinal Bernardino López served as an absentee bishop for two years. His short tenure was then followed by the thirty-year ecclesiastical rule of Bishop Gutierre de Vargas Carvajal (r. 1524–59), Bernardino's nephew. He was a modest reformer who anticipated the Council of Trent by convening a diocesan synod in Jaraicejo in 1534.[114] Along with the reforms to church practices, Gutierre extended the family confederation's reach into the Americas by funding a naval expedition to South America's Río de La Plata from 1536 to 1539.[115] That reach was made possible by the initiative and efforts of Cardinal Bernardino and Lorenzo Galíndez de Carvajal.

AT THE CENTER OF EUROPEAN AND EARLY AMERICAN AFFAIRS

Perhaps more than any other event of the late fifteenth and early sixteenth centuries, Cristóbal Colón's encounter with the Americas in 1492 transformed and blended the historical trajectories of Spain, Europe, and the Americas. In their capacity as ecclesiastical leaders and royal administrators, Carvajal–Santa María family members performed indispensable and vital duties on behalf of King Ferdinand and Queen Isabel in their early efforts to establish a presence in the Americas. In essence, this converso family was critical for Spanish imperial plans for the Americas.

Bernardino López labored to collect papal bulls to verify the Spanish monarchs' rights in America, while his brother, Garci López de Carvajal y Sande, negotiated an independent Spanish treaty with Portugal to divide the Americas between the two Iberian kingdoms. As these two men guided Spanish affairs for the crown during the 1490s, their younger cousin, Dr. Lorenzo Galíndez de Carvajal, was completing his legal degree at the University of Salamanca and readying to join the royal court in Valladolid as a judge. Collectively, these men represented a fully transmuted Spanish converso identity that was concurrently committed to advancing extended family ties while suppressing outsiders' knowledge of their mixed Jewish-Christian ancestry.

Four years before Colón reached the Americas, Bernardino López, then bishop of Badajoz, returned to Rome as the monarchs' ambassador to Pope Innocent VIII.[116] Once there, he found himself heavily engaged in the messages flowing between the monarchs and the pope. In 1488, in a papal bull congratulating the Catholic monarchs on their victories over Islamic Granada and their capture of the palace and fortress of the Alhambra, the pope was keen to note that their "beloved son," Bernardino, had been the one to communicate the good news to him.[117] Likewise, when Innocent VIII died in 1492, Bernardino relayed news of the pope's death and the election of Pope Alexander VI (the Spaniard Rodrigo Lanzol y de Borja) to Ferdinand and Isabel.[118]

At the papal court, Bernardino was one of the critical Spanish leaders attempting to secure the pope's blessing of Spanish discoveries in the Americas. On May 3 and 4,

Table 7.1. Carvajal–Santa María Family Confederation in the Cathedral of Plasencia, 1470s–1530s (All color-coded cells are confederation members.)

Decade	Bishop	Other Family	Archdeacon of Plasencia and Béjar	Archdeacon of Trujillo and Medellín	Archdeacon of Coria	Cantor	Treasurer
1470s			Carvajal	Salamanca	Carvajal	Salamanca	Carvajal
1480s		Rodrigo de Ávila	Sancho de Carvajal	Ruy García de Salamanca Diego de Lobera	Diego de Carvajal	Ruy García de Salamanca Diego de Lobera	Álvaro de Carvajal
1490s		Rodrigo de Ávila Gutierre Álvarez de Toledo	Sancho de Carvajal Garci López de Carvajal II	Juan Castellanos de Villalva	Diego de Carvajal	Diego de Lobera	Álvaro de Carvajal
1500s		Gutierre Álvarez de Toledo	Garci López de Carvajal II	Bernardino de Carvajal (of Trujillo only)	Archdeacon no longer organized in the Diocese Plasencia.	Diego de Lobera	Bernardino de Carvajal
1510s		Gómez de Solís y Toledo	Garci López de Carvajal II	Francisco de Carvajal (of Medellín only) Luis de Cáceres (of Trujillo only) Francisco de Carvajal (of Medellín only)	n/a n/a n/a	Juan Castellanos de Villalva Juan Castellanos de Villalva Cristóbal de Villalva	Rufrio de Sande
1520s	Bernardino López de Carvajal Gutierre de Vargas Carvajal	Gómez de Solís y Toledo	Bernardino de Carvajal	Luis de Cáceres (of Trujillo only) Francisco de Carvajal (of Medellín only) Gabriel de Carvajal Pizarro (of Medellín only)	n/a n/a n/a	Cristóbal de Villalva	Álvaro de Sande
1530s	Gutierre de Vargas Carvajal		Bernardino de Carvajal	Luis de Cáceres (of Trujillo only) Gabriel de Carvajal Pizarro (of Medellín only)	n/a	Cristóbal de Villalva	Álvaro de Sande

1493, Bernardino and other Spanish officials at the papal court obtained the *Inter caetera* bull from Pope Alexander VI, as well as two other bulls, granting Spain the authority to "certain lands" not possessed by Christians.[119] Specifically, the May 3 *Inter caetera* communicated the pope's recognition and approval of Spain's discoveries and economic interests in the New World. However, it also included stipulations that Spain teach Christianity to the lands' inhabitants, as well as recertify Portuguese claims in Africa and Guinea. After further lobbying on the part of the Spanish ambassadors to Rome, a superseding May 4 *Inter caetera* was prepared to enhance and distinguish the rights and privileges of Spain vis-à-vis Portugal. With this additional papal authorization, Spain secured all lands west of the Azores and Cape Verde islands, and Portugal captured all lands to the east of these islands. This Spanish-Portuguese demarcation, depicted in Alberto Cantino's world map of 1502, granted Spain all of North America, Central America, the Caribbean, and most of South America.

Pope Alexander VI's personal sympathies, allegiances, and family interests likely influenced his favorable treatment of Spanish claims. First, the pope was originally from the Kingdom of Aragón and at the Roman Curia tended to surround himself with Spaniards.[120] Second, Bishop Bernardino López was a favorite of the pope and thus likely had significant political influence that allowed him to negotiate the best terms for the Spanish crown.[121] In June 1493, Bernardino, the preferred Castilian ambassador at the Vatican, had the privilege of personally presenting the pope with King Ferdinand and Queen Isabel's gift of gold from the Americas.[122] The pope used a portion of these American monies for his own interests, specifically to patronize his titular church. At the time of the Spanish encounter with the New World, the pope was funding the restoration of Santa María Maggori's church ceiling, which bore his family's coat of arms.[123] Previously the pope's family had enjoyed other benefits extended by the Spanish monarchs. Several years before the discovery of the Americas, in 1485, King Ferdinand had generously "invested" the pope's eldest son, Pedro Luis Borgia, with the Duchy of Gandia near Venice, thus making Pedro a superior member of the nobility.[124]

Shortly after Bernardino presented the Spanish monarch's monetary gift to Pope Alexander VI, the Carvajal–Santa María family confederation's prominence in international affairs reached new heights. In fall 1493, the pope named Bernardino López cardinal of San Pedro and Marcellinius, and the Spanish king and queen dispatched Ambassador Garci López de Carvajal y Sande to the Portuguese royal court to begin negotiations with King Juan on the division of the Americas.[125] While Garci López's embassy fell short of its goal, namely, securing a Spanish-Portuguese treaty to validate the papal *Inter caetera*, his diplomatic efforts contributed to a yearlong dialogue that produced the Treaty of Tordesillas in 1494.[126] This treaty reset the demarcation of Spanish and Portuguese lands in the Americas "at the distance of 370 leagues west of the Cape Verde Islands" and established a collaborative endeavor to map the boundary by qualified ship pilots, astrologers, and sailors.[127]

Key to the family confederation's ability to participate in these crucial historical events in the Americas and Europe was Cardinal Bernardino López's access to insiders in the Spanish royal court and his involvement with international leaders. In the 1490s, he routinely exchanged correspondence with Canon Pedro Mártir de Anglería of the Cathedral of Granada, who had regular access to the Catholic monarchs, Fernando and Isabel, who resided at the Alhambra.[128] Pedro Mártir owed his position to Cardinal Pedro González de Mendoza, his mentor.[129] This canon had first gained access to the Catholic monarchs when he served as the chaplain to Princess Juana "La Loca" (the Mad) and subsequently as chaplain to her parents, King Ferdinand and Queen Isabel.[130] From Pedro Mártir's letters, it is clear that Bernardino was a close associate of Pedro González, who in early 1495 was near death and would soon relinquish his title as cardinal of the Church of Santa Croce en Gerusalemme in Rome.[131] When Mártir wrote to congratulate Bernardino on his recent appointment by Pope Alexander VI as the new cardinal of Santa Croce, he said, "In front of our king and queen, Cardinal Mendoza . . . stated he preferred you, among all others, to receive the red cardinal's hat."[132] Thus Bernardino and the family confederation had mastered their position as elite conversos who represented the ideal hybrid identity: excellent Old Christian credentials coupled with over one hundred years of family transformation. Roman Catholic Church leaders and Spanish courtiers both knew of and respected Bernardino's position in papal and state affairs.

Through correspondence with Pedro Mártir, the strength of Bernardino's character and his interconnectedness with Spanish and papal affairs becomes apparent. In Mártir's eleven letters to the cardinal, sent from 1495 to 1500, Bernardino received congratulations on his personal accomplishments, news of the royal family, and Spanish insights on international affairs. Pertaining to the royal family, this correspondence included details of the unusual character of Spanish Princess Juana, Queen Isabel's concerns about her daughter's health, and news of the marriage of the princess to Felipe "el Hermoso" (the Handsome), who was the son of Holy Roman Emperor Maximilian I.[133] Regarding state affairs, Mártir relayed notes about embassies sent from Milan and Naples to Spain, royal concerns about the quality and "disorder" of Spanish troops protecting the frontier against a hostile France, and French king Charles VIII's military plans to take Naples.[134]

Likewise, from five of Pedro Mártir's letters penned from June 1495 to September 1497, Bernardino learned fascinating elements of what Colón had experienced in the Americas. The letters spoke of Admiral Colón's reports from Cuba, as well as Hispañola, where he believed he had located the gold mines of King Solomon.[135] Mártir's correspondence pertaining to the Americas also demonstrates the substantive nature of the intelligence that Bernardino regularly received and how this information would position the family confederation to exploit new American opportunities. Although the letters contained many inaccuracies, they constituted the best knowledge available at the time. His reports, developed from his personal relationships with Colón, Vasco de

Gama, Cortés, Magellan, and Cabot, allowed him to publish *Décadas del nuevo mundo* (Decades of the New World), one of the first chronicles describing the New World.[136]

Along with the reports contained in these letters came praise for Bernardino, thereby revealing the growing stature of the Carvajal family.[137] In a short note to Bernardino, Mártir wrote about meeting Garci López de Carvajal y Sande:

> Garci López, your brother, came to visit us at the royal court not too long ago. He is a distinguished man and of clear talent. . . . He composed in our native language some delicious verses, oozing with dense juices and weighty ideas. It has satisfied me very much to get to know him. However, I do not hold him in great esteem just because of your personal merits or because he is your brother. Nor does he think of me as a lesser, as he can see I am devotedly yours, especially as . . . he instructs me how you have forged . . . your own talents.[138]

With these brief phrases, Pedro Mártir negotiated a delicate balance between bestowing praise on the cardinal's brother and reaffirming his loyalty to and admiration of the cardinal. A creature of the royal court himself, Mártir demonstrated that Bernardino López was a man worthy of generous words, especially because he could dispense favors to his friends and associates. In fact, in the same year that Bernardino became cardinal of Santa Croce and bishop of Sigüenza, he appointed Mártir as his personal representative, his vicar and provisor, in the Diocese of Sigüenza.[139] He also extended patronage positions to his own family members. As the cardinal of Santa Croce, Bernardino named Rodrigo de Carvajal, his nephew, patriarch of his titular church in Rome.[140] Ultimately, though, Bernardino owed his elevated ecclesiastical status and his access to lucrative patronage opportunities to Pope Alexander VI.

Bernardino proved to be a good investment for the pope, especially in January 1495 when he defended the papacy from Charles VIII's demands for property and treasure in return for not attacking Rome.[141] Chronicled in Andrés Bernáldez's early sixteenth-century work, *Memorias del reinado de los reyes católicos* (Memoirs of the Catholic Kings), the events of early 1495 reveal that it was in Bernardino's nature to confront unusually difficult situations. To a great extent, Pope Alexander VI was the instigator of his conflict with the French. In his endeavor to conquer the Kingdom of Naples, the pope first turned to France to assist him.[142] However, after French troops entered the Italian peninsula and it became apparent that Cardinal Giuliano della Rovere, the pope's rival and eventual successor, had the ear of the French, Alexander VI became increasingly concerned that the French king would turn against him.[143] The pope's suspicions of the French turned out to be valid, eventually prompting him to make peace with Naples.

Unfortunately for the pontiff, he was unable to prevent the French army from entering Rome.[144] In January 1495, before Alexander VI could form a defensive Holy

League to shield himself from the French, he first had to confront the forces that were ransacking much of the Italian countryside and threatening to destroy Rome.[145] With the French blockading Rome by land and sea, combined with the poor military performance of the allied Neapolitan troops, King Charles VIII demanded that the pope surrender the Castle of San Angelo in Rome, as well as the papacy's treasury.[146] Faced with an imminent French invasion of the city, the pope sent Cardinal Carvajal as an ambassador to Charles VIII. Bernardino defiantly argued that that the king

> had promised through his faith to neither anger the Church nor demand a single thing from the Church [and] . . . that his demands are against the Holy Mother Church and what he wanted could not be given to him. . . . In no way or in any manner could he have the Castle of San Angelo nor the Church's treasury because the castle belongs to the Church and the treasury is made up of crosses, chalices, and saintly bodies.[147]

After hearing Bernardino's statement, Charles VIII responded, "My Barons will acquaint the Pope with my will," and he promised to take the castle by force of artillery, if necessary.[148] Yet, within days, Charles VIII and Alexander VI came to an agreement that produced little for the French but preserved the papacy's power and protected its assets.[149] Two months after Bernardino's bold stand, the pope formed a defensive alliance with the Italian kingdoms, the Austrian Holy Roman Emperor Maximilian, and the Spanish monarchs, which was intended to shield the Italian peninsula from further harassment by the French as well as the Turks.[150]

After demonstrating his unyielding loyalty to Pope Alexander VI during the papal conflict with the French, international leaders perceived Bernardino as a critical actor in European affairs. In 1497, the pope granted Bernardino the privilege of notifying King Ferdinand and Queen Isabel of his decision to extend a papal bull certifying the Spanish king and queen as "los reyes católicos" (the Catholic Monarchs), perhaps the single most iconic title the Spanish crown ever received.[151] Likewise, in the 1490s and 1500s, Bernardino advised the Catholic monarchs in numerous letters of the need for them to commit additional armies to fight the French.[152] Bolstering Pope Alexander VI was not left just to the Carvajal–Santa María church leaders. In 1503, at Rocasecca, Italy, a Spanish cavalry contingent of twelve hundred men was led by the Extremaduran Villalva, Carvajal, and Pizarro captains in the Spanish armies.[153] This was an integrated family using every political, religious, and military resource at its disposal to protect Spanish interests.

In other cases, Bernardino wrote to Ferdinand and Isabel to inform them of papal bulls relating to the Spanish conquest of the Canary Islands, as well as to arrange for a papal audience with them.[154] In this manner, he was consistently involved as an intermediary and adviser in multiple aspects of Spanish affairs of state.

BERNADINO'S QUEST FOR THE PAPACY

Bernardino would especially need his influential relationships when his friend Pope Alexander VI died in 1503. Alexander VI's successor, Pope Julius II, came to power during a period of constantly shifting state alliances between the papacy, Ferdinand and Isabel's Spain, Louis XII's France, and Maximilian I's Holy Roman Empire.[155] This chaotic period created the conditions for Cardinal Bernardino López de Carvajal to seek the papacy.

In 1508, these four crucial European powers forged a short-term alliance, the League of Cambrai, against Venice.[156] In less than a year the military successes of the league came to fruition. After it forced Venice to capitulate and cede many of its territories to the victors, the alliance quickly fell apart.[157] In 1509, Pope Julius II decided it was better to have a weakened Venice than one annihilated by French occupation forces.[158] As a result, the pope left the league and joined forces with his former enemy, Venice, so that the papacy could prevent France from overtaking all of the Italian peninsula.[159] It was within this politically contested environment that Cardinal Carvajal found the opportunity to challenge his old nemesis, Pope Julius II, for the papacy.

Bernardino's dislike for Pope Julius II (r. 1503–13), and perhaps his willingness to confront him, had roots in Pope Alexander VI's tenure (1492–1503).[160] Julius II, born Giuliano della Rovere, was a consistent rival of Bernardino's friend and papal patron.

Cardinal Carvajal acted against Pope Julius II after a series of key conflicts weakened the pope's position with Spain, France, and the Holy Roman Empire. In a repeat of the Investiture Controversy of the twelfth century, since 1507 the Spanish monarchs had repeatedly disputed the pope's authority to appoint bishops in Spain.[161] King Ferdinand was so displeased with Pope Julius II over this issue and other matters that, in 1507, while in route to Savona, Italy, the monarch refused to stop in Ostia to meet with him.[162] Instead he proceeded to Savona to meet King Louis XII, where the two monarchs renewed their temporary peaceful relations.[163] Further complicating the weakened position of the pontiff in 1510 and generating a previously unexpected opening for Cardinal Carvajal to advance his own interests was the encroachment of French armies on Italian soil.[164] As the French were cognizant of "the pope's wish to divide" Maximilian I from his ally, Louis XII, they were ready to support a new candidate for the papacy, Cardinal Carvajal.[165] Likewise, as Cardinal Carvajal was "one of Maximilian I's most faithful friends at the Roman Court," it seems likely that the Holy Roman Emperor backed the cardinal.[166]

At the Council of Pisa in 1511, Bernardino López de Carvajal aspired to attain the family's greatest title, pope of the Roman Catholic Church, thus completing the clan's successful rise in the Castilian as well as the European world.[167] Bernardino convened the schismatic Council of Pisa, along with Cardinals Borgia, Briconnet, de Prie, and Sanseverino, in hopes of convincing other ecclesiastical leaders and monarchs to support the initiative to unseat Pope Julius II.[168] At the council, Bernardino accepted the office of pope (or "antipope").[169] In the city of Pisa, the local residents referred to him as "Papa Bernardino."[170] However, due to unforeseen political circumstances, including the rapid recovery of Pope Julius II from a nearly fatal illness and King Ferdinand's withdrawal of support of Cardinal Carvajal's endeavor, the council failed to force the pope out of office.[171] Further, although Maximilian I had initially supported Bernardino's grasp for the pontificate, he too renounced the actors at the Council of Pisa.[172]

Unable to hold a viable coalition together, the French and Cardinal Carvajal's co-conspirators concluded the Council of Pisa without success. To penalize the five schismatic cardinals for their actions, Pope Julius II excommunicated each of them at the Fifth Lateran Council of 1512.[173] Although the pope deprived Bernardino of his ecclesiastical titles and his income from the Diocese of Sigüenza for a short period, in 1513, Bernardino and his associates rehabilitated themselves when Pope Julius II died and Pope Leo X assumed the mantle of the papacy. Pope Leo X reconciled Bernardino and the four other men to the church and restored them to their status as cardinals.[174]

During the 1510s, Bernardino returned to a vigorous life as a cardinal. He participated as a critical actor in the conclaves that elected Popes Adrian VI (r. 1522–23) and Clement VII (r. 1523–34), and he oversaw the Spanish monarchs' construction of the Basilica de San Croce de Jerusalem in Rome.[175] At the election of Adrian VI, he almost succeeded once again in claiming the papacy for himself and his family, and his actions are worthy of telling because they show the Carvajal–Santa María family confederation was always a useful tool of the Spanish monarchy.

Perhaps remembering how Maximilian I had undercut his efforts at the 1511 Council of Pisa, Cardinal Carvajal wrote to the newly elected emperor, Carlos V, to inform him that the Medici pope Leo X had died at eight o'clock on the evening of December 1, 1521, and asked for his advice pertaining to the forthcoming conclave.[176] Without the benefit of a copy of the emperor's reply, we know that the actions of the conclave of cardinals indicate that Carvajal was seriously considered by his fellow princes of the church to be a worthy choice. Reports from the emperor's ambassador in Rome also reveal that these holy men were fighting a vicious battle for the position. The ambassador, Juan Manuel, was at the conclave and reported, "There cannot be so much hatred and so many devils in hell as among these cardinals. . . . The cardinals quarrel with one another, and do not yet assemble in conclave. Some of them wish to bring about a schism."[177]

Not until the end of December, on the twenty-eighth, did thirty-nine cardinals convene the conclave to elect a new pope at the Vatican's Apostolic Palace.[178] Noticeably

Table 7.2. Papal Conclave Records of Scrutiny, December 30, 1521–January 9, 1522

Scrutiny	Top Five Candidates	Scrutiny	Top Five Candidates
December 30 First and second scrutiny	C. of Sabina (N. Fiesco) – 10 votes C. Grimani – 10 votes **C. of Ostia (Carvajal) – 9 votes** C. Jacobacius – 7 votes C. de Grassis – 6 votes	January 1 Third scrutiny	**C. of Ostia (Carvajal) – 10 votes** C. of Como – 7 votes C. of Sabina – 7 votes C. Jacobacius – 7 votes C. Piccolomini – 7 votes C. Ursini – 7 votes
January 2 Fourth scrutiny	C. Sanctorum Quatuor (L. Puccio) – 14 votes C. of Ancona – 8 votes **C. of Ostia (Carvajal) – 8 votes** C. Fiesco – 7 votes C. Jacobacius – 7 votes C. St. Sisto – 7 votes	January 3 Fifth scrutiny	C. of Volterra (F. Soderini) – 12 votes C. of Sabina – 9 votes C. of Tortosa (absent) – 8 votes C. of Ancona – 7 votes C. Jacobacius – 7 votes C. Monte – 7 votes C. of York (absent) – 7 votes
January 4 Sixth scrutiny	**C. of Ostia (Carvajal) – 9 votes** C. of Sabina – 9 votes Cardinal of Sion – 8 votes C. Sanctorum Quatuor – 8 votes C. Jacobacius – 8 votes C. Araceli – 8 votes	January 5 Seventh scrutiny	C. of Sabina – 9 votes C. of Sion – 8 votes C. Sanctorum Quatuor – 7 votes C. Vitus – 7 votes **C. of Ostia (Carvajal) – 6 votes** C. of Ancona – 6 votes C. of Bologna – 6 votes C. de Medici – 6 votes C. Jacobacius – 6 votes
January 6 Eighth scrutiny	**C. Tusculi (A. Farnese) – 12 votes** Initially, Cardinal Farnese declared pope, but the vote was called into question.	January 7 Ninth scrutiny	C. of Sabina – 10 votes C. of Porto (D. Grimani) – 10 votes **C. of Ostia (Carvajal) – 9 votes** C. of Sion – 8 votes C. Jacobacius – 8 votes
January 8 Tenth scrutiny	C. Jacobacius – 11 votes **C. of Ostia (Carvajal) – 10 votes** C. of Sabina – 10 votes (tie) C. of Sion – 10 votes (tie) C. of Porto – 10 votes (tie)	January 9 Eleventh scrutiny	**C. of Ostia (Carvajal) – 15 votes** **C. of Tortosa – 15 votes** By consensus, the conclave elected Adriian Florensz, Cardinal of Tortosa (Spain), as Pope Adrian VI.

Source: Bergenroth, *Calendar of Letters, Despatches, and State Papers.*

absent from the opening of the gathering of the College of Cardinals was Adriaan Florensz, a Flemish cardinal who at the time was the bishop of Tortosa in Spain. Over the course of a week and a half, the cardinals proceeded through eleven votes, or scrutinies at the Sistine Chapel (table 7.2; fig. 7.6). On the first three scrutinies, the votes demonstrated that the politicking men had a definite preference for an Italian; however, the Portuguese and Spanish had their candidates too. Cardinal Carvajal (always recorded

FIGURE 7.6. Sistine Chapel, Apostolic Palace. Creative Commons. Used with permission.

as the "Cardinal of Ostia") garnered an impressive third-place finish in the first and second scrutinies, but in the third scrutiny, he received most of the votes. For unknown reasons, perhaps with the knowledge that the election would require many more ballots, in the third scrutiny "one ticket nominated fourteen persons. Some of the cardinals were indignant at such a joke, and desired to open the ticket[;] however, [this] was not done."[179] Voting dragged on through Sunday, January 5. Consistently, Bernardino placed in the top preferred papal candidates during six of the seven ballot tabulations. However, there was still no black smoke wafting from the chimney near the Sistine Chapel.

On January 6, "Papam habemus," "We have a pope," was declared when Cardinal Alessandro Farnese of Tusculi garnered two-thirds of the required ballots. Chaos ensued when Cardinal Cesarini "forsook him" and verbally changed his vote to Cardinal Egidio.[180] Unable to resolve the conflict, the conclave announced "et Papam non habemus," "and we do not have a pope." The gathering was so unsettled by what was described as a "malicious" environment that Cardinal Grimani "retired from the conclave because he felt his conscience much troubled by what had passed," after which Cardinal Egidio proceeded to circulate the chapel and tell "very bad stories about Farnese." As Egidio had been Farnese's confessor for many years, he had knowledge of Farnese's sinful nature.

Three more scrutinies were required to elect the new pope, and repeatedly the cardinal of Ostia, Bernardino, appeared in the top three. Just steps away from the stove that would reveal the *fumata bianca* (white smoke) and the selection of the new pope, Bernardino must have felt the weight of history on his shoulders. About two weeks before January 6, Bernardino had received instructions from Carlos V to vote for another Spanish cardinal in the papal election. Yes, the cardinals would select their pope, but their actions reflected greater European and Spanish political events. This papal election was held less than two months after the resolution of the Comuneros Revolt of 1519–21. That nativist Spanish rebellion against Carlos V's absentee rule—and a genuine fear of the decreasing prominence of Spanish cities and nobility in his Flemish-dominated royal court—had required a substantial military response from the emperor.[181] Tasked with the effective toppling of the revolt had been Carlos V's own childhood tutor and native son of Flanders, Bishop Adriaan Florensz.[182] It seems likely that the emperor owed a great debt to Adriaan. There are strong indications that Bernardino knew he could not become pope and that, as always, the Carvajal–Santa María family confederation served at the pleasure of the king and owed its prosperity to him. It was not Bernardino's destiny to become pope.

On the day before Christmas in 1521, just days before Pope Leo X's certain death and the opening of the conclave, the emperor's ambassador in Rome, Juan Manuel, dispatched a briefing to Carlos V. In his many notes to the monarch, Juan Manuel revealed that the emperor had instructed several cardinals to vote for a particular papal candidate. Juan Manual letter to the emperor stated:

> The cardinals who are ready to serve his (the Emperor's interests) are Cardinals Vich, Valle, Siena, Jacobacius, Campegio, de Medicis, Sion, Santiquatro, and Farnese. Other cardinals are also ready to be useful to him, but as they are only the servants of others, it is not worthwhile to speak of them. I think Cardinal Santa Croce will do his duty.[183]

On the final scrutiny, the eleventh, on January 9, 1522, the cardinal of Ostia had fifteen votes and the cardinal of Tortosa, now physically present at the conclave, had fifteen votes. Understanding they were at the moment of truth, the Cardinal of St. Sisto "praised the virtues and learning of the Cardinal of Tortosa, went to him, and begged the other cardinals to do the same."[184] Appearing to be the second man to do so, Bernardino López walked over to Adriaan Florensz, the Cardinal of Tortosa, and indicated his vote with his feet. At 5:00 p.m. on that January evening, Adriaan was elected Pope Adrian VI, and Bernardino had done his duty.

Bernardino's fruitless quest for the papacy and his subsequent restoration as a cardinal reveal both the limits and the nature of political alliances and converso families. On the first occasion that he sought the papacy, during the Council of Pisa in 1511, he could not claim victory without the cohesive efforts of King Louis XII of France, Holy Roman Emperor Maximilian I, and King Ferdinand of Spain. Pope Julius II could not be removed from office. Further, due to the constant shifting of European alliances during this period, Bernardino had to traverse political quicksand to reach the papacy. Once again, in 1522, his quest for the papacy was likely cut short by Emperor Carlos V's desires and the failure of the Comuneros Revolt.

Faced with these difficulties, his initiative demonstrates that no individual or family was an island unto itself and that only with a broad network of social and political support could individuals attain their goals. The elite converso family confederation had reached its apex. Conversos could serve the Roman Catholic Church, but no amount of personal ambition, family fortitude, or political intrigue would allow them to become popes.

EXPUNGING THE RECORD AND ERASING MEMORY

Just as Bernardino's efforts were cresting, a new generation of Placentino family confederation leaders was beginning to make its presence felt in Spain. These new family leaders of the sixteenth century were consummate creatures of the Spanish royal court and Roman Catholic Church, who, while ambitious, never overextended their roles as loyal servants. They included Lorenzo Galíndez de Carvajal (royal judge, historian, and member of the Consejo de Indias), Juan Suárez de Carvajal (future bishop of Lugo and also member of the Consejo de Indias), and Gutierre de Vargas Carvajal (future bishop of Plasencia).[185]

During the remaining years of the early 1500s, Lorenzo Galíndez would shoulder the task of serving the Catholic monarchs while also advancing the interests of the Plasencia family confederation. In 1505, he assisted Dr. Alfonso Díaz de Montalvo in the promulgation of the Laws of Toro, which facilitated the transfer of entailed lands (or primogeniture) to first sons in Spain's most elite noble class of the sixteenth century, the Grandeza (Grandees), as well as other lower nobles.[186] In Lorenzo's capacity as an adviser to the Catholic monarchs, he standardized, mediated, and "censored" the Castilian royal chronicles into an official state history.[187] Further, Lorenzo used these accounts to incorporate the Carvajal lineage and heritage into Spain's history of elite noble families.[188] Notably absent were any Jewish ancestries for his family. As an important counselor to the Spanish monarchy, Lorenzo advanced letrados, like himself, at the expense of elite noble knightly families, like the Mendoza, that had traditionally populated the royal administration.[189] Last, named correo mayor of the Consejo de Indias in 1514, Lorenzo helped define early Spanish American policies and promoted the placement of his own family in key exploration and conquest roles in the Americas.[190]

For his efforts, he was well compensated by various religious institutions that were effectively an extension of the royal government. After his long association with the Cathedral of Salamanca and its university, he began to receive new benefits in the early 1500s. In 1507, he obtained a supplemental salary, as well as all other privileges, as the overseer of the local hospital, Casa de San Lázaro de Salamanca.[191] Although his primary activities during the 1500s involved the Consejo Real and the Consejo de Indias, in 1521, Lorenzo received a royally approved annual salary from Emperor Carlos V of 150,000 maravedís that was paid by the Cathedral of Salamanca.[192] The matter of Lorenzo's salary was so important to the emperor that he dispatched his order, via Spanish royal treasurer Francisco de Vargas, from the distant city of Worms, Germany. Of course, the Carvajal–Santa María family confederation was always willing to facilitate transactions such as these; Vargas was married to Lorenzo's cousin from Plasencia, Inés de Carvajal, a daughter of Francisco de Carvajal, second señor de Torrejón.[193] These relationships were further reinforced through family connections in Salamanca, where Lorenzo's uncle, Dr. Martín de Ávila, was on the faculty at the university.[194]

Compensation came from other institutions as well, even those tangentially connected to Lorenzo. In 1516, Carlos V ordered Cardinal Cisneros of the Diocese of Toledo to pay Lorenzo a salary, even though he "will not be able to serve the cathedral."[195] Two years later, the emperor wrote from Zaragoza instructing his ambassador in Rome and Lorenzo's uncle, Martín de Ávila, to appoint him titular head of the Abadía de San Juan de Poyo.[196] The abbey was located in the far-flung province of Pontevedra (present-day Galicia).

Thus, by the opening of the sixteenth century, the Carvajal–Santa María family confederation had thoroughly and collectively transformed itself into an elite converso family of royal and ecclesiastical decision makers in Spain. Yet its identity was fundamentally problematic, because its converso lineage, and that of all other elite New Christians, was suspect in sixteenth-century Spain. While Cardinal Francisco Mendoza y Bobadilla's sensational text, *El tizón de la nobleza*, would not appear until the late 1560s, the Spanish royalty during the early 1500s moved aggressively to expunge the record of its tainted bloodlines. This was essential because by the early sixteenth century limpieza de sangre laws excluded all New Christians, whether of Jewish or Muslim origin, from royal or church service. This issue of blood lineage exposes a crucial question in the formation of early modern Spain.

Early modern Spanish history is simultaneously imperial and majestic but also culturally trangressive because of the mixed heritage of Jews, Christians, and Muslims in the Iberian Peninsula. Was Spain European or Mediterranean? Relating its late fourteenth- through sixteenth-century history is complicated and disjointed because of competing narratives that struggle to explain whether Spain was actually a unified Spanish Christian state with one people by 1500 or a social organism that was much more culturally and religiously hybridized. Castilians had created institutional rules—such as blood purity laws—that few families could measure up to. Many nobles simply could not claim pure Old Christian blood lineages and thus were cognizant of the need to destroy records documenting New Christian ties and to fabricate new ones that showed ancient Christian roots.

Exploring the creation and fate of the Carvajal–Santa María family confederation is therefore two stories of identity: one of mixed Jewish-Christian heritages and another of brutal determination to eliminate a problematic lineage and to manifest an idealized Christian one. Just as the family confederation had created a formidable fraternal history in the personages of Cardinal Juan de Carvajal and Cardinal Bernardino López de Carvajal, it also had to suppress other less desirable aspects of its lineage. There was no other early sixteenth-century family member more involved in this endeavor to manage the history and memory of the entire Spanish nobility than Lorenzo Galíndez de Carvajal. His role in the editing of royal chronicles and other documents that might reveal the Jewish, Muslim, and lowly origins of the royalty and nobility is virtually certain. Further, Lorenzo was highly aware of his actions and his role on behalf of the Catholic monarchs and, later, Emperor Carlos V. In many of his personal letters, Lorenzo characteristically concluded with a personal hallmark that communicated some sense of his personal and professional character and approach to his duty to others: "I have done only what you commanded."[197]

What was the doctor commanded to do by Spain's royal leadership? To clarify that Spain's ancestry was Christian and did not suffer from any Jewish or Muslim defects. Due to their elevated position in the Castilian world, many noble clans came to benefit from Lorenzo's reworking of official chronicles and genealogical treatises that celebrated their ancestral lineages and accomplishments. Among his most significant works from the first decades of the 1500s were *Crónica de los reyes católicos desde 1468 hasta 1518*; *Anales breves de los reyes católicos Don Fernando y Doña Isabel*; *Genealogía de los Reyes de Castilla, desde don Pelayo hasta don Juan II*; *Crónica de Juan II*; *Crónica de Enrique IV*; and *Adiciones genealógicas a los Claros varones de Castilla, de Fernán Pérez de Guzmán, señor de Batres*.[198]

In terms of their relevance to the particular question of the Jewish origins, and for that matter, Muslim origins, of some of the Castilian nobility, these official state creations are known to present falsified genealogies. In his unpublished manuscript, "Vida y obras maestras del Dr. D. Lorenzo Galíndez de Carvajal," the distinguished historian and member of the Royal Academy of History, Rafael Floranes (1743–1801), argues,

"We know of the defects he [Lorenzo] created and introduced into the chronicles, which were not present during earlier reign's [versions]. . . . [D]uring the time of the Catholic Monarchs, he was censor and judge of the works of prior chroniclers . . . as well a master editor [of those works]."[199]

The sterilizing efforts of Lorenzo are most apparent in the collected annals of Castilian history (the previously mentioned chronicles). These annals conspicuously excluded the four most illustrious men of the preceding two hundred years: King Ferdinand of Aragón, Constable Ruy López Dávalos, Admiral Alonso Enríquez, and Royal Chanciller Pedro López de Ayala.[200] These genealogies were not properly documented until the 1517 publication of *Adiciones genealógicas a los Claros varones de Castilla, de Fernán Pérez de Guzmán, señor de Batres.*

By tampering with earlier chronicles, especially those pertaining to the period when New Noble and converso families were actively shaping Castile's political and cultural agenda (the reigns of Juan II, 1406–54, and Enrique III, 1454–74), Lorenzo began a process of religious cleansing of Spain's past.[201] In doing so, he was actually altering the work of his own kinsmen, such as Alvar García de Santa María, a royal administrator for King Juan II. A principal endeavor involved creating "confusion" around the royal Trastámaran dynasty's bloodlines and other noble ancestries, as well as redacting the prologue from Fernán Pérez de Guzmán's *Crónica de Juan II.* These redactions eliminated "the genealogy of Bishop Don Alonso de Burgos [a converso] and his consanguinity with this king [Juan II]."[202] With the stroke of the pen, Lorenzo the chronicler excised the Jewish and converso bloodlines that connected the ha-Levi/Santa María, Álvaro de Luna, and Pérez de Guzmán clans to Castilian King Juan II. Those same ancestries would come to link the Carvajal family to the Trastámaran dynasty as well via their intermarriage with the Santa María in Plasencia.

One of the few well-documented examples where historians know that Lorenzo Galíndez was actively manipulating the identities of Spain's illustrious families is the case of the converso Antonio de Nebrija, author of the first Castilian grammar, *Gramática de la lengua castellana.*[203] Published in 1492, this critical work was the first grammar published for any European language, excluding Latin. Included in *Adiciones genealógicas,* prepared and presented by Lorenzo on behalf of the deceased Catholic monarchs in 1517 (during the minority rule of Carlos V), were the king's ancestry and many notable families' lineages, as well as the ancestral blood lineage of Nebrija, himself a New Christian.[204] On final preparation of the manuscript, which was printed in the northern Castilian city of Logroño, Nebrija noted that his family history was incorrect. Rafael Floranes shares an account that was relayed to the king regarding the final publication of *Adiciones genealógicas.*

The chronicle came out of the press in Logroño at the same time that the treatise [*Adiciones genealógicas*?] and its first three collections of additions and notes was printed. Then this one [Nebrija] took a sample volume [from the press] and returned to his study to examine it. He then compared it with the [original] manuscript he had given to the printer or another of the same version. He noted in the margin the many errors that the printer had committed, among the more substantial ones were certain genealogical notes that spoke of him [Nebrija] and of his blood lineage. He recorded all this with the intent of fixing them [the errors] in a second edition because he did not personally concur with this one. This supervisor [of the press] said he had printed as he was told[,] . . . cautioning these were the notes and corrections of Galíndez and the volume would be used.[205]

Floranes's account of Nebrija's experience seems plausible, given the need to "fix" lineages. After all, how could the Catholic monarchs justify and continue to enforce blood purity laws across every institution if their own lineages, and that of the nobility, were so corrupted?

Floranes concludes his analysis of *Adiciones genealógicas* with supplementary notations that suggest Lorenzo "corrected" many other noble genealogies. In addition to referencing Francisco Mendoza y Bobadilla's contemporary text, *El tizón de la nobleza*, Floranes laments how "through this invention of Dr. Galíndez, our history has been taken from our hands."[206] This systematic manipulation of nobility genealogies concurs with the historical findings of this author and the many other scholars cited in this book.

A careful inspection of the Carvajal family lineage written by Lorenzo in *Adiciones genealógicas* validates that his history excluded the many Jewish and converso relations the Carvajal family shared with the ha-Levi/Santa María clan. Instead, Lorenzo only highlights strategic interrelations that present himself and the house of Carvajal in the most positive light. For example, he records:

They also had another daughter who was named Doña Elvira de Toledo, who married, in Talavera, Diego de Carvajal, Señor de Sobrinos, who was the son of Licenciado Álvaro de Carvajal and Doña Leonor de la Torre. [Diego] is the grandson of Alvar García de Orellana "El Rico" and Dona Mencia González de Carvajal, Señores de Orellana "La Nueva," my grandparents.[207]

This type of selective presentation of genealogies, that is, eliminating Jewish and well-known converso ancestors, was the norm for converso noble families, and Lorenzo seemed to master the process for his family and many other notables. For example, even though I present considerable evidence of the family confederation's intermarriage and close family coordination, the doctor chose to exclude the Carvajal–Santa María intermarriages and coordinated actions in *Adiciones genealógicas*. Even the family confederation's primary competitors—the Estúñiga—were spared public shaming.[208] Thus, if anything held elite conversos together, it was a commitment to eliminate their Jewish past.

In 1525, Lorenzo retired to his native Plasencia and returned to his home across the street from the Cathedral of Plasencia.[209] Before his death in 1528, he knew his extended family members would safeguard the future of the clan and their secret. With Bishop Gutierre de Vargas Carvajal now leading the Cathedral of Plasencia, and other Carvajal, Sande, and Villalva family members occupying every other important position in the cathedral chapter, the Carvajal–Santa María family confederation's future seemed secure. Through duty, devotion, and service, they were well positioned for Spain's imperial and Catholic future. They had buried their past.

8

COMPLICATIONS FROM THE PAST
THREATEN THE FUTURE

The sixteenth and seventeenth centuries brought complications for the Carvajal–Santa María family confederation in Spain and the Americas. After the formal expulsion of all Jews from Spain and Portugal, disparate outcomes emerged for those who remained in Spain and those who settled in colonial Spanish America. As Jewish families were expelled from Plasencia, the family confederation did little to forestall their departure. Some assisted in the transferring of gold and silver funds to those who were expelled, but for the most part these conversos made a convincing, public break with Judaism. While they continuously labored to remove any public doubts about their constructed Old Christian religious personae, there was and is little reason to doubt that the majority of the family confederation were staunch Christians. However, some extended family members returned to the practice of Judaism and paid with their lives.

In this concluding chapter, I briefly investigate how the Carvajal–Santa María family confederation fared during the first 150 years after the Spanish encounter with the Americas, roughly 1500 to 1650. Universally, the family confederation in Plasencia and in colonial Spanish America focused on public denials of their Jewish ancestry and any connection to Jewish religious practices. While the Spanish and Bolivian families largely avoided more extensive investigations into their blood purity and questions pertaining to the sincerity of their Christian practices, in Mexico the story was entirely different. There the identities of the family confederation were on full trial. New archival research I present here suggests that the staunchest of the Christian family confederation members in Mexico actively participated in the quieting and ultimate execution of the Jewish branches of the extended clan. The Carvajal–Santa María family committed fratricide.

AT HOME IN SPAIN: CHRISTIAN IDENTITIES IN QUESTION

The Placentino Family Confederation, 1492–1570

Within the community of Plasencia, the family confederation deployed Old Christian Carvajal surnames and other lesser-known Old Christian surnames to mask the converso identities of extended family members such as the Santa María. In fact, on April 5, 1561, when Bishop Gutierre de Vargas Carvajal and his fellow churchmen in the Cathedral of Plasencia gathered to enact a new blood purity statute that excluded the descendants of Jewish families from their ranks, the men perpetuated the centuries-old myth regarding their Old Christian lineage. Along with his full complement of canons, almost all of whom were his relatives, the bishop and these guardians of the Christian faith conveniently chose not to acknowledge what they all knew to be true: their own bloodlines carried what Spanish Christians considered anathema—the ancestral stain of Judaism. Together, they declared:

> We order . . . presently and in the future that none shall be admitted into this church as an official, dignitary, canon, ractioner, brother, chaplain, notary, nor crier. Not one or any descendant of the lineage of conversos, Jews, Muslims. Nor any Old Christian who is their descendant. This includes any who relapsed to their prior faiths and were reconciled or penanced by the Holy Office of the Inquisition.[1]

Among those family confederation members who signed the statute, which applied to everyone in the cathedral chapter, were Archdeacon Fabián Carvajal Monroy, Archdeacon Gabriel Pizarro, Master Martín González de Carvajal (whose memorial chapel in the new Cathedral of Plasencia displayed Carvajal and Santa María heraldic devices), Cantor Pedro Bermúdez de Villalva, Canon Francisco de Vargas, Canon Salvador Sánchez de Tamayo, and Canon Francisco de Carvajal. This exceptional moment captured the convoluted and contradictory blending of Jewish blood and Christian faith for these Placentino families. Simply put, Placentino family members denied their converso background.

As the early sixteenth century unfolded, the family confederation in Plasencia fared well during the Inquisition's efforts to identify backsliding New Christians. The Inquisition court with jurisdiction over Plasencia, about 200 kilometers to the south and based in Llerena, expressed little interest in investigating the family. If there were flaws in the family's religious armor, it was only exposed when clan members chose to reveal the Jewish backgrounds of other family members, as in the case of churchman Luis de Carvajal.

Luis was an inquisitor and official in the Cathedral of Plasencia and appears frequently in the *Actas capitulares*, the day-to-day business records of the church, in the early sixteenth century. He was exceptional in that he made it his responsibility to purify the blood of the church. As early as 1518, it is apparent that Luis was fully engrossed in the examination of accusations against conversos and Jews, including his uncle, Diego de Vargas, who resided in Talavera.[2] Further, it seems that Luis de Carvajal was so exceedingly harsh as an inquisitor that that Emperor Carlos V wrote to him on September, 10, 1518, chastising him and ordering him to relinquish his position under penalty of incurring royal indignation and its full effects.[3] As Juan Antonio Llorente noted in *Historia crítica de la Inquisición en España*, the emperor was aghast at Luis's activities, writing to him, "[You are] using such novel methods not seen or heard of since the Holy Sanctified Office of the Inquisition began its operations."[4] As a result, Luis was forced to resign his position as inquisitor.[5]

Where Luis de Carvajal was sure that it was his mission to rectify the problem of the Jewish ancestry of his own relatives, Miguel de Carvajal, a Christian converso playwright, was equally indignant over his fellow conversos' hypocritical stance on the limpieza de sangre statutes and public hatred of Jews and New Christians. The playwright's willingness to challenge Christian norms likely reduced his place in Spanish Golden Age literature. The story of Miguel de Carvajal is intertwined with his controversial play, *Tragedia Josephina*, which he brought to the stage in Plasencia, Spain, on Corpus Christi Day sometime in the 1530s.[6] Miguel's play was problematic because, in order to speak to the plight of conversos, he allegorized the biblical story of Joseph being sold into bondage by his brothers.[7] He thereby engaged his audiences to consider the relationship between Christian brothers—old and new.[8]

Before proceeding with the play itself, let us first consider the ancestry of Miguel, who was the son of Alonso de Carvajal and Teresa Núñez de Almaraz of Plasencia (see ch. 3).[9] While there is little known about his father, Miguel's paternal uncle and patron, Hernando de Carvajal, was a conquistador who resided in Santo Domingo del Puerto in the Isla Española de las Indias in 1528.[10] Hernando was also a member of the family confederation that assisted Francisco de Carvajal with the restoration of Plasencia to royal rule in 1488 (see ch. 7). Thus, Miguel was well connected to the family confederation in Plasencia as well as to those engaged in the military conquests in the Americas. Miguel's New Christian status is also argued by David Gitlitz, who documented that he was likely related to Ana María de Almaraz, a converso investigated by the Spanish Inquisition.[11]

Tragedia Josephina, which was apparently popular as it went through four versions, touched a raw nerve in blood purity–obsessed Spain.[12] The performance told the story of how Joseph's brothers sold him into slavery, which was an indirect indictment of the Old Christians' persecution of the new converts to Christianity, but more remarkably it gave Miguel's character, Faraute, the opportunity to address the audience directly before each act of the play.[13] Through the vehicle of these prologues Miguel confronted his audience. Appearing in a stereotypical Jewish costume, Faraute addresses the audience in act 1 as follows:

Just listen, ladies and gentlemen, what an intelligent group! A lot of people are griping because Jews and their costumes always seem to butt into these affairs. And I have to admit they have a point, because all those black gabardines couldn't possibly be healthy in this summer heat. Nevertheless, I cannot help suspecting that it takes one to know one.[14]

Miguel de Carvajal's provocative tone simultaneously impeached the audience because they recognized "Jews" and coded a message about the playwright's mixed-blood origins. This denunciation of Spanish mores was carried to fruition in Miguel's prologue to act 3. Faraute, speaking to the viciousness of Spanish civil society, states:

Ladies and gentlemen, I come before you both embarrassed and very upset. Embarrassed by the behavior of the actors and the audience. Upset seeing you upset, or rather angry. You've no business getting angry at me, for I have performed in the Roman Coliseum before the pope and cardinals[,] ... before the King of England[,] ... the king of France[,] ... and those illustrious audiences have always listened to me with pleasure. . . . You, on the other hand, seem ready to attack and decapitate a saint! Well, I'm putting you on notice that these days there are no saints worth decapitating.[15]

Again, Miguel grasped the audience's moral sensibilities and exposed the social hostility of the Spanish, even to those conversos who might display saintly qualities. His reference to the Roman Coliseum suggests that he was referring to the early life of Christianity in pagan Rome, when Christians were sentenced to death in a public spectacle. Now Old Christians—those who inhabited the Holy Office of the Inquisition—were the spectators who threw New Christians to the metaphorical lions.

Tragedia Josephina continued to entertain and provoke audiences into the 1530s but was ultimately censored by the Inquisition and condemned in 1559. It appears that just as Cardinal Francisco Mendoza y Bobadilla revealed Jewish, Muslim, and other humble origins of the Spanish aristocracy in *El tizon de la nobleza*, Miguel was able to focus Spaniards' attention on the duplicity surrounding discriminatory blood purity norms in Spain.

Distant Family Relations in Spain

Placentino family members were exceptionally successful at mitigating the impact of the blood purity statutes and the Inquisition's activities. There are several explanations for this outcome: both royal and local ecclesiastical authorities effectively shielded them, and their Christian beliefs and practices appeared to be sincere. Nevertheless, the Holy Office investigated some individuals who may have been distantly related to the Carvajal–Santa María. The incomplete record of Inquisition cases (*procesos*) preserved in the Archivo Histórico Nacional in Madrid shows at least two Carvajal-surnamed individuals who were brought before tribunals. These cases present genealogies but do not conclusively indicate a relation, or, for that matter, a nonrelation to the Placentino family confederation.

The first case involves the inquisitorial tribunal in Salamanca, which called Alonso de Carvajal, a member of the town council of Sigüenza, before it on January 24, 1492, on unspecified grounds.[16] Alonso claimed he was falsely accused by Friar Juan Lopes and in his own defense stated, "It is wrong to say that in this Inquisition there are no false accusations."[17] Although the case was initiated, the tribunal did not continue to review Alonso's background.

Just two years later, in 1494, the Inquisition implicated another Carvajal. In that case, King Ferdinand and Queen Isabel intervened directly by dictating the blood purity legitimacy of Juan de Carvajal's wife, Catalina Sánchez, who came under suspicion in Salamanca.[18] Even though she was accused of being a Judaizing converso, Catalina was granted mercy by the monarchs and confirmed as not being a heretic.[19] Given the long association of the Placentino family confederation with the city of Salamanca and the direct intervention of the monarchs, it seems likely that Juan and Catalina were related to the family confederation.

These two relatively innocuous cases demonstrate that the Carvajal–Santa María family confederation did experience official inquisitorial scrutiny, but it was quite limited. No other cases for potentially related Carvajal-surnamed family members appear in the records of the Spanish Holy Office of the Inquisition. However, in the Americas, the family confederation experienced further inspection by prying Christian eyes. Disparate fates awaited the converso family confederation in the Americas.

THE AMERICAS, SIXTEENTH AND EARLY SEVENTEENTH CENTURIES

During the early sixteenth century, members of the family confederation successfully settled in Nueva España (Mexico) and Charcas (present-day southern Peru, Bolivia, and northern Argentina). Although Emperor Carlos V's 1522 decree stated, "Not one new convert to our Catholic faith, no Moor, no Jew, nor their children, are allowed to pass into the Indies," the family confederation exploited their royal administrative access, ecclesiastical connections, and military expertise to fan out across the Caribbean, Mexico, and South America.[20]

Mexican Identities

After Cristóbal Colón's entry into the Americas in 1492, Spain focused on the dismemberment of the Aztec Empire (1519–21), centered in present-day Mexico, and the Inca Empire (1532–72), located in the Andean highlands of Peru and Bolivia.

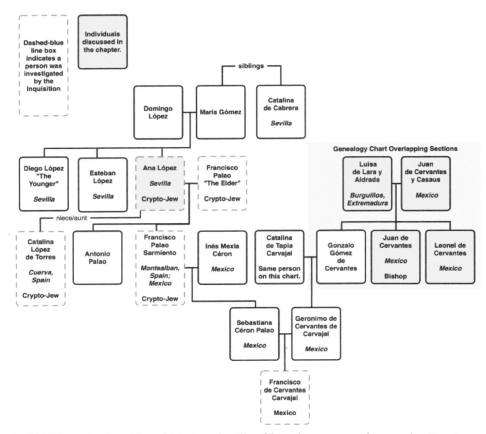

FIGURE 8.1.A. Spanish and Mexican families, fifteenth–seventeenth centuries. Part 1.

Accompanying Cortés's invasion force were likely family confederation members represented by "first conqueror" and conquistador Antonio de Carvajal "the Elder," reportedly from Zamora, Spain, but whose brother (Rodrigo) indicated the family originated from the clan's ancestral stronghold of Trujillo (approximately 80 kilometers south of Plasencia).[21] (See figs. 8.1a–b.) Although Antonio's paternity cannot be precisely determined, it is probable that he and his siblings, Rodrigo and Regina, were directly related to the Plasencia Carvajal via the Álvarez de Toledo and Carvajal intermarriages in Talavera de la Reina.[22] On the other hand, Antonio's spouse, Catalina de Tapia, was the daughter of María de Peralta, a family well known for its role in the persecution of crypto-Jews during the Mexican Inquisition, and conquistador Bernardino Vásquez de Tapia. The Vásquez clan had married into the converso Inés de Cabrera and Juan Alonso de Sosa lineages of Córdova.[23] The Cabrera/Cabreros were descendants of the Santa María family. Thus it can be concluded that the Spanish and Mexican families were, at minimum, extended relations (first or second cousins) or, more likely, direct descendants of the Placentino Carvajal–Santa María family confederation.

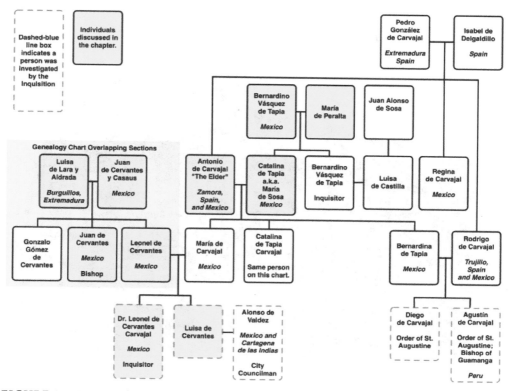

FIGURE 8.1.B. Spanish and Mexican families, fifteenth–seventeenth centuries. Part 2.

Another fountainhead of the interlinking families in México was the conquistador Juan de Cervantes y Casaus and his wife, Luisa de Lara y Aldrada, from Burguillos in the Spanish Extremadura.[24] From these families emerged multiple documentable intraclan marriages, such as Catalina de Tapia Carvajal and Gonzalo Gómez de Cervantes and Leonel de Cervantes and María de Carvajal.[25] When the family confederation arrived in Mexico as conquistadors, it quickly populated the royal administrative world, primarily as city councilmen and churchmen. For example, Dr. Leonel Cervantes de Carvajal, the grandson of Antonio, served as archdeacon and headmaster of the Cathedral School of Santa Fe in Mexico City, as well as a distinguished member of the Holy Office. Other grandsons of Antonio would serve as bishops, such as Diego de Carvajal, bishop of Guamanga in Peru, and Agustín de Carvajal, a member of the Order of St. Augustine and the Holy Office.[26]

Although the family held the reins of key church and royal institutions in the Americas, during the sixteenth and seventeenth centuries the Inquisition repeatedly scrutinized their religious pedigree and practices. One such occurrence that may have exposed the family's converso roots was a formal inquiry launched by the Holy Office in Cartagena de las Indias (Colombia) in 1616. An investigation into Leonel Cervantes's

FIGURE 8.2. Inquisitorial Palace, Mexico City. Creative Commons. Used with permission.

limpieza de sangre was initiated after genealogical questions arose relating to his sibling, Luisa de Cervantes, who was a resident of Cartagena, and his first cousin, Friar Agustín de Carvajal, at the time bishop of Guamanga in northern Perú.[27] Two years later, the Holy Office in Mexico City took up the investigation and began what amounted to a routine but also revealing proceeding to record the maternal ancestry of Leonel (fig. 8.2).

On January 17, 1618, the inquisitional commission set about the task of mapping and verifying the family's pedigree via testimony from knowledgeable persons. Testifying first was Baltasar de Latadena, who at the time was eighty years old and had lived in Mexico City for four decades and thus was in an excellent position to know a great deal about the family. His testimony was not extraordinary; it simply confirmed that he knew that Leonel's parents were Leonel de Cervantes and María de Carvajal, both born in Spain. Likewise, María's parents were Antonio de Carvajal "the Elder" and Catalina de Tapia Carvajal, both from Spain as well. All were "old Christians without the stain of either the Moorish or Jewish *converso* race . . . nor castigated or penanced by the Holy Office of the Inquisition."[28]

Other details on the extended relations of Leonel Cervantes came into focus, especially the broader reach of the Carvajal, from the witness Hernando de Laserna.[29] Hernando related that the clan had long-held ties in Pánuco, where Leonel's paternal grandfather, Juan de Cervantes y Casaus, was a knight commander and royal official. His maternal grandfather, Antonio, was a city councilman in Mexico City. The witness also asserted that Leonel's ecclesiastical connections flowed from his mother's side of the family and that he was a first cousin to Bishop Agustín de Carvajal of Guamanga.[30] The bishop was originally from Spain and had traveled with his order, the Order of St. Augustine, first through Panamá and later to Perú. Similarly, the record highlights that Agustín's brother, Diego de Carvajal, later served as bishop of Guamanga.[31]

Others who were officially questioned added that Leonel Cervantes's family "was not only a clean, Old Christian one, but also of a lineage of hidalgo caballeros," yet none of these witnesses knew from where in Spain the Carvajal had come; this seemed to be an unknown or omitted detail that no one could answer.[32] To not have this important piece of such a well-known and royally connected family's lineage fully explored indicates the clan's effectiveness in shielding more prominent members from sustained inquiries. In this respect, the family confederation's identity, while potentially suspect, was always viewed as an Old Christian one, despite its concealed ancestry. Given that the family confederation in the Americas was the by-product of extensively intermarried New Noble and converso families of the Spanish Extremadura, additional Holy Office inquiries suggest they barely escaped complete familial disaster.

Those American investigations, which took place at the beginning of the seventeenth century, exposed undesirable details about the family confederation on both sides of the Atlantic Ocean. For example, in the Spanish regions of Toledo and Talavera de la Reina, a focal point of the Carvajal-Toledo-Cervantes intermarriages, the Holy Office encountered a debased Jewish pedigree. In February 1632, the family's Jewish background was finally exposed just three generations into the past when Mexican inquisitors opened an inquiry of Francisco de Cervantes Carvajal, a native of Mexico City, who was a second cousin of Leonel Cervantes.[33] They initiated the scrutiny after a fellow churchman publicly called Francisco "a Jew." The records of the inquiry indicate numerous witnesses were of the opinion that Francisco's maternal great-grandmother, Ana López, "was not an Old Christian" and that his great-grandmother, María Gómez, was a Jewish convert.[34] In the proceso the inquisitors recorded marginalia directing the reader to "bad" findings—proof of Ana's Jewish blood. Witnesses such as Juan Gómez de Ocaña divulged that Ana López was "not of a clean lineage, that the family was not clean, but that they did not know or understand the basis of this bad opinion."[35] Another individual called to testify, Melchor López, stated, "People speak vulgarly and think badly of the quality and cleanliness of Ana López's blood."[36] Others, such as Gregorio Paxua Ramírez, added that Ana López's family "was descended from Jews . . . and condemned or penanced by the Holy Office with San Benito garb [the penitential gown of a reconciled crypto-Jew]."[37] In short order, the family confederation's blood lineage and identity was on full trial. Without the benefit of full control of ecclesiastical institutions, such as in their native Extremadura, the family was in deep trouble.

Broader transatlantic familial relationships soon appeared, linking families in Montealbán, Spain (a stronghold of the Álvarez de Toledo side of the clan), and Cuerva, Spain (in the vicinity of Toledo). Ana López's niece, Catalina López de Torres, had also been previously investigated and incarcerated by the Holy Office for crypto-Jewish beliefs.[38] Demonstrating how damaging family testaments could be to a clan intent on obscuring its full lineage, the Holy Office was able to use a personal will to discover that another accused relative, Francisco Palao, was also known as Francisco Palao Sarmiento.[39] These findings only led to further questions from the Inquisition as the family's identity began to unravel.

During a fourteen-year investigation of Álvaro de Cervantes y Loaysa and Elena de Cervantes of Talavera de la Reina, who were married first cousins, the Holy Office learned that multiple family members were reconciled Christians who had practiced Judaism.[40] Álvaro claimed ties to the Carvajal via his grandmother, Isabel Girón de Carvajal, still perceived as Old Christian, and his grandfather, Rodrigo de Carranza, whose family originally came from Burgos, Spain. This connection to Burgos is telling as it was a fourteenth-century heartland of the Santa María branch of the family confederation, as well as where Álvaro's great-great-uncle Pedro de Carranza, a physician, had confessed to being a practicing secret Jew. In later cases, the inquiries into clan lineages often found their way back to the Extremaduran and Sevillian Cabrera(o)s family, specifically, Catalina de Cabrera of Sevilla who was a convicted secret Jew, further indicating the weblike connections of the extended Carvajal–Santa María family confederation.[41] Fortunately for the family, the Atlantic Ocean served as a robust buffer between the American and European branches of the confederation. While knowledge of Judaizing elements of the family confederation in Spain did flow into the Americas, it failed to undo the American clan's Old Christian identity. Likewise, the Placentinos in Spain never seemed to feel the tight grasp of the Inquisition due to their effective public demonstration of Christianity via their religious endowments and prominent role in the Spanish church.

The most thought-provoking and perplexing element of the family confederation's identity relates to the infamous Inquisition case and execution of Luis de Carvajal "the Younger" and many members of his family in Mexico City starting in 1596. These cases, and the specific actions of the family confederation, suggest tangible ties between Christian and crypto-Jewish family members in the Americas. In short, in late sixteenth-century Mexico the family found it progressively more difficult to shield themselves and their relations from the suspicious eyes of Old Christians and their competitors.

Earlier Old World relationships and competitions may have contributed to the unpleasant complications that the Carvajal–Santa María family confederation encountered in Mexico. In 1580 and precisely at the same location that the "first conqueror" Antonio de Carvajal had settled, the region of Pánuco, Luis de Carvajal y de la

Cueva "the Senior" arrived; he was the uncle of the younger Luis. Previously, King Philip II of Spain had granted the senior Luis permission to settle Portuguese and Spanish newcomers in Mexico; as many as two-thirds of them were conversos, according to Stan Hordes, author of *To the End of the Earth*.[42] After first finding his footing in Pánuco, Luis planned to pacify the indigenous peoples and settle the new region, called the Kingdom of Nuevo León, with 259 colonists.[43]

Among those Mexican elites who assisted Luis in the movement of these families into the region was the Cervantes-Carvajal clan. Specifically, Hernando de Medina, Sebastián Rodríguez, Leonel de Cervantes, and Simón de Coca lent Luis 8,000 ducats so that he could pay a mandatory bond to the government.[44] Put simply, the Old World family confederation may have been operating at full force in Mexico during this era because Leonel de Cervantes was the father of the inquisitor Leonel Cervantes de Carvajal and the brother of Bishop Juan de Cervantes. It appears that, at minimum, both sets of Carvajal families shared business and political interests, and perhaps more intimate ones as well.

Another Old World connection between Spain and Mexico was the Carvajal–Santa María family confederation's old nemesis, the Estúñiga (Zúñiga) family. At the time of the senior Luis's "pacification" of the native Mexican peoples, the viceroy of New Spain was Álvaro Manrique de Zúñiga, duke of Béjar. It seemed that old scores from Plasencia, Spain, would now be settled in Mexico when Zúñiga accused Luis of rebellious acts and mistreatment of the native peoples.[45] In a stunning fall, both the senior and younger Luises, their immediate families, and many colonists were brought to the attention of the Mexican Inquisition. Martin A. Cohen's seminal work, *The Martyr: The Story of a Secret Jew and the Mexican Inquisition in the Sixteenth Century*, documents the undoing of these conversos. However, what has remained unknown until present was the potential connection of those who were executed and those who ordered the executions.

In 1596, the younger Luis de Carvajal was sentenced to death for practicing Judaism. Although scholars have presumed that Luis and his immediate family did not belong to the Carvajal–Santa María lineage in Mexico City, in fact, it appears that they at least shared extended relations. Those family confederation members leading the investigation of this seemingly unrelated family were Leonel Cervantes de Carvajal; Bishop Juan de Cervantes, an uncle of Leonel; and inquisitor Alonso de Peralta, the cousin of Leonel. The bishop personally informed Luis that he would be tortured until he confessed, and Alonso signed the execution order for Luis in 1596.[46]

While Luis and most of his family members received the death penalty in 1596, the Holy Office and one of the family's defense attorneys, Dr. García Figueroa de Carvajal, placed Luis's surviving sister, Maríana, in the protective custody of the Vásquez de Tapia family in Mexico City.[47] Cohen notes that this family was connected to the Inquisition's community of local informants and officials. However, unknown to Cohen and other scholars is the new, unsettling finding that the Holy Office did not place Mariana in the home of strangers but instead in the protective custody of the converso Carvajal–Santa María family confederation lineage that hailed from the Spanish Extremadura. In 1596, Mariana resided in the home of Luisa de Castilla, who was Leonel de Cervantes's great- aunt and conquistador Antonio de Carvajal's sister-in-law. (See fig. 8.1b.) Thus the reconciled crypto-Jew, Mariana, was to be rehabilitated and reintegrated into Christian society by her extended relatives who shared a Jewish ancestry.

From this unusual incident it seems highly plausible to conclude that Maríana was an extended relation of the family confederation and that while the the latter was unable to save all members of its crypto-Jewish branch, it did initially shield Mariana from a deadly auto-da-fe in 1596. However, four years after this affair, the Holy Office returned to Mariana's case and determined that she had relapsed into the practice of Judaism and thus must pay her religious debt to the Inquisition with her life. Leonel Cervantes, Juan Cervantes, and García Figueroa did not act a second time to protect Mariana. It appears that the family confederation actively participated in the elimination of relatives— perhaps distant—who jeopardized the survival and success of the extended clan. The Carvajal–Santa María family confederation in late sixteenth-century Mexico City did the unthinkable—they executed every last family member who betrayed Christianity and embraced Judaism—and buried their secret clan history.

After this shocking event, just as they did in Spain, the family confederation appeared to expunge the official record of its Jewish ancestry. It concealed and destroyed evidence in Mexico City, especially after the unpleasant series of inquisitional investigations into its lineage and the executions of the crypto-Jewish clan in the 1590s. Leonel Cervantes's own career was negatively colored by his effort to censor an inquisitional record from public view. In 1642, at which time Leonel was now an elder, established member of the Mexico City community of local elites, potentially harmful details about his professional practices came to the attention of his church colleagues. In a sworn statement taken in Guatemala, an anonymous informant reported on what he had overhead in the house of Bishop Bartolomé González of Guatemala.[48] The informant, a servant or resident in the bishop's home, had clandestinely listened to the bishop and Juan Sáenz, an Inquisition authority, discussing how Leonel had manipulated records of the Holy Office. The details of Leonel's activities probably made it to Guatemala from Mexico after García Figueroa de Carvajal, the defense attorney for the deceased Mariana, was promoted to a judicial position in the Real Audiencia in Guatemala.[49] In the brief report, the informant stated the bishop and the official discussed how "[Leonel Cervantes] seized and embargoed papers from the records of the Holy Office. Within these papers, he changed various names of persons as well as their contents under the pretense that he was searching for errors."[50]

What exactly the doctor removed from the files and destroyed was impossible for the Holy Office to determine, but Bishop González and Juan Sáenz agreed that officials should search for any missing investigation files, guard them, and return them to the

Holy Office. However, Leonel Cervantes's colleagues in the Mexican Inquisition never followed up with a review of the doctor's actions. This event suggests that Leonel, as a senior member of the Inquisition, could operate without fear of professional recriminations or a new wave of inquisitorial investigations.

The event also exposes how a local Inquisition and its leaders could elect to avoid contentious issues that might incriminate their own members and families. For example, Alonso de Peralta, the inquisitor who had signed off on the execution of the crypto-Jewish Carvajal, was a close relative of Leonel Cervantes via the Vásquez de Tapia–Peralta lineage.[51] Thus, by protecting the Carvajal name, Alonso was safeguarding the family's Old Christian identity.

It seems plausible that Leonel's motivation for destroying and manipulating records was to suppress evidence relating to his or extended family members' ancestry and limpieza de sangre—an ancestry that he was certain to know was polluted with a Jewish lineage and that would, at best, preclude his retaining his position as headmaster of the Cathedral School of Santa Fe and as a member of the Holy Office in Mexico City. At worst, further investigations might provoke a more thorough evaluation of the Christian religiosity and identity of the family. In light of the 1596 execution of Luis de Carvajal and other immediate family members, Leonel Cervantes's destruction of case records raises the question of what type of evidence may have existed that linked the Carvajal–Santa María family confederation to Mexico's secret Jews.

Bolivian Identities

Unlike their experiences in Spain and Mexico City, the family confederation in Charcas experienced little harassment from the Holy Office as the church failed to institute a commission in the region. During the sixteenth and early seventeenth century, the Charcas clan generated an image and identity as a potent Old Christian family in military, royal bureaucratic, and religious affairs.

The earliest branches of the South American family included Garci López de Carvajal, Diego de Vargas Carvajal, and Francisco "the Demon of the Andes" Carvajal, who served under Francisco and Gonzalo Pizarro in their conquest of South America.[52] Prior to his departure from Spain and to the Andes, Francisco collaborated with Dr. Lorenzo Galíndez de Carvajal (correo mayor of the Consejo de Indias) in the royal court in Spain and often reported to family members in Plasencia about their relatives' efforts in South America.[53]

After an unsuccessful attempt to explore the South American coast in 1524, Francisco Pizarro regrouped in Toledo in 1529, taking with him Garci López and 180 men into Incan Peru.[54] Francisco Carvajal can later be found in South America in 1546 as the field marshal to Gonzalo Pizarro.[55] He also served as Gonzalo's henchman during the 1540s Spanish civil wars of Peru.[56] Diego de Vargas, the son of Lorenzo Galíndez, was married to Gonzalo Pizarro's sister, Inés Rodríguez. He was a soldier and participated in the siege of Cuzco in 1536. Participating in the Spanish endeavors to evangelize the indigenous population in Perú, Bolivia, and Tucumán was family member Gaspar de Carvajal, a Dominican friar who in 1549 was named an official "protector" of the Native Americans.[57] In this manner, the Carvajal–Santa María family confederation operated at the military and religious vanguard of the Spanish invasion of South America.

After the initial conquest, the family secured territory, political posts, and economic benefits, in spite of the fact that its Jewish past should have denied it entry into the Americas. For example, in 1539 licentiate Illan Suárez de Carvajal reported from Cuzco to Emperor Carlos V that Francisco Pizarro was en route to Kollasuyu and Charcas to establish new cities.[58] Participating in the 1540 foundation of La Plata, the royal administrative city for Charcas, was Juan de Carvajal, who was granted a "solar," or a land parcel, on which to build his noble home.[59]

The family confederation also embedded themselves in the economic exploitation of the Andes, in particular, Cerro Rico's abundant silver resources. In 1556 it was Diego Huallpa, an indigenous man who worked in the *repartimiento* (colonial forced labor system) of licentiate Benito Suárez de Carvajal in Cuzco, who informed the Spanish about the mining potential of Cerro Rico, the silver-laden mountain in Potosí, Bolivia (fig. 8.3).[60]

Soon thereafter, Diego de Vargas, in 1561, and a different Francisco de Carvajal, in 1573, participated in the exploitation of indigenous labor and resources in Potosí and La Plata.[61] Concurrently, the Spanish began to explore and establish the province of Tucumán in northern Argentina. Under the direction of Viceroy García Hurtado de Mendoza, the province was populated by a large number of the family confederation's clans, including the Cabrera/os, Carvajal, Gutiérrez, Sosa, Suárez, and Vásquez.[62] Diego de Villarreal, whose lineage is uncertain, founded its first town, San Miguel de Tucumán, in 1565, and eight years later the converso Jerónimo Luis de Cabrera settled Córdoba.[63] Jerónimo was a descendant of none other than Cardinal Mendoza, author of *El tizón de la nobleza*, and Andrés de Cabrera, the first marques of Moya.[64]

There are strong indications that the Plasencia-based Cabreros family was related to the Cabrera clan from Córdoba, Spain, because both intermarried with the Porras and Gutiérrez lineages.[65] Reassembling these relationships is difficult to accomplish because converso families were highly cognizant of the need to cleanse records pertaining to their ancestry. This is exactly what the fifteenth-century bishop, Francisco de Cabrera of Ciudad Rodrigo, did when he altered his testament to eliminate references to his relatives in Toledo and Segovia.[66]

New archival research exposes a robust interrelated converso community in Charcas at the end of the seventeenth century and well into the eighteenth, which included the Gutiérrez, Ulloa, Cabreros, and Carvajal families. For example, during the 1580s and 1590s, Ventura Gutiérrez, a royal official, made two trips back to Spain; Pedro de Ulloa managed "the business of war" and "pacification" of the "frontiers"; licentiate

FIGURE 8.3. View of Cerro Rico from Potosí, Bolivia. Photo by author.

Antonio Gutiérrez de Ulloa investigated a case of bigamy, Christóbal de Mendoza y Cabreros secured rights to new lands in the Tucumán, and Luis de Carvajal oversaw the silver mines in Potosí as its alcalde mayor.[67] In many cases, such as in the operations of the mines, family members such as Ventura Gutiérrez and Luis de Carvajal coordinated their enrichment.[68]

In the Charcas during the 1590s, the family confederation guided religious life as it did in Plasencia, Spain. Pedro Gutiérrez de Oropesa served as a member of the chapter of the Cathedral of La Plata and as its vicar to La Paz.[69] Furthermore, clansmen such as Dr. Diego de Trejo made significant inroads into leadership roles in the Cathedral of La Plata. First entering the cathedral chapter in 1590s, Diego graduated from cantor to provisor and vicar by 1605.[70] An extended family relation from Mexico joined soon thereafter. In 1609, Alonso de Peralta, related to the Mexican lineage of Carvajal inquisitors and conquistadors, came to serve as Charcas's new bishop.[71]

Spaniards also left the guarding of Christianity in Charcas to converso family confederation members. While there was no formally established Holy Office of the Inquisition in Charcas, high-level inquisitors circulated among the elite colonial population. Directed by the king in 1592, Antonio Gutiérrez relocated from Lima to La Plata with the instructions that the Real Audiencia not "disturb or impede" the Inquisition's efforts to identify and punish heretics in La Plata.[72] Once in the area, Antonio, a descendant of the family from Plasencia, was not a particularly aggressive inquisitor; there is no indication that he ever sought to investigate Jewish heresies in the region. Rather, cases of bigamy and failed business agreements (which did not appear to be connected to issues of faith) seemed to have occupied his time.[73] Unlike Mexico City's robust persecution of conversos, the Inquisition in the region floundered throughout the 1590s and early 1600s because of the absence of Inquisition officials.[74]

The family confederation found its strongest footing in the Andean highlands in the 1620s under the aegis of Dr. Juan de Carvajal y Sande. A direct descendant of the Carvajal–Santa María family confederation of Plasencia, Juan was a member of the king's Sevilla-based Consejo de Indias and an official visitor and member of the Real Audiencia of La Plata.[75]

When the Real Audiencia in the Andean city of La Plata received a letter on March 1, 1638, from King Felipe IV, Juan was among the officials who received it. He could not have been surprised by the dispatch's contents and claims. In it, the king noted that an unnamed Inquisition official had reported:

> In the Province of Tucumán [northern Argentina] there are many and innumerable Hebrews. They evaded [the official] before and now do so in growing numbers in these parts. Not only are they infected with their evil faith, but also defile our faith. And with boldness and great harm they have desecrated one of the churches and its religious images.[76]

Accordingly, King Felipe IV ordered, "The most efficient remedy to this rot and these actions is to establish a Tribunal of the Inquisition in one of the cities of the province."[77] The king's instructions were clear: identify and eliminate the Jewish threat that now demeaned his Andean kingdom.

Now charged with the responsibility of routing out Jews in colonial Bolivia and Argentina, Juan and his fellow administrators knew that the king's reference to "Hebrews" was a conventional euphemism for Portuguese conversos, who had immigrated to and were conducting business in South America.[78] However, what neither Juan de Carvajal nor other members of the Real Audiencia would publicly admit was that the king had addressed his letter to another group of conversos: many members of royal government. According to the normative beliefs of the period, the family confederation was simultaneously Christian in the public sphere and hiding its Jewish lineage in the private sphere.

Interestingly, the Andean government responded to Felipe IV's instructions in the well-documented Spanish American administrative tradition, "I obey, but I do not comply." In 1648, ten years after King Felipe IV's demand to eliminate the presence of "Hebrews" in Charcas, Juan ascended to the position of president of the Audiencia.[79] As a capable royal administrator, he earned the vigorous praise of his contemporaries, such as the Andean chronicler licenciate Pedro Ramírez del Águila. In his 1639 text, *Noticias políticas de indias y relación descriptiva de la ciudad de la Plata*, Pedro highlighted what most contemporary Spaniards cared about: the production of precious metals from Cerro Rico in Potosí. According to Pedro, Juan de Carvajal had advanced mining efforts and commerce in Potosí by channeling multiple water sources into a more effective waterway.[80] It is within this political and economic development context that Spanish history remembers Juan de Carvajal y Sande and not his converso origins. The family confederation always put duty to the Spanish crown ahead of itself, and for that service, its members were rewarded and shielded.

One element of the religious lives of the converso family confederation in Charcas that is difficult to interpret is its role in the creation of and participation in the religious brotherhood known as the Cofradía de Vera Cruz (Confraternity of the True Cross) in Potosí. As it was founded sometime before 1612 and in connection with Convent of Saint Francis, several prominent ecclesiastical and lay conversos initiated the special devotional organization that simultaneously integrated related family members and promoted their social status in colonial society. Among its more public activities was a special religious procession that occurred on Holy Thursday preceding the celebration of Easter.[81] Those confraternity members who may have been related to the broader family confederation were Vicar Diego Zanbrana de Villalobos, Bartolomé Martínez de Tapia, Dr. Bartolomé de Cervantes, Diego de Vargas, Pedro Osorio, and Alonso Cotel Carvajal.[82] Even though some evidence suggests that Spanish religious brotherhoods were utilized by conversos to practice the Jewish faith in private, there is no immediate indication that this occurred in the Cofradía de Vera Cruz.

On the other hand, the Cofradía's actions were an overt public display of Christian religiosity. Just as the family confederation had utilized religious foundations (chapel masses, chapel endowments, and monastic foundations) to bolster its Christian credentials in fifteenth-century Plasencia, so did the members of the Cofradía in Potosí. The Cofradía provided the ideal public venue for colonial elites to communicate their Christian identity in an overt manner. In sum, like their predecessors in Plasencia and their contemporaries in Mexico City, the Andean family confederation consistently practiced a public Christianity—with the secret knowledge that they were descended from Sephardic Jews.

CONCLUSION

The archival record from Spain, Mexico, and the Andes establishes with little doubt that the Carvajal–Santa María family confederation was of converso origins, even though it toiled aggressively to bury this truth in blood purity and lineage-obsessed Spain and colonial Spanish America. Moreover, the family confederation retained knowledge of its late fourteenth-century Jewish ancestry late into the seventeenth century. Collectively, family members promoted their lineage as an Old Christian one, although their actions and practices reveal their hybridized identity that retained limited Jewish cultural and religious understanding but ultimately was explicitly and decisively Christian in the public arena. Their determination signaled a deep-seated desire to rid themselves of their Jewish bloodlines through acts of intense Christian faith.

Elite conversos such as the Carvajal–Santa María family confederation were highly effective at hiding in plain sight and remain an understudied community in Spain and the New World. This comprehensive study establishes that elite Jewish converts to Christianity—and the Old Christians with whom they intermarried—did more than survive the anti-Jewish sentiment and prohibitions of the late medieval and early modern periods but assertively sought and expanded their political, ecclesiastical, and economic opportunities, especially in colonial Mexico and the Andes. Conversos, while careful to guard their genealogical pasts from Old Christians, steadfastly fostered and nurtured their Old World extended family and filial relationships with a certain level of impunity. Furthermore, these conversos operated across thousands of miles of ocean and three continents.

To limit their exposure to the Inquisition, the conversos continued publicly to promote familial Christian piety, as the evidence suggests. Because of their efforts to conceal their identities, it is difficult for modern scholars to ascertain their religious beliefs. Surprisingly, although conversos' official positions and personal fortunes were subject to loss due to their minority religious ancestries, they were relatively unsympathetic and not above the exploitation of politically weak indigenous populations. In particular, the family confederation's wealth-building efforts in Mexico and Bolivia/Peru centered on the mining of precious minerals, which often resulted in deadly human and environmental impacts on the indigenous population. The family confederation in the Americas remained elites intent on guarding and promoting their status in colonial Spanish America, regardless of the outcomes for indigenous peoples.

Elite conversos remained vulnerable to the Holy Office well into the seventeenth century. In most cases Spanish and Andean conversos could outmaneuver the Holy Office, but those in Mexico encountered more difficulties and sometimes fatal outcomes. While alienated from their Jewish past, conversos had not forgotten their Jewish roots and actively sought to remain connected to and protect their extended family members. But these relationships were complicated, and it was not unheard of for conversos to oversee the elimination of extended family members who continued to be practicing Jews.

In sum, the convoluted history of the Carvajal–Santa María family confederation is reflective of the religious and status preoccupations of the late fourteenth through early seventeenth centuries in Spain and the Americas. Conversos adeptly utilized the same institutions intended to exclude them from public and religious life to advance their interests and well-being. Their history adds to a more comprehensive explication of the Jewish diaspora after the Edict of Expulsion of 1492 and the long-term survival of conversos in the Spanish world. Essentially, Jews converted and Old Christians intermarried, and they collectively concealed bloodlines as they moved west toward the Americas. In an extraordinary and entirely unexpected manner, they seem to have followed Moses Maimonides's twelfth-century advice to convert temporarily and flee to safety so that they might live another day. Jewish elements of the Carvajal–Santa María family confederation may have heeded this advice, but their path forward during the early modern period offered them no realistic return to Judaism. For their Old Christian partners, those who chose to become conversos through intermarriage with Jews and other conversos, the future would be tied to perpetual doubts about their Christian identities. Together, their identities would always remain encumbered by blood and faith.

NOTES

INTRODUCTION

1. Bernáldez, *Memorias del reinado*, 572; Pastor, *History of the Popes*, 6:367, 372.
2. Pastor, *History of the Popes*, 6:375.
3. Ibid., 6:374; RAH, Colección Pellicer, tomo 9/4070, fol. 142.
4. Bernáldez, *Memorias del reinado*, 643–45; Pastor, *History of the Popes*, 7:44–45; RAH, Colección Pellicer, tomo 9/4070, fol. 143.
5. Bernáldez, *Memorias del reinado*, 643–45; Pastor, *History of the Popes*, 7:44–45; RAH, Colección Pellicer, tomo 9/4070, fol. 143; Gerber, *Jews of Spain*, 127.
6. Bernáldez, *Memorias del reinado*, 643–45; Pastor, *History of the Popes*, 7:44–45; RAH, Colección Pellicer, tomo 9/4070, fol. 143; Gerber, *Jews of Spain*, 127, 140.
7. Phillips and Phillips, *Concise History of Spain*, 112, 115, 121; Gerber, *Jews of Spain*, ix–x, 140.
8. Hillgarth, "Spanish Historiography," 25.

CHAPTER 1.   ORIGINS

1. Defining identity through the persecution of others is not a uniquely European or Spanish phenomenon but appears to be a universal element of the human condition.
2. Nirenberg, *Communities of Violence*, 21.
3. Ibid.
4. Ibid., 11–14.
5. Moore, *Formation of a Persecuting Society*, 5.
6. Given, Review of Moore's *The Formation of a Persecuting Society*.

263

7. Ibid.

8. Rubin, Review of Moore's *The Formation of a Persecuting Society*, 1025.

9. Baer, *History of the Jews*, 111.

10. Ibid., 306, 354.

11. Ibid., 355–56.

12. Bloch, *Feudal Society*, 1:123.

13. Ibid., 123–24.

14. Ibid.

15. Duby, "Diffusion of Cultural Patterns," 6; Duby "La diffusion du titre cheval-reque," 39–70.

16. Duby, "Diffusion of Cultural Patterns," 6.

17. Harney, *Kinship and Marriage*, 8, 12. (I am grateful to Professor Harney for bringing the world of Spanish civilization to life for me as an undergraduate at the University of Texas at Austin.)

18. Ibid., 36–37, 58, 66, 72, 74.

19. Bisson, *Tormented Voice*, 34.

20. Ibid., 120.

21. The incontestability of family is related in countless Spanish historical works focusing on noble houses, such as Simon R. Doubleday's *The Lara Family: Crown and Nobility in Medieval Spain*, José Manuel Gutiérrez Rodríguez's *Oropesa y los Álvarez de Toledo*, J. M. Lodo de Mayoralgo's *Viejos linajes de Cáceres*, Vicente Paredes y Guillén's *Los Zúñigas, señores de Plasencia*, and Luis Salazar y Castro's *Historia genealógica de la casa de Haro*. Even converso family histories, such as Francisco Cantera Burgos's *Alvar García de Santa María y su familia de conversos: Historia de la judería de Burgos y sus conversos mas egregious* and Luciano Serrano's *Los conversos: D. Pablo de Santa María y D. Alfonso de Cartagena*, fit into this category of scholarship that reinforces the presence of clan in the formation of a group's self-perception.

22. Gerbet, *La noblesse dans royaume de Castille*, 106.

23. Ibid., 106–7.

24. Nader, *The Mendoza Family in the Spanish Renaissance*, 27.

25. Ibid., 4.

26. Amador de los Ríos, *Historia social, política y religiosa*, 312.

27. Fuente, "Christian, Muslim and Jewish Women," 163–69.

28. Ida Altman impressively evaluates the transatlantic history of the Carvajal and Sande families in *Emigrants and Society* (1989), but my work differs substantially from hers in that I uncover and investigate the Jewish and converso origins and development of these families.

29. Greenblatt, *Renaissance Self-Fashioning*, 83.

30. Ibid., 82.

31. Astarita, *Continuity of Feudal Power*, 4, 160–61.

32. ACP, Legajo 129, doc. 11, fol. 3–3v.

33. Safran, *Second Umayyad Caliphate*, 158.

34. Kennedy, *Muslim Spain and Portugal*, 56.

35. Ibid., 115, 237, 246. Note that historians of Christian Spain and Islamic Spain often use different naming conventions for the Almohad caliph Abu Yusuf Ya'qub al-Mansjur (1184–99). From a Christian historical perspective, this caliph's name is commonly shortened to "Ya'qub I," whereas scholars of Islamic Spain typically refer to him as "Ya'qub al-Mansur." For clarity, I use the caliph's full name in all references pertaining to him. Further, I would like to thank L. J. Andrew Villalón for pointing out that the name "al-Mansur," often translated as "the victorious," is commonly associated with the Spanish Umayyad ruler Muhammad b. Abi 'Amir (981–1002), who took the title "al-Mansur."

36. ACP, Legajo 129, doc. 11, fol. 2; González Cuesta, *Obispos de Plasencia*, 13. Correas Roldán attributes the commencing of his work to the year 1579 on folio 5 of ACP, Legajo 129, doc. 11. Correas Roldán appears to be the author of another early manuscript, ACP, Legajo 129, doc. 10, on the history of the Cathedral of Plasencia, titled "Noticias de los señores obispos de esta ciudad de Plasencia."

37. Fernández, *Historia y anales*, 7.

38. The earliest medieval accounts of the city spell the name of the river "Jerete"; the modern spelling is "Jerte." The names are used interchangeably here and are cited as they appear in the original source document.

39. Sánchez Loro, *Historias placentinas inéditas*, A:37–38; González Cuesta, *Obispos de Plasencia*, 23.

40. Fernández, *Historia y anales*, 2.

41. Ibid.

42. Ibid.

43. Paredes y Guillén, *Los Zúñigas*, 66–67; Santos Canalejo, *El siglo XV en Plasencia*, 105–7.

44. BUS, MS 2.650, fol. 14v.

45. BUS, MS 2.650, fols. 7, 13.

46. Kennedy, *Muslim Spain and Portugal*, 246.

47. ACP, Legajo 129, doc. 11, fols. 2–3; Benavides Checa, *Prelados placentinos*, 287–89.

48. Benavides Checa, *El Fuero de Plasencia*, 42, 45, 46, 54, 69, 76, 77, 105, 106, 107, 108, 133, 155.

49. Ibid., 42.

50. Ibid., 76.

51. Ibid., 106.

52. ACP, Legajo 129, doc. 11, fols. 3–3v; Benavides Checa, *Prelados placentinos*, 287–89.

53. ACP, Legajo 129, doc. 11, fols. 3–3v; Benavides Checa, *Prelados placentinos*, 287–89.

54. BUS, MS 2.650, fols. 25–26.

55. The map presented here is the author's original work and is based on the following sources: Fernández, *Historia y anales*, 153–55; Benavides Checa, *Prelados placentinos*, 147; a map titled "Plasencia en 1400" in the Spanish Servicio Geográfico del Ejercito library and referenced in Santos Canalejo, *El siglo XV en Plasencia*, 58.

56. ACP, *Actas capitulares*, tomo 1, fols. 264–71v.

57. ACP, *Actas capitulares*, tomo 1, fols. 32, 55.

58. Benavides Checa, *Prelados placentinos*, 147–48; Santos Canalejo, *El siglo XV en Plasencia*, 58.

59. ACP, Legajo 1, doc. 6; Benavides Checa, *Prelados placentinos*, 147; Benavides Checa, *El Fuero de Plasencia*, 11.

60. ACP, Legajo 129, doc. 11, fol. 2; Fernández, *Historia y anales*, 30; González Cuesta, *Obispos de Plasencia*, 13; Codero Alvarado, *Plasencia: Heráldica, histórica y monumental*, 60.

61. ACP, *Actas capitulares*, tomo 1, fols. 57v–58.

62. ACP, *Actas capitulares*, tomo 1, fols. 57v–58.

63. ACP, Legajo 282, "El portazgo de Plasencia"; ACP, Legajo 270, doc. 15.

64. ACP, *Actas capitulares*, tomo 1, fols. 56v–57, 67v–69.

65. Santos Canalejo, *El siglo XV en Plasencia*, 58.

66. Ibid.

67. Benavides Checa, *Prelados placentinos*, 139.

68. Ibid.

69. ACP, Legajo 7, doc. 22; ACP, Legajo 14, doc. 42.

70. ACP, Legajo 282, doc. 11.

71. ACP, Legajo 12, doc. 10; ACP, Legajo 14, doc. 1.

72. Sánchez Loro, *Historias placentinas inéditas*, A:402; González Cuesta, *Obispos de Plasencia*, 40.

73. Sánchez Loro, *Historias placentinas inéditas*, A:45; González Cuesta, *Obispos de Plasencia*, 51.

74. Fernández, *Historia y anales*, 37.

75. Ibid.

76. Ibid., 37–38; García Carraffa and García Carraffa, *Diccionario heráldica y genealógico*, 22:268–69.

77. Sánchez Loro, *Historias placentinas inéditas*, A:37–38.

78. RAH, Colección Salazar y Castro, tomo C-20, fol. 204v.

79. RAH, Colección Salazar y Castro, tomo C-20, fols. 204v–215v; Fernández, *Historia y anales*, 39–40. Additional documentation on these intermarriages is presented throughout this book and is derived from testaments, codicils, property sales, business transcriptions, memorials, foundations, and church records.

80. Fernández, *Historia y anales*, 41.

81. Ibid., 43.

82. Ibid.

83. Ibid., 41.

84. Ibid., 52.

85. Ibid., 52–54.

86. Ibid., 53.

87. Ibid., 28.

88. González Cuesta, *Obispos de Plasencia*, 33; Fernández, *Historia y anales*, 29.

89. ACP, Legajo 129, doc. 10, fol. 10; González Cuesta, *Obispos de Plasencia*, 40–41.

90. Codero Alvarado, *Plasencia: Heráldica, histórica y monumental*, 69.

91. Ruiz, *Spain's Centuries of Crisis*, 28–29.

CHAPTER 2.   CRISIS AND IMPETUS

1. Phillips and Phillips, *Concise History of Spain*, 83, 97.

2. Olea and Christakos, "Duration of Urban Mortality for the Fourteenth-Century Black Death Epidemic," 291.

3. Pamuk, "Black Death and the Origins of the 'Great Divergence,'" 294.

4. Cohn, "Black Death and the Burning of Jews," 4.

5. Ibid., 8.

6. Rosell, *Crónicas de reyes de Castilla*, tomo primero, 390.

7. In his valuable work, *Mayorazgo*, Bartolomé Clavero argued that prior to the civil war there were old noble clans and after its conclusion came a new generation of noble houses known as the New Nobility.

8. Hillgarth, *Spanish Kingdoms*, 2:374–76.

9. Singer and Adler, *Jewish Encyclopedia*, s.v. "Spain," 493.

10. Cantera Burgos, *Sinagogas del Toledo, Segovia, y Córdoba*, 49.

11. Ibid., 494.

12. Rosell, *Crónicas de reyes de Castilla*, tomo primero, 431.

13. Ibid.

14. Ruiz, *Spain's Centuries of Crisis*, 79.

15. Villalón, "Cut Off Their Heads," 153, 174–75.

16. Ibid., 175.

17. Rosell, *Crónicas de los reyes de Castilla*, tomo primero, 481–83, 499; Villalón, "Cut Off Their Heads," 164.

18. Ruiz, *Spain's Centuries of Crisis*, 80.

19. Hillgarth, *Spanish Kingdoms*, 2:372, 385.

20. Singer and Adler, *Jewish Encyclopedia*, s.v. "Spain," 494.

21. Hillgarth, *Spanish Kingdoms*, 2:375.

22. Ibid., 375, 380.

23. Rosell, *Crónicas de reyes de Castilla*, tomo primero, 589.

24. Ibid.

25. Ibid. 591.

26. Ibid.

27. Ibid., 592.

28. Ibid.

29. Phillips and Phillips, *Concise History of Spain*, 83.

30. Hillgarth, *Spanish Kingdoms*, 2:386.

31. Ibid., 387.

32. Ibid., 388.

33. Clavero, *Mayorazgo*, 116.

34. Ibid.

35. Hillgarth, *Spanish Kingdoms*, 2:374–75.

36. Special thanks to L. J. Andrew Villalón for sharing Clavero's work with me.

37. Clavero, *Mayorazgo*, 28.

38. Ibid.

39. Ibid.

40. Ibid.

41. de Moxó, "La nobleza castellana en el siglo XIV," 495.

42. Ibid.

43. Ruiz, *Spain's Centuries of Crisis*, 89.

44. Ibid., 82.

45. AHCB, vol. 46, fol. 424.

46. RAH, Colección Salazar y Castro, tomo C-20, fols. 211–213v.

47. Fernández, *Historia y anales*, 37–38; García Carraffa and García Carraffa, *Diccionario heráldico y genealógico*, 22:268–69.

48. Sánchez Loro, *Historias placentinas inéditas*, A:402; Fernández, *Historia y anales*, 37–38; García Carraffa, *Diccionario heráldico y genealógico*, 22:268–69.

49. Fernández, *Historia y anales*, 37–38.

50. Ibid.

51. Ibid.

52. ACP, Legajo 14, doc. 25.

53. ACP, Legajo 14, doc. 25.

54. RAH, Colección Salazar y Castro, C-20, fols. 211–212v; García Carraffa and García Carraffa, *Diccionario heráldico y genealógico*, 22:271; Mendoza y Bobadilla, *El tizón de la nobleza española*, 142–45.

55. AHNSN, Ovando, Caja 35, doc. 1993, no folio.

56. ACP, Legajo 270, doc. 13.

57. AHNSN, Torrejón, Caja 7, doc. 10; ACP, Legajo 1, doc. 34; ACP, Legajo 14, doc. 4; ACP, Legajo 14, doc. 23; ACP, Legajo 14, doc. 25; ACP, Legajo 14, doc. 1; ACP, Legajo 1, doc. 21; ACP, Legajo 2, doc. 21; ACP, Legajo 12, doc. 16; ACP, Legajo 14, doc. 38.

58. Serrano, *Los conversos*, 52, 62; Cantera Burgos, *Alvar García de Santa María*, 304.

59. RAH, Colección Floranes, B-16, fols. 14 (282), 17 (287).

60. Lea, *History of the Inquisition of Spain*, 1:115–16.

61. Serrano, *Los conversos*, 21, 25.

62. Ibid., 23.

63. Roth, *Conversos, Inquisition, and the Expulsion*, 138.

64. Ibid.

65. Ibid., 139.

66. Ibid., 139–40.

67. Ibid., 139.

68. Ibid., 144.

69. Amador de los Ríos, *Historia social, política y religiosa*, tomo 2, 493–95.

70. Ibid., 496–502.

71. Ibid., 12, 42, 618–26.

72. Baer, *History of the Jews*, 2:169.

73. Rosell, *Crónicas de reyes de Castilla*, tomo segundo, 177.

74. AHMB, Legajo HI-2960, no folio.

75. Lea, "Ferrand Martínez," 216; Cantera Burgos, *Alvar García de Santa María*, 24–25.

76. AHMB, Legajo HI-2960, no folio.

77. AHCB, vol. 48, fol. 250; AHCB, vol. 46, fol. 424; AHCB, vol. 5, fols. 51–51v.

78. AHNSN, Osuna, Caja 300, docs. 8 (6), 9 (5), no folio; AHNSN, Osuna, Caja 299, docs. 1 (4), 1 (6), 2 (1), no folio; AHNSN, Osuna, Caja 303, doc. 51, no folio; AHNSN, Osuna, Caja 303, doc. 42, no folio; Santos Canalejo, *El siglo XV en Plasencia*, 79; Hervás, *Historia de los judíos de Plasencia*, 2:174–80.

79. There is a debate about whether Alvar García de Santa María was the son or the brother of Pablo de Santa María. The historian Francisco Cantera Burgos raises this issue in *Alvar García de Santa María y su familia de conversos*. He argues that Alvar García de Santa María was the brother of Pablo de Santa María and cites other historians who agree with him, including Mariana, Flórez, Floranes, Amador de los Ríos, Anibarro, and A. Paz y Meliá. Luciano Serrano, author of *Los conversos*, is the only one who disagrees with this finding, suggesting instead that Alvar García was Pablo's son. Curiously, Cantera Burgos attributes this error in genealogy to the royal chronicler and adviser to the *reyes católicos*, Dr. Lorenzo Galíndez de Carvajal, a descendant of the Plasencia Carvajal family who had intermarried with the Santa María. See Cantera Burgos, *Alvar García de Santa María*, 60–61.

80. ACP, *Actas capitulares*, tomo 1, fols. 29–29v; ACP, Legajo 270, doc. 13, no folio.

81. ACP, *Actas capitulares*, tomo 1, fols. 46–46v, 99–100v, 105, 116, 161.

82. ACP, *Actas capitulares*, tomo 1, fols. 29–29v.

83. ACP, Legajo 143, doc. 12; ACP Legajo 270, doc. 13. Juan González de Santa María was likely the brother of Alfonso García de Santa María, archdeacon of Trujillo and Medellín during the 1430s. Two additional sources document Alfonso García's church position in Plasencia, as well as name his siblings: ACP, *Actas capitulares*, tomo 1, fols. 217v–219; and Cantera Burgos, *Alvar García de Santa María*, 524, 532, which notes that Alfonso García worked in the service of Bishop Gonzalo de Santa María at the Cathedral of Plasencia. Cantera Burgos also notes that Alfonso García had two brothers, Pedro García de Santa María and Juan González de Santa María. Thus Juan González seems to be the same individual named in the archive of the Cathedral of Plasencia and in Cantera Burgos.

84. ACP, Legajo 143, doc. 12; ACP, Legajo 270, doc. 13.

85. ACP, *Actas capitulares*, tomo 1, fol. 313v.

86. AHCB, Registro 2, fols. 240v–241.

87. Estúñiga is the spelling of the family's surname during the 1300s and 1400s; Zúñiga is the modern variant. I have used the family's original surname as it appears in the manuscripts.

88. AHCB, Registro 2, fols. 240v–241.

89. AHNSN, Osuna, Caja 213, doc. 19 (21), fols. 253–59, 347. See these folios for the Estúñiga family genealogy recorded in Diego López de Estúñiga's testament.

90. AHNSN, Osuna, Caja 213, docs. 19 (20)–19 (21), fols. 239–59; Villalobos y Martínez-Pontremuli, "Los Estúñiga," 331–33.

91. AHNSN, Osuna, Caja 213, doc. 19 (21), fols. 253–59; Martínez Moro, *La renta feudal en la Castilla*, 53–71.

92. Martínez Moro, *La renta feudal en la Castilla*, 116.

93. Fernández, *Historia y anales*, 164–68.

94. Paredes y Guillén, *Los Zúñigas*, 44.

95. AHNSN, Osuna, Caja 213, docs. 19 (20), fol. 258; Cantera Burgos, *Alvar García de Santa María*, 130, 285.

96. AHNSN, Osuna, Caja 213, docs. 19 (20), fol. 348.

97. Teresa de Estúñiga and Rodrigo Ponce de León were reported to be married in the testament of Juan Ponce de León, conde de Arcos y la Ciudad de Cadiz. See AHNSN, Osuna, Caja 124, doc. 2.

98. Mendoza y Bobadilla, *El tizón de nobleza española*, 12.

99. Ibid., 57.

100. Ibid., 12, 59.

101. Ibid., 75, 95

102. Ibid., 109.

103. Gutiérrez Rodríguez, *Oropesa y los Álvarez*, 14–17.

104. AHNSN, Frías, Caja 1764, doc. 31; ACP, Legajo 270, N. 1.

105. Franco Silva, "Oropesa, nacimiento de un señorío toledano," 299–314.

106. Ibid., 308–11.

107. Ibid., 310–11.

108. AHNSN, Frías, Caja 1762, docs. 3, 4, fol. 3.

109. Rabade Obrado, "La invención como necesidad," 511.

110. Mendoza y Bobadilla, *El tizón de nobleza española*, 63–64, 68, 121.

111. Amador de los Ríos, *Historia social, política y religiosa*; Lea, *History of the Inquisition of Spain*; Baer, *History of the Jews*.

112. Amador de los Ríos, *Historia social, política y religiosa*, tomo 2, 349–50.

113. Lea, *History of the Inquisition*, 1:107.

114. Gerber, *Jews of Spain*, 113; Roth, *Conversos, Inquisition, and the Expulsion*, 33.

115. Baer, *History of the Jews*, 2:97, 100–101.

116. Netanyahu, *Origins of the Inquisition*, 127.

117. Danvila, "El robo de la judería de Valencia," 364, 365, 371, 374; de Garganta and Forcada, *Biografía y escritos de San Vicente Ferrer*, 172–73.

118. Maccoby, "The Tortosa Disputation, 1413–14, and Its Effects," 23.

119. Klener, "Introduction: Spanish Jewry at the Eve of the Expulsion," in *The Expulsion of the Jews and Their Emigration to the Southern Low Countries*, XIV.

120. Pacios López, *La disputa de Tortosa*, 1:49–51; Maccoby, "The Tortosa Disputation, 1413–14, and Its Effects," 28.

121. Roth, *Conversos, Inquisition, and the Expulsion*, 55.

122. Pacios López, *La disputa de Tortosa*, 1:44; Amador de los Ríos, *Historia social, política y religiosa*, tomo 2, 432.

123. Roth, *Conversos, Inquisition, and the Expulsion*, 55–58.

124. AHNSN, Osuna, Caja 298, doc. 3 (17); Hervás, *Historia de los judíos de Plasencia*, 2:86–92, 100–102; 1:38–50.

125. de Garganta and Forcada, *Biografía y escritos de San Vicente Ferrer*, 172–73.

126. Ibid.; Benavides Checa, *Prelados placentinos*, 154. While there is no explicit evidence of Ferrer's travels in the Diocese of Plasencia, the Estúñiga family would later construct a monastery bearing his name in Plasencia's La Mota.

127. AHNSN, Osuna, Caja 298, doc. 3 (17), fol. 42v.

128. AHNSN, Osuna, Caja 298, doc. 3 (17), fol. 42v.

129. AHNSN, Osuna, Caja 298, doc. 3 (17), fols. 45–46v; Hervás, *Historia de los judíos de Plasencia,* 1:42.

130. AHNSN, Osuna, Caja 298, doc. 3 (17), fol. 77v.

131. AHNSN, Osuna, Caja 298, doc. 3 (17), fol. 78.

132. AHNSN, Osuna, Caja 298, doc. 3 (17), fols. 90–90v.

133. AHNSN, Osuna, Caja 298, doc. 3 (17), fol. 91.

134. AHNSN, Osuna, Caja 298, docs. 3 (13) and 3 (14); Hervás, *Historia de los judíos de Plasencia,* 2:100–102.

135. AHNSN, Osuna, Caja 298, docs. 3 (13) and 3 (14); Hervás, *Historia de los judíos de Plasencia,* 2:100–102.

136. For example, in 1257, Artal de Luna refused to pay these church tariffs to the bishop of Zaragoza. See Burns, "A Mediæval Income Tax," 445.

137. Vassberg, *Land and Society in Golden Age Castile,* 220.

138. Gerbet, *Noblesse dans royaume de Castille,* 136–39.

139. Ibid., 274–75.

140. Clavero, *Mayorazgo,* 28.

141. Gerbet, *Noblesse dans royaume de Castille,* 250–51.

142. Martínez Moro, *La renta feudal,* 25–26; Gerbet, *Noblesse dans royaume de Castille,* 251.

143. Vaquero, Marín Martínez, and Gatell, *Diccionario de historia eclesiástica de España,* s.v. "Diezmo." Although the *Diccionario* does not cite potential Islamic antecedents of this agricultural tax, it should be noted that diezmos resemble the Islamic practice of collecting the *kharāj.* For more information on the kharāj, see Cooper, "The Assessment and Collection of Kharāj Tax," 365–82.

144. Bishop Domingo's surname is not known. ACP, Legajo 282, doc. 1, "Constituciones sinodales publicadas," no folio.

145. ACP, Legajo 282, "Privilegio del Rey D. Alfonso XI," no folio.

146. See ACP, *Actas capitulares,* tomo 1 (1399–1453), fols. 1–29, for the 1390s accounting of cathedral properties.

147. ACP, *Actas capitulares,* tomo 1 (1399–1453), fols. 1–29.

148. A review of the *Actas capitulares* reveals that none of these families had kin on the governing cathedral chapter.

149. ACP, *Actas capitulares,* tomo 1, fols. 5v–6v, 15–15v, 16–16v, 18–19v, 20–23v.

150. ACP, *Actas capitulares,* tomo 1, fols. 1–29.

151. See n. 146 above.

152. ACP, *Actas capitulares,* tomo 1, fols. 8–8v, 15–15v, 17–18v.

153. ACP, *Actas capitulares,* tomo 1, fols. 8–8v.

154. ACP, *Actas capitulares,* tomo 1, fols. 20–27.

155. ACP, Legajo 282, "Real provisión de D. Enrique España," no folio; ACP, *Extractos del inventario de papeles del archivo,* tomo 3, doc. 338.

156. ACP, Legajo 282, "Real provisión de D. Enrique España," no folio; ACP, *Extractos del inventario de papeles del archivo,* tomo 3, doc. 338.

157. ACP, Legajo 282, "Real provisión de D. Enrique España," no folio; ACP, *Extractos del inventario de papeles del archivo*, tomo 3, doc. 338.

158. RAH, Colección Salazar y Castro, tomo C-20, fols. 211–213v.

159. ACP, Legajo 282, doc. 3, no folio.

160. ACP, Legajo 129, doc. 10, fols. 15–15v; Fernández, *Historia y anales*, 132–33; González Cuesta, *Obispos de Plasencia*, 81–85.

161. ACP, Legajo 282, "Real Provisión de D. Enrique España," no folio; ACP, *Extractos del inventario*, tomo 3, doc. 338.

162. ACP, *Extractos del inventario*, tomo 3, doc. 338.

163. ACP, *Extractos del inventario*, tomo 3, doc. 338.

164. ACP, *Extractos del inventario*, tomo 3, doc. 338.

165. ACP, *Extractos del inventario*, tomo 3, doc. 338.

166. ACP, Legajo 282, "Real provisión de D. Enrique España," no folio; ACP, *Extractos del inventario*, tomo 3, doc. 338.

167. ACP, Legajo 45, doc. 13.

168. RAH, Colección Salazar y Castro, tomo C-20, fol. 212v.

169. ACP, Legajo 45, doc. 13. No surname is provided for Fernando the bishop.

170. ACP, Legajo 45, doc. 13.

171. ACP, Legajo 45, doc. 13.

172. ACP, Legajo 45, doc. 14. Alfonso López, the sixth co-conspirator, is named and absolved but is not required to pay a financial penalty. Note that there are some monetary discrepancies between the transcribed and original documents. Specifically, the original states that Juan Sánchez owes 730, not 430, maravedís.

CHAPTER 3.   OPPORTUNITY

1. Paredes y Guillén, *Los Zúñigas*, 66–67; Santos Canalejo, *Historia medieval*, 105–7.

2. Burckhardt, *Civilization of the Renaissance in Opportunity Italy*, 98.

3. Greenblatt, *Renaissance Self-Fashioning*, 1.

4. Martin, *Myths of Renaissance Individualism*, ix.

5. Ibid., 15.

6. Ibid., 36.

7. Ruggiero, *Machiavelli in Love*, 21.

8. Ibid.

9. For an expert treatment of Herbert Grundmann's impact on the historiography of medieval Christian Europe, see Van Engen, "Christian Middle Ages," 519–52.

10. Van Engen, "Christian Middle Ages," 523.

11. Ibid., 519, 521, 522.

12. Pulido Serrano, "Los judíos en obra," 46.

13. Caro Baroja, *Los judíos en España*, 1:133.

14. Ibid., 1:132–33.

15. See the excellent historiographical reviews presented in David Graizbord's *Souls in Dispute* and Renée Levine Melammed's *A Question of Identity*. My own work employs these texts as a basic framework for discussing Sephardic history and adds discussion pertaining to the wider realm of scholarship on identity.

16. Llorente, *Historia crítica de la Inquisición*, 124–25.

17. Gerber, *Jews of Spain*, xii.

18. Ibid.

19. Graizbord, *Souls in Dispute*, 8–9.

20. Ibid.

21. Ibid., 9.

22. Hordes, *To the End of the Earth*, 109.

23. AHNSN, Ovando, Caja 35, doc. 1993, no folio.

24. ACP, Legajo 270, doc. 13, no folio.

25. ACP, Legajo 143, doc. 12; ACP, Legajo 270, doc. 13. Juan González de Santa María was likely the brother of Alfonso García de Santa María, the cathedral's archdeacon of Trujillo and Medellín during the 1430s. Two additional sources document Alfonso García's church position in Plasencia, as well as name his siblings: ACP, *Actas capitulares*, tomo 1, fols. 217v–219, detail Alfonso's church position; and Cantera Burgos, *Alvar García de Santa María*, 524, 532, notes that Alfonso García worked in the service of Bishop Gonzalo de Santa María at the Cathedral of Plasencia. Cantera Burgos also notes that Alfonso García had two brothers, Pedro García de Santa María and Juan González de Santa María. Thus, Juan González seems to be the same individual named in the archive of the Cathedral of Plasencia and in Cantera Burgos's text.

26. ACP, Legajo 143, doc. 12; ACP, Legajo 270, doc. 13.

27. ACP, *Calendario o libro de aniversarios de la Santa Iglesia placentina*. In 2007, this previously unknown text was located by don Juan Manuel Ramos Berrocoso, at the time director of the Archivo de la Catedral de Plasencia, and is not cataloged. The *Calendario*, which records anniversary masses before the late sixteenth century, includes twenty-six masses for men and women who were not clergy (*seculares*). Although as many as ten masses might be said for a donation, this occurred for just one benefactor, doña Gracia González. The vast majority of donations produced one anniversary mass for the benefactor. As Leonor Sánchez's donation was not accepted, due to the judge's decision in favor of María Gómez, her anniversary masses were not recorded.

28. Leonor Sánchez also described Juan González de Santa María as her "family relation"; therefore, Sánchez was related to María Gómez through extended marital ties and was related to Juan through unspecified blood relations (i.e., uncle, aunt, grandparent).

29. ACP, Legajo 270, doc. 13, no folio.

30. ACP, Legajo 270, doc. 13, no folio.

31. ACP, Legajo 270, doc. 13, no folio.

32. ACP, Legajo 270, doc. 13, no folio.

33. See these testaments and genealogical records: AHNSN, Luque, Caja 160, doc. 9; AHNSN, Osuna, Caja 300, doc. 9 (7); ACP, Legajo 270, doc. 13; ACP, Legajo 14, doc. 25; ACP, Legajo 6, doc. 50; Sánchez Loro, *Historias placentinas inéditas*, B:275–76.

34. ACP, Legajo 269, doc. 25.

35. AHNSN, Luque, Caja 159, docs. 3, 6, 7, 8, 9, 15, 17, 18, 19, 20, 21, 22; AHNSN, Luque, Caja 160, doc. 8.

36. Mencía Álvarez de Carvajal and Diego García de Ulloa were the parents of Juan de Carvajal. See AHNSN, Ovando, Caja 35, doc. 2006, fols. 1, 4v, 9.

37. ACP, *Actas capitulares*, tomo 1, fols. 46–46v, 99–100v, 105, 116, 161.

38. ACP, Legajo 3, doc. 22, no folio.

39. ACP, Legajo 14, doc. 2, no folio.

40. McGaha, *Story of Joseph in Spanish Golden Age Drama*, 17.

41. According to Michael McGaha, the story of Joseph in Genesis 37–50 is a critical component of the Jewish people's epic and speaks to its most formative moment—the exodus from Egypt. See McGaha, *Story of Joseph in Spanish Golden Age Drama*, ix, 19.

42. ACP, *Extractos del inventario de papeles del archivo*, tomo 1, 282v–285; ACP, *Extractos del inventario de papeles del archivo*, tomo 2, 10v–11; Gitlitz, "Conversos and the Fusion of Worlds," 146–48.

43. An extensive review of the archival indexes of the Archivo de la Catedral de Plasencia and all its legajos, libros, and extractos pertaining to the Carvajal family produced no evidence of the Carvajal family serving as churchmen in the Diocese of Plasencia before 1400. Further, an investigation of the genealogy and nobility records held by the Real Academia de Historia (Madrid, Spain), especially its Colección Salazar y Castro and Colección Floranes, and the Archivo histórico nacional–sección nobleza and its pertinent collections (Alba de Yeltes, Baena, Bornos, Castrillo, Fernán-Núñez, Frías, Luque, Mocejón, Osuna, Ovando, and Torrejón) yielded similar findings.

44. Gonzalo de Estúñiga and Pedro de Estúñiga were the sons of Diego López de Estúñiga, the justicia mayor of King Juan I and a member of his royal council. Their mother was the conversa Juana García de Leyva. See Sánchez Loro, *Historias placentinas inéditas*, B:368.

45. Peter Linehan notes disagreements between the bishop and the cathedral chapter in Burgos, Palencia, and many other communities during the 1260s. Jodi Bilinkoff documents similar economic and patronage conflicts between the bishop of Ávila and the cathedral chapter during the 1450s. See Linehan, *Spanish Church and Papacy in the Thirteenth Century*, 177, 256; Bilinkoff, *Ávila of Saint Teresa*, 29.

46. See "Cabildos," in Aldea Vaquero, Martínez, and Gatell, *Diccionario de historia eclesiástica*, tomo 1, 299–300.

47. See "Iglesia y estado," in Aldea Vaquero, Martínez, and Gatell, *Diccionario de historia eclesiástica*, tomo 2, 1117–19.

48. Burns, "Organization of a Mediæval Cathedral Community," 14.

49. "Iglesia y estado."

50. Linehan, "Segovia," 481–82.

51. For example, see comparative evidence for absentee bishops in Ávila. Bilinkoff, *Ávila of Saint Teresa*, 29.

52. ACP, *Actas capitulares*, tomo 1, fols. 1–79.

53. ACP, Legajo 129, doc. 10, fols. 15–16v.

54. ACP, *Actas capitulares*, tomo 1, fol. 79.

55. ACP, *Actas capitulares*, tomo 1, fol. 79.

56. ACP, *Actas capitulares*, tomo 1, fols. 31v, 32–33, 50–50v, 98–98v, 114v, 168.

57. ACP, Legajo 129, doc. 10, fol. 10.

58. See "Dignidades eclesiásticas," in Aldea Vaquero, Martínez, and Gatell, *Diccionario de historia eclesiástica*, tomo 2, 758–59.

59. In 1424, the archdeacon of Coria was a member of the Plasencia cathedral chapter. However, this jurisdiction was later moved into the Diocese of Cáceres. See ACP, *Actas capitulares*, tomo 1, fols. 98–98v; "Cabildos."

60. "Cabildos."

61. ACP, *Actas capitulares*, tomo 1, fols. 35–35v, 65v, 274v–279.

62. When the cathedral chapter had a named attorney (*abogado*), as in 1442, it also named a canon, such as Ruy García de Salamanca, with the proper legal credentials to handle the office. Ruy García took on these additional duties and its supplemental salary. See ACP, *Actas capitulares*, tomo 1, fols. 249v–252.

63. ACP, *Actas capitulares*, tomo 1, 60v–65v; Herbermann et al., *The Catholic Encyclopedia*, s.v. "Vicar General."

64. Bilinkoff, *Ávila of Saint Teresa*, 30–31; Burns, "Organization of a Mediaeval Cathedral Community," 18.

65. For two examples of the superior status of archdeacons, see the March 6, 1445, bishop's statute regarding misuse of church resources and a property sale/exchange from January 2, 1441. ACP, *Actas capitulares*, tomo 1, fols. 274v–279, 291–297v.

66. Men who held dual roles in the chapter and served short periods as the dean included Prebendary Gil Gutiérrez de la Calleja (1406–7), Canon Diego Blásquez (1408), Sacristan Juan Sánchez (1417), Prebendary Diego Martínez (1417), Canon Sancho Ortiz de Estúñiga (part of 1424), Archdeacon Gonzalo García de Carvajal (part of 1424), Canon Ruy González (1434), Canon Álvaro de Monroy (1437–38), and Canon Álvaro de Salazar (1445, 1453). See ACP, *Actas capitulares*, tomo 1, fols. 29v, 47v–48, 65v–66, 69, 75–76v, 98–98v, 243v–245v, 284v–291, 363v–368, 424–26.

67. ACP, *Actas capitulares*, tomo 1, fols. 31v, 33–33v, 50–50v.

68. Burns, "Organization of a Mediaeval Cathedral Community," 16–17.

69. Kettering, "Patronage and Kinship," 408–9, 412.

70. Ibid., 408.

71. Ibid., 408–9, 412.

72. ACP, Legajo 129, doc. 10, fol. 15; Fernández, *Historia y anales*, 132–33; González Cuesta, *Los obispos de Plasencia*, 81–85.

73. ACP, Legajo 282, doc. 3, no folio.

74. ACP, Legajo 282, doc. 3, no folio.

75. The Gutiérrez de la Calleja family was part of the converso Santa María family. See chapter 2 for more details of their familial relationships.

76. In addition to the Fernández family, the following men were members of the cathedral chapter: Diego Blásquez, dean; Juan Sánchez, cantor; and Pedro "Cardenal de España," treasurer. See ACP, Legajo 129, doc.10, fol. 15v.

77. ACP, Legajo 282, doc. 9, "Testamento del Bachiller," no folio. Archdeacon Fernández served as a tutor to his brother's son, Martín de St. Esteban. The affinity that the archdeacon had for this nephew was so great that he would later name him his "universal heir" in his last testament.

78. ACP, Legajo 129, doc. 10, fols. 15–15v; ACP, *Calendario o libro de aniversarios de la Santa Iglesia placentina*, fol. 1.

79. ACP, Legajo 129, doc. 10, fols. 15v–16.

80. ACP, Legajo 129, doc. 10, fols. 15v–16; ACP, Legajo 282, doc. 7, "Constituciones del Señor Obispo," no folio.

81. ACP, Legajo 45, docs. 13–16; ACP, Legajo 282, doc. 2, "Real provisión de don Enrique," no folio.

82. ACP, Legajo 45, docs. 13–16.

83. ACP, Legajo 129, doc. 10, fol. 16.

84. ACP, *Actas capitulares*, tomo 1, fol. 29v.

85. ACP *Actas capitulares*, tomo 1, fols. 35–35v.

86. The cathedral chapter used the titles "dean" and "mayordomo" interchangeably from the 1390s until at least the 1430s. See ACP, *Actas capitulares*, tomo 1, fols. 1, 29–29v, 62.

87. ACP, *Actas capitulares*, tomo 1, fol. 29v.

88. ACP, *Actas capitulares*, tomo 1, fols. 35–35v.

89. Not until 1424, when Gonzalo García de Carvajal was appointed archdeacon of Plasencia and Béjar, does another Carvajal or Santa María appear in the *Actas capitulares* as a church official. See ACP, *Actas capitulares*, tomo 1, fols. 1–97v.

90. ACP, *Actas capitulares*, tomo 1, fols. 60v–65v.

91. ACP, *Actas capitulares*, tomo 1, fols. 60v–65v; ACP, Legajo 25, doc. 18, "Estatutos antiguos," fols. 51–53.

92. ACP, *Actas capitulares*, tomo 1, fols. 61v–62.

93. ACP, *Actas capitulares*, tomo 1, fol. 313.

94. ACP, Legajo 129, doc. 10, fols. 16–16v; ACP, *Actas capitulares*, tomo 1, fols. 98–98v.

95. ACP, Legajo 282, doc. 9, "Testamento del Bachiller en Decretos D. Martín Fernández de Soria, Arcediano de Plasencia y Béjar 4 de Octubre 1424," no folio.

96. ACP, Legajo 129, doc. 10, fol. 16v.

97. Sánchez Loro, *Historias placentinas inéditas*, B:369.

98. Fernández, *Historia y anales*, 164–68.

99. RAH, Colección Salazar y Castro, C-20, fols. 197–217. This statement is based on my review of sources in the RAH, AHHSN, and ACP.

100. Nader, *Mendoza Family in the Spanish Renaissance*, 40.

101. Herlihy, "Three Patterns of Social Mobility," 639–41.

102. See chapters 1 and 2 for a discussion of the Carvajals' caballero origins, lower noble status, and modest wealth.

103. Herlihy, "Three Patterns of Social Mobility," 632–33.

104. The Mendoza family did not aggressively advance into the church service until King Juan II's 1458 appointment of Pedro González de Mendoza as bishop of Calahorra. Even though the Mendozas recognized the importance of ecclesiastical service in the pursuit of higher social stations, the family only accepted the king's offer of the bishop's posi-

tion after they understood the king would not provide them with what they truly desired—new seigniorial titles. See Nader, *Mendoza Family in the Spanish Renaissance*, 49–51.

105. RAH, Colección Salazar y Castro, tomo C-20, fol. 212v.

106. RAH, Colección Salazar y Castro, tomo C-20, fol. 212v.

107. Cantera Burgos, *Alvar García de Santa María*, 385. Alonso Rodríguez de Maluenda was the son of María Núñez and Juan Garcés Rodríguez Maluenda. María Núñez, a Jewish convert to Christianity, was the sister of Pablo de Santa María.

108. ACP, Legajo 129, doc. 10, fols. 16v–17; ACP, Legajo 129, doc. 11, fol. 15.

109. ACP, *Actas capitulares*, tomo 1, fol. 29v; ACP, Legajo 129, doc. 10, fols. 16–16v.

110. ACP, *Actas capitulares*, tomo 1, fol. 114v.

111. ACP, *Actas capitulares*, tomo 1, fols. 65v, 66, 67v–69, 75–76, 98–98v, 99v–100v, 105, 114v, 119, 121v–122, 143v, 151. The Santa María include the de Calleja, Maluenda, and Salamanca families. The Santa María and Gómez de Almaraz families had intermarried during this period: María Gómez de Almaraz was married to Juan González de Santa María sometime during 1406–21. See ACP, Legajo 143, doc. 12; ACP, Legajo 270, doc. 13. In addition, Bishop Gonzalo García de Santa María had three pages or servants whom he paid but who were not members of the chapter: Gonzalo de la Calleja, Gonzalo de Salamanca, and Gabriel Sánchez.

112. During the sixteenth century, the Cabrero and López de Calatayud families utilized their dominance over the Diocese of Ávila's cathedral chapter for advancement and benefit. However, the events in Ávila occurred more than one hundred years after the Carvajal–Santa María family confederation's activities in Plasencia, and neither of the Ávila families came from a knightly background. See Bilinkoff, *Ávila of Saint Teresa*, 29–33.

113. Bishop and royal counselor Pablo de Santa María had recommended to the king that Gonzalo de Estúñiga be appointed bishop of Plasencia from 1415 to 1422. See Serrano, *Los conversos*, 62.

114. ACP *Actas capitulares*, tomo 1, fols. 121v–122.

115. ACP *Actas capitulares*, tomo 1, fols. 60v–65v; "Vicar General."

116. "Iglesia y estado."

117. Ibid.

118. ACP, Legajo 282, doc. 1, "Constituciones Sinodales publicadas," no folio.

119. ACP, *Actas capitulares*, tomo 1, fols. 75–76.

120. ACP, Legajo 14, doc. 14.

121. ACP, Legajo 14, doc. 14; ACP, Legajo 282, doc. 1, "Constituciones sinodales publicadas," no folio.

122. ACP, Legajo 14, doc. 14.

123. ACP, *Actas capitulares*, tomo 1, fols. 75–76.

124. ACP, *Actas capitulares*, tomo 1, fols. 114v–116.

CHAPTER 4.   INNOVATION

1. Amador de los Ríos, *Historia social, política y religiosa*, tomo 2, 493–95.

2. Ibid., 496–502.

3. Bilinkoff, *Ávila of Saint Teresa*, 24–27; Phillips, *Ciudad Real 1500–1700*, 98.

4. ACP, Legajo 282, "El portazgo de Plasencia"; ACP, Legajo 270, doc. 15.

5. See "Diezmo," in Aldea Vaquero, Martínez, and Gatell, *Diccionario de historia eclesiástica*, 2:757–58; O'Callaghan, *Cortes of Castile-León 1188–1350*, 51, 144–45; Payne, *History of Spain and Portugal*, 2:282.

6. ACP, Legajo 282, "El portazgo de Plasencia"; ACP, Legajo 270, doc. 15.

7. ACP, Legajo 282, "Real provisión de D. Enrique España," no folio; ACP, *Extractos del inventario*, tomo 3, doc. 338.

8. ACP, Legajo 143, doc. 3; ACP, Legajo 14, docs. 38, 48, 56; ACP, Legajo 14, doc. 25. In addition, it appears that Francisco de Trejo, another son of Gutierre González de Trejo, was married to another Sevilla López de Carvajal. Sevilla's pedigree cannot be established, but she may have been the same woman married to Luis de Trejo. Perhaps Luis de Trejo died and Sevilla married his brother, Francisco de Trejo. See ACP, Legajo 13, doc. 24.

9. ACP, *Actas capitulares*, tomo 1, fol. 252.

10. ACP, Legajo 270, doc. 18.

11. ACP, *Actas capitulares*, tomo 1, fols. 264–271v.

12. It should be noted that these wine taxes were different from internal trade levies (portazgo).

13. ACP, *Actas capitulares*, tomo 1, fols. 264–271v.

14. ACP, *Actas capitulares*, tomo 1, fols. 264–271v.

15. ACP, *Actas capitulares*, tomo 1, fols. 264–271v.

16. ACP, *Actas capitulares*, tomo 1, fols. 264–271v. According to John Edwards, an *azumbre* is a "liquid measure: 2 liters, or 3.5 liters." See Edwards, *Christian Córdoba*, 193.

17. ACP, *Actas capitulares*, tomo 1, fols. 264–271v.

18. ACP, Legajo 129, doc. 10, fols. 17–17v; ACP, Legajo 282, doc. 5, "Estatutos de la Catedral de Plasencia."

19. The altar boys ranged from 13 to 18 years of age, indicating these were young men preparing for church service.

20. For a selection of typical one-time donations to the church, see ACP, *Calendario o libro de aniversarios*; ACP, Legajo 282, doc. 13, *Calendario de misas traslado*, fols. 1v, 2, 3v, 5, 6v ff.

21. ACP, *Calendario o libro de aniversarios*; ACP, Legajo 282, doc. 13, *Calendario de misas traslado*, fols. 2v, 5.

22. ACP, *Calendario o libro de aniversarios*; ACP, Legajo 282, doc. 13, *Calendario de misas traslado*, fols. 2v, 5.

23. ACP, *Calendario o libro de aniversarios*; ACP, Legajo 282, doc. 13, *Calendario de misas traslado*, fols. 2v, 5.

24. The church provided funerary services for all cathedral chapter members for nine months after death.

25. ACP, Legajo 282, doc. 1, "Estatutos y sínodos," no folio.

26. Duggan, "Unresponsiveness of the Late Medieval Church," 24–25.

27. ACP, Legajo 282, doc. 1, "Estatutos y sínodos," no folio; ACP, *Actas capitulares*, tomo 2, fol. 146. Tomo 2 of the *Actas capitulares* is lost; however, Legajo 282 provides this specific reference to that text.

28. See ch. 2 for the financial irregularities that contributed to the decline of the Fernández family in the cathedral chapter.

29. ACP, Legajo 25, doc. 14, fols. 6–6v; ACP, *Actas capitulares,* tomo 2, fol. 46.

30. ACP, *Actas capitulares,* tomo 1, fols. 35–35v.

31. ACP, *Actas capitulares,* tomo 1, fols. 249v–252.

32. ACP, *Actas capitulares,* tomo 1, fols. 249v–252.

33. ACP, *Actas capitulares,* tomo 1, fols. 249v–252.

34. ACP, *Actas capitulares,* tomo 1, fols. 363v–368.

35. ACP, *Actas capitulares,* tomo 1, fols. 363v–368.

36. These lease rates, and others reported here, were calculated using 139 separate church contracts in ACP, *Actas capitulares,* tomo 1, fols. 29v–428.

37. ACP, *Actas capitulares,* tomo 1, fols. 29v–428.

38. ACP, *Actas capitulares,* tomo 1, fols. 67v, 98.

39. ACP, *Actas capitulares,* tomo 1, fol. 59. Gil Gutiérrez de la Calleja leased a home in which Fernán Sánchez resided.

40. ACP, *Actas capitulares,* tomo 1, fol. 59.

41. ACP, *Actas capitulares,* tomo 1, fol. 59.

42. After 1431, the Carvajal–Santa María family confederation acquired fewer leases for newly available church properties. However, it did not relinquish the church leases it had previously secured from 1424 to 1431. This change in leasing practices corresponded to the family's efforts to impose church reforms in the Cathedral of Plasencia.

43. ACP, *Actas capitulares,* tomo 1, fols. 75–76.

44. ACP, *Actas capitulares,* tomo 1, fols. 3–4; ACP, Legajo 5, docs. 29, 30. For instance, in the late 1390s, the Jewish noble Don Abraen owned a vineyard in the village of Trujillo that was adjacent to vineyards owned by the Carvajal. Likewise, the Jewish Molho and Aruso families owned vineyards in the vicinity of Plasencia.

45. ACP, *Actas capitulares,* tomo 1, fols. 340–45, 361v–363v; AHNSN, Osuna, Caja 298, doc. 3 (17); Hervás, *Historia de los judíos de Plasencia,* 2:86; ACP, Legajo 270, doc. 1. In addition to being wine producers, Jewish families in Plasencia were arms dealers and makers (the Escapa), shoemakers (the Aruso), and blacksmiths (the Daza). Wealthier Jewish individuals, such as Yucef Bejarano and Jacob Faralon, would lease the king's tax collection authority from the municipal council at a set price, thereby hoping to collect more in tax proceeds than they paid for purchasing this taxation authority.

46. ACP, *Actas capitulares,* tomo 1, fols. 99v–101v, 103–103v, 116, 132–33, 155v–158, 161.

47. ACP, *Actas capitulares,* tomo 1, fol. 116.

48. ACP, *Actas capitulares,* tomo 1, fols. 101–101v, 103–103v.

49. ACP, *Actas capitulares,* tomo 1, fols. 99v–101v, 103–103v, 132–33, 155v–158, 161–64.

50. ACP, *Actas capitulares,* tomo 1, fols. 382v–387.

51. ACP, *Actas capitulares,* tomo 1, fols. 158–59.

52. ACP, *Extractos del inventario,* tomo 2, fols. 10–10v.

53. During the fourteenth and fifteenth centuries, the Cathedral of Plasencia used the words *caballerías* and *yugadas* interchangeably, as evidenced in ACP, *Actas capitulares,* tomo 1, fols. 161–64. In colonial Spanish American history, *caballería* refers to a specific measurement of land. Carrerra Stampa, in "The Evolution of Weights and Measures in New Spain," 5,

cites colonial Mexican sources that describe a caballería of land as "a width of 192 varas of the said measure and double this, that is, 384 varas for the length." However, in Plasencia during the fourteenth and fifteenth centuries, the term *caballería* did not appear to communicate this level of specificity. The *Diccionario de la lengua español* (*DEL*, 1729) clarifies that this specific measurement pertained to "las Indias" and not to peninsular Spain. The only definition of *caballería* that relates to financial or territorial compensation in peninsular Spain is the following: "In Aragon they were known as certain lands that the rich men would spilt among the knights and men of war who were their vassals, and others who served them, when they left the service of the kings." The Cathedral of Plasencia's mixed use of the terms *caballería* and *yugada* complicates this discussion because the *DEL* indicates that a yugada was an imprecise amount of tillable land; its size depended on the oxen and the man leading them. Here both are defined as variable areas of workable agricultural land that were most likely given by a king to a caballero for services rendered. See Carrera Stampa, "Evolution of Weights and Measures in New Spain," 2–24.

54. ACP, *Actas capitulares*, tomo 1, fols. 380–382v.

55. ACP, *Actas capitulares*, tomo 1, fols. 99v–100v, 155v–157, 161–64.

56. Typically, the Castilian king rewarded his knights for their successful military service in two ways: with plunder and with grants of lands. During military campaigns these knights accumulated materials such as precious metals, clothing, horses, oxen, and cattle. In addition, the king compensated his knights with short-term land tenancies, as well as grants of land. With these lands, also known as caballerías, knights could generate income through property rents, agricultural production, and animal husbandry. In the late fourteenth century, elite Castilian families who had accumulated extensive property collections converted much of it into inalienable family entailed lands (mayorazgos) that the eldest son (sometimes daughter) of each successive generation would inherit. See Doubleday, *The Lara Family*, 28–29, for an example of how the Lara family collected booty and lands during the Spanish Reconquest. Also see Powers, *Society Organized for War*, 104–7, for a discussion of thirteenth-century land compensation provided by the king to his knights and soldiers in Extremadura. See Clavero, *Mayorazgo*, 71, 102–9, for a discussion of feudal lands (their value and uses) and the creation of mayorazgos. See Nader, *Mendoza Family in the Spanish Renaissance*, 112–15, for a discussion of the Mendoza family's use of agricultural and sheepherding lands.

57. ACP, *Actas capitulares*, tomo 1, fol. 145.

58. ACP, *Actas capitulares*, tomo 1, 98–98v.

59. ACP, *Actas capitulares*, tomo 1, fols. 31v, 83–83v. Fernán Álvarez de Montealbán was later known as Fernán Álvarez de Toledo, señor de Oropesa.

60. ACP, *Actas capitulares*, tomo 1, fols. 145–51. This property agreement for 8,500 maravedís covered several pieces of land. Therefore, I have treated this lease agreement as a single property lease for the purposes of calculating the total number of cathedral property leases.

61. Kagan, *Students and Society in Early Modern Spain*, 202.

62. Ibid., 88.

63. Nader, *Mendoza Family in the Spanish Renaissance*, 37.

64. Ibid., 128–29.

65. RAH, Colección Pellicer, tomo 9/4070, fol. 1; RAH, Colección Salazar y Castro, tomo C-20, fols. 212–212v.

66. Nader, *Mendoza Family in the Spanish Renaissance*, 37.

67. ACP, *Actas capitulares*, tomo 1, fols. 231v–235v, 264–271v.

68. ACP, *Actas capitulares*, tomo 1, fols. 252–56.

69. ACP, *Actas capitulares*, tomo 1, fols. 116–116v. On only one previous occasion, in 1425, did Bishop Santa María oversee church affairs relating to the lease of a house and storehouse to his "family member," Gil Gutiérrez de la Calleja.

70. ACP, *Actas capitulares*, tomo 1, fols. 114v–116. For example, in 1425, Bishop Santa María communicated with the cathedral chapter via letter that Archdeacon Gonzalo García de Carvajal was responsible for collecting papal-ordered funds for the Castilian king.

71. Unfortunately, Bishop Santa María never elaborated on the services that Garci López de Carvajal performed for the Cathedral of Plasencia.

72. A review of church records, specifically, ACP, *Actas capitulares*, tomo 1, indicates this was the only occurrence of a church gift of land to an individual between 1399 and 1453. The Cathedral of Plasencia's limited archival records for the period before 1399 also indicate this was the first occurrence of such a gift.

73. ACP, *Actas capitulares*, tomo 1, fols. 393–94. For example, a collection of ancestral homes with corrals on Calle de Rua rented for 400 maravedís a year.

74. ACP, Legajo 270, doc. 13, no folio.

75. ACP, *Actas capitulares*, tomo 1, fols. 172v–174v, 205–206v.

76. ACP, *Actas capitulares*, tomo 1, fols. 172v–174v, 205–206v.

77. ACP *Actas capitulares*, tomo 1, fols. 197v–198v; ACP, Legajo 282, doc. 4, "Libro III," fols. 4v–8; ACP, Legajo 282, doc. 9, "Traslado de autos hechos," fols. 1–1v. Why Gonzalo Gutiérrez de la Calleja's son's surname was Fernández de Cabreros is an interesting question. Juan's mother's name was Teresa de Porras. As the Gutiérrez de la Calleja surname was known to the community of Plasencia as a converso one, it appears that the family chose to change their name to begin the process of masking their converso identity. The Fernández de Cabreros name was transformed throughout the late fifteenth century and became simply Cabreros or Cabrero in the early sixteenth century.

78. Codero Alvarado, *Plasencia: Heráldica, histórica y monumental*, 145.

79. ACP, *Actas capitulares*, tomo 1, fols. 391v–392v.

80. ACP, *Actas capitulares*, tomo 1, fols. 168–168v.

81. ACP, *Actas capitulares*, tomo 1, fols. 284v–291.

82. ACP, Legajo 14, doc. 25. The Heredad de Rio Bermejo comprised 40 yugadas, according to the record. Garci López owned only 2.5 yugadas. Diego González de Carvajal, his cousin, also owned portions of it.

83. The fifteenth-century Spanish word *criado* should not be confused with the modern connotations "servant" or "maid." Rather, a criado during the fifteenth century was often a nephew or a younger relative in the service of an older family member in order to learn a profession or acquire business and political experience. The criado was expected to provide good service, while the older family member was responsible for training, educating, and readying the young man for his adult life.

84. Beltrán de Heredia, *Bulario de Universidad de Salamanca*, 2:410; ASAV, Reg. Suppl. 319, fol. 85.

85. ACP, *Actas capitulares*, tomo 1, fols. 291–97.

86. ACP, *Actas capitulares*, tomo 1, fols. 291–97.

87. ACP, *Actas capitulares*, tomo 1, fols. 197v–313; ACP, Legajo 282, doc. 3, "Prebendados y dignidades," no folio.

88. ACP, *Actas capitulares*, tomo 1, fols. 217v–219.

89. ACP, *Actas capitulares*, tomo 1, fols. 217v–219.

90. ACP, *Actas capitulares*, tomo 1, fols. 236v–237.

91. ACP, *Actas capitulares*, tomo 1, fols. 274v–279.

92. ACP, *Actas capitulares*, tomo 1, fols. 333–335.

93. ACP, *Actas capitulares*, tomo 1, fols. 229v–300, 99v Alfonso was the son of Diego Fernández Braicio and Isabel de Carvajal.

94. ACP, *Actas capitulares*, tomo 1, fols. 229v–300; ACP, Legajo 45, doc. 41, no folios.

95. Ruiz, *Spain's Centuries of Crisis*, 91.

96. Ibid.

97. ACP, Legajo 25, "Estatuto para que viernes se celebrarse Cabildo, hecho el viernes 12 de Octubre de 1431."

98. Gitlitz, *Secrecy and Deceit*, 319, 320.

99. Ibid.

100. Ibid, 322–23.

101. Ibid.

102. Ibid., 331.

103. Serrano, *Los conversos*, 108.

104. Ibid.

105. Singer and Adler, *The Jewish Encyclopedia*, s.v. "Feast of Tabernacles"; Katsh, "Poems from Barcelona Mahzor," 350–51.

106. Katsh, "Poems from Barcelona Mahzor," 350–51.

107. For personal reasons, I have elected to use the New American Bible, which was presented to me by St. Thomas More Catholic Church in Caracas, Venezuela, upon my confirmation on May 27, 1984; John 7.

108. ACP, Legajo 25, doc. 14, fols. 53v–54; ACP, *Actas capitulares*, tomo 2, fol. 134.

109. ACP, *Actas capitulares*, tomo 1, fol. 67v.

110. ACP, *Actas capitulares*, tomo 1, fols. 384v–387, 391v–392v.

111. ACP, Legajo 25, doc. 14, fols. 53v–54; ACP, *Actas capitulares*, tomo 2, fol. 134.

112. ACP, Legajo 25, doc. 14, fols. 53v–54; ACP, *Actas capitulares*, tomo 2, fol. 134.

113. ACP, Legajo 25, doc. 14.

114. ACP, Legajo 25, doc. 14, fols. 197v–313.

115. ACP, Legajo 25, doc. 14, fols. 309–13.

116. ACP Legajo 282, doc. 3, "Prebendados y dignidades," no folios. Successive archdeacons of Plasencia and Béjar (1420–1578): Gonzalo García de Carvajal, Rodrigo de Carvajal, Garci López de Carvajal, Bernardino de Carvajal, Francisco de Carvajal, and Alvaro de Carvajal.

117. Glick, "Convivencia: Introductory Note," 1.

118. Gerber, *Jews of Spain*, 113.

119. López de Ayala, *Crónica de Enrique III*, 24.

120. AHMB, Legajo HI-2961.

121. AHCB, vol. 48, fol. 250; AHCB, vol. 46, fol. 424; AHCB, vol. 5, fols. 51–51v.

122. AHNSN, Osuna, Caja 300, docs. 8 (6), 9 (5); AHNSN, Osuna, Caja 299, docs. 1 (4), 1 (6), 2 (1); AHNSN, Osuna, Caja 303, docs. 42, 51; Santos Canalejo, *El siglo XV en Plasencia*, 79; Hervás, *Historia de los judíos de Plasencia*, 2:174–80.

123. Paredes y Guillén, *Los Zúñigas*, 66; Santos Canalejo, *El siglo XV en Plasencia*, 105.

124. Paredes y Guillén, *Los Zúñigas*, 67; Santos Canalejo, *El siglo XV en Plasencia*, 106–7.

125. ACP Legajo 2, doc. 55; ACP Legajo 3, doc. 22.

126. See note 36 above. The specific Jewish and Muslim contracts identified in this analysis are found in ACP, *Actas capitulares*, tomo 1, fols. 52v–53, 112–13, 200–202v, 223v–225v, 319–326v, 326v–328, 340–45, 361–363v, 378v–380v. The only individual belonging to a religious minority who rented a home from the Cathedral of Plasencia between 1401 and 1424 was Don Arradamen, a Muslim master carpenter. Arradamen leased his house on the Plaza Mayor, adjacent to the Iglesia de San Esteban, for 150 maravedís a year.

127. ACP, *Actas capitulares*, tomo 1, fols. 52v–53, 112–13, 200–202v, 223v–225v, 319–326v, 326v–328, 340–45, 361–363v, 378v–380v; AHNSN, Osuna, Caja 298, doc. 3 (17); Hervás, *Historia de los judíos de Plasencia*, 2:86–92, 100–102; Hervás, *Historia de los judíos de Plasencia*, 1:38–50.

128. ACP, *Actas capitulares*, tomo 1, fols. 319–23.

129. ACP, *Actas capitulares*, tomo 1, fols. 340–45.

130. As Çag Escapa was the sole proprietor, not an apprentice to a craftsman, he was likely an older adult. If he was from Plasencia, then the cathedral would not have required him to provide a cosigner. Because Escapa had to produce the rabbi, a senior member of the local Jewish community, as cosigner, this contract suggests that he was not a native of the city.

131. ACP, *Actas capitulares*, tomo 1, fols. 31v, 83–83v. Most church agreements that required a cosigner pertained to property transactions conducted by first-time renters, such as archpriest Pedro Fernández de Soria, who was the nephew of prebendary Juan Rodríguez de Fuenteveros, and by individuals who lived outside of Plasencia, such as Fernán Álvarez de Montealbán.

132. ACP, Legajo 14, doc. 25; ACP, Legajo 14, doc. 42; ACP, Legajo 4, doc. 6; ACP, Legajo 270, doc. 13; ACP, Legajo 6, doc. 48.

133. Benavides Checa, *Prelados placentinos*, 139 n. 1.

134. Ibid.

135. ACP, Legajo 3, doc. 20; ACP, Legajo 7, doc. 22. A YouTube.com video flyover of this area is accessible at www.youtube.com/watch?v=DH_KonA0GY; the immersive Unity-3D model can be explored on the RCCP website's Virtual Plasencia Portal (http://revealing cooperationandconflict.com/virtual-plasencia-portal/).

136. ACP, *Actas capitulares*, tomo 1, fols. 340–45.

137. The RCCP, created in 2012, is a scholarly initiative that reexamines historical cases of medieval and early modern Jewish, Christian, and Muslim interaction as well as an

activist endeavor intent on buttressing humanistic reflection in academia and among the general public. RCCP developed Virtual Plasencia, an Internet-deployed 3D world and educational initiative that engages scholars and the public in a vigorous evaluation and dialogue on cooperation and conflict in the Spanish community of Plasencia (1300–1600). This community, the first of several cities that will be re-created, is of universal interest because its residents of different faiths and social classes struggled to maintain intercultural respect and cooperation just as Europeans were growing increasingly hostile to Jews and Muslims and intolerant of assimilated minorities (converts to Christianity). The project is an international collaboration involving nine universities in Spain, Switzerland, and the United States. Roger L. Martínez-Dávila serves as the project director, and Victor Roger Schinazi (ETH-Zurich) is the technical leader. The project is an independent scholarly endeavor organized within MappaMundi, a digital humanities initiative of the University of Texas at Austin. MappaMundi graciously provided seed funding for the creation of Virtual Plasencia, as well as ongoing intellectual and technical counsel. In addition, RCCP secured collaborative agreements and endorsements from key Spanish institutions, including the Ayuntamiento de Plasencia; Ministerio de Educación, Cultura, y Deportes; and Centro Sefarad Israel. More information is available at http://revealingcooperationandconflict.org.

138. ACP, Legajo 3, doc. 20; AHNSN, Osuna, Caja 298, docs. 3 (13) and 3 (14); Hervás, *Historia de los judíos de Plasencia*, 2:100–102.

139. For records on the intermarriage between the Carvajal and Almaraz families, as well as their property holdings, see ACP, Legajo 4, docs. 9, 46, 47; ACP, Legajo 269, doc. 3; ACP, Legajo 12, doc. 10; Codero Alvarado, *Plasencia: Heráldica, histórica y monumental*, 129–31. For records on the intermarriage between the Carvajal and Álvarez de Toledo families, as well as their property holdings, see AHNSN, Frías, Caja 1763, docs. 3, 31, 32; AHNSN, Bornos, Caja 705, doc. 3; AHNSN, Bornos, Caja 796, doc. 2.

140. ACP, *Actas capitulares*, tomo 1, fol. 77.

141. AHNSN, Frías, Caja 1764, doc. 32. Also, it should be noted that before the Carvajal and Álvarez de Toledo families united, the Carvajal–Santa María family confederation entered into a complex regional and jurisdictional conflict with the Álvarez de Toledo (late 1420s).

142. Fernández, *Historia y anales*, 153–55; Benavides Checa, *Prelados placentinos*, 147. See also the map titled "Plasencia en 1400" that the Spanish Servicio Geográfico del Ejercito holds in its library; Santos Canalejo, *El siglo XV en Plasencia*, 58.

143. ACP, Legajo 14, doc. 25; ACP, Legajo 3, doc. 20; ACP, *Actas capitulares*, tomo 1, fols. 116, 174, 197v, 223v–225v; ACP, Legajo 270, doc. 13; Hervás, *Historia de judíos de Plasencia*, 1:96–97.

144. ACP, *Actas capitulares*, tomo 1, fols. 112–13.

145. ACP, Legajo 14, doc. 25, fols. 9v–10v.

146. ACP, Legajo 14, doc. 25, fols. 391v–392v, 393–94, 394–395v.

147. ACP, Legajo 14, doc. 25, fols. 208v–209, 217v–219, 252–56, 284v–297.

148. ACP, Legajo 14, doc. 25, fols. 208v–209, 217v–219.

149. AMP, "Casa de San Esteban sobre un moro Bejarano y tiene un testificacion de un criado de los Carvajales."

150. RAH, Colección Salazar y Castro, tomo C-12, 159v; RAH, MS L-5, fol. 106v; Sánchez Loro, *Historias placentinas inéditas*, B:461–62.

151. ACP, Legajo 7, doc. 10, fol. 1.

152. ACP, Legajo 7, doc. 10, fol. 2.

CHAPTER 5.   TURMOIL AND STRUGGLE

1. Roth, *Conversos, Inquisition, and Expulsion*, 89.

2. Ibid.

3. Ibid.; Gerber, *Jews of Spain*, 127.

4. Cartagena, *Defensorium unitatis Christianae*, 43–52.

5. Ibid., 343–56.

6. Ibid.

7. Mendoza y Bobadilla, *El tizón de nobleza española*, 12.

8. Ibid., 119.

9. Ibid., 127.

10. AMP, "Pesquisa hecha por Miguel de Sepúlveda."

11. AMP, "Pesquisa hecha por Miguel de Sepúlveda."

12. ACP, Legajo 282, "El portazgo de Plasencia"; ACP, Legajo 270, doc. 15.

13. AMP, "Pesquisa hecha por Miguel de Sepúlveda."

14. AMP, "Pesquisa hecha por Miguel de Sepúlveda."

15. ACP, Legajo 282, doc. 7.

16. Gutiérrez Rodríguez, *Oropesa y Álvarez de Toledo*, 17.

17. Paredes y Guillén, *Los Zúñigas*, 69 n. 1.

18. Beltrán de Heredia, *Bulario de Universidad de Salamanca*, 2:302–3; ASAV, Reg. Suppl. 213, fol. 19.

19. Beltrán de Heredia, *Bulario de Universidad de Salamanca*, 2:329–30; ASAV, Reg. Suppl. 244, fol. 250.

20. Beltrán de Heredia, *Bulario de Universidad de Salamanca*, 2:332; ASAV, Reg. Suppl. 244, fols. 19v–20.

21. AMP, "Pesquisa hecha por Miguel de Sepúlveda corregidor."

22. AMP, "Pesquisa hecha por Miguel de Sepúlveda corregidor."

23. AMP, "Pesquisa hecha por Miguel de Sepúlveda corregidor."

24. AMP, "Pesquisa hecha por Miguel de Sepúlveda corregidor."

25. AMP, "Pesquisa hecha por Miguel de Sepúlveda corregidor."

26. AMP, "Pesquisa hecha por Miguel de Sepúlveda corregidor"; Gutiérrez Rodríguez, *Oropesa y Álvarez de Toledo*, 17.

27. AMP, "Pesquisa hecha por Miguel de Sepúlveda corregidor"; Gutiérrez Rodríguez, *Oropesa y Álvarez de Toledo*, 17.

28. AMP, "Pesquisa hecha por Miguel de Sepúlveda corregidor"; Gutiérrez Rodríguez, *Oropesa y Álvarez de Toledo*, 17.

29. AMP, "Pesquisa hecha por Miguel de Sepúlveda corregidor"; Gutiérrez Rodríguez, *Oropesa y Álvarez de Toledo*, 17.

30. AMP, "Pesquisa hecha por Miguel de Sepúlveda corregidor"; Gutiérrez Rodríguez, *Oropesa y Álvarez de Toledo*, 17.

31. The king controlled the city council because he appointed its members, the corregidores.

32. Benavides Checa, *Prelados placentinos*, 159.

33. Fernández, *Historia y anales*, 96; Santos Canalejo, *El siglo XV en Plasencia*, 77–79; Paredes y Guillén, *Los Zúñigas*, 35–36, 44–45. In addition, in 1441, Pedro de Estúñiga appears with his new title, conde de Trujillo. See Pérez de Guzmán, *Crónica del rey Don Juan II*, 604. Further, it should be noted that Pedro was the eldest son of the deceased Diego López de Estúñiga, former chief judge for Juan II. In addition to benefiting from the extensive wealth accumulated by his father, Pedro was the heir of his father's titles (chief judge and conde de Béjar) and seigniorial lands that were widely distributed across the Kingdom of Castile and León. The most prominent of those territories were the family's newest lands in the village of Béjar, which was located in the Diocese of Plasencia. Although Pedro often found himself in constant confrontation with King Juan II's favorite, Constable Álvaro de Luna, in 1423 the men worked together in defense of the king during a Castilian civil war. King Juan II faced a significant contest for the throne, initiated by his brother, Enrique, who had the armed support of many Castilian nobles, as well as of the kings of Aragón and of Navarra. When Juan II defeated his enemies, he rewarded Pedro by granting him the title, and the lands associated with it, conde de Ledesma. Years later, in 1440, when the king wished to reclaim the village of Ledesma, he offered Pedro the village of Trujillo in compensation.

34. Elisa Carolina de Santos Canelejo notes that Gómez González de Carvajal joined "Diego de Orellana" and other knights in the armed resistance to Pedro de Estúñiga's selection as conde de Trujillo. However, it should be noted that Diego de Orellana was also known as Diego García de Bejarano Orellana "la Nueva." Diego and Gómez were brothers. See Santos Canelejo, *El siglo XV en Plasencia*, 79; Fernández, *Historia y anales*, 96; Carillo del Huete, *Crónica del halconero de Juan II*, 353.

35. Guzmán, *Crónica del rey Don Juan II*, 608.

36. Ibid.; Fernández, *Historia y anales*, 96.

37. AMP, "Pesquisa hecha por Miguel Sánchez de Sepulveda."

38. For analysis of the wine dispute of 1431, see chapter 4; and ACP, *Actas capitulares*, tomo 1, fols. 264–271v.

39. For a description of the portazgo agreement of 1428, see chapter 4; and ACP, Legajo 282, "El portazgo de Plasencia," and ACP, Legajo 270, doc. 15.

40. AHNSN, Osuna, Caja 300, docs. 8 (6), 9 (5); AHNSN, Osuna, Caja 299, docs. 1 (4), 1 (6), 2 (1); AHNSN, Osuna, Caja 303, docs. 42, 51; Santos Canalejo, *El siglo XV en Plasencia*, 79; Hervás, *Historia de judíos de Plasencia*, 2:174–80.

41. ACP, Legajo 282, "El portazgo de Plasencia"; ACP, Legajo 270, doc. 15.

42. AHNSN, Osuna, Caja 300, docs. 8 (6), 9 (5); AHNSN, Osuna, Caja 299, docs. 1 (4), 1 (6), 2 (1); AHNSN, Osuna, Caja 303, docs. 42, 51; Santos Canalejo, *El siglo XV en Plasencia*, 79; Fernández, *Historia de judíos de Plasencia*, 2:174–80.

43. AHNSN, Frías, Caja 1764, doc. 32, fols. 1, 4v.

44. ACP, Legajo 282, doc. 7.

45. Fernández, *Historia y anales*, 150–53; Paredes y Guillén, *Los Zúñigas*, 185–87.

46. AMP, "Expediente a instancia de Dona Ines María de Vargas."

47. ACP, Legajo 7, doc. 22; ACP, Legajo 3, doc. 20; AHNSN, Osuna, Caja 298, docs. 3 (13) and 3 (14).

48. AMP, "Expediente a instancia de Dona Ines María de Vargas."

49. AMP, "Expediente a instancia de Dona Ines María de Vargas."

50. See chapter 2 for a discussion of the church-knight diezmos conflicts of 1396 and 1410. See also ACP, Legajo 282, "Real Provisión de D. Enrique Espana," no folio; ACP, *Extractos del inventario de los papeles*, tomo 3, doc. 338; ACP, Legajo 45, doc. 13.

51. At this time, Estúñiga planned a threefold increase in the religious poll tax on the Jewish community. ACP, *Actas capitulares*, tomo 1, fols. 52v–53, 112–13, 200–202v, 223v–225v, 319–326v, 326v–328, 340–45, 361–363v, 378v–380v.

52. For records on the Carvajal's mayorazgos in Plasencia, see ACP, Legajo 1, doc. 29; ACP, Legajo 3, doc. 11; ACP, Legajo 3, doc. 22; ACP, Legajo 14, doc. 42.

53. AGS, *EMR*, Legajo 1; AHNSN, Osuna, Caja 215, doc. 10 (2), 58v; Hervás, *Historia de judíos de Plasencia*, 2:158–59, 181–82; Santos Canalejo, *El siglo XV en Plasencia*, 111; Ladero, "Las juderías de Castilla," *Sefarad*, 254.

54. AGS, *EMR*, Legajo 1; Hervás, *Historia de judíos de Plasencia*, 2:158–59, 181–82.

55. López de Ayala, *Crónicas de reyes de Castilla*, tomo segundo, 547–653; Round, *Greatest Man Uncrowned*, 1–31; Villalón, "Law's Delay," 232–54; Hillgarth, *Spanish Kingdoms 1250–1516*, 2:303–5.

56. Sánchez Loro, *Historias placentinas inéditas*, B:403.

57. Ibid., 410 n. 16.

58. ACP, *Actas capitulares*, tomo 1, fols. 274–79; ACP, Legajo 25, "Acuerdos del Cabildo," fols. 8v–12v; ACP, Legajo 282, doc. 1, "Estatutos y sínodos," no folio.

59. ACP, Legajo 25, "Acuerdos del Cabildo," fols. 8v–12v.

60. ACP, Legajo 25, "Acuerdos del Cabildo," fols. 8v–12v.

61. ACP, Legajo 25, "Acuerdos del Cabildo," fols. 8v–12v.

62. ACP, Legajo 25, "Acuerdos del Cabildo," fols. 8v–12v.

63. ACP, *Actas capitulares*, tomo 1, 245v–249; ACP, Legajo 25, "Acuerdos del Cabildo," fols. 8v–12v; ACP, Legajo 282, doc. 1, "Estatutos y sínodos," no folio.

64. Round, *Greatest Man Uncrowned*, 32–33.

65. López de Ayala, *Crónicas de reyes de Castilla*, 676–78.

66. Round, *Greatest Man Uncrowned*, 65.

67. Ibid., 1; Cantera Burgos, *Alvar García de Santa María*, 409–516.

68. ACP, *Actas capitulares*, tomo 1, fols. 274–79; ACP, Legajo 25, "Acuerdos del Cabildo, Cuaderno 1," fols. 8v–12v; ACP, Legajo 282, doc. 1 "Estatutos y sínodos," no folio.

69. Paredes y Guillén, *Los Zúñigas*, 27–35.

70. Fernández, *Historia y anales*, 98–99. The Carvajal knights, along with the count of Plasencia and Béjar and other knights from the region, such as Gutierre de Sotomayor, master of the Order of Alcántara, were at war with the *infantes* de Aragón and king of Navarra.

71. ACP, *Actas capitulares*, tomo 1, fols. 274–79; ACP, Legajo 25, "Acuerdos del Cabildo, Cuaderno 1," fols. 8v–12v; ACP, Legajo 282, doc. 1, "Estatutos y sínodos," no fol.

72. ACP, Legajo 25, "Acuerdos del Cabildo, Cuaderno 1," fols. 8v–12v.

73. ACP, Legajo 25, "Acuerdos del Cabildo, Cuaderno 1," fols. 8v–12v.

74. ACP, Legajo 25, "Acuerdos del Cabildo, Cuaderno 1," fols. 8v–12v.

75. ACP, Legajo 25, "Acuerdos del Cabildo, Cuaderno 1," fols. 8v–12v.

76. ACP, Legajo 25, "Acuerdos del Cabildo, Cuaderno 1," fols. 8v–12v.

77. ACP, Legajo 25, "Acuerdos del Cabildo, Cuaderno 1," fols. 8v–12v.

78. Cantera Burgos, *Alvar García de Santa María*, 208.

79. ACP, Legajo 129, doc. 10, fol. 18.

80. ACP, Legajo 129, doc. 10, fol. 18.

81. ACP, *Actas capitulares*, tomo 1, 368v–372v.

82. ACP, *Actas capitulares*, tomo 1, fols. 424–26.

83. ACP, Legajo 273, doc. 2; Hervás, *Historia de los judíos de Plasencia*, 2:218–19; Santos Canalejo, *La historia medieval de Plasencia y su entorno geo-histórico*, 479–80.

84. AMP, *Actas municipales*, 1461–65, fol. 15.

85. AMP, *Actas municipales*, 1461–65, fols. 20–26.

86. AMP, *Actas municipales*, 1461–65, fols. 17–18.

87. AMP, *Actas municipales*, 1461–65, fols. 30v–32.

88. ACP, Legajo 282, doc. 4, 1v–3, 5v–7; ACP, Legajo 99, "Girones de Talavera."

89. ACP, *Extractos del inventario de papeles*, tomo 2, fols. 32–32v; ACP, Legajo 282, doc. 4, fols. 6v–7.

90. ACP, Legajo 129, doc. 10, fol. 19.

91. This finding was determined after reviewing the five surviving books (1, 3, 4, 5, 6) of the Cathedral of Plasencia's *Chapter Acts*, or *Actas capitulares*, for the years 1390 to 1510. In addition, I consulted ACP, Legajo 282, which is a collection of transcriptions from the *Actas capitulares*.

92. The bishop was not a member of the cathedral chapter, although his personal representative, the vicar general, participated in the chapter's meetings.

93. ACP, Legajo 282, doc. 4, fols. 2–8. By 1490, the only Santa María participating in the cathedral chapter was Juan Fernández de Cabreros, a cathedral notary.

94. During the mid-fifteenth century, Castile was caught in the turbulent wake of extended and varied conflicts. The conflicts troubling the Kingdom of Castile included noble families competing with one another for control and influence over King Juan II, Castile's continuous political and military confrontations with fellow Christian kingdoms and Islamic Granada, and the fall of Juan II's most powerful adviser, the converso Álvaro de Luna. See López de Ayala, *Crónicas de reyes de Castilla*, tomo segundo, 547–653; Round, *Greatest Man Uncrowned*, 1–31; Villalón, "Law's Delay," 232–54; Hillgarth, *Spanish Kingdoms 1250–1516*, 2:303–5.

95. Roth, *Conversos, the Inquisition, and Expulsion*, 89.

96. Ibid.; Gerber, *Jews of Spain*, 127.

97. Gerber, *Jews of Spain*, 127.

98. Ibid.

99. Aronson-Friedman and Kaplan, *Marginal Voices*, 8.

100. Friedman, "Jewish Conversion, the Spanish Pure Blood Laws and Reformation," 11.

101. ACP, *Actas capitulares*, tomo 1, fols. 197v–198v; ACP, Legajo 282, doc. 4, fols. 4v–8; ACP, Legajo 282, doc. 9, "Traslado de autos hechos," fols. 1–1v.

102. Rábade Obradó, "Los judeoconversos en la Corte y en la epoca del los reyes católicos," 522, 524, 565.

103. ACP, Legajo 282, doc. 4, fols. 4v–8.

104. Poole, "Politics of *Limpieza de Sangre*," 386.

105. ACP, Legajo 282, "El portazgo de Plasencia"; ACP, Legajo 270, doc. 15; Rodríguez Martínez, *Historia del Monasterio de San Benito*, 73 n. 15.

106. ACP, Legajo 270, doc. 15.

107. López de Ayala, *Crónicas de reyes de Castilla*, tomo segundo, 572–74.

108. Several other Carvajal family members followed Juan's example, including his second cousin Bernardino López de Carvajal, who ascended to the position of cardinal and challenged Pope Julius II for the papal tiara in the 1510s; and his nephew Juan Suárez de Carvajal, who served as bishop of Lugo from 1539 to 1561 and later was a member of the Council of the Indies under Philip II. See Fernández, *Historia y anales*, 175; AHNSN, Frías, Caja 1017, doc. 3; AHNSN, Mocejón, Caja 7; RAH, Colección Pellicer, 9/4058, fols. 1–6, 100.

109. Gómez Cañedo, *Don Juan de Carvajal*, 31.

110. RAH, Colección Salazar y Castro, tomo C-12, fol. 159.

111. ACP, Legajo 129, doc. 10, fol. 18.

112. Beltrán de Heredia, *Bulario de Universidad de Salamanca*, 2:329–30; ASAV, Reg. Suppl. 244, fol. 250.

113. Beltrán de Heredia, *Bulario de Universidad de Salamanca*, 2:332; ASAV, Reg. Suppl. 244, 19v–20.

114. Gómez Canedo, *Don Juan de Carvajal*, 34.

115. Ibid.

116. Ibid.

117. Beltrán de Heredia, *Bulario de Universidad de Salamanca*, 2:379–80; ASAV, Reg. Suppl. 283, 250v–251.

118. Beltrán de Heredia, *Bulario de Universidad de Salamanca*, 2:142–43; ASAV, Reg. Suppl. 134, fol. 51.

119. Beltrán de Heredia, *Bulario de Universidad de Salamanca*, 2:381–83; ASAV, Reg. Lat. 364, fols. 247–48.

120. Beltrán de Heredia, *Bulario de Universidad de Salamanca*, 2:385; ASAV, Reg. Suppl. 290, fol. 36v.

121. Beltrán de Heredia, *Bulario de Universidad de Salamanca*, 2:385; ASAV, Reg. Suppl. 290, fol. 36v.

122. Beltrán de Heredia, *Bulario de Universidad de Salamanca*, 2:385; ASAV, Reg. Suppl. 290, fol. 36v.

123. Beltrán de Heredia, *Bulario de Universidad de Salamanca*, 2:385; ASAV, Reg. Suppl. 290, fol. 36.

124. Beltrán de Heredia, *Bulario de Universidad de Salamanca*, 2:410; ASAV, Reg. Suppl. 319, fol. 85.

125. Gómez Cañedo, *Don Juan de Carvajal*, 36.

126. Ibid.

127. González Cuesta, *Obispos de Plasencia*, 112.

128. Beltrán de Heredia, *Bulario de Universidad de Salamanca*, 2:446–47; ASAV, Reg. Suppl. 359, fols. 70v–71.

129. Levillain, s.v. "Auditor, Rota," in *Papacy: Encyclopedia*.

130. Ibid.

131. Ibid.

132. Ibid.

133. Beltrán de Heredia, *Bulario de Universidad de Salamanca*, 2:446–47; ASAV, Reg. Suppl. 359, fols. 70v–71.

134. Beltrán de Heredia, *Bulario de Universidad de Salamanca*, 2:446–47; ASAV, Reg. Suppl. 359, fols. 70v–71.

135. ACP, Legajo 129, doc. 10, fol. 18.

136. ACP, Legajo 129, doc. 10, fol. 17v; RAH, Colección Salazar y Castro, tomo C-16, fol. 306.

137. ACP, *Actas capitulares*, tomo 1, fols. 421–24.

138. ACP, Legajo 85, doc. 1; ACP, Legajo 129, doc. 10, fol. 18v; González Cuesta, *Obispos de Plasencia*, 116; González Cuesta, "Catedral de Gramática de Plasencia (1468–1852)," 105–25.

139. ACP, Legajo 45, docs. 3, 12; ACP, Legajo 129, doc. 10, fol. 18v.

CHAPTER 6.   MEMORY AND RELIGION

1. Stoler, "Racial Histories and Their Regimes of Truth," 186.

2. Ibid., 186–87, 190.

3. Mariscal, "Role of Spain in Contemporary Race Theory," 11.

4. Ibid.

5. Nirenberg, "Mass Conversion and Genealogical Mentalities," 6, 18.

6. Ibid., 18.

7. Roth, *Conversos, Inquisition, and Expulsion*, xix.

8. See Martínez, *Genealogical Fictions*.

9. Díaz Ibáñez, "Las relaciones iglesia-nobleza," 312–13; Beceiro Pita and Córdoba de la Llave, *Parentesco, poder y mentalidad*, 43, 90, 98, 100; Bilinkoff, *Ávila of Saint Teresa*, 18–19.

10. Beceiro Pita and Córdoba de la Llave, *Parentesco, poder y mentalidad*, 39; Rahn Phillips, *Ciudad real 1500–1700*, 10, 49–51.

11. RAH, Colección Salazar y Castro, tomo C-20, fols. 211–213v.

12. Fernández, *Historia y anales*, 37–38; García Carraffa and García Carraffa, *Diccionario heráldico y genealógico*, 12:268–69.

13. Sánchez Loro, *Historias placentinas inéditas*, A:402; Fernández, *Historia y anales*, 37–38; García Carraffa and García Carraffa, *Diccionario heráldico y genealógico*, 12:268–69.

14. Fernández, *Historia y anales*, 37–38.

15. Ibid.

16. Ibid.

17. See chapter 3 for discussion of these intermarriages.

18. The appearance of the Carvajal clan's multiple interconnections and intermarriage with the Villalva is especially important to understanding a major element of this investigation—the depth of the Carvajal–Santa María family confederation. This finding—that by the 1460s the Villalva, Carvajal, and Santa María were related—is the outcome of documenting the relationship between Sevilla López de Carvajal and her churchmen cousins. It demonstrates that while other Castilians were targeting high-profile conversos for exclusion from church and royal positions during the mid- to late 1400s, the Carvajal family was not only strengthening its family relations with its Santa María partners in the Cathedral of Plasencia, but the two clans merged bloodlines. See ACP, Legajo 14, doc. 4; ACP, Legajo 1, doc. 18; ACP, Legajo 14, doc. 25; ACP, Legajo 269, doc. 25; AHNSN, Luque, Caja 160, doc. 9; Codero Alvarado, *Plasencia: Heráldica, histórica y monumental*, 148–51.

19. ACP, Legajo 25, doc. 14, fols. 53v–54; ACP, *Actas capitulares*, tomo 2, fol. 134.

20. ACP, Legajo 25, doc. 14, fols. 53v–54; ACP, *Actas capitulares*, tomo 2, fol. 134.

21. Hordes, *To the End of the Earth*, 109.

22. For example, in 1455, Diego Gónzalez de Carvajal established a memorial mass for himself at the Church of Saint Nicholas and another for his deceased spouse, Catalina González, at the Monastery of San Francisco. See ACP, Legajo 14, doc. 25.

23. Serrano, *Los conversos*, 108.

24. Ibid.

25. ACP, *Calendario o libro de aniversarios*; ACP, Legajo 282, doc. 13, fols. 3–3v; ACP, *Extractos del inventario*, tomo 2, fols. 11v–12; ACP, Legajo 133, doc. 17; ACP, Legajo 143, doc. 3; ACP, Legajo 129, doc. 11, fol. 15v.

26. ACP, *Extractos del inventario*, tomo 2, fols. 11v–12; ACP, Legajo 133, doc. 17; ACP, Legajo 143, doc. 3.

27. ACP, *Extractos del inventario*, tomo 2, fols. 11v–12; ACP, Legajo 133, doc. 17; ACP, Legajo 143, doc. 3.

28. ACP, *Extractos del inventario*, tomo 2, fols. 11v–12; There is conflicting evidence regarding the identity of Dr. Garci López de Carvajal. The "extracted" records report that he was the son of Diego González de Carvajal and Sevilla López de Carvajal. Yet the property transaction records in the *Actas capitulares* definitively report that Garci López was the son of Alvar García de Bejarano-Orellana and Mencía González de Carvajal. Because the *Actas capitulares* are the actual records from the time period, as opposed to the extracts that were compiled sometime after the seventeenth century, I believe the transcriber of the extracts inserted the lineage of Garci López in the record. Therefore, I report Garci López and Gómez González de Carvajal as the sons of Alvar García de Bejarano-Orellana.

29. See chapter 5 for discussion of the cathedral reforms and initiatives that dedicated new clergy to the task of singing memorial masses.

30. For a selection of typical one-time donations to the church, see ACP, *Calendario o libro de aniversarios*; ACP, Legajo 282, doc. 13, fols. 1v, 2, 3v, 5, 6v, and other pages without folios.

31. ACP, *Calendario o libro de aniversarios*; ACP, Legajo 282, doc. 13, fols. 2v, 5.

32. The individual masses for each family member were derived from the following sources: ACP, *Calendario o libro de aniversarios*; ACP, Legajo 282, doc. 13, fols. 2, 2v, 4, 5v, 7, 10–10v, 12v, and other pages without folios; ACP, Legajo 282, doc. 4, fols. 1v–2v, 15–15v; ACP, Legajo 13, doc. 9; ACP, *Extractos del inventario*, tomo 1, fols. 154–154v; ACP, Legajo 129, doc. 11, fols. 20–22; ACP, Legajo 13, doc. 5; ACP, Legajo 13, doc. 18; Rubio Rojas, *Las disposiciones testamentarias*, 30.

33. Ibid.

34. ACP, *Calendario o libro de aniversarios*.

35. Bilinkoff, *Ávila of Saint Teresa*, 40.

36. ACP, Legajo 14, doc. 4; ACP, Legajo 89, docs. 1, 11, 12; Fernández, *Historia y anales*, 117.

37. ACP, Legajo 14, doc. 4.

38. Most likely, Sevilla López de Carvajal and her father were the cousins of the late fourteenth-century knight Diego González de Carvajal y Vargas, who was the progenitor of the Plasencia Carvajal. Although Sevilla López's exact ancestry is unknown, her immediate family intermarried with the Camargo, Trejo, Tapia, Toledo, Villalva, and Díaz de Buezo clans. Among her "cousins" were Estefanía González de Carvajal and Mencía González de Carvajal, the daughters of the primary knight studied in this investigation, Diego Gónzalez de Carvajal. Like her cousin, Mencía González de Carvajal, Sevilla was married to a Camargo clansman, Gonzalo de Camargo. Thus, Sevilla López shared close and redundant ties to the main line of the Plasencia Carvajal family. See ACP, Legajo 14, doc. 4; ACP, Legajo 1, doc. 18; ACP, Legajo 14, doc. 25; ACP, Legajo 269, doc. 25; AHNSN, Luque, Caja 160, doc. 9; Codero Alvarado, *Plasencia: Heráldica, histórica y monumental*, 148–51.

39. ACP, Legajo 14, doc. 4; ACP, Legajo 1, doc. 18; ACP, Legajo 14, doc. 25; ACP, Legajo 269, doc. 25; AHNSN, Luque, Caja 160, doc. 9; Codero Alvarado, *Plasencia: Heráldica, histórica y monumental*, 148–51.

40. See ACP, Legajo 14, doc. 4; ACP, Legajo 1, doc. 18; ACP, Legajo 14, doc. 25; ACP, Legajo 269, doc. 25; AHNSN, Luque, Caja 160, doc. 9; Codero Alvarado, *Plasencia: Heráldica, histórica y monumental*, 148–51.

41. ACP, Legajo 14, doc. 4.

42. ACP, Legajo 14, doc. 1; ACP, Legajo 85, doc. 1; ACP, *Actas capitulares*, tomo 1, fols. 208v–209, 217v–219, 252–56, 284v–297.

43. ACP, Legajo 14, doc. 4.

44. ACP, Legajo 14, doc. 4.

45. ACP, Legajo 14, doc. 4.

46. ACP, Legajo 14, doc. 4.

47. ACP, Legajo 14, doc. 4.

48. Cordero Alvarado, *Plasencia: Heráldica, histórica y monumental*, 30–34.

49. Sánchez Loro, *El convento placentino de San Ildefonso*, 24.

50. Ibid., 25.

51. ACP, Legajo 89, docs. 11, 12; Sánchez Loro, *El convento placentino de San Ildefonso*, 24–25.

52. ACP, Legajo 89, docs. 11, 12; Sánchez Loro, *El convento placentino de San Ildefonso*, 24–25.

53. Sánchez Loro, *El convento placentino de San Ildefonso*, 25; Benavides Checa, *Prelados placentinos*, 169.

54. Sánchez Loro, *El convento placentino de San Ildefonso*, 25–26; Benavides Checa, *Prelados placentinos*, 171.

55. Sánchez Loro, *El convento placentino de San Ildefonso*, 25–26.

56. Ibid; Benavides Checa, *Prelados placentinos*, 169.

57. Fernández, *Historia y anales*, 150–53; Benavides Checa, *Prelados placentinos*, 169.

58. ACP, Legajo 13, doc. 5, fol. 2v.

59. ACP, Legajo 13, doc. 5, fol. 1.

60. To compare Sancha de Carvajal's approach to will making and memorial services, I also reviewed the wills of the following extended family members: Gonzalo Lorenzo de Espadero's will of 1395 (AHNSN, Ovando, Caja 35, doc. 1993), Catalina González de Carvajal's will of 1431 (ACP, Legajo 14, doc. 38), Diego González de Carvajal's will of 1455 (ACP, Legajo 14, doc. 25), and Sevilla López de Carvajal's will of 1467 (ACP, Legajo 14, doc. 4).

61. Juan de Carvajal's focus on Mary is discussed below.

62. ACP, Legajo 13, doc. 5, fol. 1–1v.

63. For example, Diego González de Carvajal, Sancha's uncle, requested the clergy celebrate one Trinitary. ACP, Legajo 14, doc. 25.

64. ACP, Legajo 13, doc. 5, fols. 1–1v; ACP Legajo 14, doc. 25, fols. 3v–4.

65. Ibid.

66. Aríes, *Hour of Our Death*, 180.

67. ACP, Legajo 13, doc. 5, fol. 2.

68. ACP, Legajo 13, doc. 5, fol. 2.

69. ACP, Legajo 13, doc. 5, fol. 1v.

70. There are no references in the *Actas capitulares* or the indexed Legajos in the archive of the Cathedral of Plasencia that explicitly describe how Juan de Carvajal funded his church projects.

71. ACP, *Actas capitulares*, tomo 3.

72. Gonzalo Lorenzo de Espadero was a progenitor of one lineage of the Carvajal and Ulloa families in the Extremadura. See AHNSN, Ovando, Caja 35, doc. 1993, no folio.

73. Díaz Ibáñez, "Las relaciones iglesia-nobleza," 312–13.

74. ACP, *Actas capitulares*, tomo 3, fol. 44v.

75. RAH, MS L-5, "Vida del ilustrísimo," fol. 106v; Sánchez Loro, *Historias placentinas inéditas*, B:461–62.

76. ACP, *Actas capitulares*, tomo 3, fol. 44v.

77. RAH, MS L-5, "Vida del ilustrísimo," fol. 106v; Sánchez Loro, *Historias placentinas inéditas*, B:461–62.

78. ACP, *Actas capitulares*, tomo 3, fol. 44v.

79. The dean and treasurer Alvaro de Carvajal was the son of Diego González de Carvajal and his third wife, Teresa Rodríguez de Yanguas. In addition, Diego had another son serving in the cathedral at this time—Canon Gómez González de Carvajal, who was the son of his second wife, Catalina González de Carvajal. The two half brothers, Alvaro and Gómez, were first cousins of Cardinal Juan de Carvajal. See ACP, Legajo 5, doc. 37; ACP, Legajo 14, doc. 25.

80. ACP, *Actas capitulares*, tomo 3, fol. 48v.

81. Oakley, "Alleviations of Penance," 500.

82. Bossy, "Mass as Social Institution," 37.

83. ACP, *Actas capitulares*, tomo 3, 48v.

84. For a selection of typical donations of 200 to 300 maravedís for a single *capellania* mass, see *Calendario de misas traslado*, fols. 1v, 2, 3v, 5, 6v, and other pages without folios.

85. ACP, *Actas capitulares*, tomo 3, fol. 48v. A note about the value of maravedís: for a boy or a young man, the 38 maravedís would have been a substantial bonus, considering the value of the maravedís at this time. With 38 maravedís, one could purchase roughly one of the following: 25 pounds of fresh beef, 13 pounds of rice, or 1 1/3 third pounds of sugar. The approximate value of 38 maravedís was calculated using a list of the price of goods from 1462 to 1464. See Sáez, *Demostración histórico del verdadero valor de todas*, 509.

86. ACP, *Actas capitulares*, tomo 3, fol. 48v.

87. In 1469, Canon Pedro de Carvajal served in the newly created position of archdeacon of Cáceres. By 1498, Pedro's son served as a canon in the cathedral. Pedro was the son of Garcia de Carvajal and Fernán Pérez de Ulloa. Pedro's grandfather was Garci López de Carvajal, the royal adviser and a judge in King Juan II's real audiencia. See ACP, *Actas capitulares*, tomo 3, fol. 48v; ACP, Legajo 3, doc. 20; ACP, *Actas capitulares*, tomo 4, fol. 6; Lodo de Mayoralgo, *Viejos linajes de Cáceres*, 14.

88. ACP, *Actas capitulares*, tomo 3, fol. 48.

89. Blackburn, "'Te Matrem dei Laudamus,'" 57.

90. Ibid., 60; ACP, *Actas capitulares*, tomo 3, fol. 48.

91. Walker Trainor, "Salve Regina," 38 (1).

92. ACP, Legajo 129, doc. 10, fol. 18; RAH, MS L-5, "Vida del ilustrísimo," fol. 106v; Sánchez Loro, *Historias placentinas inéditas*, B:461–462; González Cuesta, *Obispos de Plasencia*, 115.

93. Benavides Checa, *Prelados placentinos*, 60.

94. Herbermann et al., s.v. "Baldachinum," in *Catholic Encyclopedia*. There are no sources describing the statue, and it has no discernible or unique characteristics. Site visits to the Museo de la Catedral de Plasencia, located in the Old Cathedral, in March 2006 and November 2006 revealed that the museum has no documentation pertaining to the retablo mayor. Likewise, texts pertaining to the Old Cathedral of Plasencia provide no details on this statue and only limited information about the retablo. Each of these relevant texts is cited in this discussion of the retablo.

95. In particular, the Gothic Italian style, the dominant artistic style in Spain during the fourteenth and fifteenth centuries, appears to have had the greatest influence on the Plasencia retablo. For instance, the Plasencia altarpiece's gilded, scalloped, and leaflike decorative elements are similar to Piero della Francesca's *Polyptych of St. Anthony* altarpiece (ca. 1460–70). Like the Plasencia retablo, it dedicates its primary center panel to a depiction of Mary with the Christ child, with a surrounding Romanesque rounded arch. In the case of Plasencia's altarpiece, both the upper and lower panels utilize Romanesque arches to frame their two subjects, Mary with Christ and the praying statue. Antonio da Negroponte's *Madonna and Child Enthroned with Angels* altarpiece (ca. 1455) also has this same motif

and Romanesque arch, in addition to incorporating an urn with vegetation flowing from the crown of the altarpiece. Both the Plasencia and Negroponte altarpieces display this urn feature. Similar to Plasencia's retablo, Antonio Vivarini and Giovanni D'Alemagna's *Triptych of St. Jerome* (ca. 1441) and Bartolomeo Vivarini's *Triptych of St. Mark* (ca. 1474) display similar winglike and vegetative elements. The Plasencia retablo presents matching pairs of wings on both sides of the lower panel, upper panel, and at its crown. On the *Triptych of St. Jerome* and *Triptych of St. Mark*, similar pairs of wings are attached above each of its three panels. Antonio Vivarini and Giovanni D'Alemagna's *Triptych of Madonna Enthroned* (ca. 1446) shares a comparable Mary with Christ child motif, with the child holding the orb, and elaborate vegetative elements. Perhaps the Plasencia's altarpiece most hybridized elements are the two columns that frame the lower panel of the altar and the four columns of the baldachin. Although the columns utilize Corinthian capitals, which can be found in Romanesque and Gothic architecture, the shaft of each pillar is covered with elaborate decorations that appear to mimic a stylized amphora. These elements include acanthus leaves and amphora handles in the lower two-thirds of each column, as well as an amphora lid in the upper one-third of each column. A similar use of urns on columns can be found in Domenico Ghirlandaio's fresco, *Birth of the Virgin*, in the Capella Tornabuoni at Santa María Novella church in Florence, Italy, (ca. 1480s) and Benozzo Gozzoli's *Tabernacle of the Madonna della Tosse* fresco (ca. 1484). In the case of Gozzoli's fresco, it too depicts an altar with Mary and the Christ child and is framed with two columns that have Corinthian capitals and acanthus leaves on the pillars. See Sturgis, "Frame, §VIII, 1: Spanish medieval (ii) Gothic retables. (a) Establishment of the form. (b) Development," in *A Dictionary of Architecture and Buildings*, Grove Art Online, Oxford University Press, February 2, 2008, http://www.groveart.com.ezproxy.lib.utexas.edu/; Sturgis, *A Dictionary of Architecture and Buildings*, 3:307–29; Taylor and Van Eck, "Piero della Francesca's Giants," 246; Friedmann, "Footnotes to the Painted Page," 17; Holgate, "Early History of Antonio Vivarini's 'St Jerome' Altar-Piece," 19–20; Pudelko, "Altarpiece by Antonio Vivarini and Giovanni d'Allemagna," 131; Cadogan, "Observations on Ghirlandaio's Method of Composition," 159, 166; Ahl, "Benozzo Gozzoli's Frescoes of the Life of Saint Augustine in San Gimignano," 212.

96. It has hues similar to Fra Angelico's *Madonna of Humility* (ca. 1433–35) and Fra Fillipo Lippi's *Madonna and Child* (ca. 1452). See Llorens, Borobia, and Alarco, *Masterworks: Museo Thyssen-Bornemisza*, 28–29; Hartt, *Art: A History of Painting, Sculpture, Architecture*, 705.

97. Llorens, Borobia, and Alarco, *Masterworks: Museo Thyssen-Bornemisza*, 38–39.

98. Ibid.

99. Ibid.

100. Sheffler, *Symbols of Christian Faith*, 75.

101. For example, in Petrus Christus's *Virgin of the Dry Tree* (ca. 1465), the orb is placed in Christ's hand. Also, it should be noted that on the Virgin's right hand, the ring and middle fingers are held together, while the index and little finger are spread outward. Other scholars have suggested this gesture by Mary may be related to the praying of the rosary or another religious practice where Mary intercedes upon behalf of humanity. See Van Baaren, "Significance of Gestures in Paintings of Hieronymus Bosch," 23–24.

102. See Llorens, Borobia, and Alarco, *Masterworks: Museo Thyssen-Bornemisza*, 34–35.

103. ACP, *Actas capitulares*, tomo 3, fol. 44v.

104. Herbermann, *Catholic Encyclopedia*, s.v. "Ecclesiastical Heraldry."

105. Ecclesiastical heraldry, such as Cardinal Juan de Carvajal's emblem, appears to become a feature of the Christian church in the late thirteenth century. The first known integration of a cardinal's galero with a family coat of arms is reportedly used on the tomb of Bernard, cardinal of Longuisel (d. 1290), who is interred at Orvieto. See Woodward, *Treatise on Ecclesiastical Heraldry*, 137.

106. RAH, MS L-5, "Vida del ilustrísimo," fol. 106v.

107. Codero Alvarado, *Plasencia: Heráldica, histórica y monumental*, 72.

108. Fernández, *Historia y anales*, 288.

109. At the opening of the sixteenth century, the following Carvajal family members were in the cathedral chapter: Garci López de Carvajal II (archdeacon of Plasencia), Diego de Carvajal (archdeacon of Coria), Bernardino de Carvajal (archdeacon of Trujillo), Rodrigo de Yanguas (canon and descendent of knight Diego González de Carvajal), and Gómez de Carvajal (prebendary). See ACP, *Actas capitulares*, tomo 4, fols. 6–9.

110. ACP, Legajo 129, doc. 10, 19v.

111. See ACP, *Actas capitulares*, tomo 4, fols. 6bis–6bis vuelto.

112. RAH, MS L-5, "Vida del ilustrísimo," fol. 106v.

113. RAH, MS L-5, "Vida del ilustrísimo," fol. 106v.

114. Benavides Checa, *Prelados Placentinos*, 58.

115. Ladner, "Medieval and Modern Understanding of Symbolism," 231.

116. Ibid., 225.

117. Ibid.

118. Ibid.

119. Ibid., 239–40.

120. Ameisenowa and Mainland, "Tree of Life in Jewish Iconography," 333.

121. Ibid., 338.

122. ACP, Legajo 129, doc. 10, fol. 18; Benavides Checa, *Prelados Placentinos*, 70.

123. Herbermann, s.v. "Benediction of Blessed Sacrament," in *Catholic Encyclopedia*.

124. Ibid.

125. Ibid.

126. Ibid.

127. Benavides Checa, *Prelados placentinos*, 70.

128. ACP, Legajo 129, doc. 11, fols. 18–18v.

129. Overall, the artifact measures 32.7 inches (83 cm) high, 11.8 inches (30 cm) wide at the tabernacle, and 12.6 inches (32 cm) at its base. See Museum label for "Custodias," Cathedral of Plasencia (Spain) Old Cathedral Museum, Plasencia, Cáceres.

130. RAH, Colección Salazar y Castro C-16, fol. 306; ACP, Legajo 129, doc. 10, fol. 18; Fernández, *Historia y anales*, 103–4; González Cuesta, *Obispos de Plasencia*, 111–12.

131. González Cuesta, *Obispos de Plasencia*, 111–12.

132. The five comparative monstrances are Jan van Eyck's painting of the Ghent Altarpiece, Wenzel von Olmutz's design for a monstrance, Alart du Hamel's design for a mon-

strance, a German monstrance with the Relic of St. Sebastian, and a Bohemian monstrance. See Eyck, "Ghent Altarpiece: Reference: Miraculous host in Monstrance, ms. 31240, fol. 21," at http://www.artstor.org (accessed October 4, 2016); Hutchison, "Early German Artists," in *The Illustrated Bartsch*, vol. 9, Commentary, pt. 2; Willshire, *Catalogue of Early Prints in British Museum*, 314–17; Anonymous, "Monstrance 1400–1410," at http://www.artstor.org (accessed October 4, 2016); Saint Oswald Reliquary Workshop, *Monstrance with the "Paten of Saint Bernwald*," CMA 1930.505, 1413–96, at http://www.artstor.org (accessed October 4, 2016).

133. Because the monstrance is placed in a sealed museum display, the backside of the tabernacle is not visible, thus obstructing the view of the fourth badge.

134. Hand, "'Saint Jerome in His Study,'" 49:2, 3.

135. Brown, *Augustine of Hippo*, 3, 380.

136. Augustine of Hippo, *City of God Against Pagans*, xi; Augustine of Hippo, *Confessions*, 11.

137. Logan, *History of the Church in Middle Ages*, 289.

138. Herbermann, s.v. "Augustine of Hippo," in *Catholic Encyclopedia*.

139. Ahl, "Benozzo Gozzoli's Frescoes of the Life of Saint Augustine in San Gimignano," 35–36.

140. Hand, "'Saint Jerome in His Study,'" 49:2, 4; Herbermann, s.v. "St. Ambrose," in *Catholic Encyclopedia*.

141. ACP, Legajo 13, doc. 7.

CHAPTER 7.   SUCCESS AND LOYALTY

1. Phillips and Phillips, *Concise History of Spain*, 107–10.

2. Lea, *History of the Inquisition*, 1:135–36; Phillips and Phillips, *Concise History of Spain*, 112, 115, 121; Gerber, *Jews of Spain*, ix–x.

3. RAH, Colección Salazar y Castro, tomo A-11, fols. 50–51.

4. Gardiner Davenport, *European Treaties Bearing on the History of the United States*, 61–62, 77.

5. RAH, Colección Pellicer, tomo 9/4070, fol. 136; Bernáldez, *Memorias del reinado*, 345; Mattingly, *Renaissance Diplomacy*, 143–44.

6. Phillips and Phillips, *Concise History of Spain*, 127

7. Bernáldez, *Memorias del reinado*, 571–72; Pastor, *History of the Popes*, 6:334–35, 367, 372, 374.

8. Phillips and Phillips, *Concise History of Spain*, 137, 138.

9. Ibid., 140.

10. AGS, Registro del Sello de Corte, June 1511, no folio; Hervás, *Historia de los judíos de Plasencia*, 2:377–95; Benavides Checa, *Prelados placentinos*, 159–61. It should be noted that the history of the Jewish community of Plasencia is expertly researched and discussed in Hervás's exhaustive *Historia de los judíos de Plasencia*.

11. Hervás, *Historia de los judíos de Plasencia*, 1:116–33, discusses the Estúñiga clan's seizure of the synagogue and the relocation of the Jewish community. While Hervás precisely

plots the locations of each individual Jewish family member, below I indicate the approximate location (usually a set of houses as opposed to a precise home) of these Jewish families. Moreover, while the forced relocation of these Jews is in itself a tragically important finding, from this author's perspective what is equally valuable is the role and approach of the Estúñiga clan versus the Carvajal–Santa María family confederation to Placentino Jews.

12. AGS, Registro del Sello de Corte, June 1511, no folio.

13. The area and distances were calculated in the chapter using the ArcGIS georeferenced map created by Roger L. Martínez-Dávila and Paddington Hodza of the Revealing Cooperation and Conflict Project. See http://revealingcooperationandconflict.com.

14. ACP, Legajo 2, doc. 55, fol. 1.

15. ACP, Legajo 2, doc. 55, fol. 2.

16. ACP, Legajo 2, doc. 55, fol. 3.

17. Hervás, *Historia de los judíos de Plasencia*, 1:129.

18. AHNSN, Frías, Caja 1764, doc. 32,

19. ACP, Legajo, 1, doc. 51, fols. 1–1v.

20. ACP, Legajo 1, doc. 42; ACP, Legajo 3, doc. 11; ACP, Legajo 14, doc. 42; ACP, Legajo 3, doc. 21; ACP, Legajo 5, doc. 42; ACP, Legajo 2, doc. 56; Hervás, *Historia de los judíos de Plasencia*, 1:116–21; 2:452–59, 472–81, 488–94, 497–501.

21. AMP, "Pertenenzias de 1.000 mrs. de renta y censo perpetuo en cada ano . . . Francisco de Paula Vargas y Carvajal"; Hervás, *Historia de los judíos de Plasencia*, 2:481–88.

22. Lea, *History of the Inquisition*, 1:135–36; Phillips and Phillips, *Concise History of Spain*, 115; Gerber, *Jews of Spain*, ix–x.

23. Beinart, *Trujillo*, 287–353; Hervás, *Historia de los judíos de Plasencia*, 2:506; AHN, Inquisición, Legajo 175; Exp. 1, fols. 17–24.

24. ACP, Legajo 6, doc. 30; Fernández, *Historia y anales*, 154.

25. Sánchez Loro, *El parecer de un deán*, 513–42.

26. ACP, Legajo 129, doc. 11, fol. 16v; González Cuesta, *Obispos de Plasencia*, 119, 125–26.

27. Gerber, *Jews of Spain*, 138.

28. AGS, Registro del sello de corte, 31 marzo 1493, fol. 65; AGS, Registro del sello de corte, 26 Junio 1493, fol. 129; Hervás, *Historia de los judíos de Plasencia*, 1:243–44.

29. Mendoza y Bobadilla, *El tizón de la nobleza española*, 12, 57.

30. Ibid., 12, 59.

31. Ibid., 107, 121.

32. Ibid., 77.

33. Llorente, *Historia crítica de Inquisición en España*, 1:185.

34. Ibid.

35. Ibid., 216.

36. Lea, *History of the Inquisition of Spain*, 1:155–56.

37. Ibid., 23, 28, 172–73.

38. Ibid., 35, 82.

39. Ibid., 114.

40. Ibid., 146–47.

41. Glick, "On Converso Identity and Marrano Ethnicity," 67.

42. Rábade Obradó, "Los judeoconversos," 507–37; Rábade Obradó, "Religiosidad y practica religiosa," 139.

43. Poole, "Politics of Limpieza de Sangre," 359–89.

44. Netanyahu, *Marranos of Spain*, 1.

45. Ibid., 2–3.

46. Ibid., 3.

47. Graizbord, *Souls in Dispute*, 8.

48. Ibid., 2, 172.

49. Yovel, *Other Within*, xii–xiii.

50. Wachtel, *Foi Duy Souvenir*, 13.

51. Melammed, *Question of Identity*, 166–68.

52. Starr-LeBeau, *In the Shadow of the Virgin*, 80–81.

53. Ibid., 83.

54. Martz, *Network of Converso Families*, 320–21. It appears that the Carvajal family may have shared relatives with the converso de Toledo and Guzmán families of Toledo during the late 1500s. Martz notes that on January 6, 1600, Elvira de Toledo y Guzmán benefited from a ruling relating to an inheritance. At the time, Don Francisco de Carvajal, a corregidor on the municipal council of Toledo and the count of Torrejón del Rubio, approved the contested will in Elvira's favor, and in return she presented Don Francisco with a loan of 12,000 reales (408,000 maravedís).

55. Ibid., 405.

56. Ibid.

57. Ibid., 401–2.

58. Ibid., 402.

59. RAH, Colección Pellicer, tomo 9/4070, fol. 134; AUS, *Libro de Claustro* 1, fol. 253; Marcos Rodríguez, *Extractos de los libros*, 6(3):182.

60. RAH, Colección Floranes, tomo B-16, fols. 257–58; RAH, Colección Salazar y Castro, tomo C-20, fol. 214.

61. Lapuya, "La Universidad de Salamanca," 28.

62. Herriott, "Thirteenth-Century Manuscript," 280.

63. Ibid.

64. Addy, *Enlightenment in the University of Salamanca*, xvii; Lapuya, "La Universidad de Salamanca," 26.

65. Herriott, "Thirteenth-Century Manuscript," 279.

66. Lobingier, "Siete Partidas," 536.

67. Addy, *Enlightenment in the University of Salamanca*, xviii; Herriott, "Thirteenth-Century Manuscript," 279.

68. Herriott, "Thirteenth-Century Manuscript," 280.

69. Ibid.

70. Ibid.

71. Ibid.

72. For evidence of the intermarriage of the Ruiz de Camargo and Carvajal families, see ACP, Legajo 14, docs. 1, 4, 25.

73. ACP, Legajo 45, doc. 41, no folio.

74. AUS, *Libro de Claustro* 2, fol. 94v; Marcos Rodríguez, *Extractos de libros,* 6(3):234–35.

75. Nader, "'Greek Commander' Hernán Núñez de Toledo," 463, 469; Castro, *Spaniards,* 486.

76. AUS, *Libro de Claustro* 2, fol. 54v; Marcos Rodríguez, *Extractos de libros,* 6(3):215.

77. AUS, *Libro de Claustro* 3, fols. 66, 125v; Marcos Rodríguez, *Extractos de libros,* 6(3):280, 307.

78. Nader, *The Mendoza Family in the Spanish Renaissance,* 128–30.

79. Ibid.

80. Ibid., 130.

81. AUS, *Libro de Claustro* 3, fol. 128; Marcos Rodríguez, *Extractos de libros,* 6(3):308.

82. AUS, *Libro de Claustro* 3, fol. 128; Marcos Rodríguez, *Extractos de libros,* 6(3):308.

83. AUS, *Libro de Claustro* 3, fol. 128; Marcos Rodríguez, *Extractos de libros,* 6(3):308.

84. AUS, *Libro de Claustro* 3, fol. 129v; Marcos Rodríguez, *Extractos de libros,* 6(3):309.

85. AUS, *Libro de Claustro* 3, fol. 130; Marcos Rodríguez, *Extractos de libros,* 6(3):309.

86. AUS, *Libro de Claustro* 3, fols. 128v, 131; Marcos Rodríguez, *Extractos de libros,* 6(3):308–9.

87. AUS, *Libro de Claustro* 3, fols. 128v, 131.

88. AUS, *Libro de Claustro* 3, fol. 78; Marcos Rodríguez, *Extractos de libros,* 6(3):86–87; Villalba, *Colección diplomática del Cardenal Mendoza,* 91.

89. Nader, *The Mendoza Family in the Spanish Renaissance,* 143.

90. BNE, MSS 23129–8, fol. 1.

91. Fernández y Sánchez, *Discutido extremeño Cardenal Carvajal,* 17; Hamburgh, "Rosso Fiorentino's Descent," 589.

92. Hamburgh, "Rosso Fiorentino's Descent," 589.

93. Ibid., 589–90.

94. Fernández y Sánchez, *Discutido extremeño Cardenal Carvajal,* 17–18.

95. RAH, Colección Pellicer, tomo 9/4070, fol. 134.

96. In 1472, Count Álvaro de Estúñiga pursued a legal claim against Estefanía González de Carvajal and her spouse, Luis de Trejo, regarding a property in Plasencia. See ACP, Legajo 1, doc. 44.

97. The tensions between the Carvajal and the Estúñiga clans were likely exacerbated by the War of Succession (1475–79). At this time, the Estúñiga family had allied with Juana "la Beltraneja" instead of Isabel. See Rades y Andrada, *Crónica de las tres órdenes y caballerías,* 54; Fernández, *Historia y anales,* 151; Sánchez Loro, *El parecer de un deán,* 551.

98. Paredes y Guillén, *Los Zúñigas,* 142.

99. Sánchez Loro, *El parecer de un deán,* 552.

100. Fernández, *Historia y anales,* 151.

101. Ibid.

102. Sánchez Loro, *El parecer de un deán,* 554.

103. Fernández, *Historia y anales,* 151.

104. Rades y Andrada, *Crónica de las tres órdenes y caballerías*, 54.

105. Ibid., 53.

106. Fernández, *Historia y anales*, 151.

107. Ibid.

108. Sánchez Loro, *El parecer de un deán*, 555–56.

109. Ibid., 152; RAH, Colección Pellicer, tomo 9/4070, fol. 116.

110. RAH, Colección Salazar y Castro, tomo C-20, fol. 213.

111. RAH, Colección Pellicer, tomo 9/4070, fols. 113–114v.

112. Fernández, *Historia y anales*, 152.

113. ACP, Legajo 282, doc. 4, fols. 2–8; Fernández, *Historia y anales*, 152; RAH, Colección Pellicer, tomo 9/4070, fols. 93–93v; ACP, Legajo 282, doc. 4, fols. 4v–8; ACP, Legajo 282, doc. 9, fols. 1–1v.

114. González Cuesta, *Obispos de Plasencia*, 152.

115. ARCV, Sala Vizcaya, Legajo 829/7; ARCV, Sala Vizcaya, Legajo 1527–18, Caja 2836; Archivo de Protocolos de Sevilla, Oficio Primero, 1.539; Dermit Martínez, "Construcción de naos," 47–68; Dermit Martínez, "Expedición del obispo," 19–40.

116. Martínez Diez, *Bulario de Inquisición*, 241.

117. Ibid.

118. RAH, Colección Salazar y Castro, tomo A-11, fols. 50–51.

119. AGI, Patronato 1, N. 3, R. 2; Davenport, *European Treaties*, 61–62, 77.

120. Vander Linden, "Alexander VI," 13.

121. Davenport, *European Treaties*, 56.

122. Olschki, "Columbian Nomenclature of the Lesser Antilles," 413–14.

123. Ibid., 411.

124. Vander Linden, "Alexander VI," 13.

125. RAH, Colección Pellicer, tomo 9/4070, fol. 136.

126. RAH, Colección Pellicer, tomo 9/4070, fol. 136.

127. RAH, Colección Pellicer, tomo 9/4070, fol. 136.

128. González Novalin, "Pedro Mártir de Anglería," 148.

129. Ibid.

130. Ibid., 150.

131. RAH, Colección Pellicer, tomo 9/4070, fol. 136v; López de Toro, *Documentos inéditos*, 9:298–99.

132. RAH, Colección Pellicer, tomo 9/4070, fol. 136v; López de Toro, *Documentos inéditos*, 9:298–99.

133. RAH, Colección Pellicer, tomo 9/4070, fol. 136v; López de Toro, *Documentos inéditos*, 317–19, 324–25, 331–32.

134. RAH, Colección Pellicer, tomo 9/4070, fol. 136v; López de Toro, *Documentos inéditos*, 298–300, 400–401.

135. RAH, Colección Pellicer, tomo 9/4070, fol. 136v; López de Toro, *Documentos inéditos*, 306.

136. Thompson, "'Cronistas de Indias' Revisited," 185.

137. López de Toro, *Documentos inéditos*, 298–99.

138. Ibid.

139. RAH, Colección Salazar y Castro, tomo A-11, fols. 82–84; RAH, Colección Pellicer, tomo 9/4070, fol. 136v; González Novalin, "Pedro Mártir de Anglería," 149.

140. RAH, Colección Salazar y Castro, tomo C-20, fol. 212.

141. Bernáldez, *Memorias del reinado*, 345; Emerich et. al., *Cambridge Modern History*, 110–11.

142. Emerich et. al., *Cambridge Modern History*, 109–10.

143. Ibid., 113–14.

144. Emerich et. al., *Cambridge Modern History*, 110; Bernáldez, *Memorias del reinado*, 345.

145. Bernáldez, *Memorias del reinado*, 345; Mattingly, *Renaissance Diplomacy*, 143–44.

146. Bernáldez, *Memorias del reinado*, 347; Pastor, *History of the Popes*, 5:445–46.

147. Bernáldez, *Memorias del reinado*, 348.

148. Ibid.; Pastor, *History of the Popes*, 5:453.

149. Pastor, *History of the Popes*, 5:458.

150. Mattingly, *Renaissance Diplomacy*, 143–44.

151. RAH, Colección Salazar y Castro, tomo A-11, fols. 139–40.

152. RAH, Colección Salazar y Castro, tomo A-11, fols. 139–40.

153. Bernáldez, *Memorias del reinado*, 442–44.

154. RAH, Colección Salazar y Castro, tomo A-11, fols. 63–65, 428–29; RAH, Colección Salazar y Castro, tomo A-12, fol. 61.

155. Emerich et al., *Cambridge Modern History*, 126, 129.

156. Hazlitt, *Venetian Republic*, 2:149–53; Pastor, *History of the Popes*, 6:299.

157. Pastor, *History of the Popes*, 6:316.

158. Cloulas, "Wars of Italy, France"; Pastor, *History of the Popes*, 6:318.

159. Pastor, *History of the Popes*, 6:321.

160. Emerich et al., *Cambridge Modern History*, 110.

161. Pastor, *History of the Popes*, 6:291.

162. RAH, Colección Salazar y Castro, tomo A-12, fol. 61; Pastor, *History of the Popes*, 6:291.

163. Pastor, *History of the Popes*, 6:291.

164. Cloulas, "Wars of Italy, France."

165. Shaw, *Julius II*, 246.

166. Pastor, *History of the Popes*, 6:295.

167. RAH, Colección Pellicer, tomo 9/4070, fol. 140.

168. Bernáldez, *Memorias del reinado*, 571; Pastor, *History of the Popes*, 6:334–35.

169. Pastor, *History of the Popes*, 6:334–35.

170. Ibid.

171. Ibid., 367, 372; Bernáldez, *Memorias del reinado*, 572.

172. Pastor, *History of the Popes*, 6:375.

173. Ibid., 374; RAH, Colección Pellicer, tomo 9/4070, fol. 142.

174. Bernáldez, *Memorias del reinado*, 643–645; Pastor, *History of the Popes*, 7:44–45; RAH, Colección Pellicer, tomo 9/4070, fol. 143.

175. Bergenroth, *Calendar of Letters, Despatches, and State Papers*, 2:384–93, 592–94; Varagnoli, *S. Croce in Gerusalemme*, 32; Humanes, *Restauración en Templete*, 22–23.

176. RAH, Colección Salazar y Castro, tomo A-21, fol. 339; Bergenroth, *Calendar of Letters, Despatches, and State Papers*, 2:381.

177. RAH, Colección Salazar y Castro, tomo A-21, fols. 406, 385.

178. RAH, Colección Salazar y Castro, tomo A-21, fol. 390.

179. RAH, Colección Salazar y Castro, tomo A-21, fol. 390.

180. RAH, Colección Salazar y Castro, tomo A-21, fol. 390.

181. Phillips and Phillips, *Concise History of Spain*, 137.

182. Ibid.

183. RAH, Colección Salazar y Castro, tomo A-21, fol. 406; Bergenroth, *Calendar of Letters, Despatches, and State Papers*, 2:385.

184. Bergenroth, *Calendar of Letters, Despatches, and State Papers*, 2:392.

185. AGI, Patronato 170, R. 18; RAH, Colección Muñoz, tomo 9/4842, fol. 265; RAH, Colección Muñoz, tomo 9/4837, fols. 57v, 77; RAH, Colección Muñoz, tomo 9/4851, fols. 53–53v; RAH, Colección Salazar y Castro, tomo A-29, fol. 553; RAH, Colección Pellicer, tomo 9/4080, fols. 135–137v.

186. Beltrán de Heredia, *Cartulario de la Universidad de Salamanca*, 3:283.

187. RAH, Colección Floranes, B-16, fols. 256–296v; BNE, MS 11.174; Torres Fontes, *Estudio sobre la "Crónica de Enrique IV,"* 9–24; BNE, MS 13.261; RAH, Colección Salazar y Castro, tomo G–17.

188. BNE, MS 10.677, fols. 72–73.

189. Rodríguez Valencia, *Isabel la Católica*, tomo 1, 108.

190. RAH, Colección Muñoz, tomo 9/4839, fols. 29, 152, 269–70, 293v; RAH, Colección Muñoz, tomo 9/4837, fol. 5; RAH, Colección Muñoz, tomo 9/4851, fol. 82; RAH, Colección Muñoz, tomo 9/4852, fols. 5–5v, 10–10v, 12v, 15v, 17v, 20, 24, 26, 27–27v, 46v–48; AGI, Patronato 170, R. 18.

191. AGS, Libros de Cámara, Lib. 14, fols. 69v–70; Beltrán de Heredia, *Cartulario de la Universidad de Salamanca*, 3:285.

192. AGS, Libros de Cámara, Lib. 57, fol. 38; Beltrán de Heredia, *Cartulario de la Universidad de Salamanca*, 3:291.

193. RAH, Colección Pellicer, tomo 9/4070, fol. 117v.

194. AGS, Casa Real, Legajo 3, fols. 143–44; Beltrán de Heredia, *Cartulario de la Universidad de Salamanca*, 3:284.

195. AGS, Libros de Cámara, lib. 318/1, fol. 188v; Beltrán de Heredia, *Cartulario de la Universidad de Salamanca*, 3:287.

196. AGS, Libros de Cámara, lib. 43, fol. 62v; Beltrán de Heredia, *Cartulario de la Universidad de Salamanca*, 3:288.

197. AGS, Cámara de Castilla 137, doc. 322; AGS, Cámara de Castilla 164, doc. 103; AGS, Cámara de Castilla 143, doc. 69; AGS, Cámara de Castilla 157, docs. 128–30.

198. BNE, MS 18.346; BNE, MS 11.174; BNE, MS 7.860; BNE, MS 945; BNE, MS 13.261; BNE, MS 677.

199. RAH, Colección Floranes, tomo B-16, fol. 13v (281v).

200. RAH, Colección Floranes, tomo B-16, fol. 18 (288).

201. RAH, Colección Floranes, tomo B-16, fols. 13v–14 (281v–282).

202. RAH, Colección Floranes, tomo B-16, fol. 14 (282), 17 (287). Alonso de Cartagena was also known as Alfonso de Cartagena or the son of Pablo de Santa María.

203. Castro, *Spaniards*, 485–86; Meyuḥas, *Between Sepharad and Jerusalem*, 22–23; Gitlitz, *Secrecy and Deceit*, 435.

204. BNE, MS 10.677.

205. RAH, Colección Floranes, tomo B-16, fol. 17 (289).

206. RAH, Colección Floranes, tomo B-16, fol. 20 (293).

207. BNE, MS 10.677, fol. 72v.

208. BNE, MS 10.677, fols. 73–74.

209. Torres Fontes, *Estudio sobre la "Crónica de Enrique IV."*

CHAPTER 8. COMPLICATIONS FROM THE PAST THREATEN THE FUTURE

1. ACP, Legajo 25, doc. 18, fols. 48–50.

2. Llorente, *Historia crítica de la Inquisición*, 1:304.

3. Ibid.

4. Ibid.

5. Cuartero y Huerta and Vargas-Zúñiga y Montero de Espinosa, *Índice de la Colección*, 14:295.

6. McGaha, *Coat of Many Cultures*, 17.

7. According to Michael McGaha, the story of Joseph in Genesis 37–50 is a critical component of the Jewish people's epic and speaks to its most formative moment—the exodus from Egypt. See McGaha, *Coat of Many Cultures*, 19.

8. Gitlitz, "*Conversos* and Fusion of Worlds," 261.

9. McGaha, *Story of Joseph*, 19; Cortes, "Miguel de Carvajal," 144.

10. Cortes, "Miguel de Carvajal," 145.

11. McGaha, *Story of Joseph*, 19.

12. Ibid., 18.

13. Ibid., 21.

14. Ibid., 26.

15. Ibid., 61.

16. Carrete Parrondo, *Fontes Iudaeorum*, 7:178.

17. Ibid.

18. Ibid., 7:136.

19. Ibid.

20. García de Proodian, *Los judíos en América*, 21.

21. AGN, Inquisición, vol. 320, exp. 12, fol. 384; AGN, Inquisición, vol. 846, exp. 15, fol. 263; AGI, Patronato 62, R. 1, fol. 1; RAH, Colección Muñoz, tomo 9/4794, fols. 236v–237v.

22. AHNSN, Frías, Caja 1764, doc. 19.

23. AGN, Inquisición, vol. 195, exp. 8, fol. 385 azul.

24. AGN, Inquisición, vol. 320, exp. 12, fol. 386.

25. AGN, Bienes Nacionales, vol. 312, exp. 8, fols. 29–29v.

26. AGN, Inquisición, vol. 320, exp. 12, fol. 385.

27. AGN, Inquisición, vol. 320, exp. 12, fols. 382–84.

28. AGN, Inquisición, vol. 320, exp. 12, fols. 387v–388.

29. AGN, Inquisición, vol. 320, exp. 12, fols. 389–389v.

30. AGN, Inquisición, vol. 320, exp. 12, fol. 390v.

31. AGN, Inquisición, vol. 320, exp. 12, fol. 417.

32. AGN, Inquisición, vol. 320, exp. 12, fol. 408.

33. AHN, Inquisición, Legajo 292, exp. 4.

34. AHN, Inquisición, Legajo 292, fols. 12v, 24v, 38v.

35. AHN, Inquisición, Legajo 292, fols. 12v, 24v, 38v.

36. AHN, Inquisición, Legajo 292, fol. 29v.

37. AHN, Inquisición, Legajo 292, fol. 17v.

38. AHN, Inquisición, Legajo 292, fols. 20–20v.

39. AHN, Inquisición, Legajo 292, fols. 29v–30.

40. AHN, Inquisición, Legajo 292, exp. 2.

41. AHN, Inquisición, Legajo 292, exp. 4, fols. 51, 55v.

42. Cohen, *Martyr*, 37, 46; Hordes, *To the End of the Earth*, 76.

43. Cohen, *Martyr*, 105; Hordes, *To the End of the Earth*, 76.

44. Temkin, *Luis de Carvajal*, 105, 218–19.

45. Cohen, *Martyr*, 110; Hordes, *To the End of the Earth*, 78.

46. AGN, Inquisición, vol. 195, exp. 8, fols. 383–404; AGN, Lote Riva Palacio 14, vol. 1489, fols. 299, 456; Schwaller, "Tres familias mexicanas," 183, 189; Costigan, *Through Cracks in the Wall*, 64.

47. Huntington Library, HM MS 35105; Cohen, *Martyr*, 259.

48. AGN, Inquisición, vol. 443, exp. 12, fol. 526.

49. AGN, Bienes Nacionales, vol. 765, exp. 10.

50. AGN, Inquisición, vol. 443, exp. 12, fol. 526–526v.

51. AGN, Inquisición, vol. 444, exp. 2; BRAH, Colección Muñoz, tomo 9/4794, fols. 243v–244.

52. Altman, *Emigrants and Society*, 45, 49, 188, 234; Vázquez Fernández, *Los Pizarros*, 211.

53. AMP, *Actas capitulares*, 1 de agosto de 1522, fol. 26.

54. Kamen, *Empire*, 106.

55. Ibid., 261.

56. Ibid., 11, 238.

57. Egana, *Historia de la iglesia*, 2:73, 109.

58. Mendoza Loza, *Obras completas*, 1:97.

59. Ibid., 1:43.

60. Fuertes López, *Creación de Villa Imperial de Potosí*, 81–82.

61. Ibid., 95, 105.

62. Levillier, *Guerras y conquistas*, 24; Lizondo Borda, *Historia del Tucumán*, 95–97, 105, 106, 113, 124.

63. Ricci, *Evolución de la Ciudad de San Miguel de Tucumán*, 15.

64. Mendoza y Bobadilla, *El tizón de la nobleza española*, 190; Rábade Obradó, "La invención como necesidad," 173.

65. ACP, Legajo 282, doc. 3; Rábade Obradó, "La invención como necesidad," 197.

66. Rábade Obradó, "La invención como necesidad," 197.

67. ABNB, Correspondencia, CaCh 22; ABNB, Correspondencia, CaCh 69; ABNB, Correspondencia, CaCh 81; ABNB, Correspondencia, CaCh 104; ABNB, Cabildo de Potosí, CPLA. 1587 I.1., fols. 295–96.

68. ABNB, Cabildo de Potosí, CPLA. 1587 I.1, fols. 295–96.

69. García Quintanilla, *Historia de Iglesia en Plata*, 4:19.

70. Ibid., 19, 27.

71. Ibid.

72. ABNB, Real Cédulas 248, fol. 1.

73. ABNB, Correspondencia, CaCh 175.

74. Martinez Lopez et al., *Cedulario de Audiencia*, 62.

75. ABNB, Real Cédulas 389; Fernández, *Historia y anales*, 37–38; García Carraffa and García Carraffa, *Diccionario heráldico y genealógico*, 12:268–69.

76. ABNB, Real Cédulas 381, fol. 1.

77. ABNB, Real Cédulas 381, fol. 1.

78. Domínguez Ortiz, *Los judeoconversos*, 132–33.

79. ABNB, Real Cédulas, 405.

80. Ramírez de Águila, *Noticias políticas de Indias*, 81–82.

81. Ibid., 2.

82. ABAMT, Cofradías Sig. 1612, fols. 1, 3v, 5, 9v, 38.

BIBLIOGRAPHY

PRIMARY SOURCES

Archives

Archivo-Biblioteca Arquidiocesanos Monseñor Taborga (Bolivia) (ABAMT)
    Cofradías Sig. 1612.
Archivo y Biblioteca Nacionales de Bolivia (ABNB)
    Cabildo de Potosí. *Libros de Acuerdos.* CPLA. 1587 I.1.
    Correspondencia de la Real Audiencia de La Plata. CaCh 22.
    Correspondencia de la Real Audiencia de La Plata. CaCh 69.
    Correspondencia de la Real Audiencia de La Plata. CaCh 81.
    Correspondencia de la Real Audiencia de La Plata. CaCh 104.
    Correspondencia de la Real Audiencia de La Plata. CaCh 175.
    Real Cédulas 248.
    Real Cédulas 381.
    Real Cédulas 389.
    Real Cédulas 405.
Archivo de la Catedral de Plasencia (Spain) (ACP).
    Actas capitulares, tomo 1 (1399–1453).
    Actas capitulares, tomo 1 (1399–1453), traslado.
    Actas capitulares, tomo 3 (1459–76).
    Actas capitulares, tomo 4 (1494–1508).
    Calendario o libro de aniversarios de la Santa Iglesia placentina.
    Extractos del inventario de los papeles del archivo, tomo 1.
    Extractos del inventario de los papeles del archivo, tomo 2.

Extractos del inventario de los papeles del archivo, tomo 3.

Legajo 1, doc. 6. "1413. Escrita de fundación de dos aniversarios en Sn. Nicolás hecha por Sancho Esteban a cuyo efecto deja una casa en la calle llamada de Don Marcos."

Legajo 1, doc. 18. "1489. Copia simple y Escrita Estefanía Gonzlz. de Carvajal del derecho que tiene la casa de sus padres a la dehesa de Valdeculebras la 3a. parte de la Dehesilla de los cuales hizo donación a su sobrino Pedro de Trejo y al hijo mayor que le sucedió."

Legajo 1, doc. 21. "1531. Escrita de venta de la dehesa de Aldeanueva de Beriggues por Franco de Carvajal a Juan de Tapia, vecino de Plasa."

Legajo 1, doc. 23. "1586. Escrita de censo anual impuesto por la Sra. Da. Juana de Solís, mujer de Diego Nieto Curadora de su hijo el clérigo Martín Nieto de Solís sobre unas casas suyas de calle del Rey y a favor del Colegio de Dn. Fabián de Monroy, Arcediano que fue de esta S. I. C."

Legajo 1, doc. 24. "s.f. [sin fecha] Papel suelto sobre una fundación de Sevilla López Carvajal."

Legajo 1, doc. 29. "s.f. [sin fecha] Relación de los bienes de diversos Mayorazgos."

Legajo 1, doc. 34. "1539. Real Ejecutoria de Dn. Carlos y Da. Juana expedida a petición de Da. Juana de Carvajal contra Pedro Gil de Villalobos y Da. Isabel de Carvajal vecinos de Plasa. sobre el mejor derecho a la herencia de Ma. Barrionuevo—Copia de una cláusula del testamento de Elvira de Carvajal, mujer de Luis de Trejo—Datos varios sobre las familias Carvajal, Villalobos y Trejos."

Legajo 1, doc. 42. "1482. Escrita. de venta de un solar que Diego de Carvajal tenía a las espaldas de sus casas principales que salen a la calle de Trujillo (que se deslindan) al judío Isay de Oropesa vecinos ambos de Plasa da por ciertos mrvs. y cuatro pares de gallinas de censoanual perpetuo."

Legajo 1, doc. 44. "1472. Ante el Escribano público de Plasa. y su tierra por el Duque Dn. Álvaro de Zúñiga comparece Juan Gonzlz. de Benavente, vo. de Casas de Millán por sí y en nombre de otros convecinos protestando de que Dn. Luis de Trejo, Señor de Grimaldo, les ha obligado a mandarle ciertas caballerías de heredad que ellos tenían arrendadas de Estefanía Gonzlz. Carvajal, mujer que fue de Pedro de Trejo y de Rodrigo Carvajal, su hermano. Solicitan del Duque que no les obligue al cumplimiento de dicho tributo."

Legajo 1, doc. 51. "s.f. [sin fecha] Varias escrituras del siglo XV incompletas de ventas."

Legajo 2, doc. 21. "1538. Cumplimiento de carta de dote que Juan de Tapia hizo a su hija Ana de Tapia al desposarse con Alonso de Carvajal vo. de Plasa—Ajuar de Ana de Tapia."

Legajo 2, doc. 55. "1477. Escrita de venta de unas casas en la calle de Zapatería por Pedro Carvajal Villalobos a Saúl Daza y Judá Fidauque, judíos—Hayn Moxudo y su mujer venden a Mahyr Cohe, judío, una casa en la Plaza en 1488."

Legajo 2, doc. 56. "1487. Venta por Isabel Rodgz. De Yanguas, vda. de Rodrigo de Carvajal al judío Mahyr Cahe de dos casas en la calle de Zapatería."

Legajo 3, doc. 11. "1482. Escrita de venta por Diego Carvajal, hijo de Rodrigo Carvajal a Juan Lozano de un solar en la calle de Trujillo—Copia simple de la misma Escrta."

Legajo 3, doc. 20. "1461. Carta de censo que el Cabo otorgó al Comendador Alonso de Béjar sobre unas casas de la Plazuela frente a Sn. Nicolás, lindantes con casa de la Cofradía de los Judíos y con la cocina del Conde."

Legajo 3, doc. 21. "1485. Escrita de venta de una casa en la calle de Trujillo por Bellida, vda. de Salomón Moldo a Jusa Surruyo."

Legajo 3, doc. 22. "1497. Carta de censo que otorga Diego de Carvajal y su mujer Elvira Gutiérrez de Trejo por sí y en nombre de Ca. Oña, Franco Jerez, Fernando de Carvajal, yerno de Sancho Avellaneda y de Da Juana, vda. del moro Abrahim Serrano y sus hijas Sera y Fátima sobre unas caballerías, de ellos y del Convento de Sn. Vicente, en la dehesa de Mari Juan, del Concejo de Serradilla."

Legajo 4, doc. 6. "1588. El Doctoral de Plasa. y Capellán de la Princesa Da. Juana, Dn. Álvaro de Carvajal compra un sitio en Sn. Nicolás con ciertas obligaciones de restauración, construcción de una Capilla etc."

Legajo 4, doc. 9. "1511. Carta de censo perpetuo otorgado por Hernando de Carvajal y Isabel de Almaraz su mujer a Franco de Tamayo sobre la 4a. parte de la dehesa que llaman de Garguera."

Legajo 4, doc. 46. "1558. Miguel, Franco y Álvaro de Carvajal, hijos de Hernando de Carvajal e Isabel de Almaraz venden al Canono. Andrés de la Cadena la casa de la Puerta de Berrozana."

Legajo 4, doc. 47. "1579. Hernando Nieto redime el censo que la casa de la Puerta de Berrozana tenía a favor de los Carvajales."

Legajo 5, doc. 29. "Venta de unas casas en la calle de la Rua y rentas unas a favor de Dean Dn. Diego de Jerez."

Legajo 5, doc. 30. "1492. Carta de compra de los dichos . . . judíos viejos y nuevos es a la puerta de Berrozana."

Legajo 5, doc. 37. "Carta de venta que hizo Doña Ester . . . de unas casas que son en calle de Zapatería."

Legajo 5, doc. 42. "Carta de censo perpetuo . . . de Diego de Carvajal."

Legajo 6, doc. 30. "1492. El Deán Dn. Diego de Jerez deja a Da. Leonor de Jerez mil ducados y ciertas alhajas."

Legajo 6, doc. 48. "1691. Sobre sepulturas de Carvajales en Sn. Nicolás."

Legajo 6, doc. 50. "1539. Relación de documentos en el pleito al Vinculo y Mayorazgo que fundó Franco de Almaraz (datos genealógicos)—Pleito entre Ma. Teresa Ibarra y Anto. de Vargas sobre dicho Mayorazgo—Cláusulas del testamento de Rodrigo Quijada Almaraz y su mujer Beatriz de Trejo—Autos seguidos en 1759 entre Dn. Anto. de Vargas, Síndico del Convento de Sn. Franco y Dn. Franco Enríquez sobre el Mayorazgo fundado por los anteriores."

Legajo 7, doc. 10. "1456. Escrita de imposición de censo por Diego Díaz en Inés Díaz su mujer sobre unas casas fronteras a Sn. Martín."

Legajo 7, doc. 22. "1488. Escrita de censo a favor de Cabo sobre unas casas en la calle de Coria frente a Sn. Nicolás que lindan con Carvajales, Cofradía de los Judíos y la pared de la Nota frente a la cocina del Conde Dn. Alvaro (Bueno para topografía Extr. 452)."

Legajo 12, doc. 10. "1536. Testamento de Elvira de Martínez Carvajal, mujer del Comendador Gonzalo de Trejo—Se manda enterrar en Sn. Martín con sus padres y que se pongan sus armas (Torre, flor de lis y la banda de los Carvajales) (Datos genealógicos y casas principales)."

Legajo 12, doc. 16. "1503. Testamento de Diego de Tapia, vo de Galisteo—Documento del cambio hecho en 1540 por Lope de la Rua y su mujer Isabel Ruiz de Tapia de las casas junto a Sn. Martín a favor de Gonzalo de Trejo y Elena de Tapia."

Legajo 13, doc. 5. "1478. Testamento de Sancha de Carvajal, fundadora de la Capilla de Cabeza Dolid—Datos de Varonas."

Legajo 13, doc. 9. "1503. Testamento de 1807 de la donación que hizo Diego Carvajal, Arcedo de Coria y Canono de Plasencia, de unas casas en la calle de Sta. Ma. a favor del Cabo—Ext. 198."

Legajo 13, doc. 18. "1782. Inventario de los bienes de Da. Teresa Juliana de Herrera mujer de Dn. Ignacio de la Vega Muñoz y Almaraz."

Legajo 13, doc. 24. "1510. Testamento de Sevilla López, esposa del Francisco de Trejo."

Legajo 14, doc. 1. "1499. Testamento de Da. Sevilla López de Carvajal."

Legajo 14, doc. 2. "1499. Fundación de la Capnia. de Diego González de Carvajal la qual se halla en el Libro de Cadena en la Iglae. de Sta. Maria."

Legajo 14, doc. 4. "1577. Testamento de Da. Ysavel de Carvajal."

Legajo 14, doc. 25. "1455. Testamento del Sor. Dn. Diego Gómez de Carvajal."

Legajo 14, doc. 38. "1431. Poder pa. Testar y Testamento de Catalina González primera mujer de Diego González de Carvajal."

Legajo 14, doc. 42. "1485. Copia simple del Testamto. De Rui Gonz. De Carvajal Hijo de Diego Gonz. De Carvajal funda Mayorazgo del tercio de bienes y señala por fintas las casas grandes que vibia en Plasencia cerca de la sinagoga de los judíos con todos los Corrales y Plaza de las Puertas de ellas."

Legajo 14, doc. 48.

Legajo 14, doc. 56.

Legajo 25, doc. "Acuerdos del Cabildo, Cuaderno."

Legajo 25, doc. "Estatuó para que viernes se celebrarse Cabildo, hecho el viernes 12 de octubre de 1431."

Legajo 25, doc. 14. "1445. Estatuó sobre nombramiento de Comisionados de xmos. y Contadores de Rentas. Ext. 836."

Legajo 25, doc. 18. "1534. Estatutos antiguos. Copias de 1534 a 1580."

Legajo 45, doc. 3. "1465. Compromiso hecho por varios vecinos de Trujillo para pagar xmo. de heredades al Cardenal Dn. Juan de Carvajal con quien habían tenido pleito sobre ello."

Legajo 45, doc. 12. "s.f. [sin fecha] Copia del allanamiento del Concejo y vecinos de Trujillo para paga de xmos. en 1410."

Legajo 45, doc. 13. "1410. Allanamiento de Diego Ga. de Orellana, de Trujillo sobre paga de xmos.—Copia posterior."

Legajo 45, doc. 14. "1410. Allanamiento de otros vecinos de Trujillo sobre paga de xmos.—Copia posterior."

Legajo 45, doc. 15. "1465. Allanamiento de otro vecino de Trujillo sobre paga de xmos.—Copia posterior."

Legajo 45, doc. 16. "s.f. [sin fecha] Allanamiento de otro vecino de Trujillo sobre paga de xmos.—Copia posterior."

Legajo 45, doc. 41. "1573. Testimonio fechado por el Notario de Trujillo por el que consta que noticioso el Cabo. de que granos de Magasquillas y Caballerías de Trujillo se entregasen al Obo. Córdoba y Mendoza se opuso pidiendo traslado de los mandatos del Vicario para poder acudir al Provisor reclamando quedó así—Ext. 652."

Legajo 85, doc. 1. "1468. Fundación en Plasa. de la Cátedra de Gramática por Dn. Juan de Carvajal, Cardenal de Sant Ángelo."

Legajo 89, doc. 11.

Legajo 89, doc. 12.

Legajo 99, doc. 21. "Girones de Talavera."

Legajo 129, doc. 10. "1766. Copia de noticias de Obispos de Plasencia."

Legajo 129, doc. 11. "s.f. [sin fecha] Notas históricas de la Sede, Obispos y pleitos—Copia del Estatuto fundamental y de los documentos diplomáticos más importantes."

Legajo 133, doc. 17. "1452. Dos escrituras de compra por el Cabo. a Luis de Trejo partes de las dehesas del Carrascal, Gorjalla, y las Hazas para su Mesa Capitular de los bienes de los Memorias que fundó el Obo. Dn. Gonzalo de Santa María—Ext. 46."

Legajo 136, doc. 26. "1400. Copia de 1807 de la donación que el Arcedo. Dn. Simón Sánchez hizo al Cabo. de la heredad del Campillo que llaman del Arcediano—Deslinde—Ext. 173."

Legajo 143, doc. 3. "1452. Copia de la compra que hizo el Cabo. de las heredades Carrasal, Gorjada, y las Mazas por las Memorias del Obo. Santa María."

Legajo 143, doc. 12. "1430. Deslinde las tierras de Blasco Ferndz. de Madrigal, vo. De Plasa.—Trueque que Juan Sánchez, vo. de Garganta la Ollas, lugar de Dn. Luis de la Cerda, Conde Medinaceli, por la que dá al Cabo. la mitad de la Torrecilla y parte de Valdefuentes por los bienes que el Cabo. tiene en Jaraíz y Garganta—Testamento de Leonor Sánchez que se manda enterrar ante Sta. Ma. La Blanca de la Catedral (datos sobre la Iglesia antigua)—Manda al Cabo. la dehesa de Corral Enmedio para que la digan 12 aniversarios—Manda a los Curas la Vinosilla y la mitad de Valsoriano y Ferrucejo y otras muchas mandas—Escrito. de 1421 por la que Leonor Sánchez 'La Ferruza,' va. de Plasa., deja al Cabo. la dehesa del Corral de Enmedio."

Legajo 269, doc. 3. "1505. Carta de pago de Diego Núñez y Pedro Núñez de Almaraz para Diego de Villalobos."

Legajo 269, doc. 25. "1448. Nombramiento como el anterior [Gonzalo García de Santa María]."

Legajo 270, doc. 1. "1405. Testimonio de haberse cobrado la tercera parte del portazgo de Tornavacas."

Legajo 270, doc. 13. "1406. Testamento de Leonor Sánchez dejando al Cabo. su dehesa de Corral del Medio. Siguen actas de posesión de dicha dehesa por el Cabo. en 1412—Otra de fundación piadosa sobre la repetida heredad en 1421."

Legajo 270, doc. 15. "1428. Declaración auténtica sobre derechos del Cabo. en el Portazgo de Plasa."

Legajo 270, doc. 18. "1385. Declaración auténtica sobre derechos del Cabo. en el Portazgo de Plasa."

Legajo 273, doc. 2. "1454. Sobre la confiscación de rentas del portazgo de la ciudad y tierra de Plasencia."

Legajo 282, doc. 11. "1418. El portazgo de Plasencia pertenecía al Cabildo Catedral."

Legajo 282, doc. 1. "Constituciones Sinodales publicadas por Señor D. Domingo I, natural de Béjar, y aprobadas por el Cabildo Placentino, en 14 de Junio de 1229. Vertidas del latín al castellano, martes 3 de abril de 1313"; "Estatutos y Sínodos."

Legajo 282, doc. 2. "Transcripciones de documentos (de Benavides Checa)"; "Real Provisión de D. Enrique España que los Sres. de los lugares no impidan el arrendamiento de los diezmos obtenida a instancia del Sr. Obispo D. Pedro"; "1346. Privilegio del Rey D. Alfonso XI dado a favor de la ciudad de Plasencia."

Legajo 282, doc. 3. "Prebendados y Dignidades desde 1189."

Legajo 282, doc. 4. "Libro III. Viejo de Actas Capitulares. Cabildos celebrados desde 1459 al 1477."

Legajo 282, doc. 5. "Estatutos de la Catedral de Plasencia editados por Don Andrés Noroña, 1615."

Legajo 282, doc. 7. "Constituciones del Señor Obispo Vicente Arias de Balboa."

Legajo 282, doc. 9. "Traslado de los autos hechos en lo de septiembre de 1524 por el Juez Lic. Gonzalo Campo, que pretendió quitar los balcones de las ventanas de las casas de Plasencia"; "Testamento del Bachiller en Decretos D. Martín Fernández de Soria, Arcediano de Plasencia y Béjar 4 de octubre 1424."

Legajo 282, doc. 11. "El Abad y Cabildo de la Universidad toman posesión de la Sinagoga de los judíos el dial de 2 de febrero de 1493 que les habían concedió los Reyes Católicos en 11 de enero de 1493."

Legajo 282, doc. 13. *Calendario de Misas Traslado.*

Archivo de la Catedral de Valladolid (Spain) (ACV)

Legajo 22, doc. 26.

Archivo General de Indias (Spain) (AGI)

Patronato 1, N. 3, R. 2.

Patronato 62, R. 1.

Patronato 170, R. 18.

Archivo General de la Nación (Mexico) (AGN)

Bienes Nacionales. Vol. 312, exp. 8.

Bienes Nacionales. Vol. 765, exp. 10.

Inquisición. Vol. 195, exp. 8.

Inquisición. Vol. 292, exp. 2.

Inquisición. Vol. 292, exp. 4.

Inquisición. Vol. 320, exp. 12.

Inquisición. Vol. 443, exp. 12.

Inquisición. Vol. 444, exp. 2.

Inquisición. Vol. 846, exp. 15.

Lote Riva Palacio 14. Vol. 1489.

Archivo General de Simancas (Spain) (AGS)

Cámara de Castilla 137, doc. 322.

Cámara de Castilla 143, doc. 69.

Cámara de Castilla 157, doc. 128.

Cámara de Castilla 157, doc. 129.

Cámara de Castilla 157, doc. 130.

Cámara de Castilla 164, doc. 103.

Casa Real, legajo 3.

Escribanía Mayor de Rentas (EMR), Legajo 1. "Contribución de la cabeza de pecho de los judíos de Plasencia, Abraham Abendi salió fiador de Pedro Rodríguez de Sevilla, recaudador mayor de las rentas del obispado."

Libros de Cámara, libro 14.

Libros de Cámara, libro 43.

Libros de Cámara, libro 57.

Libros de Cámara, libro 318/1.

Registro del Sello de Corte, 31 marzo 1493.

Registro del Sello de Corte, 26 junio 1493.

Registro del Sello de Corte, junio 1511.

Archivo Histórico de la Catedral de Burgos (Spain) (AHCB)

Registro 2.

Vol. 5.

Vol. 46.

Vol. 48.

Archivo Histórico Municipal de Burgos (Spain) (AHMB)

Legajo HI-2960.

Legajo HI-2961.

Archivo Histórico Nacional (Spain) (AHN)

Inquisición. Legajo 175, exp. 1.

Inquisición. Legajo 292, exp. 2.

Inquisición. Legajo 292, exp. 4.

Archivo Histórico Nacional, Sección Nobleza (Spain) (AHNSN)

Bornos. Caja 705, doc. 3.

Bornos. Caja 796, doc. 2.

Frías. Caja 1017, doc. 3.

Frías. Caja 1762, doc. 3.

Frías. Caja 1762, doc. 4.

Frías. Caja 1763, doc. 3.

Frías. Caja 1763, doc. 31.
Frías. Caja 1763, doc. 32.
Frías. Caja 1764, doc. 3.
Frías. Caja 1764, doc. 4.
Frías. Caja 1764, doc. 19.
Frías. Caja 1764, doc. 31.
Frías. Caja 1764, doc. 32.
Luque. Caja 159, doc. 3.
Luque. Caja 159, doc. 6.
Luque. Caja 159, doc. 7.
Luque. Caja 159, doc. 8.
Luque. Caja 159, doc. 9.
Luque. Caja 159, doc. 15.
Luque. Caja 159, doc. 16.
Luque. Caja 159, doc. 17.
Luque. Caja 159, doc. 18.
Luque. Caja 159, doc. 19.
Luque. Caja 159, doc. 20.
Luque. Caja 159, doc. 21.
Luque. Caja 159, doc. 22.
Luque. Caja 160, doc. 8.
Luque. Caja 160, doc. 9.
Mocejón. Caja 7.
Osuna. Caja 213, doc. 19 (20).
Osuna. Caja 213, doc. 19 (21).
Osuna. Caja 215, doc. 10 (2).
Osuna. Caja 298, doc. 3 (13).
Osuna. Caja 298, doc. 3 (14).
Osuna. Caja 298, doc. 3 (17).
Osuna. Caja 299, doc. 1 (4).
Osuna. Caja 299, doc. 1 (6).
Osuna. Caja 299, doc. 2 (1).
Osuna. Caja 300, doc. 8 (6).
Osuna. Caja 300, doc. 9 (5).
Osuna. Caja 300, doc. 9 (7).
Osuna. Caja 303, doc. 42.
Osuna. Caja 303, doc. 51.
Ovando. Caja 35, doc. 1993.
Ovando. Caja 35, doc. 2006.
Ovando. Caja 35, doc. 2054.
Ovando. Caja 35, doc. 2060.
Torrejón. Caja 7, doc. 10.
Archivo Histórico Provincial de Cáceres (Spain)
Paredes. Legajo 13, doc. 11.

Archivo Municipal de Plasencia (Spain) (AMP)

Actas capitulares, 1 de agosto de 1522.

Actas municipales, 1461–65.

"Casa de San Esteban sobre un moro Bejarano y tiene un testificación de un criado de los Carvajales."

"Expediente a instancia de Doña Inés María de Vargas. AMP, Plasencia, Spain. 1815."

"Expediente a instancia de Doña Inés María de Vargas por la justifica es propiedad de sus casa de la Plazuela de Ansano [2 marzo] 1815."

"Pertenenzias de 1.000 mrs. de renta y censo perpetuo en cada año . . . Francisco de Paula Vargas y Carvajal."

"Pesquisa hecha por Miguel Sánchez de Sepúlveda corregidor de la ciudad de Plasencia, en razón de las terminus y otras cosas. Fecha en 3 de septiembre de 1431, ante Martín Fernández de Logroño, escribano de esta ciudad."

Archivo de Protocolos de Sevilla (Spain)

Oficio Primero. 1.539. "Paleografía de Doña Concepción Hidalgo de Cisneros."

Archivo de la Real Chancillería de Valladolid (Spain) (ARCV)

Sala Vizcaya. Legajo 829/7. "Escritura de obligación otorgada por el coronel Ochoa de Salazar."

Sala Vizcaya. Legajo 1527–18, caja 2836. "Probanza del pleito de Lope de Barraondo, vecino de Bilbao, con Gutierre de Carvajal, Obispo de Plasencia, sobre la construcción de unas naos."

Archivo de la Universidad de Salamanca (Spain) (AUS)

Libro de Claustro 2.

Libro de Claustro 3.

Archivum Secretum Apostolicum Vaticanum (ASAV)

Reg. Lat. 364.

Reg. Suppl. 134.

Reg. Suppl. 213.

Reg. Suppl. 244.

Reg. Suppl. 283.

Reg. Suppl. 290.

Reg. Suppl. 319.

Reg. Suppl. 359.

Biblioteca Nacional de España (Spain) (BNE)

MSS 7.860. Genealogía de los Reyes de Castilla, desde don Pelayo hasta don Juan II.

MSS 10.677. Adiciones genealógicas a los Claros varones de Castilla, de Fernán Pérez de Guzmán, señor de Batres.

MSS 11.174. Anales breves de los Reyes Católicos Don Fernando y Doña Isabel.

MSS 13.261. Crónica de Enrique IV.

MSS 18.346. Crónica de los Reyes Católicos desde 1468 hasta 1518.

MSS 23.129-8. Concesión de una canonjía y prebenda de la catedral de Sevilla a D. Bernardino de Carvajal, el 11 marzo 1482, y la tesorería de la misma iglesia a D. Manuel Fernández de Córdoba, arcediano de Moya (Cuenca), el 14 marzo 1482.

MSS 945. Crónica de Juan II.

Biblioteca de la Real Academia de la Historia (Spain) (RAH)
    Colección Floranes, tomo B-16.
    Colección Muñoz, tomo 9/4794
    Colección Muñoz, tomo 9/4080.
    Colección Muñoz, tomo 9/4837.
    Colección Muñoz, tomo 9/4839.
    Colección Muñoz, tomo 9/4842.
    Colección Muñoz, tomo 9/4851.
    Colección Muñoz, tomo 9/4852.
    Colección Pellicer, tomo 9/4058.
    Colección Pellicer, tomo 9/4070.
    Colección Pellicer, tomo 9/4080.
    Colección Salazar y Castro, tomo A-11.
    Colección Salazar y Castro, tomo A-21.
    Colección Salazar y Castro, tomo A-29.
    Colección Salazar y Castro, tomo C-12.
    Colección Salazar y Castro, tomo C-16.
    Colección Salazar y Castro, tomo C-20.
    Colección Salazar y Castro, tomo G-17.
    Manuscript L-5. "Vida del Ilustrísimo y reverendísimo señor don Juan de Carvajal"
        por Bachiller Diego Martínez.
Biblioteca de la Universidad de Salamanca (Spain) (BUS)
    MSS 2.650. Descripción de la Ciudad y Obispado de Plasencia por Luis de Toro.
Huntington Library (U.S.)
    HM MSS 35105, "Proceso contra de Leonor de Cáceres."

Publications

Aldea Vaquero, Quintín, Tomas Marín Martínez, and José Vives Gatell, eds. *Diccionario de historia eclesiástica de España.* Madrid: CSIC, 1972, 4 vols.

Anonymous. *Monstrance.* 1400–1410. Rímskokatolická farnost Kuntá Hora-Sedlec. October 4, 2016. http://www.artstor.org.

Augustine of Hippo. *City of God against Pagans.* Translated by R. W. Dyson. Cambridge: Cambridge University Press, 1998.

———. *Confessions.* Translated by R. S. Pine-Coffin. Harmondsworth: Penguin Books, 1961.

Benavides Checa, José. *El Fuero de Plasencia.* Rome: Tipografía de M. Lobesi, 1896.

Bergenroth, G. A. *Calendar of Letters, Despatches, and State Papers, relating to the Negotiations between England and Spain, preserved in the Archives at Simancas and Elsewhere.* Vol. 1. London: Longmans, Green, Reader, & Dyer, 1866.

Bernáldez, Andrés. *Memorias del reinado de los reyes católicos.* Edited by Manuel Gómez-Moreno and Juan de M. Carriazo. Madrid: Blass, Tipográfica, 1962.

Carillo del Huete, Pedro. *Crónica del halconero de Juan II.* Madrid: Espasa-Calpe, 1946.

Cartagena, Alonso de. *Defensorium unitatus christianae.* Translated by P. Manuel Alonso, S. I. Madrid: CSIC, 1943.

Constable, Olivia Remie. *Medieval Iberia: Readings from Christian, Muslim, and Jewish Sources.* Philadelphia: University of Pennsylvania Press, 1997.

Eyck, Jan van. *Ghent Altarpiece: Reference: Miraculous host in Monstrance, ms. 31240, fol. 21.* 1390–1441. ARTstor. October 4, 2016. http://www.artstor.org.

Fernández, Alonso. *Historia y anales de la Ciudad y Obispado de Plasencia.* Edición facsimilar. Madrid: Cicon Ediciones, 1627.

Foster, John, trans. *The Chronicle of James I, King of Aragón.* London, 1883.

Guillaume, A., trans. *The Life of Muhammad: A Translation of Ibn Ishaq's Sirat Rasul Allah.* Lahore: Oxford University Press, 1967.

Internet History Sourcebooks Project. "Medieval Sourcebook: Pact of Umar, 7th Century— Internet History Sourcebooks Project." http://www.fordham.edu/halsall/source/pact -umar.asp.

———. "Medieval Sourcebook: Twelfth Ecumenical Council: Lateran IV 1215." http:// www.fordham.edu/halsall/basis/lateran4.asp.

López de Ayala, Pedro. *Crónica de Enrique III.* Edited by Constance L. Wilkins and Heanon M. Wilkins. Madison: Hispanic Seminary of Medieval Studies, 1992.

———. *Crónicas de los reyes de Castilla.* Tomo segundo. Biblioteca de Autores Españoles No. 68. Madrid: Estereotipia y Galvanoplastia de Aribau y Compañia, 1877.

Marcos Rodríguez, Florencio. *Extractos de los Libros de Claustros de la Universidad de Salamanca.* Siglo XV, 1463–84. Tomo 6, no. 3. Salamanca: Graficas Alfer, 1964.

Mendoza y Bobadilla, Francisco. *El tizón de la nobleza española: O maculas y sambenitos de sus linajes.* Barcelona: Empresa Literario-Editorial, 1880.

Pérez de Guzmán, Fernán. *Crónica del rey Don Juan II.* Madrid: B. A. E., 1953.

Rades y Andrada, Francisco de. *Crónica de las tres órdenes y caballerías de Calatrava, Santiago y Alcántara.* Toledo: Librerías "Paris-Valencia," 1572.

Rosell, Cayetano. *Crónicas de los reyes de Castilla desde Don Alfonso el Sabio hasta los Católicos Don Fernando y Doña Isabel.* Tomo primero. Madrid: Biblioteca de Autores Españolas, 1953.

Sánchez Loro, Domingo. *Historias placentinas inéditas: Primera parte catalogus episcoporum ecclesiae Placentinae.* Vol. A. Cáceres: Institución Cultural "El Brocense" Diputación Provincial de Cáceres, 1982.

———. *Historias placentinas inéditas: Primera parte catalogus episcoporum ecclesiae Placentinae.* Vol. B. Cáceres: Institución Cultural "El Brocense" Diputación Provincial de Cáceres, 1983.

Scott, Samuel Parsons. *Las siete partidas.* Chicago: Comparative Law Bureau of the American Bar Association, 1931.

SECONDARY SOURCES

Acton, John Emerich Edward Dalberg Acton, Baron, Adolphus William Ward, G. W. Prothero, Stanley Mordaunt Leathes, and E. A. Benians. *The Cambridge Modern History.* New York: Macmillan Co., 1902.

Addy, George M. *The Enlightenment in the University of Salamanca.* Durham, NC: Duke University Press, 1966.

Ahl, Diane Cole. "Benozzo Gozzoli's Frescoes of the Life of Saint Augustine in San Gimignano: Their Meaning in Context." *Artibus et Historiae* 7, no. 13 (1986): 35–53.

Altman, Ida. *Emigrants and Society: Extremadura and America in the Sixteenth Century.* Berkeley: University of California Press, 1989.

Amador de los Ríos, José. *Historia social, política y religiosa de los judíos de España y Portugal.* Tomos 2 and 3. Madrid: Imprenta de T. Fortanet, 1876.

Ameisenowa, Zofja, and W. F. Mainland. "The Tree of Life in Jewish Iconography." *Journal of the Warburg Institute* 2, no. 4 (April 1939): 326–45.

Arìes, Phillipe. *The Hour of Our Death.* Translated by Helen Weaver. New York: Oxford University Press, 1981.

Aronson-Friedman, Amy, and Gregory B. Kaplan, eds. *Marginal Voices.* Leiden: Brill, 2012.

Astarita, Tommaso. *The Continuity of Feudal Power: The Caracciolo di Bienza in Spanish Naples.* Cambridge: Cambridge University Press, 1992.

Baer, Yitzhak. *A History of the Jews in Christian Spain.* 2 vols. Philadelphia: Jewish Publication Society of America, 1961.

Barnadas Guillermo Calvo A., Josep M. *Archivo-Biblioteca Arquidiocesanos Monseñor Taborga guia general preliminar.* Sucre: Instituto de Cultura, Fundación MAPFRE, 2006.

Beceiro Pita, Isabel, and Ricardo Córdoba de la Llave. *Parentesco, poder y mentalidad: La nobleza castellana siglos XII–XV.* Madrid: CSIC, 1990.

Beinart, Haim. *Trujillo: A Jewish Community in Extremadura on the Eve of the Expulsion from Spain.* Jerusalem: Magnes Press, 1980.

Beltrán de Heredia, Vicente. *Bulario de la Universidad de Salamanca (1218–1549): Introducción.* Salamanca: Universidad de Salamanca, 1966.

———. *Bulario de la Universidad de Salamanca (1219–1549).* Vol. 2. Salamanca: Universidad de Salamanca, 1966.

Benavides Checa, José. *Prelados placentinos.* Plasencia: Excmo. Ayuntamiento de Plasencia, 1999.

Benítez Sanchez-Blanco, Rafael, Francisco Chacón Jiménez, and Juan Hernández Franco. *Poder, familia y consanguinidad en la España del antiguo régimen.* Barcelona: Anthropos Editorial del Hombre, 1992.

Bilinkoff, Jodi. *The Ávila of Saint Teresa: Religious Reform in a Sixteenth-Century City.* Ithaca, NY: Cornell University Press, 1989.

Bisson, Thomas. *Tormented Voice: Power, Crisis, and Humanity in Rural Catalonia 1140–1200.* Cambridge, MA: Harvard University Press, 1998.

Blackburn, Bonnie J. "'Te Matrem dei Laudamus': A Study in the Musical Veneration of Mary." *Musical Quarterly* 53, no. 1 (January 1967): 53–76.

Bloch, Marc. *Feudal Society.* Vol. 1: *The Growth of Ties of Dependence.* Translated by L. A. Manyon. Chicago: University of Chicago Press, 1997.

Bloom, Jonathan, and Sheila Blair. *Islam: A Thousand Years of Faith and Power.* New Haven, CT: Yale University Press, 2002.

Bodian, Miriam. *Dying in the Law of Moses: Crypto-Jewish Martyrdom in the Iberian World.* Bloomington: Indiana University Press, 2007.

Bossy, John. "The Mass as a Social Institution." *Past and Present,* no. 100 (August 1983): 29–61.

Brown, Peter. *Augustine of Hippo: A Biography.* Berkeley: University of California Press, 2000.

Bulliet, Richard W. *Islam: The View from the Edge.* New York: Columbia University Press, 1994.

Burckhardt, Jacob. *The Civilization of the Renaissance in Italy.* London: Penguin, 1990.

Burns, R. Ignatius. "A Mediæval Income Tax: The Tithe in the Thirteenth-Century Kingdom of Aragon." *Speculum* 41, no. 3 (July 1966): 438–52.

———. "The Organization of a Mediæval Cathedral Community: The Chapter of Valencia 1238–1280." *Church History* 31, no. 1 (March 1962): 14–23.

Caballero-Navas, Carmen, and Esperanza Alfonso, eds. *Late Medieval Jewish Identities: Iberia and Beyond.* New York: Palgrave, 2010.

Cadogan, Jean K. "Observations on Ghirlandaio's Method of Composition." *Master Drawings* 22, no. 2 (Summer 1984): 159–72.

Cañizares-Esguerra, Jorge. *How to Write the History of the New World: Histories, Epistemologies, and Identities in the Eighteenth-Century Atlantic World.* Stanford, CA: Stanford University Press, 2002.

Cantera Burgos, Francisco. *Alvar García de Santa María y su familia de conversos: Historia de la judería de Burgos y sus conversos más egregios.* Madrid: Instituto Arias Montano, 1952.

———. "Juderías medievales de la provincia de León." *Archivos Leóneses: Revista de Estudios y Documentación de los Reinos Hispano-Occidentale* 55–56 (1974): 85–155.

———. *Sinagogas del Toledo, Segovia y Córdoba.* Madrid: Instituto Arias Montano, 1973.

Caro Baroja, Julio. *Los judíos en la España moderna y contemporánea.* Vol. 1. Madrid: ISTMO, 2000.

Carrera Stampa, Manuel. "The Evolution of Weights and Measures in New Spain." *Hispanic American Historical Review* 29, no. 1 (February 1949): 2–24.

Carrete Parrondo, Carlos. *Fontes iudaeorum regni castellae.* Vol. 7. Salamanca: Universidad Pontificia de Salamanca, 1997.

Carson, Thomas, and Joann Cerrito, eds. *New Catholic Encyclopedia.* Detroit: Thomson Gale, 2003.

Castro, Américo. *The Spaniards: An Introduction to Their History.* Translated by Willard F. King and Selma Margarettan. Berkeley: University of California Press, 1971.

Clavero, Bartolomé. *Mayorazgo: Propiedad feudal en Castilla 1369–1836.* Madrid: Siglo XXI de España Editores, 1974.

Codero Alvarado, Pedro. *Plasencia: Heráldica, histórica y monumental.* Plasencia: Excmo. Ayuntamiento de Plasencia, 1997.

Cohen, Martin A. *The Martyr: The Story of a Secret Jew and the Mexican Inquisition in the Sixteenth Century.* Philadelphia: Jewish Publication Society of America, 1973.

Cohn, Samuel M., Jr. "The Black Death and the Burning of Jews." *Past and Present,* no. 196 (August 2007): 3–36.

Coleman, David. *Creating Christian Granada: Society and Religious Culture in an Old-World Frontier City, 1492–1600.* Ithaca, NY: Cornell University Press, 2003.

Collantes de Teran Sanchez, Antonio. *Sevilla en la baja edad media: La ciudad y sus hombres.* Seville: Sección de Publicaciones del Excmo. Ayuntamiento de Sevilla, 1977.

Collins, Roger. *The Arab Conquest of Spain 710–797.* Oxford: Blackwell, 1995.

Cooper, Richard S. "The Assessment and Collection of Khar j Tax in Medieval Egypt." *Journal of the American Oriental Society* 96, no. 3 (July–September 1976): 365–82.

Cortes, Narciso Alonso. "Miguel de Carvajal." *Hispanic Review* 1, no. 2 (April 1993): 141–48.

Costigan, Lucia Helena. *Through the Cracks in the Wall: Modern Inquisitions and New Christian Letrados in the Iberian Atlantic World.* Leiden: Brill, 2010.

Cuartero y Huerta, Baltasar, and Antonio de Vargas-Zúñiga y Montero de Espinosa. *Índice de la colección de don Luis de Salazar de Castro* 14. Madrid: Real Academia de la Historia, 1956.

Danvila, Francisco. "El robo de la judería de Valencia en 1391." *Boletín de la Real Academia de la Historia* 8 (1886): 358–96.

Davenport, Frances Gardiner. *European Treaties Bearing on the History of the United States and Its Dependencies to 1648.* Washington, DC: Carnegie Institution of Washington, 1917.

Dequeker, Luc, and Werner Verbeke, eds. *The Expulsion of the Jews and Their Emigration to the Southern Low Countries (15th–16th C.).* Leuven: Leuven University Press, 1998.

Dermit Martínez, Pedro Jose. "La construcción de las naos del obispo de Plasencia en Vizcaya." *Derroteros de la Mar Sur* 11 (2003): 47–68.

———. "La expedición del Obispo de Plasencia III parte: En busca del Arauco." *Derroteros de la Mar Sur* 13 (2005): 19–40.

Díaz Esteban, Fernando, ed. *América y los judíos hispanoportugueses.* Madrid: Sociedad Estatal de Conmemoraciones Cultures, 2009.

Díaz Ibáñez, Jorge. "Las relaciones iglesia-nobleza en el Obispado de Cuenca durante la baja edad media." *La España Medieval,* no. 20 (1997): 281–319.

Domínguez Ortiz, Antonio. *Los judeoconversos en España y América.* Madrid: Ediciones ISTMO, 1978.

Doubleday, Simon R. *The Lara Family: Crown and Nobility in Medieval Spain.* Cambridge, MA: Harvard University Press, 2001.

Duby, Georges. "La diffusion du titre chevalreque sur le versant mediterraneen de la Chetiente latine." In *La noblesee au Moyen Age: XIe–XVe siècles: Essais a la memorie de Robert Boutruche,* edited by Philippe Contamine, 39–70. Paris: PUF, 1976.

———. "The Diffusion of Cultural Patterns in Feudal Society." *Past and Present,* no. 39 (April 1968): 3–10.

Duggan, Lawrence G. "The Unresponsiveness of the Late Medieval Church: A Reconsideration." *Sixteenth Century Journal* 9, no. 1 (April 1978): 3–26.

Edwards, John. *Christian Cordoba: The City and Its Region in the Late Middle Ages.* Cambridge: Cambridge University Press, 1982.

Egana, Antonio de. *Historia de la iglesia en la América española: Desde el descubrimiento hasta comienzos del siglo XIX.* Vol. 2: *Hemisferio sur.* Madrid: Bibliotecas de Autores Cristianos, 1966.

Fernández y Sánchez, Teodoro. *El discutido extremeño Cardenal Carvajal.* Cáceres: Institución Cultural "El Brocense" de la Excma. Diputación P. de Cáceres, 1981.

Franco Silva, Alfonso. "Oropesa, el nacimiento de un Señorío Toledano a fines del siglo XIV." *Anuario de Estudios Medievales*, no. 15 (1985): 299–314.

Friedmann, Herbert. "Footnotes to the Painted Page: The Iconography of an Altarpiece by Botticini." *Metropolitan Museum of Art Bulletin*, n.s., 28, no. 1 (Summer 1969): 1–17.

Friedman, Jerome. "Jewish Conversion, the Spanish Pure Blood Laws and Reformation: A Revisionist View of Racial and Religious Antisemitism." *Sixteenth Century Journal* 18, no. 1 (Spring 1987): 3–30.

Fuente, María Jesúus. "Christian, Muslim and Jewish Women in Late Medieval Iberia." In *Al-Andalus, Sepharad, and Medieval Iberia: Cultural Contact and Diffusion*, edited by Ivy A. Corfis, 163–69. Leiden: Brill, 2009.

Fuertes López, José Antonio. *Creación de la Villa Imperial de Potosí: La Capitulación de 1561.* Potosí: Biblioteca del Bicentenario, 2010.

Gampel, Benjamin R. "Jews, Christians, and Muslims in Medieval Iberia: Convivencia through the Eyes of Sephardic Jews." In *Convivencia: Jews, Muslims, and Christians in Medieval Spain*, edited by Vivian B. Mann, Thomas F. Glick, and Jerrilynn D. Dodds. New York: Jewish Museum, 1992.

García Carraffa, Alberto, and Arturo García Carraffa. *Diccionario heráldico y genealógico de apellidos españoles y americanos.* Vol. 12. Madrid: Imprenta de Antonio Marzo, 1926.

García de Proodian, Lucia. *Los judíos en América: Sus actividades en los Virreinatos de Nueva Castilla y Nueva Granada s. XVII.* Madrid: Arte Gráficas Resma, 1966.

García Quintanilla, Julio. *Historia de la iglesia en La Plata.* Vol. 4: *Historia del Cabildo Metropolitano, 1582–1799.* Sucre: ABAMT, 1999.

Garganta, José M. de, and Vicente Forcada. *Biografía y escritos de San Vicente Ferrer.* Madrid: Biblioteca de Autores Cristianos, 1956.

Gerber, Jane S. *The Jews of Spain: A History of the Sephardic Experience.* New York: Free Press, 1992.

Gerbet, Marie-Claude. *La noblesse dans le royaume de Castille: Étude sur ses structures sociales en Estrémadure 1454–1516.* Paris: Publications de la Sorbonne, 1979.

Gillman, Stephen, and Edmund L. King. *An Idea of History: Selected Essays of Américo Castro.* Columbus: Ohio State University Press, 1977.

Gitlitz, David M. "La actitud cristiano-nueva en 'Las cortes de la muerte.'" *Segismundo* 9 (1974): 141–64.

———. "Conversos and the Fusion of Worlds in Micael de Carvajal's *Tragedia Josephina*." *Hispanic Review* 40, no. 3 (1972): 260–70.

———. *Secrecy and Deceit: The Religion of the Crypto-Jews.* Albuquerque: University of New Mexico Press, 2002.

Given, James. Review of *The Formation of a Persecuting Society: Power and Deviance in Western Europe, 950–1250*, by R. I. Moore. *American Historical Review* 94, no. 4 (October 1989): 1017–72.

Glick, Thomas F. "Convivencia: An Introductory Note." In *Convivencia: Jews, Muslims, and Christians in Medieval Spain*, edited by Vivian B. Mann, Thomas F. Glick, and Jerrilynn D. Dodds, 1–10. New York: Jewish Museum, 1992,

———. *Islamic and Christian Spain in the Early Middle Ages.* Princeton, NJ: Princeton University Press, 1979.

————. "On Converso Identity and Marrano Ethnicity." In *Crisis and Creativity in the Sephardic World, 1391–1648*, edited by Benjamin Gampel, 59–76. New York: Columbia University Press, 1997.

Gómez Canedo, Lino. *Don Juan de Carvajal: Un español al servicio de la Santa Sede.* Madrid: CSIC, 1947.

González Cuesta, Francisco. "La Catedral de Gramática de Plasencia 1468–1852." *Memoria Ecclesiae* 12 (1997): 105–25.

————. *Los obispos de Plasencia.* Plasencia: Excmo. Ayuntamiento de Plasencia, 2002.

González Novalín, José Luis. "Pedro Mártir de Anglería y sus 'triunviros' 1506–1522." *Hispania Sacra* 33, no. 67 (1981): 148.

Graizbord, David. *Souls in Dispute: Converso Identities in Iberia and the Jewish Diaspora.* Philadelphia: University of Pennsylvania Press, 2004.

Greenblatt, Stephen. *Renaissance Self-Fashioning: From More to Shakespeare.* Chicago: University of Chicago Press, 1980.

Gutiérrez Rodríguez, José Manuel. *Oropesa y los Álvarez de Toledo.* Toledo: Diputación Provincial, 1985.

Halkin, Abraham, and David Hartman. *Crisis and Leadership: Epistles of Maimonides.* Philadelphia: Jewish Publication Society of America, 1985.

Hamburgh, Harvey E. "Rosso Fiorentino's Descent from the Cross in a Franciscan Context." *Sixteenth Century Journal* 19, no. 4 (Winter 1988): 577–604.

Hand, John Oliver. "'Saint Jerome in His Study' by Joos van Cleve." *Record of the Art Museum, Princeton University* 49, no. 2 (1990): 2–10.

Harney, Michael. *Kinship and Marriage in Medieval Hispanic Chivalric Romance.* Turnhout: Brepols, 2001.

Hartdegen, Stephen J., ed. *The New American Bible.* New York: Catholic Book Publishing, 1968.

Hartt, Frederick. *Art: A History of Painting, Sculpture, Architecture.* New York: Harry N. Abrams, 1989.

Hazlitt, William Carew. *The Venetian Republic: Its Rise, Its Growth, and Its Fall 421–1797.* Vol. 2. London: Adam and Charles Black, 1900.

Herbermann, Charles George, Edward A. Pace, Conde Benoist Pallen, Thomas J. Shahan, John J. Wynne, and Andrew Alphonsus MacErlean. *The Catholic Encyclopedia: An International Work of Reference on the Constitution, Doctrine, Discipline, and History of the Catholic Church.* New York: Robert Appleton Co., 1907.

Herlihy, David. "Three Patterns of Social Mobility in Medieval History." *Journal of Interdisciplinary History* 3, no. 4 (Spring 1973): 623–47.

Herriott, J. Homer. "A Thirteenth-Century Manuscript of the Primera Partida." *Speculum* 13, no. 3 (November 1929): 279–94.

Hervás, Marciano de. *Historia de los judíos de Plasencia y su tierra.* Vol. 1: *De los orígenes a la Inquisición siglos XII–XVII.* Sevilla: Objetivó 4, Medios Audiovisuales, 2001.

————. *Historia de los judíos de Plasencia y su tierra.* Vol. 2: *Colección diplomática 1187–1823.* Sevilla: Objetivo 4, Medios Audiovisuales, 2001.

Hillgarth, J. N. "Spanish Historiography and Iberian Reality." *History and Theory* 24, no. 1 (February 1985): 23–43.

———. *The Spanish Kingdoms 1250–1516*. Vol. 2. Oxford: Clarendon Press, 1978.

Holgate, Ian. "The Early History of Antonio Vivarini's 'St Jerome' Altar-Piece and the Beginnings of the Renaissance Style in Venice." *Burlington Magazine* 143, no. 1174 (January 2001): 19–22.

Hordes, Stanley M. *To the End of the Earth: A History of the Crypto-Jews of New Mexico*. New York: Columbia University Press, 2005.

Humanes, Luisa F. *Restauración en el templete de Bramante-Roma*. Madrid: Construcciones Angel B. Beltrán, 2002.

Hutchison, Jane Campbell. *The Illustrated Bartsch*. Vol. 9, Commentary Part 2. New York: Abaris, 1991.

Kagan, Richard L. *Students and Society in Early Modern Spain*. Baltimore: Johns Hopkins University Press, 1974.

Kamen, Henry. *Empire: How Spain Became a World Power, 1492–1763*. New York: HarperCollins, 2003.

Katsh, Abraham I. "Poems from Barcelona Mahzor of the 13th Century." *Jewish Quarterly Review* 57 (1967): 347–59.

Kennedy, Hugh. *Muslim Spain and Portugal: A Political History of al-Andalus*. Harow: Pearson Education, 1996.

Kettering, Sharon. "Patronage and Kinship in Early Modern France." *French Historical Studies* 16, no. 2 (Fall 1989): 408–35.

Klener, Julien. "Introduction: Spanish Jewry at the Eve of the Expulsion." In *The Expulsion of the Jews and Their Emigration to the Southern Low Countries (15th–16th C.)*, edited by Luc Dequeker and Werner Verbeke, IX–XIX. Leuven: Leuven University Press, 1998.

Kunin, Seth S. *Juggling Identities: Identity and Authenticity among the Crypto-Jews*. New York: Columbia University Press, 2009.

Ladero, M. A. "Las juderías de Castilla según algunos 'servicios' fiscales." *Sefarad* 31, no. 2 (1971): 249–64.

Ladner, Gerhart B. "Medieval and Modern Understanding of Symbolism: A Comparison." *Speculum* 54, no. 2 (April 1979): 223–56.

Lapidus, Ira M. *A History of Islamic Societies*. Cambridge: Cambridge University Press, 2002.

Lapuya, Isidoro L. "La Universidad de Salamanca y la cultura española en el siglo XIII." In *Conferencia inaugural primera de las de lengua castellana*, December 8, 1897, Sorbonne, Paris. Paris: Sorbonne, 1900.

Lascaris Comneno, Constantino. *Colegios mayores*. Madrid: Editorial Magisterio Español, 1952.

Layna Serrano, Francisco. *Historia de Guadalajara y sus Mendozas en los siglos XV y XVI*. 4 vols. Madrid: Aldus, 1942.

Lea, Henry Charles. "Ferrand Martínez and the Massacres of 1391." *American Historical Review* 1, no. 2 (January 1896): 209–16.

———. *History of the Inquisition of Spain*. 3 vols. New York: Macmillan, 1907.

León Tello, Pilar. *Judíos de Ávila*. Ávila: Excma. Diputación Provincial de Ávila, 1963.

Levillain, Philippe, ed. *The Papacy: An Encyclopedia*. New York: Routledge, 2002.

Levillier, Roberto. *Guerras y conquistas en Tucumán y Cuyo: Fundación de Mendoza, San Juan, San Miguel de Tucumán y Córdoba por españoles del Chile y Charcas 1554–1574*. Buenos Aires: Imprenta Porter Hnos, 1945.

Linehan, Peter. "Segovia: A 'Frontier' Diocese in the Thirteenth Century." *English Historical Review* 96, no. 380 (July 1981): 481–508.

———. *The Spanish Church and the Papacy in the Thirteenth Century*. Cambridge: Cambridge University Press, 1971.

Lings, Martin. *Muhammad: His Life Based on the Earliest Sources*. Rochester, NY: Inner Traditions International, 1983.

Lizondo Borda, Manuel. *Historia del Tucumán: Siglo XVI*. Tucumán: Universidad Nacional de Tucumán, 1942.

Llorens, Tomás, Mar Borobia, and Paloma Alarco. *Masterworks: Museo Thyssen-Bornemisza*. Madrid: Museo Thyssen-Bornemisza, 2000.

Llorente, Juan Antonio. *Historia crítica de la Inquisición de España: Obra original conforme lo que resulta de los Archivos del Consejo de la Suprema y de los tribunales de provincia*. Barcelona: J. Pons, 1870.

Lobingier, Charles S. "Las Siete Partidas in Full English Dress." *Hispanic American Historical Review* 9, no. 4 (July 1938): 529–44.

Lodo de Mayoralgo, J. M. *Viejos linajes de Cáceres*. Cáceres: Editorial Extremadura, 1971.

Logan, F. Donald. *A History of the Church in the Middle Ages*. London: Routledge, 2002.

López de Toro, José. *Documentos Inéditos para la historia de España, Epistolario, Pedro Mártir de Angleria*. Vol. 9. Madrid: Imprenta Góngora, 1955.

Maccoby, Hyam. "The Tortosa Disputation, 1413–14, and Its Effects." In *The Expulsion of the Jews and Their Emigration to the Southern Low Countries (15th–16th C.)*, edited by Luc Dequeker and Werner Verbeke, 23–34. Leuven: Leuven University Press, 1998.

MacCormack, Sabine. *On the Wings of Time: Rome, the Incas, Spain, and Peru*. Princeton, NJ: Princeton University Press, 2007.

Mariscal, George. "The Role of Spain in Contemporary Race Theory." *Arizona Journal of Hispanic Cultural Studies* 2 (1998): 7–22.

Martin, John Jeffries. *Myths of Renaissance Individualism*. New York: Palgrave Macmillan, 2004.

Martínez, María Elena. *Genealogical Fictions: Limpieza de Sangre, Religion, and Gender in Colonial Mexico*. Stanford, CA: Stanford University Press, 2008.

Martínez-Dávila, Roger Louis. "From Sword to Seal: The Ascent of the Carvajal Family in Spain: 1391–1516." PhD dissertation, University of Texas at Austin, 2008.

———. "Jews, Catholics, and Converts: Reassessing the Resilience of Convivencia in Fifteenth Century Plasencia, Spain." *Journal of Spanish Portuguese and Italian Crypto Jews* 1 (Spring 2009): 95–119.

———. "Trans-Atlantic 'Hebrew' and *Converso* Networks: Conquistadors, Churchmen, and Crypto Jews in the Spanish Extremadura and Colonial Spanish America." *Journal of Spanish Portuguese and Italian Crypto Jews* 4 (Spring 2012): 135–66.

Martínez-Dávila, Roger L., Josef Díaz, and Ron D. Hart. *Fractured Faiths / Las fes fracturadas: Spanish Judaism, the Inquisition, and New World Identities / El judaismo español, la Inquisicion y identidades nuevo mundiales*. Albuquerque, NM: Fresco Books / SF Design, 2016.

Martínez Diez, Gonzalo. *Bulario de la Inquisición española*. Madrid: Editorial Complutense, 1997.

Martínez López, María del Carmen, José Enciso Contreras, José Arturo Burciaga Campos, and Raúl Castrellon Reyes. *Cedulario de la Audiencia de La Plata de Los Charcas: Siglo XVI.* Sucre: Archivo y Biblioteca Nacionales de Bolivia, 2005.

Martínez Moro, Jesús. *La renta feudal en la Castilla de siglo XV: los Stúñiga [sic].* Valladolid: Gráficas Andrés Martín, 1977.

Martz, Linda. *A Network of Converso Families in Early Modern Toledo: Assimilating a Minority.* Ann Arbor: University of Michigan Press, 2003.

———. "Relations between Conversos and Old Christians in Early Modern Toledo: Some Different Perspectives." In *Christians, Muslims, and Jews in Medieval and Early Modern Spain: Interaction and Cultural Change,* edited by Mark D. Meyerson and Edward D. English, 220–40. Notre Dame, IN: University of Notre Dame Press, 2000.

Mattingly, Garrett. *Renaissance Diplomacy.* Boston: Houghton Mifflin, 1955.

McGaha, Michael D. *Coat of Many Cultures: The Story of Joseph in Spanish Literature 1200–1492.* Philadelphia: Jewish Publication Society, 1997.

———. *The Story of Joseph in Golden Age Drama.* Lewisburg: Bucknell University Press, 1998.

Melammed, Renée Levine. *A Question of Identity: Iberian Conversos in Historical Perspective.* New York: Oxford University Press, 2004.

Mendoza Loza, Gunnar. *Obras completas.* Vol. 1. Sucre: Archivo y Biblioteca Nacionales de Bolivia, 2005.

Meyerson, Mark D. *A Jewish Renaissance in Fifteenth-Century Spain.* Princeton, NJ: Princeton University Press, 2004.

Meyuḥas Ginio, Alisa. *Between Sepharad and Jerusalem: History, Identity and Memory of the Sephardim.* Leiden: Brill, 2014.

Moore, R. I. *The Formation of a Persecuting Society: Power and Deviance in Western Europe, 950–1250.* New York: B. Blackwell, 1987.

Moxó, Salvador de. "De la nobleza vieja a la nobleza nueva: La transformación nobiliaria castellana en la baja edad media." *Cuadernos de Historia* 3 (1969): 1–195.

———. "La nobleza castellana en el siglo XIV." *Anuario de Estudios Medievales* 7 (1970): 493–511.

Nader, Helen. "'The Greek Commander' Hernán Núñez de Toledo, Spanish Humanist and Civic Leader." *Renaissance Quarterly* 31, no. 4 (Winter 1978): 463–85.

———. *The Mendoza Family in the Spanish Renaissance 1350–1550.* New Brunswick, NJ: Rutgers University Press, 1979.

Netanyahu, Benzion. *The Marranos of Spain.* New York: American Academy for Jewish Research, 1966.

———. *The Origins of the Inquisition in Fifteenth-Century Spain.* New York: Random House, 1995.

Nieto Cumplido, M., and C. L. de Tena y Alvear. "El Alcázar Viejo, una repoblación cordobesa del siglo XIV." *Axerquía* 1 (1980): 231–73.

Nirenberg, David. *Communities of Violence: Persecution of Minorities in the Middle Ages.* Princeton, NJ: Princeton University Press, 1998.

———. "Mass Conversion and Genealogical Mentalities: Jews and Christians in Fifteenth-Century Spain." *Past and Present* 174 (2002): 3–41.

————. *Neighboring Faiths: Christianity, Islam, and Judaism in the Middle Ages and Today.* Chicago: University of Chicago Press, 2014.

Oakley, Thomas P. "Alleviations of Penance in the Continental Penitentials." *Speculum* 12, no. 4 (October 1937): 488–502.

O'Callaghan, Joseph F. *The Cortes of Castile-León 1188–1350.* Philadelphia: University of Pennsylvania Press, 1989.

Olea, Ricardo A., and George Christakos. "Duration of Urban Mortality for the Fourteenth-Century Black Death Epidemic." *Human Biology* 77, no. 3 (June 2005): 291–303.

Olschki, Leonardo. "The Columbian Nomenclature of the Lesser Antilles." *Geographical Review* 33, no. 3 (July 1943): 413–14.

Pacios López, A. *La disputa de Tortosa.* 2 vols. Madrid and Barcelona: Instituto Arias Montano, 1957.

Pamuk, Sevket. "The Black Death and the Origins of the 'Great Divergence' across Europe, 1300–1600." *European Review of Economic History* 11, no. 3 (December 2007): 289–317.

Paredes y Guillén, Vicente. *Los Zúñigas, señores de Plasencia.* Cáceres: Tipografía Encuadernación y Liberia de Jiménez, 1903.

Pastor, Ludwig. *The History of the Popes.* Vols. 5–7. London: Routledge & Kegan Paul, 1950.

Payne, Stanley G. *A History of Spain and Portugal.* Vol. 2. Madison: University of Wisconsin Press, 1973.

Perry, Mary Elizabeth. *The Handless Maiden: Moriscos and the Politics of Religion in Early Modern Spain.* Princeton, NJ: Princeton University Press, 2005

Phillips, William D., Jr., and Carla Rahn Phillips. *A Concise History of Spain.* Cambridge: Cambridge University Press, 2010.

Poole, Stafford. "The Politics of Limpieza de Sangre: Juan de Ovando and His Circle in the Reign of Philip II." *The Americas* 55, no. 3 (January 1999): 359–89.

Powers, James F. *A Society Organized for War: The Iberian Municipal Militias in the Central Middle Ages, 1000–1284.* Berkeley: University of California Press, 1988.

Pudelko, Georg. "The Altarpiece by Antonio Vivarini and Giovanni d'Allemagna, Once in S. Moise at Venice." *Burlington Magazine for Connoisseurs* 71, no. 414 (September 1937): 130–33.

Pulido Serrano, Juan Ignacio. "Los judíos en la obra de Julio Caro Baroja." *Historia Social,* no. 55 (2006): 45–60.

Rábade Obradó, María del Pilar. "La invención como necesidad: Genealogía y judeoconversos." *En la España Medieval* 29, no. 1 (2006):183–202.

————. "Los judeoconversos en la Corte y en la época de los reyes católicos: Una interpretación de conjunto." *Espacio, Tiempo y Forma, serie IV, Historia Moderna,* tomo 6 (1993): 25–38.

————. "Religiosidad y práctica religiosa entre los conversos castellanos (1483–1507)." *Boletín de la Real Academia de la Historia* 194, no. 1 (1997): 83–141.

Rahn Phillips, Carla. *Ciudad Real 1500–1700: Growth, Crisis, and Readjustment in the Spanish Economy.* Cambridge, MA: Harvard University Press, 1979.

Ramírez del Águila, Pedro. *Noticias políticas de Indias y relación descriptiva de la Ciudad de La Plata.* Sucre: Imprenta Universitaria, 1978.

Ray, Jonathan. *The Sephardic Frontier: The Reconquista and the Jewish Community in Medieval Iberia.* Ithaca, NY: Cornell University Press, 2006.

Ricci, Ricardo. *Evolución de la ciudad de San Miguel de Tucumán.* Tucumán: Universidad Nacional de Tucumán, 1967.

Rodríguez, Florencio Marcos. *Extractos de los libros de Claustros de la Universidad de Salamanca, siglo XV (1463–1484).* Vol. 6, no. 3. Salamanca: Universidad de Salamanca, 1964.

Rodríguez Martínez, Luis. *Historia del Monasterio de San Benito el Real de Valladolid.* Valladolid: Caja de Ahorros Popular de Valladolid, 1981.

Rodríguez Valencia, Vicente. *Isabel la católica en la opinión de españoles y extranjeros, siglos XV al XX.* Vol. 1. Valladolid: Instituto "Isabel la católica" de Historia Eclesiástica, 1970.

Roth, Norman. *Conversos, Inquisition, and the Expulsion of the Jews from Spain.* Madison: University of Wisconsin Press, 1995.

Round, Nicholas. *The Greatest Man Uncrowned: A Study of the Fall of Don Álvaro de Luna.* London: Tamesis Books, 1986.

Rubin, Miri. Review of *The Formation of a Persecuting Society: Power and Deviance in Western Europe, 950–1250,* by R. I. Moore. *Speculum* 65, no. 4 (October 1990): 1025–27.

Rubio Rojas, Antonio. *Las disposiciones testamentarias de don Francisco de Carvajal, arcediano de Plasencia y Mecenas de Cáceres, su villa natal.* Cáceres: Imp. T. Rodríguez Santano, 1975.

Rucquoi, Adeline. *Valladolid en la edad media: El mundo abreviado 1367–1474.* Valladolid: Junta de Castilla y León Consejería de Educación y Cultura, 1997.

Ruggiero, Guido. *Machiavelli in Love: Sex, Self, and Society in the Italian Renaissance.* Baltimore, MD: Johns Hopkins University Press, 2010.

Ruiz, Teofilo F. *Spain's Centuries of Crisis 1300–1474.* Malden, MA: Wiley-Blackwell, 2011.

Sáez, Liciniano. *Demostración histórico del verdadero valor de todas las Moneda que corrían en Castilla durante el reynado del Señor Don Enrique IV, y de su correspondencia con las del Señor D. Cárlos IV.* Madrid: Imprenta de Sancha, 1805.

Safran, Janina M. *Defining Boundaries in al-Andalus: Muslims, Christians, and Jews in Islamic Iberia.* Ithaca, NY: Cornell University Press, 2013.

———. *The Second Umayyad Caliphate: The Articulation of Caliphal Legitimacy in Al-Andalus.* Cambridge, MA: Harvard University Press, 2000.

Saint Oswald Reliquary Workshop. *Monstrance with the "Paten of Saint Bernwald," CMA 1930.505.* 1413–96. Cleveland Museum of Art. October 4, 2016. http://www.artstor.org.

Salazar y Castro, Luis. *Historia genealógica de la Casa de Haro.* Madrid: Archivo Documental Español, 1959.

———. *Historia genealógica de la Casa y Lara.* 4 vols. Madrid: Imprenta Real por Mateo de Llanos y Guzmán, 1694–97.

Sánchez Loro, Domingo. *El convento placentino de San Ildefonso.* Cáceres: Publicaciones del Departamento Provincial de Seminarios de F. E. T. y de las J. O. N. S., 1956.

———. *El parecer de un deán: Don Diego de Jerez, consejero de los Reyes Católicos, servidor de los duques de Plasencia, deán y protonotario de su Iglesia Catedral.* Cáceres: Publicaciones del Departamento Provincial de Seminarios de F. E. T. y de las J. O. N. S., 1959.

Santos Canalejo, Elisa Carolina de. *La historia medieval de Plasencia y su entorno geo-histórico.* Cáceres: Instituto Cultural "El Brocense," 1986.

———. *El siglo XV en Plasencia y su tierra: Proyección de un pasado y reflejo de una época.* Cáceres: Instituto Cultural "El Brocense," 1981.

Schwaller, John Frederick. "Tres familias mexicanas del siglo XVI." *Historia Mexicana* 31, no. 2 (October–December 1981): 171–96.

Schwartz, Stuart B. *All Can Be Saved: Religious Tolerance and Salvation in the Iberian Atlantic World.* New Haven, CT: Yale University Press, 2008.

Scott, S. P., ed. *The Visigothic Code Forum Judicum.* Boston: Boston Book, 1910.

Serrano, Luciano. *Los conversos: D. Pablo de Santa María y D. Alfonso de Cartagena.* Madrid: Escuela de Estudios Hebraicos, 1942.

Shaw, Christine. *Julius II: The Warrior Pope.* Oxford: Blackwell, 1993.

Sheffler, Alva William. *Symbols of the Christian Faith.* Grand Rapids, MI: Eerdmans, 2002.

Silva, Alfonso Franco. "Oropesa, el nacimiento de un señorío toledano a fines del siglo XIV." *Anuario de Estudios Medievales* no. 15 (1985): 299–314.

Singer, Isidor, and Cyrus Adler. *The Jewish Encyclopedia: A Descriptive Record of the History, Religion, Literature, and Customs of the Jewish People from the Earliest Times to the Present Day.* New York: Funk and Wagnalis, 1905.

Starr-LeBeau, Gretchen D. *In the Shadow of the Virgin: Inquisitors, Friars, and Conversos in Guadalupe, Spain.* Princeton: Princeton University Press, 2003.

Stoler, Ann Laura. "Racial Histories and Their Regimes of Truth." *Political Power and Social Theory* 11 (1997): 183–206.

Sturgis, Russell. *A Dictionary of Architecture and Buildings: Biographical, Historical, and Descriptive.* Vol. 3. New York: Macmillan, 1902.

———. "Frame, §VIII, 1: Spanish medieval (ii) Gothic retables. (a) Establishment of the form. (b) Development." In *A Dictionary of Architecture and Buildings.* Grove Art Online. Oxford University Press. http://www.groveart.com.ezproxy.lib.utexas.edu/. Accessed February 2, 2008.

Szombathy, Zoltan. "Genealogy in Medieval Muslim Societies." *Studia Islamica,* no. 95 (2002): 11–13.

Taylor, Paul, and Caroline Van Eck. "Piero della Francesca's Giants." *Journal of the Warburg and Courtauld Institutes* 60 (1997): 243–47.

Temkin, Samuel. *Luis de Carvajal: A Biography.* Santa Fe, NM: Sunstone Press, 2011.

Thompson, Donald. "The 'Cronistas de Indias' Revisited: Historical Reports, Archeological Evidence, and Literary and Artistic Traces of Indigenous Music and Dance in the Greater Antilles at the Time of the 'Conquista.'" *Latin American Music Review / Revista de Música Latinoamericana* 14, no. 2 (Autumn–Winter 1993): 181–201.

Torres Fontes, Juan. *Estudio sobre la "Crónica de Enrique IV" del Dr. Galíndez de Carvajal.* Murcia: CSIC, 1946.

———. "Los judíos murcianos a fines del siglo XIV." *Miscelánea Medieval Murciana* 8 (1981): 57–117.

Twinam, Ann. *Public Lives, Private Secrets: Gender, Honor, Sexuality, and Illegitimacy in Colonial Spanish America.* Stanford, CA: Stanford University Press, 1999.

Valdeavellano, Luis G. de. *Curso de historia de las Instituciones españoles.* Madrid: Ediciones de la Revista de Occidente, 1968.

Van Baaren, Th. P. "The Significance of Gestures in the Paintings of Hieronymus Bosch." In *Visible Religion*. Vol.7 of *Genres in Visual Representation*, edited by Werner-Reimers-Stiftung, 23–24. Leiden: Brill, 1982.

Van Engen, John H. "The Christian Middle Ages as a Historiographical Problem." *American Historical Review* 91 (1986): 519–52.

Vander Linden, H. "Alexander VI and the Demarcation of the Maritime and Colonial Domains of Spain and Portugal, 1493–1494." *American Historical Review* 22, no. 1 (October 1916): 1–20.

Varagnoli, Claudio. *S. Croce in Gerusalemme: La basilica restaurata e l'architettura del Settecentro romano*. Rome: Bonsignori Editore, 1995.

Vassburg, David E. *Land and Society in Golden Age Castile*. Cambridge: Cambridge University Press, 1984.

Vázquez Fernández, Luis. *Los Pizarros, la Merced, el convento de Trujillo (Cáceres) y Tirso*. Madrid: Estudios, 1984.

Villalba, F. Javier. *Colección diplomática del Cardenal Mendoza 1454–1503, cuadernos de historia medieval, sección colecciones documentales, I*. Madrid: Universidad Autónoma de Madrid, 1999.

Villalobos y Martínez-Pontremuli, María Luisa de. "Los Estúñiga: La penetración en Castilla de un linaje nueva." *Cuadernos de Historia* 6 (1975): 331–33.

Villalón, L. J. Andrew. "Cut Off Their Heads, or I'll Cut Off Yours." In *The Hundred Years War (Part II)*, edited by L. J. Andrew Villalón and Donald J. Kagay, 153–84. Leiden: Brill, 2008.

———. "The Law's Delay: The Anatomy of an Aristocratic Property Dispute 1350–1577." PhD dissertation, Yale University, 1984.

Wachtel, Nathan. *La foi duy souvenir: Labyrinthes marranes*. Paris: Editions du Seuil, 2001.

Walker Trainor, Millie. "Salve Regina: Hail Holy Queen." *Catholic Insight* 13, no. 11 (December 2005): 38.

Willshire, William Hughes. *Catalogue of Early Prints in the British Museum*. London: Longmans, 1883.

Woodward, John. *A Treatise on Ecclesiastical Heraldry*. Edinburg: W. & A. K. Johnston, 1894.

Yovel, Yirmiyahu. *The Other within the Marranos: Split Identity and Emerging Modernity*. Princeton, NJ: Princeton University Press, 2009.

INDEX

ROGER LOUIS MARTÍNEZ-DÁVILA

is associate professor of history

at the University of Colorado, Colorado Springs,

and is a UC3M CONEX-Marie Curie Fellow

at the Universidad Carlos III de Madrid.

CPSIA information can be obtained
at www.ICGtesting.com
Printed in the USA
LVHW06*1908120918
589926LV00002B/54/P